BUYING A *HOUSE IN*

SCOTLAND

Nicola Taylor

Distributed in the USA by
The Globe Pequot Press, Guilford, Connecticut

D1382394

Published by Vacation Work, 9 Park End ~~~~, ~~~~
www.vacationwork.co.uk

BUYING A HOUSE IN SCOTLAND
by Nicola Taylor

First edition 2006

Copyright © 2006

ISBN 13: 978-1-85458-348-2
ISBN 10: 1-85458-348-4

Cover design by mccdesign ltd

Illustrations by Mick Siddens

Typeset by Guy Hobbs

Cover photograph: painted houses on Tobermory waterfront

Printed and bound in Italy by Legoprint SpA, Trento

CONTENTS

PART I
SCOTLAND THE BRAVE

LIVING IN SCOTLAND

RESIDENCE & ENTRY

PART II
LOCATION, LOCATION...

WHERE TO FIND YOUR IDEAL HOME

PART III
THE PURCHASING PROCEDURE

PART IV
WHAT HAPPENS NEXT

ACKNOWLEDGEMENTS

The author would like to thank all those people who provided information, advice and encouragement during the writing of this book. In particular, Caroline Deacon, Sharon Blackie, Bill Herbert and Charlie Whittaker who provided lively accounts of their experiences for my case studies, as well as good advice and encouragement for those who may wish to follow in their footsteps. My thanks are also due to David Woodworth and Charles James for their technical and editorial expertise. Finally, for his constant support even when I was seemingly permanently welded to my PC, I would like to thank my husband Charlie Taylor.

Photographs in colour section by Highland Dreams.

TELEPHONE NUMBERS

International Telephone Codes. Throughout this book, UK telephone codes have been used. For those calling UK numbers from abroad, the international code is +44 (or 00 44) and the initial 0 is dropped. So 0131-222 5555 is +44 131-222 5555 when calling from outside the UK.

FOREWORD

Scotland has long been a favourite holiday destination for people across the world, who come for the stunning scenery, the sporting and outdoor activities, the history and the whisky.

In recent years, however, increasing numbers of people have come to see the advantages of moving permanently to this unique country, or buying a second home to give them a bolthole when they need a break from their busy lives elsewhere. These advantages are many and varied, but the main thing that people moving to Scotland seem to be looking for is a place where they can avoid many of the stresses and strains of modern living and still feel they have some elbow room. Scotland retains a slower pace of life than the rest of the UK, particularly in the rural areas. Even the cities are smaller, less surrounded by urban sprawl, more 'user-friendly', so commuting times are shorter and the countryside is never far away. The air is clean, the people are friendly and have time for each other. All round, it provides a better quality of life.

Whether you are looking for the solitude of a rural retreat, or the buzz of living and working in a lively city environment, properties are still relatively affordable compared with other areas of the UK, which has attracted many buyers from the south of England. For the price of a modest house in the London area, it's possible to find a large property with some land and have change left over.

The Scottish housing market is not simple: the types of properties for sale vary greatly between the city centres, where apartment-living is the norm; the towns of the central belt, where terraced and semi-detached houses with small gardens predominate; and rural areas where properties range from small single-storey dwellings, often with an acre or more of land, to large elegant estate houses set in many more acres.

This book is a guide to anybody who is considering buying property in Scotland. Part I gives an overview of the history and culture of the country, plus practical details regarding how to relocate to Scotland from abroad and the way of life once here. Part II describes the differences between the main regions of the country, and the types and prices of property available in each area. Part III guides the reader through the whole process of selecting and buying a property. Many buyers from elsewhere in the UK are put off by the fact that the Scottish system is different from the one they are used to. The system, from putting in an offer through the conveyancing and purchasing process, to final settlement, is explained clearly and simply. Finally, Part IV looks at post-purchasing practicalities, including restoring and renovating properties, dealing with local builders, house removals and how to make money from your property.

Nicola Taylor, Glasgow
February 2006

Part I

SCOTLAND THE BRAVE

LIVING IN SCOTLAND

RESIDENCE & ENTRY

LIVING IN SCOTLAND

CHAPTER SUMMARY

- **Immigration.** Around 30,000 people a year relocate to Scotland from outside the UK.
  - Scotland's immigrant population has grown by over one third in the last decade.
- Scotland's legal, political and education systems are different from the rest of the UK.
- **Population.** The average population density of Scotland is only 65 people per square kilometre.
  - 90% of the population live within one hour's drive of Perth in the Central Belt.
- **Geography.** Over 25% of the country is protected by environmental designations including National Parks, National Scenic Areas, Sites of Special Scientific Interest, National, Local and Forest Nature Reserves.
  - Scotland has about 790 islands and islets in total, only 130 of which are inhabited.
- Much of Edinburgh, the capital city, is a World Heritage Centre.
- In the middle of June, the north of Scotland never experiences complete darkness, with an extended twilight between 11pm and 4am.
- The Scots tend to have socialist principles: the Labour and Liberal Democratic parties are far more popular than the Conservatives.
- The number of Gaelic speakers has fallen by 75 per cent in the last 100 years.
- **Getting There.** It is far easier and cheaper to fly to Scotland than it once was.
  - There are five main airports in Scotland, at Edinburgh, Glasgow, Prestwick, Aberdeen and Inverness.
- Broadband internet connections are now available throughout Scotland.
- **Education.** The Scottish Credit & Qualifications Framework rewards achievement for all learners, from those with Learning Difficulties through to Doctorate level.
  - The secondary school system includes nine Centres of Excellence for gifted children.

> ○ All Scottish residents are entitled to free healthcare through the National Health Service.

INTRODUCTION – FLOWER OF SCOTLAND

Scotland provokes strong emotions in people. Many love it, some hate it, but few seem to be indifferent to it. A country of contrasts, it evokes contradictory reactions in people in many areas. One stereotypical view has characterised the Scotsman as mean and dour, but those who know and love the country find they are generally friendlier and more generous than their counterparts south of the border. This has much to do with Scotland being a smaller, less crowded, country. People still have time to stop and have a *blether* (chat) and to help their neighbours.

The weather is another aspect of Scotland that generally receives a bad press – but equally, visitors rave over the beautiful scenery, the lochs and the mountains, and their changing aspect from hour to hour. And of course, the weather is part and parcel of this natural environment – one shapes the other.

Again, there are conflicting reports about the food of Scotland. On the one hand, the Scots are notorious for having one of the worst diets in the world, yet on the other, it also has a reputation for some of the highest quality luxury foods you will find anywhere: Scottish salmon, venison, beef and, of course, whisky, are all highly valued the world over.

The fact that Scotland and its people retain a wildness in their land and their soul, makes some imagine them as a somewhat uncivilised lot, rough and uneducated to a degree, a view coloured by memories of their warlike history. Yet Scotland has produced some of the world's great minds in the fields of literature and the arts, science, exploration and engineering, to name but a few fields of endeavour. From Dr Livingstone to Dr Alexander Fleming, Sir Walter Scott to Dame Muriel Spark, Alexander Graham Bell to John Logie Baird, the Scots have made a contribution to world progress out of proportion to their small size.

The Scottish education system is still the best in the UK, while Glasgow was selected as the European City of Culture in 1999 and Edinburgh was named in 2004 as the first UNESCO world city of literature.

Tourism has long been a staple industry of Scotland, with an illustrious history going back many years. Both Samuel Johnson and Queen Victoria made famous tours of Scotland, their thoughts and impressions saved permanently in the diaries made of their trips. The Royal Family has continued their love affair with Scotland, Balmoral being their favourite 'bolthole' for family holidays and breaks from affairs of state.

Many other tourists emulate them, indulging in their love of salmon fishing in the superb rivers, while others are attracted by the other great Scottish gift to the world, golf. Many more just come to get away from it all and to walk in the endless countryside.

There is no doubt that the majority of people who develop the desire to move permanently to Scotland do so after holidaying there. They want the chance to experience the scenic beauty and more relaxed lifestyle all year round.

In the 21st Century, Scotland seems more popular as a place to live than it ever was. This has been brought about by several factors which have brought this small country to prominence in the eyes of the world. First and most notably is the historic event of Scotland regaining its own parliament for the first time since 1707. Since its first sitting in 1999, the Scottish Parliament has discussed and passed much legislation destined to firm up the individual character of Scotland. It has always seen itself as more than just part of the United Kingdom – indeed, in many ways its psyche has more links with European than English thought, a trait which goes back many centuries to the Auld Alliance between Scotland and France in which the two countries specifically and deliberately defied the English.

The new Parliament has not been an unalloyed success – surveys show that a large minority of the Scottish people are disappointed with their performance thus far, and there has been a furore over the mishandling of the project to build the new parliament building at Holyrood, leading to it running massively over-budget and taking years longer to complete than originally stated – but this is surely to be expected of any new administration. Although they may not admit it, overall one suspects that the Scottish people are proud of their newly devolved status. Anything to distance themselves from the auld enemy – the English – is likely to go down well with most Scots!

On a perhaps more frivolous level, the profile of Scotland, its history and landscape, has been raised in the eyes of the world by Hollywood blockbusters of recent years, such as *Braveheart* and *Rob Roy*, while within Great Britain, the English have shown great enthusiasm for programmes such as *Hamish Macbeth*, *Monarch of the Glen* and the *Para Handy Tales* which all have the Scottish Highlands as a breathtaking backdrop to tales of loveable Scottish characters. Films such as *Trainspotting*, set amongst the drugs sub-culture of Edinburgh, have shown a more controversial and gritty view of the realities of life in urban Scotland – again, the contrasts are what make this such an intriguing place to live.

Scotland boasts one of the few remaining genuine wilderness areas of Europe, and what people move here for more than any other reason is its natural beauty and the sense that here there is a slower pace of life, clean air and more room to follow one's own desires. It has long been a popular place to retire to, but the massive growth in modern technology of recent years, most notably the internet, has allowed many younger people to live and work in the remote areas and maintain the standard of living they had been used to in the urban south of Britain. There has been a veritable stampede of incomers buying property in Scotland, particularly in rural areas and in Edinburgh.

In 2000, there were over 400,000 English-born people living in Scotland, a significant percentage in a country of only 5 million, and in the same year nearly 29,000 people came to Scotland from outside the UK. Of these, one in ten immigrants came from America while 43 per cent of the rest came from Europe, mainly Germany, France, Spain and Ireland. There were also significant numbers arriving from Australia, Canada, South Africa, China, Holland and New Zealand. Although overall Scotland is suffering, along with other western countries, from a declining birthrate, Scotland's immigrant population has grown by more than one third in the last decade.

There is also a significant movement of Scots out of the country. In 2000, there were almost twice as many Scots-born people living in England as English-born people living in Scotland, while Scots and their descendants have long been found in many other corners of the world. They are renowned for their tendency to travel and settle elsewhere in the world, perhaps a tendency to be found in many small, historically poor, countries. There are particularly large populations of Scots and their descendants in places such as Canada, Australia and New Zealand, partly due to such disgraceful episodes in the Scotland's history as the Highland Clearances of the late 18th and early 19th Centuries when large landowners moved whole communities off the land to make way for grazing for sheep and stalking and shooting for the gentry. Even before this, the tendency of the Scot to emigrate, for a variety of reasons, is well-documented. Many Scottish soldiers travelled abroad to fight – as many as ten thousand Scots served for France in the Hundred Years War between 1337 and 1453, while Louis XI had his own Scots Guard during his reign of 1461-1483. Two centuries later, Scottish soldiers fought for Gustavus Adolphus of Sweden in the Thirty Years War of 1618-48.

The other impetus, apart from fighting, for the Scots to leave their homeland, was the search for a better life elsewhere, as the quality of the land and high rents made life in Scotland hard and poverty-stricken. After the union of the crowns in 1603, Scots were banned from travelling to England without permission, which encouraged them to travel further afield. Places such as Nova Scotia ('New Scotland') in Canada are a lasting monument to these Scottish pioneers. Predating the Highland Clearances, in 1650 Cromwell deported five thousand Scots to the American colonies. When Bonnie Prince Charlie was exiled to the continent after the Jacobite Rebellion of 1745, many loyal Scotsmen followed him. In the late 18th Century, many Scots were given high positions within the Indian Government.

Despite their tendency to roam the world, Scotland continues to exert a pull on its sons and daughters, however. Of the 29,000 immigrants in 2000, one quarter were Scots-born, and of the 3099 moving from Australia, as many as 40 per cent were Scots born. Many more of those incomers from around the world – and indeed from England – have some Scots blood in their veins. So many people with Scottish ancestry are attracted to the auld country, seeing their move as 'coming home' as much as escaping from somewhere else.

Scotland has seen its share of ups and downs, going through periods of historical and political upheaval, and of grinding poverty. As recently as the 1960s and 70s the country saw its rural areas become depopulated as people moved south for better jobs and higher incomes, while areas of the cities of Glasgow and Dundee in particular were notorious for the poverty and slum properties to be found there. At that time, crofts in the Highlands could be snapped up for a pittance – although it has to be said that some buyers had their fingers burned, unaware that the purchase of a croft house didn't necessarily mean that they would have unrestricted use of the land on which it stood. Crofting is a legal minefield, and anybody contemplating buying a croft needs to be aware of the pitfalls even today. Today, crofts are far harder to come by, and those which do come on to the market excite huge interest and change hands for large sums. In the cities the slum tenements have now been either pulled down or renovated into desirable apartments, and wholesale regeneration is taking place, attracting young, ambitious workers from across the globe. The Scottish Executive is encouraging this with its Fresh Talent initiative designed to encourage high calibre foreign students to make their homes and follow their careers in Scotland. There are signs that this strategy is paying off – of the immigrants who move to Scotland, 37% of them hold a higher level qualification and the number falling into the 'high-earner' bracket is almost twice the UK average.

HISTORY

The Origins of the Scottish People

The area we now know as Scotland has been inhabited for around 8,000 years. The earliest inhabitants of whom any trace has been found were Mesolithic (Middle Stone Age) people who moved north into the north west Highland region and the Inner Hebrides in around BC7000. They spread slowly to other areas, including Kintyre further south, and Fife, Deeside and the Forth estuary on the east. Nomadic hunters and fishermen, these people left no evidence of permanent settlements.

It was the Neolithic (New Stone Age) people who formed the first fixed homes. Evidence of about a dozen of their hamlets has been found, dating from around BC4000. It is these people to whom we owe the stone-built chambered tombs, barrows, cairns and burial mounds which have been found in many areas of Scotland. The items they contained, grave goods intended to accompany the deceased to the afterlife, give an insight into their daily lives.

Although these sort of cairns and tombs have been found in many parts of continental Europe, stone circles, created by the Megalithic peoples, are peculiar to the British Isles. The most famous of these is, of course, Stonehenge in Wiltshire, England, but Scotland has its own very impressive circles, in particular the Callanish Standing Stones in Lewis, and the Ring of Brodgar, Orkney.

From about BC2500 a wave of migration from Europe began, these people being known as the Beaker People, because of their earthenware pottery. Then in BC2000 the use of bronze appears, thought to have been introduced to Scotland from Ireland.

By BC500 iron was beginning to be used, allowing production of stronger, sharper tools and weapons.

From BC900 there were successive waves of Celtic migration. These people came from north west Europe, first spreading through Germany, France and Belgium, then crossing the channel to Britain and Ireland. These Celtic settlers were known as Picts, and the land above the line of the Forth and the Clyde as Caledonia, a name still used today, particularly in the Highlands, and not just poetically. Scottish Premier League football team, Inverness Caledonian Thistle, is perhaps the most notably non-poetic use of the ancient name for Scotland.

The modern name of the country derives from the Scoti, a Celtic tribe who came from Ireland in the fifth century. They settled on present-day Argyll on the west coast, forming the ancient Gaelic-speaking kingdom of Dalriada.

Romans in the Gloamin'

Once they had successfully conquered the south of Britain in 43AD, the invading forces of the Romans then set about occupying other areas, pushing west into Wales and north as far as Yorkshire. In 80AD Agricola, a Roman general, launched an attack on the northern lands beyond that, and succeeded in reaching the Tay estuary in southern Scotland, finding the lowland tribes easily subjugated. The first Roman roads were laid as they went, and a network of forts linked by military roads was built across the country between the Forth and the Clyde, the aim being to keep out the northern Pictish tribesmen.

Although the Picts were a more difficult enemy than the southern tribes, their amateurish enthusiasm and aggression was no match for the organised professionalism of the Roman legions, and there were several decisive battles where the Romans decimated the Caledonian fighters. However, despite this, the Romans eventually gave up the northern lands, finding the Picts impossible to pacify. Making discretion the better part of valour, the Romans withdrew south.

Things didn't go well for them even here, as the Caledonians continued to make forays south to attack the Roman legions. In around 105AD the Romans moved even further south, below a line between the Solway and the Tyne. The reason for the abrupt removal is not known, but it is known that the Ninth Legion disappeared without trace about this time, some speculating that the war-like Caledonians overcame them, filling the bodies of the dead Romans with stones and sinking them in a loch.

In 121AD the Emperor Hadrian had his famous wall erected, running between Carlisle and South Shields, and designed to keep out the northern tribesmen who continued to invade the Roman-occupied areas. Around 139AD a new wall was constructed further north, between the forth and the Clyde, along the route of the forts and military roads established by Agricola 60 years before, and named the Antonine Wall after the current Emperor Antoninus Pius.

Despite various campaigns to subdue and conquer the northernmost parts of

Britain, the Romans, never seemed to have their hearts in it – maybe the weather and the midges were too much for their southern blood to stand! Whatever the reason, Scotland was never a Roman stronghold in the way England was, and after 401AD the Romans left the country well alone.

Birth of a Nation

All this time, while they were more or less of one mind in their desire to oust the Romans, the various peoples of Scotland were also fiercely protective of their separate identities, and there was as much conflict between them as against further threats from beyond their borders. The various waves of immigration had resulted in four main groups of peoples sharing the country: the Scots in Argyll and the Inner Hebrides; the Picts in the north; the Britons of Strathclyde; and the Angles who occupied a southern area known as Bernicia, (now Northumbria in England). It was not until 843AD that a united Scottish/Pictish kingdom was established, largely brought about by the Christianising of the people.

Emperor Constantine the Great had made Christianity the official religion of the Roman Empire in 325AD. The gospel spread to Britain through the offices of a handful of missionaries. One of the earliest was St. Ninian. Born of Romano-British parents who had converted to the new faith, he travelled to Rome as a young man, later returning to Britain and establishing a monastery on the Solway coast. His brand of Christianity spread slowly northwards through Galloway and Strathclyde, and by the time he died in 432AD, he had sent missionaries into eastern Scotland, and north to the Shetland Islands.

St. Patrick, patron saint of Ireland, was actually born in Dumbarton, Scotland and was sold into slavery in Ireland after being taken prisoner during a raid by the Irish king Niall Noigiallach in 401AD.

Continuing the cross-fertilisation between Scotland and Ireland, the Abbot St. Columba travelled to Scotland in 563 on a mission to convert the heathen Scots. He built a monastery on Iona, just off the western tip of the Isle of Mull in the Inner Hebrides. From here he brought the Celtic Christian Church to the mainland.

FIRST SIGHTING OF NESSIE

St Columba is also renowned – or notorious, depending on one's standpoint – as the first recorded Loch Ness Monster spotter. The story goes that he told one of his monks to swim across the River Ness to fetch a boat. When he was partway there, the monster appeared, threatening to attack the monk. On hearing Columba admonishing the beast, shouting at him to go back and not touch the man, the monster fled and has never since harmed a living soul.

The Christianising of Scotland continued through the offices of a growing number of missionaries and monasteries, with followers spreading their religion – and the Gaelic language – throughout the country.

The Viking plunderers from Norway first arrived on Scottish soil in 794. They raided the Hebrides, attracted by the wealth of the monasteries, and succeeded in sacking the sacred monastery at Iona in 802. In this period they also raided Ireland, and eventually settled there, building their power and wealth. By the middle of the ninth century they had established a Hiberno-Norse empire stretching from Shetland and Orkney to the Isle of Man, taking in all the western isles of Scotland as well as large areas of Ireland..

By 843, with the Pictish central lands weakened by Norse raids, Kenneth McAlpin, Scottish Lord of Kintyre, was proclaimed king of both Picts and Scots. The ceremony took place in the church of Scone, near Perth, on the sacred Stone of Destiny which had been brought from Ireland for the occasion. McAlpin's descendants had won control of most of the land now known as Scotland by the middle of the 11th century.

There were still threats to them from the Britons and the Angles, and from the Norsemen who had settled Orkney, Shetland and the Outer Hebrides, but they were little match for their strength.

Kenneth McAlpin died in 858, and the Scottishisation of the country continued over the next 200 years. These were bloody and warlike years, with two-thirds of the 15 kings who followed Kenneth meeting their deaths violently. Throughout these years of struggle, the final shape of Scotland was gradually emerging.

King Duncan, whose reign began in 1034, was the first king to rule over the lands of the Picts and Scots, Lothian and Strathclyde, and was thus the first true king of a unified mainland Scotland. It was another 400 years before the offshore islands came under the Scottish crown. In 1266, King Eric of Norway ceded the Hebrides to Scotland, then finally, in 1469, Orkney and Shetland became Scottish, through the marriage of James III to Anne of Denmark. The islands were her dowry.

Scotland & England: Union & Disunity

Once Duncan assumed his role as King of a consolidated mainland Scotland, it paved the way for a more peaceful era. Unfortunately, this was not to be. The next 700 years were characterised by battles against the English kings who wanted power over Scotland. Gaining control of Strathclyde and Lothian in the south brought about an influx of Anglo-Norman noblemen who bore an allegiance to the English king, so there was also much civil unrest within Scotland. The fate and fortunes of Scotland wavered, depending on the relative strengths of the Scottish and English kings on their respective thrones at any particular time.

David I, who came to the throne in 1124, and had been educated in France, did much to introduce Anglo-Saxon and Norman practices into Scotland. As well as granting land to his friends from the south, he introduced an English-style feudal system to the country. Gradually, the English language and Norman French spread into the Lowlands, while Gaelic became confined to the Celtic Highlands.

A decisive period in Scotland's relationship with England occurred in 1296.

Edward I of England had succeeded in imposing John Balliol on the Scottish throne, a weak man who pledged allegiance to the English throne. Edward proclaimed himself Superior and Lord Paramount of Scotland and proceeded to treat Balliol in a humiliating manner, ordering him to surrender his chief castles and involving him in petty lawsuits. The Scots saw Balliol as weak-willed and as no more than a vassal of Edward's.

In 1295, the power and land-hungry Edward invaded France. Balliol, in an attempt to show his people that he had some strength of character, negotiated an alliance with the French against their common enemy, England. This was the famous Auld Alliance which continued until the death of Mary of Guise, mother of Mary Queen of Scots, in 1560.

Balliol invaded Cumberland, and in response Edward besieged Berwick, massacring women and children as well as the Scottish army, then went on to defeat them at Dunbar, after which Roxburgh, Edinburgh and Stirling surrendered to him. Balliol abdicated the throne and went into exile, leaving Edward, known by this time as 'the Hammer of the Scots', to put Scotland under English military administration. As his final act of humiliation he removed the sacred Stone of Destiny, ultimate symbol of Scottish sovereignty, from Scone Palace to Westminster Abbey.

In 1297, William Wallace, one of the heroes of Scottish history, especially since the Hollywood portrayal of him by Mel Gibson in Braveheart, led an army to victory against the English at Stirling Bridge. Wallace ruled Scotland for a year in the name of the deposed John Balliol, but then faced Edward's army again at Falkirk. This time he was defeated. Wallace continued to be a thorn in Edward's side, travelling to the continent to enlist the help of France against Edward. Gradually, over the next few years, Edward gained the upper hand again, and Wallace was captured and executed in 1305.

Robert Bruce was the next hero to come along. With revolutionary fervour still alive in the land after the barbarous execution of William Wallace, Bruce seized Dumfries Castle and, in defiance of Edward, was crowned King of Scotland at Scone in 1306. Edward I was ill by this time, and no longer had the strength to oppose Robert Bruce. His successor, Edward II, was weak and no match for the warlike Scots. He made no attempt to subdue the Scots during the early years of his reign, which allowed Bruce to go from strength to strength, culminating in the decisive Battle of Bannockburn in 1314, when English forces were comprehensively beaten. In 1320, King Robert succeeded in getting the Scottish barons to sign up to a declaration of independence at Arbroath. It was another 14 years before Edward II was finally persuaded to recognise Scotland as an independent sovereign nation, ruled by a king who owned no fealty to any other ruler. This was the Treaty of Northampton of 1328. Many of the English, however, felt that surrendering Scotland in this way was humiliating, and they called it the 'Shameful Peace.'

Scottish Independence proved to be a fragile thing, and the fortunes of Scotland continued to wax and wane over succeeding years. Periodically the Scottish Nobles, many of them with Anglo-Norman connections, rose against the Scottish throne and the English were always willing to side with them to regain the northern lands they had lost. Various marriage alliances were made between the Scottish and English thrones during this period, which strengthened the ties between the two, with Scotland forever suffering under the superior size and strength of England.

By 1567 a Union of the Crowns had been established, whereby a series of six monarchs, starting with James VI of Scotland and ending with Queen Anne in 1714, ruled on both sides of the border. The growing interdependence of the two countries led many to see that political union would be desirable. Many, of course, still hankered after the glorious days of Scottish Independence.

Finally, in 1707, those who had been pressing for political union between the countries finally won the day, and the Act of Union was passed, guaranteeing Scotland 45 Members of Parliament in the House of Commons in London, and 16 Peers in the House of Lords.

The strongest opponents of the Act of Union within Scotland were the Jacobites, who continued to bear allegiance to the House of Stewart after James VII was deposed and replaced by the Hanoverian William and Mary. Their loyalty to the Stewarts passed to James's son, James Francis Edward, known as the Old Pretender, and to his grandson Charles Edward, the Young Pretender, more famously known as Bonnie Prince Charlie. Between 1689 and 1745 the Jacobites, predominantly Highlanders, rebelled five times, ending with the famous rising of 1745 led by Bonnie Prince Charlie, at the head of an army of over 1,000 men. After a number of skirmishes, they succeeded in entering Edinburgh and Charles took up residence at Holyrood. This did not long go unchallenged, and regiments were recalled from fighting on the continent to attack the Jacobites. Their last stand was at Culloden Moor near Inverness on 17th April 1746, where the government troops overwhelmed them. After going on the run through the Highlands, Charles finally escaped to France in September, never to return to Scotland.

In order to prevent such uprisings again, the government introduced a raft of measures, including the banning of the wearing of traditional tartan and playing the bagpipes, which effectively destroyed the Highland Clan system.

Industrialisation, Innovation and Intellectuality

Then followed a period of largely uninterrupted peace. The stability within the country allowed progress in many areas, introducing a period of innovation and prosperity. Scotland became a centre for textile production, with linen becoming its chief export. Scotland's coal and iron deposits were exploited to further the Industrial Revolution, in which James Watt had a major part to play with his ground-breaking improvements on the steam engine.

Improvements were also seen in agriculture, with more efficient methods introduced, and in communications, with new roads, bridges and canals aiding the transport of goods throughout the country.

In the late eighteenth century a period of intellectual blossoming began, with Scotland producing artists, writers, scientists and philosophers who were the envy of the world. The universities at St Andrews, Glasgow, Aberdeen and Edinburgh had a far more liberal admissions policy than Oxford and Cambridge, accepting poor but talented students from around the world. The universities produced high calibre graduates who went on to become widely-renowned doctors, engineers and entrepreneurs. Robert Burns and Sir Walter Scott, Scotland's two most famous authors, were both writing at this time too and both had a far-reaching influence on the learned classes, spreading their vision of romantic 'Scottishness' to Europe and beyond.

However, while these exciting developments were taking place in the Lowlands, the Highlands were suffering. The population was already devastated by the great losses during the years of war and rebellion, while the poor quality of the land meant the life of the highlander was hard and poverty-stricken. In the 1760s, many highlanders had emigrated to Canada, seeking a better life in the new world. During this period, many Highland chiefs moved south to Edinburgh or London, interested in their vast estates only for the rents they brought them, the welfare of their clansmen being a very low priority.

With a growth in the demand for wool as the textile industry grew, they found that sheep were far more lucrative than people. Thus began the infamous Highland Clearances. In order to clear the lands of the people who were taking up valuable grazing space, being a drain on resources rather than a source of significant income, many estate owners started a forced scheme of emigration, laying on ships in which entire communities were shipped off to Canada. Many other highlanders, taking the least line of resistance as their landlords made life more and more difficult for them, using force to drive them out of their homes and burning their cottages, chose to move themselves. Thus began the movement of the Scottish people throughout the world, to America, Australia and New Zealand. Others moved to find work in the industrial centres further south, in Glasgow and Dundee.

Once vast tracts of the Highlands were cleared for sheep, estate owners began to introduce deer and encourage the breeding of game birds such as grouse for rich Londoners to come and hunt, which proved even more lucrative than the income from wool. Further communities were cleared to provide these killing fields.

Queen Victoria did much to popularise the Highlands. She visited them for the first time in 1822 and after that made regular trips north. In 1852 she bought Balmoral Castle, immediately making the Highlands a fashionable place for the gentry to visit. Thus began the tourist industry in Scotland, an industry which today is one of the largest earners for the country.

Emigration from the Highlands continued throughout this period, as the thousands of sheep over-grazing the land made the soil less fertile. Those who did remain had to subsist on tiny parcels of land and were living from hand to mouth. Rents for these pitiable packets of land were increased to untenable levels and finally in 1882 the Highland Land League was set up to force reform, organising riots and other forms of agitation to make their case. In 1886 the Crofters' Commission was set up, which guaranteed fair rents, security of land tenure for the crofters and other benefits.

The Modern Era

It can be seen that throughout its history, the Scots have had a leaning towards radicalism – not surprising, given the injustices that have been visited on them from the south over the centuries. Their political awareness was only increased by the Economic Depression which followed the First World War, a war during which the Scots sent numbers of men, and suffered losses, out of all proportion to their population in comparison to the English contribution of manpower.

The Scottish nationalist mentality, which had persisted ever since the abortive battles for independence in earlier centuries, developed into Socialism in the latter years of the 19th Century. The Scottish Labour party was set up in 1888 and in 1892 Keir Hardie became the first working man to enter the House of Commons, as a Labour member. It was, however, the Liberal Party who, by 1894, were advocating Home Rule for Scotland. After the war, with Scotland suffering from the loss of the shipbuilding and heavy engineering which had created a mini-boom during the war years, there was little heart left in the campaign for an independent Scotland. However, by 1928 there was a resurgence in interest in traditional Scottish culture and language and the Scottish National Party was founded. Over ensuing years it worked, with only minor successes, at producing a significant movement towards Independence for the nation.

Only after the second world war, in 1945, did Scottish nationalism begin to make any headway, and even then the majority of the Scots people had no interest in it. An SNP Member was briefly elected to Parliament in a by-election, but he was defeated at the general election a few months later. In 1947 a group of students with Nationalist sympathies made a daring raid on Westminster Abbey, succeeding in liberating the Stone of Destiny and briefly hiding it in Scotland, before it was recovered by the police and returned to London.

It was 1970 before the next SNP Member of Parliament was elected, followed in 1974 by them taking seven seats, and increasing this to 11 the following year. Although many Scots remained lukewarm about complete Independence from the United Kingdom, many saw Devolution, advocated by the Labour Party, as an acceptable way forward. In 1996 the conservative UK Government agreed to the repatriation of the Stone of Destiny to Scotland, and in 1999, a Scottish Parliament with limited powers of self-government was elected.

POLITICAL STRUCTURE

Devolution

So it can be seen that the main theme of Scotland's history over the centuries has been its relationship with England. In contemporary times, this theme has not changed.

After hundreds of years of falling in and out of union and allegiance with England, throughout the 20th century the question of Scotland gaining political and economic independence, to one degree or another, has been discussed at length, both by political parties and Joe McPublic. Despite the fervour shown by the Scottish Nationalist movement, the general mood of the people of Scotland has long been that they don't really want full independence from the United Kingdom. A pragmatic and practical race, they recognise that there are many advantages to be gained through retaining strong links with England which, although not the world power it once was, nonetheless is still comparatively rich and powerful, a strong ally worth hanging on to. At the same time, the Scots, along with many other small countries in the modern world, were eager to gain some measure of autonomy, to assert their independence of thought and character in a more formalised way than was possible without the means of a certain degree of self-government.

And finally this did come to pass. On 6th May 1999 the people of Scotland voted for devolution, electing the first parliament to sit in Scotland since 1707. Devolution came into full effect on 1st July 1999 when the first session of the Scottish parliament took place.

There are 129 Members of the Scottish Parliament (MSPs) who are elected for a fixed term of four years. In the second election, in May 2003, the majority of MSPs returned to the Scottish Parliament represented the Labour Party, with 50 MSPs, followed by the Scottish Nationalist Party with 27, the Conservatives with 18, and the Liberal Democrats with 17. The remaining MSPs are independents, or represent a variety of small parties.

Devolution gave Scotland the authority to legislate on certain specified issues, including local government, planning and economic development, criminal and civil law, criminal justice and the prosecution system, police and fire services, education, health, social work and housing, environment, natural and built heritage, forestry, agriculture and fisheries, food standards, tourism, some aspects of transport, sport and the arts.

This is not to say that devolution has been an unmitigated success – Scots are still divided on whether it has made any change for the better. Only just over half the population believe that devolution has brought about an improvement in the way Scotland is governed, and while around 60% would like to see the Scottish Parliament have their powers increased, there is a feeling in many quarters that maybe the MSPs are not up to the job. This sense of unease has not been helped by the fiasco surrounding the construction of the new Scottish Parliament building at Holyrood. Dogged by controversy and claims of mismanagement from the start, the building finally opened in 2004, three years late, having cost well over £400 million, around 11 times the original estimate.

It is perhaps a lack of confidence in the calibre of their elected members which prevents the Scottish people from embracing the idea of a completely independent Scotland. Even Alex Salmond, leader of the Scottish Nationalist Party, whose raison d'être has always been independence for Scotland, has now conceded that most Scots do not want this.

There is some evidence that the view of Scots outside their homeland is somewhat different. A study of national identity following the establishment of the Scottish Parliament found that as many as 70% of middle-class Scots living in England felt they would think twice before returning to Scotland. Now that everyday life in Scotland is run in a different way they thought they would find it more difficult to fit back in and that they would have a sense of cultural isolation were they to return.

However, although they may not admit it, overall one suspects that the Scottish people are proud of their newly devolved status. Anything to distance themselves from the auld enemy, the English, is likely to go down well with most Scots!

AULD ENEMIES DIE HARD

When Scotland and England became unified in 1707, this did little to heal the long-standing rivalry between the two nations. Scotland had long had a closer relationship with continental Europe, in particular the Auld Alliance with the French, than with their nearest neighbours in England. This rivalry has continued through the centuries and is still evident today. Pope Pius 11, no less, noted this back in 1435, asserting, 'There is nothing the Scots like better to hear than abuse of the English.'

Here is just a selection of the insults traded over the years.

- *Lang beards heartless, painted hoods witless, gay coats graceless, mak' England thriftless.* (Early Scottish view of the English)
- *A greedy, dark, degenerate place of Sin*
  For th' Universe to shoot her rubbish in...
  Pimps, Bullies, Traitors, Robbers, 'tis all one,
  Scotland, like wide-jaw'd Hell, refuses none. (Anonymous, 1705)
- *Yes, sir, the Englishman is amiable. He is the mildest mannered man ever to have scuttled ship or cut a throat.* (James Bridie)
- *Scotland is of all other countries in the world, perhaps the one in which the question 'What is the use of that?' is most often asked.* (William Hazlitt)
- *God help England if she had no Scots to think for her!* (George Bernard Shaw)
- *No McTavish*
  Was ever lavish. (Ogden Nash)

In the end, I think we can say honours are pretty much even between the nations! For much more on the subject, see the entertaining book *Auld Enemies* by David Ross (Birlinn 2002)

Relationship with the UK and Europe

The Scottish Executive is subordinate to the UK Government, which retains control over all non-devolved matters relating to Scotland. In addition to MSPs, Scotland still elects representatives to Westminster (MPs), which represent their 72 Scottish constituencies in relation to these non-evolved matters.

Some politicians and voters feel this puts Scottish MPs in an anomalous position. Some Conservatives in particular, have a problem with the fact that Scottish MPs can vote on matters at Westminster which relate purely to English legislation, while they can also vote on devolved Scottish matters which English MPs can have no say in.

A row broke out in the ranks of Scottish Conservatives in May 2005, when James Gray, the Shadow Scottish Secretary, suggested that all MSPs should lose their jobs, with Holyrood being turned into a part-time home for Scottish MPs. Although the Scottish Conservative leader, David McLetchie, immediately demanded he be sacked because it was against the party's policy, there was some sympathy for his views, with one of his shadow cabinet colleagues saying, 'I see no good reason why James should be sacked for this – what he was saying was perfectly reasonable and represents what a lot of voters believe.'

Scotland is classed as a separate region within the European Parliament, with eight MEPs (Members of the European Parliament). However, it is down to the UK Government to represent Scottish interests in the European Council of Ministers, even in relation to those matters which are devolved to the Scottish Parliament within the UK.

Local Government

Scotland's local government is divided into 29 unitary authorities and three Islands councils. Local authorities are made up of directly elected councillors. The geographical area covered by each local authority, or local council, is divided into a number of areas, called 'wards', and a councillor is elected for each ward.

Local authorities are responsible within their areas for education; social work; strategic planning; roads provision and repair; consumer protection; flood prevention; coast protection; valuation and rating; the police and fire services; emergency planning; electoral registration; public transport; registration of births, deaths and marriages; housing; leisure and recreation; building control and planning; environmental health; licensing; public conveniences; the administration of district courts.

In addition, there are over 1,000 community councils throughout Scotland, which are intended – with a variable degree of success – to express the view of the communities which they represent on a range on matters pertaining to local government and other local services. They are made up of locally elected unpaid community councillors.

GEOGRAPHICAL INFORMATION

Physical Features

Scotland is bordered to the south by England, with the Atlantic Ocean to the north and west, and the North Sea to the east. The country comprises the mainland and many islands including the Hebrides, the Orkneys and the Shetlands. Scotland covers

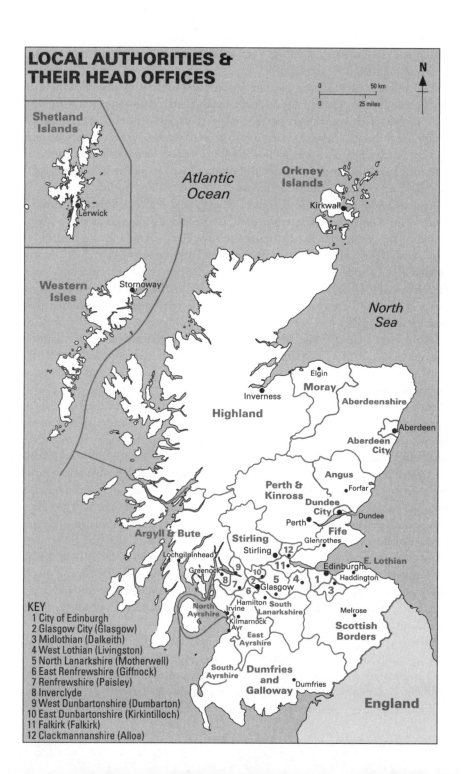

LOCAL AUTHORITIES & THEIR HEAD OFFICES

N

| 0 | 50 km |
| 0 | 25 miles |

Shetland Islands

Lerwick

Atlantic Ocean

Orkney Islands

Kirkwall

Western Isles

Stornoway

North Sea

Elgin

Moray

Inverness

Aberdeenshire

Aberdeen

Highland

Aberdeen City

Angus

Perth & Kinross

Forfar

Dundee City

Dundee

Perth

Fife

Glenrothes

Argyll & Bute

Stirling

Stirling

12

Lochgilphead

9   10   11

Greenock

8   7

Edinburgh

E. Lothian

Haddington

5   4   1

2

6   Glasgow

3

Hamilton   South Lanarkshire

Melrose

North Ayrshire

Irvine

Kilmarnock

Ayr   **East Ayrshire**

Scottish Borders

South Ayrshire

Dumfries and Galloway

Dumfries

England

KEY
1 City of Edinburgh
2 Glasgow City (Glasgow)
3 Midlothian (Dalkeith)
4 West Lothian (Livingston)
5 North Lanarkshire (Motherwell)
6 East Renfrewshire (Giffnock)
7 Renfrewshire (Paisley)
8 Inverclyde
9 West Dunbartonshire (Dumbarton)
10 East Dunbartonshire (Kirkintilloch)
11 Falkirk (Falkirk)
12 Clackmannanshire (Alloa)

around one third of the area of the United Kingdom, but its population is only one twelfth of the total UK population.

The low population density, plus the unsurpassed scenery, of unspoiled mountains and glens and vast areas of inland waters, make Scotland a beautiful and appealing place to live. The importance of preserving the wild nature of the landscape is recognised formally, with over five million acres of the land protected under various environmental designations including National Parks, National Scenic Areas, Sites of Special Scientific Interest, National, Local and Forest Nature Reserves. Together they make up over 25% of the land mass.

Mainland Scotland falls into three topographical regions. Stretching from the border with England, to the south of Glasgow and Edinburgh, are the southern uplands. The countryside here is characterised by fertile farmland and gentle hills.

The central lowlands are formed by the valleys of three rivers, the Clyde, the Forth and the Tay. Despite the name, the hills here increase in height, forming dramatic steep-sided glens, with many forests and lochs in the beautiful Trossachs. The lowlands spread to the fishing villages of the east coast and the more rugged west coast around Argyll.

North from here are the Highlands, which are themselves divided into the southern and northern Highlands along a line between Inverness and Fort William by the Great Glen, a major geological fault, along much of which runs Loch Ness, of monstrous fame.

The many islands to the north and west of the mainland have their own distinct topography. To the west of the mainland are the Outer Hebrides, now known as the Western Isles. There are about 200 islands in total, but only 14 of these are inhabited. The largest of them are Lewis and Harris, technically one landmass but treated as two distinct islands. They are renowned for their fine sandy beaches and their rugged nature. The Inner Hebrides, nearer to the mainland, include the dramatic Isle of Skye and the gentler isles of Mull and Arran. The Orkney islands, whose southernmost tip are only 6 miles (9 km) from the north coast of Scotland at Duncansby Head, are a fertile area, one reason why they were the first group of islands to be extensively settled. The Shetland islands are 50 miles (80 km) north of the Orkneys and are largely barren, with the islanders historically getting much of their food from the sea. Both were settled by the Scandinavian tribes – and at times ruled by Scandinavian kings – so they are the least 'Scottish' parts of Scotland in their culture and temperament.

Although administratively there are 29 mainland and three island councils, geographically, Scotland is divided into 12 larger regions, which do not always follow the administrative divisions. These are Shetland, Orkney, Western Isles, Highland, Grampian, Tayside, Fife, Lothian, Borders, Central, Strathclyde, Dumfries & Galloway. These regional divisions will be profiled in more detail in Part II.

SCOTLAND'S GEOGRAPHY: FACTS & FIGURES

Total area: 30,420 sq. miles/78,789 sq. km.

Inland water area: 653 sq. miles/1,692 sq. km.

Length of mainland, (Mull of Galloway to Cape Wrath): 274 miles/441 km.

Width of mainland, (Buchan Ness to Applecross): 154 miles/246 km.

Mountains: there are 284 Scottish mountains over 3000 ft/914m high, known as the Munros since Sir Hugh Munro listed them in 1891.

Highest mountain: Ben Nevis 4406 ft/1343 m.

Longest loch: Loch Fyne 42 miles/26 km.

Largest inland loch: Loch Lomond 27.46 sq. miles/71.12 sq. km.

Deepest inland loch: Loch Ness 800 ft/244m.

Islands: there are about 790 islands and islets in total, only 130 of which are inhabited.

Largest island: Skye 643 sq. miles/1648 sq. km.

Population

The population of Scotland is approximately 5.06 million, a figure which is falling. With a lower birth rate and net migration from the country, it is predicted that the population may fall below 5 million by 2021. As this includes a greater loss in the younger age groups, with the 60 plus group increasing in size, this could have dramatic consequences for the provision of services in the country. Spending on schools may fall, while social and health service provision for the elderly is destined to increase greatly. With a proportionately smaller working population, as the economically active age groups shrink, this will put a greater burden on tax-payers if these social costs are to continue to be met via personal taxes.

There was some good news in the 2005 figures for births and deaths in Scotland, with the Registrar General announcing that the number of births during the first six months of the year was at a higher level than they had been for six years. In addition, the number of deaths was 0.7% per cent lower than one year earlier. For Scotland as a whole, deaths slightly exceeded births, by 0.1%, but a good sign was that births outnumbered deaths in seven out of the 15 Health Board areas. Although these changes defer the date when Scotland's population is forecast to fall below five million, this is just a temporary halt on the downward trend, and it does imply an even greater increase in the elderly as a proportion of the whole. Scotland's total school roll will fall by around 14,000 in 2005.

In order to try to halt, or at least slow down, the population decrease, which is recognised as a great threat to the country's future prosperity, the Scottish Executive have introduced a 'Fresh Talent' initiative to encourage well-qualified immigrants to the country to work. The aim is to encourage an additional 8,000 migrants a year between 2004 and 2009. However, there are inherent difficulties in this scheme. Even if Scotland succeeds in encouraging more migrants, there is no practical way, with open borders, to ensure they remain in Scotland and do not move elsewhere in the UK. This at a time when England and Wales are trying to cut down on immigration – it seems UK-wide immigration policy will almost certainly militate against the Scottish desire to increase population.

One significant element in immigration to Scotland which the Scottish Executive seem to rather overlook, is the large numbers of people who move to the country from elsewhere in the UK, which of course is not subject to Government immigration policy. There are close to half a million UK-born people living in Scotland, and there are many more who would move if it were easier to find land and property in the north west highlands, a place which attracts many for its unique style of life. In recent years, however, land and property prices have soared and there is now a distinct shortage of both – not because the land isn't there, but because the land ownership and planning laws make new building so difficult. In addition, it is now easier than ever for European nationals to move to Scotland. Perhaps the Scottish Executive should be doing more to address these issues and attract families to depopulated areas which would only benefit from an influx of permanent residents.

One thing which is significant about Scotland's population is that population densities vary enormously across the country. It is a remarkable fact that 90% of the population live within one hour's drive of Perth in the Central Belt. While the population density for the whole of Scotland is around 65 people per square kilometre, the average density for the eastern and Glasgow area councils is 656, while for those on the west and the Islands the average is 41. Compare this with the Highlands, which has a population density of eight people per square kilometre.

It is the rural areas which currently attract inward migration, while many urban areas, in particular Glasgow, are seeing an overall and continuing decline in numbers. There are strong indications that younger people of child-bearing age are favouring rural locations: during 2003, Scotland's island communities recorded the highest birthrates, exceeding those in inner-city areas significantly. In Shetland 251 babies were born, giving a general fertility rate (GFR) of 61.4 per 1,000 women of child-bearing age, while in the Western Isles 255 babies were born, a GFR of 57.3. This compares with Edinburgh's GFR of 42.2, and Aberdeen's GFR of 43.1. This pattern can be seen again in the fact that rural areas surrounding the cities reported higher birthrates than in the cities themselves, suggesting that many couples are moving out of town, but staying within commuting distance, in order to give their children the benefits of a rural upbringing while still maintaining their urban earning capacity.

Climate

Scotland has a temperate climate, without generally experiencing great extremes of weather, however there is evidence that in recent years, as result of global warming, more periods of extreme weather have been seen. The severe storms across the country, and particularly in the Highlands and Islands, in January 2005, are the most recent example of such unusual conditions. It is predicted by long term weather forecasters that these sorts of extreme weather – excessive rainfall and very high winds in particular – will increase in frequency.

The main variation in climate occurs between the east and the west, rather than between north and south as might be expected. This is because the Gulf Stream, a warm current of the North Atlantic Ocean, has a significant influence on the seas off the west coast, making them far warmer than the North Sea. As a result, the west of the country experiences milder, wetter weather than the colder, drier east.

Although it is true that Scotland has plenty of rain, it is not a great deal wetter than the rest of Great Britain. The Highlands have a comparable annual rainfall to the English Lake District, the Welsh mountains and Cornwall, while it rains about the same amount in Edinburgh as it does in London.

It is a characteristic of Highland weather that, because of the region's topography, conditions can vary greatly within very small areas. Each loch tends to experience its own microclimate which means that while it might be raining where you are, the next village along might be bathed in sunshine. You should expect areas where there are large lochs headed by high mountains to be noticeably wetter on average than nearby areas with smaller lochs surrounded by lower land. For this reason, both Fort William, at the head of Loch Linnhe with Ben Nevis dominating the skyline, and Ullapool, on Loch Broom below the An Teallach range, are very wet areas.

Although snow lies on the highest mountains for the best part of six months of the year, from October to April, on the west coast there are generally no more than a handful of snowy days during the winter, whereas on the north east very cold, snowy conditions should be expected regularly during the winter months.

Despite Scotland being cloudier than England, the lack of air pollution means the country enjoys extremely good visibility. An exception to this is the phenomenon of the thick, cold fog called haar which comes in off the North Sea during April to September – on these occasions visibility is extremely poor!

Sunshine hours vary greatly in different parts of Scotland – both Nairn on the east coast near Inverness, and the island of Tiree, in the Inner Hebrides, have a reputation as very sunny places. Winter days in the north of Scotland are slightly shorter than those in London, but no more than about half an hour. In the summer, however, the days are far longer than those experienced further south. In the middle of June, the north of Scotland never experiences complete darkness, with the sun not going down before 11pm, and rising again by 4am, with an extended twilight between these hours.

SCOTLAND'S CLIMATE: TYPICAL FACTS & FIGURES

Month	Max °C	Min °C	Mean °C	Sunshine hrs	Rainfall mm
JANUARY					
Scotland	5.9	0.9	3.4	30.2	208.1
North	5.6	0.7	3.1	24.3	240.1
East	5.5	0.3	2.9	36.4	131.1
West	6.7	1.7	4.2	31.5	248.6
FEBRUARY					
Scotland	6.4	-0.2	3.1	81.4	108.1
North	6.0	-0.5	2.8	63.3	152.3
East	6.2	-0.4	2.9	92.2	64.5
West	7.1	0.4	3.8	94.8	95.2
MARCH					
Scotland	8.2	1.3	4.7	110.0	98.3
North	8.0	1.4	4.7	112.4	106.5
East	8.1	0.7	4.4	108.9	68.9
West	8.6	1.7	5.2	107.5	119.3
APRIL					
Scotland	10.8	4.1	7.4	104.9	122.9
North	10.3	4.1	7.2	97.2	130.5
East	10.9	3.7	7.3	100.9	106.6
West	11.2	4.6	7.9	119.5	130.8
MAY					
Scotland	14.2	5.7	9.9	183.9	61.5
North	13.4	5.5	9.3	186.5	66.7
East	14.7	5.4	10.0	192.2	50.2
West	14.8	6.2	10.4	196.1	66.8
JUNE					
Scotland	15.6	8.6	12.1	119.1	130.9
North	14.6	8.3	11.4	99.3	134.8
East	16.4	8.5	12.4	137.5	119.5
West	16.2	9.2	12.6	126.5	138.7
JULY					
Scotland	16.5	9.1	12.8	132.3	75.8
North	15.8	9.0	12.4	121.1	78.0
East	17.0	8.7	12.8	135.2	61.4
West	16.9	9.7	13.3	143.9	88.9
AUGUST					
Scotland	18.0	11.0	14.5	147.4	188.1
North	17.4	10.6	14.0	153.2	157.7
East	18.0	10.8	14.3	140.6	198.4

West	18.7	11.7	15.2	146.2	219.7
SEPTEMBER					
Scotland	15.1	8.3	11.7	119.3	175.0
North	14.6	7.9	11.2	117.9	212.1
East	15.4	8.0	11.7	129.8	88.1
West	15.4	9.3	12.3	109.4	219.2
OCTOBER					
Scotland	10.5	4.9	7.7	61.1	203.7
North	10.0	4.7	7.4	49.6	199.1
East	10.6	4.9	7.7	65.1	198.9
West	11.2	5.3	8.2	72.5	216.2
NOVEMBER					
Scotland	8.7	3.5	6.1	43.3	115.2
North	8.4	3.3	5.8	34.4	149.2
East	8.6	2.8	5.7	54.8	67.2
West	9.2	4.5	6.8	43.0	120.4
DECEMBER					
Scotland	7.4	1.5	4.4	35.9	188.8
North	7.4	1.8	4.5	25.7	240.5
East	7.0	0.6	3.8	50.0	95.1
West	7.8	2.2	5.0	34.6	220.1

AREAS REFERRED TO IN CLIMATE TABLE

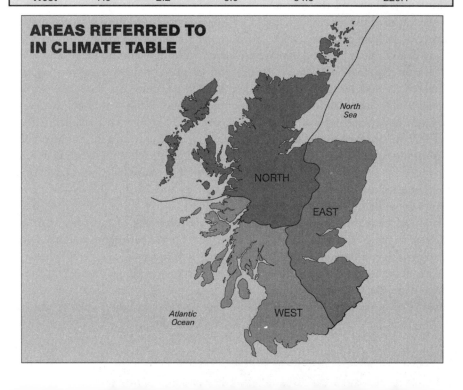

North Sea

NORTH

EAST

WEST

Atlantic Ocean

THE SCOTS: WHAT ARE THEY LIKE?

Modern Scotland is a multi-cultural society with a large proportion of the population living and working in towns and cities in modern industries, but probably the historical image of the Scotsman as a hard-drinking, kilt-wearing, mountain-dweller is the one which still holds sway in the rest of the world. The Scots themselves probably only have themselves to blame for the perpetuation of this stereotype, with their 'whisky, tartan and shortbread' approach to marketing the country to the rest of the world. Although many Scots now feel uncomfortable with this outdated and largely irrelevant picture of the country, there is still an annual Tartan Week held in the USA to encourage American visitors to Scottish shores, and if you walk down the main street of any holiday area in the country you will inevitably find shops filled with shortbread in tartan-decorated tins, tartan tam o' shanters, mini Loch Ness Monsters and row upon row of whiskies.

Historically the Scots have been characterised as tight-fisted and taciturn, but this owed more to the way the English chose to see the Scots – long the 'Auld Enemy' – than to any real facet of the Scottish character.

So is it possible to identify a Scottish national character? Well, as with most stereotypes, there is of course a grain of truth there. The kilt is still worn on high days and holidays – well, at weddings, anyway – and on such occasions plenty of drink will be drunk. Alcoholism is still a problem, even though the Scottish Executive is taking steps to address the issue and to promote a healthier lifestyle.

The image of the Scotsman as mean goes back centuries to the days when it was a very poor, peasant economy, where frugality was the order of the day – which is not to say that the little they did have wasn't shared with those around them. And many an uneducated crofter in the Highlands and Islands is not the most forthcoming of talkers, his conversation with strangers limited to comments about the weather linked with long pauses and plenty of 'ayes'. But his wife is likely to be able to chatter for hours on any subject under the sun – especially if it involves her neighbours!

The Scottish people are, in the main, far less class conscious than the English. There is generally a more democratic feel to daily life, where people tend to be taken more for who they are than where they stand in society. They have long had a tradition of socialist leanings in their politics, with the Labour and Liberal Democratic parties always doing better than the Conservatives.

Coupled with this democratic approach is a greater lack of formality than one finds in England. You will quickly be on first name terms with those you meet, even strangers. Very often a surname (family name) will not even be offered when you ask somebody their name, whether in person or on the telephone. In the Highlands, where doors are still safely left unlocked, it is customary to just drop in at people's homes. It is quite normal just to walk into your neighbour's house when you call on them – they look at you strangely if you knock at the door.

KEEPING IT IN THE FAMILY

Family roots are very important – and in a country as small as Scotland, where the clan system enshrines ancient alliances, family relationships are far-reaching. It is not unusual to get talking to someone in Glasgow and within a few minutes of mentioning you stayed in a small village in the Highlands for some years, you discover they are related to your ex-next door neighbour. So if you find you have a mutual acquaintance with somebody, beware saying anything critical about them for fear that you might be bad-mouthing one of their relatives. If you kick one member of the family, as they say, they all limp.

Equally, the town or village a Scot comes from is very important, a fact that is inherent linguistically in the Scottish phrase 'I belong to Gairloch/Edinburgh' while the English would say 'I come from Preston/London.' Hence the old music hall song 'I belong to Glasgow, Dear old Glasgow town.'

There has been a general liberalisation of attitudes over recent years. There is no doubt that Scotland is no longer the somewhat backward country, twenty years behind London in its attitudes, it undoubtedly was thirty years ago. It is now, certainly in the Central Belt, up there with the most progressive European countries. In fact, in 2004 a survey of global businessmen voted Scotland the European Region of the Future, the best place to do business based on 33 criteria including GDP growth, transport infrastructure and availability of good quality homes.

Along with this change in outlook, attitudes to women have become more egalitarian. Women work alongside men and are increasingly reaching the top jobs. Glasgow in particular, with its traditional heavy industry, has long had a masculine image, but this is changing, with 53% of the city's population and 52% of the workforce now women. This has softened the image of the city, with it now being seen as a centre of art and culture, shopping and nightlife, rather than being dominated by a culture of heavy drinking and football – which does still go on, of course. This change continues to attract more women to the city, so continuing the modernisation of a city which is learning to show its feminine side. This trend is also seen in the business world throughout Scotland, with the numbers of women heading their own businesses increasing.

English people moving to Scotland are often apprehensive that they may come across some 'anti-English' feeling. Despite the occasional incident, which is sure to be well-publicised in the English (and Scottish) media, such cases are few and far between. Any rivalry between the two nations is more likely to be on the level of good-humoured bantering than anything more malicious.

Although there is anecdotal evidence that some people living close to the border with England may display some anti-English sentiment, it is difficult to back this up with hard facts and figures. More often one gets the impression that, because there has been a long history of cross-border migration, with people on either side of the Scots-English border crossing to the other for work, shopping or leisure activities, there is a greater bond between them than between the Scots and the English generally.

Since Devolution, any resentment of one nation by the other is more common on the English side. Not that they have anything against the Scots per se, but they see the Scottish Executive spending money to improve the Scottish infrastructure, while Westminster tends to see the north of England as a far lower priority than the south, due to its distance from the seat of government in London. This is clearly demonstrated by the public expenditure per resident in these different regions. In 1999-2000, for example, this worked out at £5,271 per capita in Scotland; £5,035 in London; but just £4,837 in the north east of England, and £4,628 in the north west.

On the other hand, there are some signs that there is less antipathy from the Scots towards the English since devolution. Before, it was easy to blame the UK government for overlooking Scotland and the English having things all their own way. Now the Scots have seen at first hand that their own elected representatives don't always seem to have the interests of their people at heart, wasting time and money on things which are seen as non-essentials, a phenomenon which was writ large in the debacle over the outrageous mismanagement of, and overspend on, Holyrood, the new Scottish Parliament building.

With a comparatively low level of immigrants in Scotland, racial intolerance has not historically been a big problem. However, recent influxes of asylum seekers to Scottish cities from Eastern Europe and elsewhere have brought about some racial intolerance in certain areas, particularly the poorer areas of inner cities where these asylum seekers often end up. Some of the local population have felt that the immigrants are treated more favourably than themselves, with inevitable discord and some racial abuse.

Marriage has shown a steady decline over recent decades, with 30,755 marriages in Scotland in 2003, compared with over 40,000 per year in the 1960s. However, in 2004 there was the first increase for many years, with 32,200 marriages. With it becoming very common for couples to cohabit without getting married, there is little stigma attached to it nowadays, nor to children born out of wedlock.

Prejudicial attitudes to those 'living in sin' are more likely to be encountered in rural areas, but social attitudes for the whole of the UK have changed so dramatically in recent years that even in the Highlands and Islands hardly an eyebrow will be raised.

Making Friends

Anybody who visits the country, whatever preconceptions they come with, goes away having discovered that the Scots are actually very friendly and welcoming, prepared to put themselves out for others. When you move to the country permanently you will find it is not difficult to get to know people. In an urban or a rural setting you will find many opportunities for meeting others, and hopefully making friends with some of them. If you go out to work, this is a good place to get to know new people. It is usual to go out for lunch or after work with work colleagues and this may lead to closer friendships. If you are a parent, your children make it difficult to avoid meeting new people! Children make friends very easily, so it is inevitable that you will soon make contact with the parents of your children's friends. If you frequent a local bar or pub you may meet people there who become friends.

In rural areas it is considered rude not to be friendly with your neighbours. If you move into a new area, it is likely that you will be visited by them. If not, they will be delighted if you call on them to introduce yourself and make their acquaintance. Expect to be offered tea or coffee with biscuits, cake and even sandwiches.

There are plenty of clubs and other activities you can get involved in. Whether you join a leisure club in town or a golf club in the country; whether you fancy indulging your thespian leanings by joining the local drama group or prefer the offerings of the Scottish Women's Rural Institute; whether you want to find about more about Scottish culture by taking classes in Scottish dancing or learning a traditional instrument such as the bagpipes; or whether you join a local church, all these will give you ample opportunity to meet like-minded people who could become your friends.

It has to be said that the Scots do like a party. The Scottish New Year celebration, Hogmanay, is built on this. The ritual of 'first-footing' is still important, especially in the Highlands. It requires you to share a drink or three with all your friends, relations and acquaintances on the first occasion you meet them after the turn of the New Year. This can be an excuse for days – or even weeks – of calling on people with an open bottle of whisky!

Dances and parties don't generally start until late and certainly don't get going properly until after the pubs close. Having started in the pub, people will go on to the dance or the party, then they will continue to drink all night. Generally public dances will have a late licence so the bar stays open until the early hours of the morning. If not, no matter – there's sure to be an informal after-dance party to go on to!

Much of Scotland retains old-fashioned community values. It is still a country where people will help their neighbours and always find time to have a 'blether' and you will generally be treated courteously in shops and hotels, whether in the cities or the country. If you are moving permanently to the rural areas, you may find it takes a while to feel part of the community, but you will always be treated politely while they weigh you up. If you are not found wanting, and don't do anything to upset them, they will eventually invite you into their homes and take you to their hearts.

150 YEARS OF CHANGE

In July 2005, the Registrar General's 150th Annual report gave a fascinating glimpse at how Scotland has changed over a century and a half.

Population
- The population in 1851 was 2.89 million. In 2004 it was 5.08 million.
- In 1861, Scotland's residents accounted for 12.5 per cent of the UK population. In 2001 this figure had fallen to 8.6 per cent.

Births, Deaths & Marriages

- In the mid-19th century there were 35 births per year per 1,000 population. By the end of the 20th century the birth rate was 10 per 1,000.
- In 1855, 93,000 babies were born. In 2004 only 54,000 were born.
- In 1855 the death rate was 24 people per 1,000 population. In 2004 the rate was 11 per 1,000.
- Between 1910 and 1960, there were about 20 centenarians in the country. Today there are almost 300 Scots aged 100 or more.
- In 1855 there were 19,680 marriages. In 2004 there were 32,154.
- Civil marriages were introduced in 1940, when they accounted for ten per cent of all marriages. In 2004 half of all marriages were civil ceremonies.

Immigration

- In 1861, 75 per cent of Scottish residents came from Ireland. By 2001, less than 10 per cent did.
- In 1901, most residents born outside the British Isles came from Europe and America. In 2001 most came from Asia and Europe.

Language

- The number of Gaelic speakers has fallen by 75 per cent in the last 100 years.

Average Scot in 1850	Average Scot in 1999
Called John Smith or Mary MacDonald	Called Lewis Brown or Emma Smith.
One in seven chance of dying before first birthday	One in 200 chance of dying before first birthday.
Lived almost two to a room	Two rooms to every person.
Men married at 27, women at 25	Men married at 32, women at 29.
One in three chance of being married in their 20s	One in seven chance of being married in their 20s.
Life expectancy 40 for men, 44 for women	Life expectancy 74 for men, 79 for women.

GETTING THERE

It is far quicker and easier to reach Scotland than it used to be. The roads are far better than they were even ten years ago, and there is plenty of new road building still going on, with new long and short distance links being built in many parts of the country, particularly in the central belt. There are plans to improve the transport links between Glasgow and Edinburgh airports, while Glasgow (Prestwick) Airport in Ayrshire is now just 30 minutes drive from Glasgow, thanks to new roads.

Not before time, both domestic and international air routes are being opened up, with it now being possible to take a range of international flights direct from Scotland. Previously all international flights involved travelling from airports in

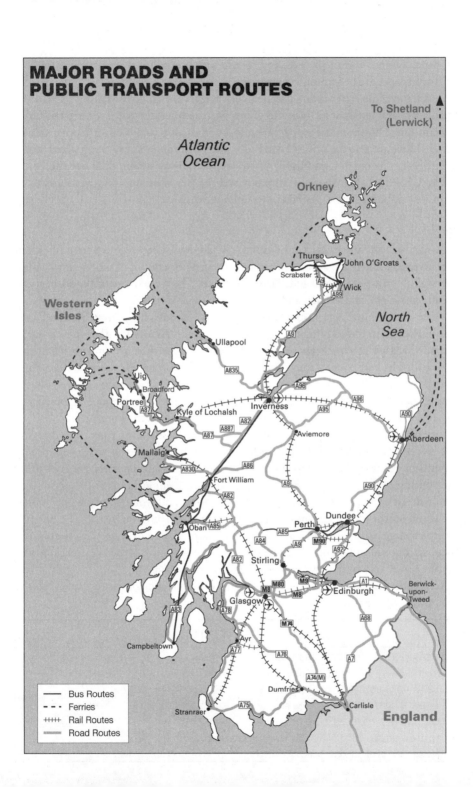

MAJOR ROADS AND
PUBLIC TRANSPORT ROUTES

To Shetland
(Lerwick)

*Atlantic
Ocean*

Orkney

*Western
Isles*

*North
Sea*

Thurso
John O'Groats
Scrabster
A9
Wick
A99

A9

Ullapool

A835

A96

A96

Uig
Broadford
Portree
A87
Kyle of Lochalsh
A82
A887
Inverness
A95
A90
Aberdeen
A87
Aviemore

Mallaig
A86
A830
A9
A90
Fort William
A82
Dundee
Oban A85
Perth
A85
A9
A92
A84
M90
A82
Stirling
M80
M9
A1
M8
Berwick-
upon-
Tweed
Glasgow
M8
Edinburgh
A78
M74
A68
Ayr
A77
A76
A7
Campbeltown
A83
A74(M)
Dumfries
Stranraer
A75
Carlisle

England

——	Bus Routes
- - -	Ferries
++++	Rail Routes
~~	Road Routes

England. Flights within the UK and to selected international destinations, mainly within Europe, are becoming far cheaper.

Coach travel too is becoming cheaper, with at least one company taking a leaf out of the book of the low-cost airlines and offering cheap inter-city travel within the UK.

Train fares, however, are not following suit, and this is still an expensive way to travel. There are also regions of Scotland where train routes are very restricted, and a large part of the north west Highlands where the railway system does not run.

The UK Public Transport Information website (www.pti.org.uk) gives links to all forms of public transport available throughout Scotland.

By Air

The main airports are situated at Edinburgh, Glasgow, Glasgow (Prestwick), Aberdeen and Inverness. There are also small airports at Barra, Benbecula, Campbeltown, Islay, Kirkwall, Stornoway, Sumbrugh, Tiree and Wick. There are frequent flights between the mainland and the islands, and regular inter-island services.

There is currently a huge upsurge in the numbers of airlines flying from Scotland. Low cost airlines seem to be springing up all over the place. As a result, they are having to compete hard with each other to secure their market share so there are some great bargains to be had. The best prices – some as low as £3.98 (plus airport taxes) for a return flight from Scotland to the continent! – are available if you book well in advance. Generally, the shorter the time between booking and flying, the higher will be the price. In practically all cases, the easiest and cheapest way of booking flights is via the Internet.

It is difficult to see how all these new airlines will survive, especially charging the low prices they do, so it is possible that some will go to the wall over coming months or years, and doubtless others will emerge. In addition, they are constantly introducing new flights and negotiating space at different airports.

British Airways fly to the longest list of destinations, but you will pay higher prices. However, on the plus side, you will get free meals and drinks on board. The no-frills airlines charge extra for drinks and snacks on board. BA do have low cost flights, but these are mainly to UK destinations from within Scotland. Other destinations will involve travel via London, with onward flights to Scotland.

Remember that the basic cost of the flight does not include airport taxes, so the final price will be higher.

MAIN AIRLINES OPERATING IN SCOTLAND

Air Scotland: ☎ 0141-222 2363; www.air-scotland.com.
British Airways: ☎ 0870-850 9850; www.ba.com.
bmi: ☎ 0870-6070555; www.flybmi.com.
Easyjet: ☎ 0871-7500 100; www.easyjet.com.
flybe: ☎ 0871-700 0535; www.flybe.com.
Flyglobespan: ☎ 0870-556 1522; www.flyglobespan.com.
Ryanair: ☎ 0818-303030; www.ryanair.com

Sample prices for return flights in November 2005 (booked 1 month in advance)	
Easyjet *(airport taxes extra)*	
Aberdeen – London (Luton)	£38.48
Edinburgh – Amsterdam	£104.98
Glasgow – Belfast	£29.98
Inverness – Bristol	£38.48
Ryanair *(airport taxes extra)*	
Aberdeen – Dublin	£29.98
Glasgow (Prestwick) – Milan	£3.98
Glasgow (Prestwick) – Stockholm	£9.98
British Airways *(prices include airport taxes)*	
Edinburgh – New York	£390.80
Inverness – Paris	£158.00
Glasgow – Sydney	£897.00

Although there are some very cheap flights to the continent, flights within Scotland are, unfortunately, not such a cheap matter. In fact, they are among the most expensive journeys on earth. For example, a mid-week flight from Edinburgh to Kirkwall Airport in Orkney can cost up to £430 return – over £1 per mile – while a weekend trip from Edinburgh to Lerwick in Shetland is £172, more expensive than flying from Edinburgh to Prague or Amsterdam. The Scottish Executive is looking at introducing subsidies to bring down the price of air travel to the Highlands and Islands by designating them vital lifeline routes, which will allow them to place them under Public Service Obligation orders. They intend to spend about £12 million pounds per year on such subsidies.

By Sea

Of the many passenger ferry operators sailing to Great Britain from continental Europe and Ireland, very few sail into Scottish ports, on a small number of routes. These include Stena Line, Smyril Line, Superfast Ferries and P&O Irish Sea. There is a far wider choice of destinations if you sail to England or Wales then travel on to Scotland by other means of transport. Dogs may be taken, at the ferry operator's discretion.

FERRY ROUTES FROM SCOTLAND	
From	**To**
Stranraer	Belfast
	Larne
Troon	Belfast
	Larne

Lerwick	Bergen
	Seysdisfjordur
Aberdeen	Bergen
Cairnryan	Larne
Rosyth	Zeebrugge

Ferries within Scotland. There are numerous ferry services within Scotland, running between the mainland and the islands, between the islands, and also short hops across some sea lochs on the mainland, which are far quicker than travelling by road. There are also inter-island ferries in Shetland and Orkney. The main operators running ferry services within Scotland are Caledonian MacBrayne and P&O Scottish Ferries.

FERRY SERVICES WITHIN SCOTLAND

From	To
Aberdeen	Lerwick (Shetland)
	Stromness (Orkney)
Ardrossan	Brodick (Arran)
Claonaig (Kintyre)	Lochranza (Arran)
Colintraive (Argyll)	Rhubodach (Bute)
Colonsay	Port Askaig (Islay)
Fionnphort (Mull)	Iona
Gourock	Dunoon (Cowall)
	Kilcreggan
	Helensburgh
Kennacraig	Port Ellen (Islay)
	Port Askaig
Largs	Cumbrae
Lochaline (Lochaber)	Fishnish (Mull)
Mallaig	Armadale (Skye)
	Eigg, Muck, Rum, Canna
Oban	Castlebay (Barra)
	Colonsay
	Craignure (Mull)
	Lismore
	Lochboisdale (S.Uist)
	Tobermory (Mull)
	Coll, Tiree
Berneray (N.Uist)	Leverburgh (Harris)
Sconser (Skye)	Raasay
Scrabster	Stromness (Orkney)
Tarbert (Kintyre)	Portavadie (Cowal)

Tayinloan	Gigha
Tobermory	Kilchoan
Uig (Skye)	Tarbert (Harris)
	Lochmaddy (N.Uist)
Ullapool	Stornoway (Lewis)
Wemyss Bay	Rothesay (Bute)

Ferry Companies

Caledonian MacBrayne: ☎ 08705-650000; www.calmac.co.uk.
Hebridean Cruises: ☎ 01756-704704; www.hebridean.co.uk.
Northlink Ferries: ☎ 0845-600 0449; www.northlinkferries.co.uk.
Orkney Ferries Ltd: ☎ 01856-872044; www.orkneyferries.co.uk.
P&O Irish Sea: ☎ 0870-242 4777; www.poirishsea.com.
P&O Scottish Ferries: ☎ 08705-202020; www.poferries.com.
Smyril Line: ☎ +298-345900; www.smyril-line.com.
Stena Line: ☎ 08705-707070; www.stenaline.co.uk.
Superfast Ferries: ☎ 0870-234 0870; www.superfast.com.
Viking Sea Taxis: ☎ 01595-692463 or 859431.
Comprehensive details of routes and operators, plus links to ferry operators' websites, are on www.seaview.co.uk and www.ferry-to-scotland.com.

By Rail

All the major Scottish cities can be reached by train from the south, but connections to smaller areas are not always available, or where they are may not be very frequent. In the Highlands, to the north and west of the line from Kyle of Lochalsh to Thurso, the railway has never reached. As bus services are also limited in this area, a car is pretty much essential.

Trains between Glasgow, Edinburgh, Aberdeen and Inverness and London run from either Kings Cross or Euston. Depending on the route, Scottish rail services are run by First ScotRail, Great North Eastern Railway and Virgin Trains.

First ScotRail run the Caledonian Sleeper service between London Euston and Glasgow, Edinburgh, Fort William, Aberdeen and Inverness. There are other stops along the way – see the website for full details of the routes. Travel on the sleeper can be taken in single berth or twin berth cabins, or in a reclining seat for a cheaper price. If you book at least seven days in advance, you may get a reduced price Apex fare, but these are limited. Family tickets are available for families of one adult and three children or two adults and two children, travelling in two inter-connecting twin berth cabins. Prices start at £30 single, £40 return, for an Apex seated sleeper ticket between Edinburgh or Glasgow and London. A family ticket for the same route is £155 single, £270 return. The first class individual fare is £130 single, £190 return. Dogs can be taken in cabins for extra cost, although guide dogs travel free.

Through-tickets from all Sleeper stations to Lille, Paris or Brussels are available from First ScotRail telesales 08457-550033.

For information about train times and fares telephone the national rail enquiries service on 08457-484950 or see www.firstgroup.com/scotrail. Train tickets for all UK services can be bought on-line at www.thetrainline.com. Tickets may also be booked by telephone with rail companies, or by telephone or in person from railway stations.

Great North Eastern Railway: ☎ 08457-225333; www.gner.co.uk.

First ScotRail: ☎ 0845-601 5929; www.firstgroup.com/scotrail.

Virgin Trains: ☎ 0870-789 1234; www.virgintrains.co.uk.

Eurostar: ☎ 08705-186186; www.eurostar.com.

Eurotunnel: ☎ 08705-353535 (UK); 0321-006100 (France); 070-223210 (Belgium); 0900-5040540 (Netherlands); 01805-000248 (Germany); www.eurotunnel.com.

By Road

Although there are coach and bus services throughout Scotland, these are few and far between in some places, so for the purposes of house hunting a car is essential.

There are just eight motorways in Scotland, all in the southern half of the country. The main trunk road in the Highlands is the A9 which runs from Falkirk to Thurso. There are still many single-track roads in the Highlands and Islands. Small lay-bys called passing places are used to allow oncoming traffic to pass and to allow faster traffic to overtake.

UK vehicles are right-hand drive and motorists drive on the left. Overtaking is permissible only on the right. Speed limits are generally 70 miles per hour (mph) (112 kph) on motorways and dual carriageways, 60 mph (96 kph) on unrestricted single carriageways and 30 mph (48 kph) or 20 mph (32 kph) in built-up and residential areas. Camper vans and caravans are restricted to a maximum of 50 mph (80 kph).

However, there is a national campaign to improve road safety in the UK and you will find that lower speed limits are indicated on certain stretches of roads. In recent years hundreds of speed cameras have been installed throughout the UK to catch speeding drivers, so it is essential to be vigilant while driving, as you can be fined heavily for exceeding the speed limit.

Seat belts must be worn by drivers and passengers of cars and crash helmets by drivers and passengers of motorcycles.

It is illegal to drive on a public road without a current driving licence, vehicle excise duty, vehicle insurance cover and MoT certificate of roadworthiness.

The full rules of the road can be found in *The Highway Code*, price £1.49 available from The Stationery Office: 71-73 Lothian Road, Edinburgh EH3 9AZ; ☎ 0870-6065566; www.tso.co.uk.

COMMUNICATIONS

The Post Office

In the past, even the smallest communities had their own local Post Office, but over the past decade or so, the Post Office has closed down branches in some rural and suburban communities. More recently, it has come to see that this isn't always a good move, because today it does not have the monopoly over services that they used to have, so if people have to travel to the next town to visit a Post Office, they may use other businesses to deliver their parcels, or for other services.

The tide seems to have turned somewhat as a result of this, and the Post Office is now trying to woo back customers by offering an increased range of services. As well as the traditional services available through the Post Office, including the collection of pensions and social security benefits; payment of bills such as gas, electricity, telephone; paying for motor vehicle and TV licences; applying for passports, buying foreign currency, they are now offering many more services. You can withdraw cash from your bank, buy travel and house insurance, take out a loan or sign up for their own HomePhone telephone service, to name a few of the services on offer.

Postal deliveries are normally made to households and business premises once a day, Monday to Saturday. Mail is posted in post boxes which are found outside post offices, by the side of roads and in some large shops or shopping centres throughout the country. Collections are made several times a day from large town centre post-boxes, while in rural communities one collection every day except Sunday is the norm.

Letters can be sent either first class or second class, which vary in their cost and speed of delivery. First class mail, costing 30p for a standard letter, is usually delivered the next working day, while second class mail, at 21p is usually delivered within three working days. Although these delivery times are what the Royal Mail aims at, and in most cases achieves, they are not guaranteed. In remote areas delivery times may be slower.

Recorded or Special Delivery are useful if you are posting important documents, valuable items or documents which must be delivered quickly. Both require a receipt from the post office on posting and a signature of the receiver on delivery, while Special Delivery guarantees delivery the next working day. Compensation is paid for non-delivery of items.

Royal Mail aim to deliver airmail letters within three working days inside Western Europe, four days to eastern Europe and five working days to destinations outside Europe. Small packets and printed papers may be sent by surface mail, and should be delivered within two weeks in Western Europe, four weeks to eastern Europe and up to eight weeks outside Europe.

Postage stamps can be purchased from post offices and in a wide range of shops. Stamps can also be bought in bulk through the Royal Mail website. Parcel Post rates vary on a sliding scale based on the weight and destination of the parcel.

Royal Mail: ☎ 08457-740740; www.royalmail.com.

Post Office: telephone numbers of local branches are in the telephone book; www. postoffice.co.uk.

Telephone

For many years, British Telecom (BT) and its forerunners had an absolute monopoly in the area of telephone provision. In the 1980s the door was opened for other telephone companies to operate, and since that time there has been a huge growth in the industry. The consequent competition, together with advances in technology, have driven down prices and extended the range of services available.

Mobile phone usage too has grown massively, and the technology is advancing so quickly now that it seems one needs to replace one's phone every other week to keep up with the latest developments. The latest models include camera and video facilities, email and text messaging just for starters.

Generally, your phone bill will include an element of regular monthly charge, plus a cost per minute for all calls made, with cheaper calls available in the evening and at weekends. Local, regional and international calls are charged at different rates and there are, at the time of writing, the first tentative steps being made by some providers to offer free local calls at off-peak times.

Mobile phones are available either on contract or pay as you go basis. With a contract, the handset is usually free but the customer commits to keeping the phone for at least 12 months at a set fee per month. This fee will include a specified number of free phone calls and text messages, after which these are charged at a rate per minute. With pay as you go, the customer buys a handset, then buys electronic 'top-ups' which allow a certain value of calls and texts to be made from the phone. Top-ups are sold in units of £5, £10, £20 and £50. Calls from landline phones to mobile phones are charged at a higher rate, and calls between mobiles on different networks are more expensive. Some mobile phone providers offer free calls and texts to other phones on their network.

New technology is destined to change the way telephone calls are made and paid for in the not too distant future. With access to broadband in most homes, systems such as Skype and Freecall are now available which allow people to make local, national and international telephone calls across the internet, either free or at a fraction of the price charged by traditional companies.

Telephone Numbers. Landline telephone numbers are composed of an area code followed by a local number. If phoning a number in the same local area, the area code does not need to be dialled.

Mobile phone numbers are 11 digit numbers, always beginning with 07.

Public Telephones. With the growth of mobile phone usage, these are becoming less well used and BT are removing many of them. They can still be found in places such as airports, railway stations and hotel reception areas, and BT are obliged to keep at least one operating in most communities, where they will be found alongside residential streets, often close to a post office or other shop.

Emergency services. The fire service, police, ambulance, coastguard, mountain rescue or cave rescue can be contacted on 999 or 112.

Internet

In 2004, 43 per cent of Scottish households had access to the internet, a figure that continues to rise as high speed Broadband connections become available across the country.

Connection to the Internet is available through any one of a large number of Internet Service Providers (ISPs). These fall broadly into two groups: 'free' services which charge no monthly subscription, with telephone call charges applied for the time you are connected; and the others which charge a monthly subscription with no call charges.

Dial-up internet connection over a standard telephone line is currently being replaced by broadband connections allowing connection to the Internet and email many times faster than through dial-up..

Broadband is delivered to homes and business using various technologies, including high speed ADSL telephone lines via telephone exchanges, wireless connections using radio repeater stations, satellite and cable systems. By the end of 2005 it should be available to everybody in the UK who wants it.

FOOD & DRINK

Food. There are conflicting reports about the food of Scotland. On the one hand, the Scots are notorious for having one of the worst diets in the world, yet on the other, it also has the reputation for some of the highest quality luxury foods you will find anywhere: Scottish salmon, venison, beef and, of course, whisky, are all highly valued the world over.

And now porridge is having its heyday, having been dismissed in the past – mainly by the English – as inedible peasant food. Oats, the traditional Scottish staple, have seen something of a renaissance in recent years, with their health benefits being recognised by the new generation of food faddists. In the US a cafe chain 'Cereality' has opened, serving only porridge and other cereals. Elsewhere, both oats and wild salmon, Scottish to their core, are included in the list of 14 'Superfoods', claimed to be the best for health and longevity.

It may be true that some years ago it was rare to find good quality food in restaurants at a reasonable price. But things have changed dramatically over the past decade. Egon Ronay, of the famous restaurant guide, has recently described Scotland as 'gastronomically the UK's most impressive region', with proportionately more good restaurants in Scotland than elsewhere.

Traditionally a conservative race as far as foreign food is concerned, the Scots are now becoming far more adventurous. Indian, Chinese and Italian restaurants in particular abound, as well as the ubiquitous burger chains, but you can now find, in the larger towns and cities, such exotica as Japanese Sushi Bars, Spanish Tapas bars or French restaurants. Sadly, even now, one of the hardest things to find is probably good quality traditional Scottish fare! The most likely place to find haggis, salmon and venison dishes is in hotels or good standard guest houses in the tourist areas. You'll also find the traditional Scottish breakfast of porridge and kippers here.

While there has undoubtedly been an improvement in both the quality and quantity of eating places, the diet of the average Scot still has a lot to answer for. Although the range of fruits, vegetables and other healthy foods is now far wider than was traditionally the case, this doesn't mean that the locals are necessarily going to eat a healthier diet than they did traditionally. The Scottish love of all things fried is still rooted deeply in their hearts. A symbol of the depths of unhealthiness the diet of some Scots can reach is the deep-fried Mars Bar. In the English media, whether this delicacy actually exists is open to as much debate as the Loch Ness Monster. I'm reserving my judgement on Nessie, but I can confirm unequivocally that you can indeed buy deep-fried Mars Bars in certain selected chippies.

A fairly recent way of spending an evening with friends is the dinner party – even now, young Scots are far more likely to go out for a night 'on the booze' than eating. Although the Scots apparently hold fewer dinner parties than the rest of the UK, (an average of 8 per year against 11 elsewhere) when they do have them they spend more on both food and drink, spending more to get better quality ingredients. Others prefer to go out to eat, especially in the cities where there is greater choice and it can work out cheaper than shouldering all the cost yourself by entertaining at home,

Drink. The Scottish male is renowned for his liking for alcohol, with beer and whisky, not surprisingly, being popular. In most places outside the cities and some larger towns, the local bar is quite likely to be in a hotel, or to be a serious drinking den with little gesture towards comfort or attractiveness. The English-style quaint oak-beamed pub, where you would happily take your wife, is a completely different animal, and such places are few and far between in Scotland.

However, things have changed in recent years. The cities have introduced large, lively bars where young people go to socialise, and even in smaller, less up to the minute places, bar owners have realised that a make-over of their premises will help them attract a wider range of people, in particular women. More and more bars now also serve food, and some have remodelled themselves as 'gastropubs' where the food is at least as important as the drink.

At the time of writing, pubs and clubs are allowed to serve alcohol between 11am-11pm on Monday to Saturday, 12.30-2.30pm and 6.30-11pm on Sundays. Where special licences are granted, normally in city centres, pubs can stay open until 1am while nightclubs can stay open until 3am. However, recently the Glasgow licencing board has been allowing licences until 3am for so-called 'hybrid bars' which provide dance floors and DJs.

You must be 18 or over to buy and consume alcohol on licensed premises. Children aged 14 or over are allowed on licensed premises if they do not consume alcohol. If the establishment has a children's certificate, under 14s are allowed into specified parts of the establishment in order to consume a meal, as long as they are accompanied by an adult.

There is currently consultation in progress on a new Licensing Bill which aims to allow 24 hour drinking, subject to local licensing decisions. There are arguments both for and against such a dramatic change, and in the end a political decision will doubtless be taken. The Bill will probably be enacted in 2008-2009.

EDUCATION

One of the reasons often given by people for moving to Scotland from other areas of the UK is the quality of the education system. Since long before devolution, Scotland has designed and administered its own system of education, distinct from that in England and Wales, and it has been recognised as a well-educated country for centuries. The university system was established in the fifteenth century and ever since that time the Scots have been acknowledged as the producer of great inventors, engineers and scientists who have had an influence on world progress far beyond Scottish shores.

It has to be said that the Scottish reputation for high educational standards has suffered slightly in recent years, largely as a result of cutbacks in public spending. Since devolution, the Scottish Executive has resolved to return Scotland to its rightful place as a world leader in education and has increased spending on education from pre-school through to university level.

Structure

It is compulsory for all children between five and 16 years to attend school. They can then either leave or continue at school for another one or two years. During these additional years pupils study and take examinations in vocational subjects to prepare them for specific careers, or in academic subjects to allow them entry to university.

The academic year runs from mid-August to the end of June, and children start primary school in the August after their fifth birthday. They stay in primary education for seven years, then move to secondary school at the age of 12, where they stay for four to six years.

Primary Schools

In most of Scotland's 2,217 primary schools children are taught in separate year groups, but in small rural schools where there may only be a few pupils in a year group, one or two teachers may teach mixed age classes. The average class size in primary schools is around 24, but there is a great variation in actual sizes between large city schools and rural schools – in the Highlands and Islands many primary schools have 50 pupils or less.

Children may take their primary education in 'Gaelic medium units' within some mainstream primary schools, when all their lessons are taught in Gaelic, and English is just one subject on offer. There is one dedicated Gaelic medium primary school in Glasgow

Secondary Schools

Children start secondary school when they are 12 and stay until they are at least 16. In the 386 secondary schools in Scotland, around 76 per cent of pupils stay on beyond the earliest school leaving age of 16. These pupils will study vocational or academic courses for one or two years, and then go on to higher education or to take a job.

Most Scottish secondary schools take both boys and girls (there are only a few single sex state schools) and all provide a full range of courses appropriate to all levels of ability from first to sixth year. Unlike in England and Wales, there is no national curriculum in Scotland. Subjects taught in schools are the responsibility of education authorities and individual headteachers. However, they follow national guidelines giving recommended hours of study for core subjects including Maths, English and languages.

Gaelic is taught in many schools and pupils may study all their subjects in Gaelic at secondary schools with Gaelic medium units. A Gaelic medium secondary school is due to open in Glasgow in 2006, alongside a Gaelic medium pre-school and primary school. This will for the first time allow children to study all their education, from three to 18, in Gaelic.

Secondary schools, usually called either high schools or academies, take pupils of all levels of attainment. There is no selection in state schools on an academic basis, although there are a few academies which, as well as providing the standard Scottish education for all their pupils, are centrally funded to specialise in certain fields. There are nine of these 'centres of excellence' which gifted children, from all over Scotland, are selected to attend and receive extra training with top class exponents in the field, alongside their normal academic studies.

CENTRES OF EXCELLENCE
Music
Douglas Academy, East Dunbartonshire
Broughton High School, Edinburgh
Various schools in Fife
Dyce Academy
Traditional Music, Plockton High School, Highlands
Sport
Bellahouston Academy, Glasgow
Dance
Knightswood High School, Glasgow
Language
International Languages, Shawlands, Glasgow
Modern Languages, various schools in East Ayrshire, North Ayrshire, Argyll and Bute.

As part of a programme of modernisation of Scotland's secondary schools, the Scottish Executive is investing over £2 billion in new and refurbished school buildings, extra teachers, and extra sport, music and vocational studies. Included in the programme is the award of at least £100,000 each for specific schools which have shown a commitment to improve their educational provisions in specific areas.

Private Schools

Most Scottish schools are public (or state) schools and charge no fees to pupils, being funded by national and local government. About four per cent of children attend private (or independent) schools which receive no public money and charge fees to pupils. Independent schools cater for all age groups and include day and boarding schools. They offer a similar range of courses to state schools and enter pupils for the same examinations. The average cost of sending a child to private senior school is around £7,000 per year.

In addition, there are some grant-aided schools, mainly providing education for those with special educational needs, which receive grants direct from the Scottish Executive.

International Schools

There are a handful of international schools in Scotland, open to both local and expatriate children. Some of these schools offer the International Baccalaureate, an internationally recognised two-year pre-university course and examination. Others offer Scottish national qualifications. For further details contact the schools direct.

The International School of Aberdeen: 296 North Deeside Road, Aberdeen AB13 0AB; ☎ 01224-732267; fax 01224-735648; www.isa.aberdeen.sch.uk.

Ecole Total Oil Marine: 1-5 Whitehall Place, Aberdeen AB2 4RH; ☎ 01224-645545; fax 01224-645565.

Hamilton School: 80-84 Queen's Road, Aberdeen AB1 6YE; ☎ 01224-317295; fax 01224-317165.

Shawlands Academy International School: 31 Moss-side Road, Glasgow G41 3TR; ☎ 0141-582 0210; fax 0141-582 0211; www.shawlands.academy.glasgow.sch.uk.

Scottish Council of Independent Schools (SCIS): 21 Melville Street, Edinburgh EH3 7PE; ☎ 0131-220 2106; fax 0131-225 8594; www.scis.org.uk.

Universities

There are 13 conventional universities in Scotland, which were all established in one of three periods: the original four were established in the Middle Ages, with the next four not constructed until 400 years later, in the 1960s, a time of huge and rapid expansion in higher education across the UK. The remaining five started life as other forms of higher education colleges, mainly polytechnics, which were all upgraded to university status in the 1990s.

There are two other sources of university education in Scotland. One is the Open University which has been providing home study degree-level courses throughout the UK for over 30 years. The other is the newest institution of Higher Education in the UK, the University of the Highlands and Islands (UHI) which made its first tentative steps towards providing a new form of education in 1998. It operates through a network of over 50 learning centres, colleges and research institutions across the Highlands and Islands. Courses are conducted both face to face and through distance learning using modern technology including video, internet and PC. UHI was designated a Higher Education Institution in 2001 and aims to achieve full university status in 2007.

SCOTLAND'S ANCIENT UNIVERSITIES
The University of St Andrews – established 1411
The University of Glasgow – established.1451
The University of Aberdeen – established 1495
The University of Edinburgh – established 1583

The Guardian newspaper compiles an annual league table of the 126 universities across the UK. In 2004, they ranked the Scottish universities as follows:

UNIVERSITY RANKINGS		
Scottish Ranking	University	UK Ranking
1	St Andrews	10
2	The University of Edinburgh	11
3	Heriot-Watt (Edinburgh)	24
4	Glasgow	30
5	Aberdeen	35
6	Abertay (Dundee)	47
7	Stirling	53
8	Napier University (Edinburgh)	58
9	Paisley	60
10	Strathclyde	64
11	Dundee	75
12	Glasgow Caledonian	91
13	Robert Gordon (Aberdeen)	99

Scottish Credit & Qualifications Framework (SCQF). In order to allow comparison of achievements across different types of qualification, all educational qualifications are part of the SCQF. A recently introduced framework, it exemplifies the Scottish democratic nature, by formally acknowledging achievements throughout the whole spectrum of ability. Level 1, for learners with learning difficulties, is shown alongside level 12, for doctoral studies. The various courses leading to these qualifications are studied within secondary schools, colleges of further and higher education, at local authority evening classes, and in universities.

LEVELS IN THE SCOTTISH CREDIT & QUALIFICATIONS FRAMEWORK			
SCQF level	SQA National Qualifications	Higher Education	SVQs
1	Access 1	–	–
2	Access 2	–	–
3	Access 3/Foundation Standard Grade	–	–
4	Intermediate 1/General Standard Grade	–	SVQ1
5	Intermediate 2/Credit Standard Grade	–	SVQ2
6	Higher	–	SVQ3
7	Advanced Higher	Higher National Certificate	–
8	–	Higher National Diploma/ Diploma in Higher Education	SVQ4
9	–	Ordinary degree/Graduate Diploma/Certificate	–
10	–	Honours degree/Graduate Diploma/Certificate	–
11	–	Masters	SVQ5
12	–	Doctorate	–

HEALTH

Scotland has long been notorious as the 'sick man of Europe' due to its historically high rates of heart attack, strokes and cancer. Due to a concerted effort by the Scottish Executive, this is improving slowly. There are health education initiatives ongoing in an attempt to cut down on the levels of drinking and smoking within the population, and to improve the nation's diet. This has led to a fall in mortality rates due to heart disease and strokes, and a reduction in cancer deaths, but there is still a long way to go. As those areas of health improve, there are more people than ever dying of alcohol-related causes. Although more people are aware of the need to eat fresh fruit and vegetables, changing long-ingrained habits is hard, and obesity in adults and children is on the rise.

One of the most dramatic and controversial decisions the Scottish executive has made since devolution is to impose a total ban on smoking in enclosed public spaces from 26th March 2006. It is hoped that this will be a big step towards cutting levels of smoking generally among the population, as well as minimising the effects of passive smoking on those non-smokers who previously had to work in smoky surroundings.

National Health Service

The major healthcare provider in Scotland is The National Health Service (NHS), which allows residents of the UK to access free healthcare services. The cost of running the NHS has risen inexorably over time, in no small part due to the fact that so many more conditions can be treated now than in the past, some of them with the use of extremely expensive medicines and other treatments; that people are living longer; and that they have come to demand better levels of medical care as the standard of living has risen generally, due to the UK becoming more prosperous. In order to help to balance the books, there are now charges for some NHS services, such as prescriptions and some dental and ophthalmic treatments. However, children, the elderly, pregnant and nursing women, people with certain chronic health problems, and those on low incomes, are exempt from all or some of these charges.

The NHS has a workforce of around one million people, making it Europe's biggest organisation. In 2004, the NHS spent about £1,700 per capita in Scotland. Every resident of the UK, including immigrants, is entitled to use NHS services.

Family doctors (called General Practitioners or GPs), dentists and opticians are accessible throughout the country, even in the remotest areas. GP practices run regular surgeries – typically Monday to Friday with urgent cases seen at a Saturday morning surgery. They also carry out house calls for more serious cases or for the elderly who have difficulty attending the surgery. You need to register with a GP practice before using their services, although any GP will see non-registered patients in an emergency.

In order to visit your GP you will need to make an appointment. It may be several days before you can have an appointment, but if you have an urgent need to see a doctor, you should always be able to see a doctor the same day, as long as you are prepared to sit and wait until there is a break in his/her scheduled workload.

For treatment and advice outside surgery hours your call to the surgery will be diverted to the telephone service NHS24, introduced in 2004. They will take your details and arrange for a nurse to call you back and give you advice or arrange for a doctor to visit. However, NHS24 regularly finds itself overloaded, resulting in delays. Doctors and patients alike are disappointed in the standard of service available, which currently falls far short of that promised. It remains to be seen how quickly the situation can be improved – it is to be hoped that the criticisms are being taken on board, and that the service improves, before a tragedy occurs and the NHS are forced, too late, into doing what is needed.

> If you have a severe medical emergency you should phone the emergency services on 999 or 112

For more specialised treatment, GPs will refer patients to NHS hospitals as either outpatients (attending clinics) or inpatients (staying in the hospital while tests and treatments are carried out). In these cases, the patient will be put onto a waiting list, which can be many months for certain less serious conditions. Hospital waiting lists are on the increase and the government is trying hard to address the issue by increasing funding to improve provision of resources and staff across the board.

Accident and emergency departments operate on a first come, first served basis – although life-threatening emergencies will obviously jump the queue. This can mean long waits in these departments.

The NHS is in something of a crisis at present, as the service becomes overloaded and doesn't always respond to modern needs. To attempt to address some of the problems for the coming decades, and to modernise the approach taken to medical treatment in line with current thinking, a framework for the future of the NHS in Scotland was devised in 2005. This proposes a radical new model of health care, aimed at improving both the functioning of the organisation and its responsiveness and effectiveness in treating patients. However, it may be many years before the recommendations of this new-style NHS are implemented.

Private Healthcare

There is a relatively small provision of private healthcare within Scotland. However, this is on the increase. Lengthy waiting lists and the perceived poor state of some hospitals have led to many more affluent Scots taking out private health insurance. There has been a 60% increase in three years, with a predicted half million Scots having private health insurance by the end of 2005 – nearly 11 per cent of the population.

Private health insurance may be part of an employer's package when you take a job, although this would generally only be for employees at executive level or above. Private insurance typically costs between £40 and £130 per month for an individual, with the elderly paying the higher rates. Most private health insurance schemes pay only for specialist and hospital treatment, and don't include routine visits to GPs and dentists. These you will have to pay for yourself if you do not wish to be treated under the NHS.

Long waiting lists is one of the main reasons for patients choosing private medicine over the NHS. In most cases the quality of medical treatment and care will be no better, although private patients benefit from non-essentials such as private rooms with TV, telephone, en-suite bathrooms and room service.

NHS GPs are not permitted to take private patients, but there are doctors in private practice who may be consulted for specialist matters. Private clinics offer a range of services including second opinions, health checks and screening. As they become more acceptably mainstream, there is a growth in people paying for complementary and alternative health therapies.

Registering with a Doctor

In order to become a patient of a particular GP practice, you must first register with that practice. This involves completing a form with your personal details. Take your NHS medical card, if you have one. If you do not have one, you will be issued with an NHS number when you register. This number will stay with you whenever you access NHS treatment or when you transfer to another GP. GPs are not obliged to accept everybody who wishes to register on to their lists, if they have a good reason for refusing you – for example, each practice has a maximum number of patients they can take, so if they are over-subscribed, they may refuse to accept you as a patient. Sometimes they may agree to take you as a temporary patient. In these cases, it's worth trying another practice nearby as they may have spare capacity.

All those who are classed as 'ordinarily resident' in the UK are entitled to free treatment on the NHS, by GPs or in hospitals. In practice, this means those who live for at least six months per year in the UK. There are no charges to anyone who has lived here permanently for more than a year, or for residents of the European Economic Area (EEA) NHS services can be accessed by other overseas visitors, but they will be charged for all services with the exception of accident and emergency treatment.

Dentists

Every dentist is allowed to provide both NHS and private dental care. However, they have a quota of NHS patients they can take, and if the dentist you choose has filled his quota he may only be able to take you as a private patient. For NHS treatment you need to register using your medical card, as with a GP. There is currently something of a crisis amongst dentists in Scotland, with many refusing to treat any NHS patients because they feel the remuneration is not worthwhile. There are stories of entire regions where NHS treatment is just not available, necessitating long trips to other regions to find a dentist who will treat NHS patients. At the time of writing, the Scottish Executive has just 'imported' 32 qualified dentists from Poland in order to address the shortage in the worst affected areas including Fife, Forth Valley and Argyll and Clyde.

Dental treatment on the NHS is not free, but it is subsidised. There are a number of exemption categories, generally in line with the exemptions from prescription charges. A basic examination costs around £6, and an extensive examination around £9 with additional charges if any treatment is needed. A patient who is not eligible for free treatment or help with payment will pay 80 per cent of the cost up to £384 per course of dental treatment.

Local dental practices can be found in the telephone directory or through your local Health Board. Contact them if you have difficulty finding a dentist who can treat you on the NHS.

British Dental Association:.BDA Scotland, Forsyth House, Lomond Court, Castle Business Park, Stirling FK9 4TU; ☎ 01786-433810; fax 01786-431810; www. bde-dentistry.org.uk.

Opticians

You do not need to register with an optician. Their addresses can be found in the telephone directory. You must have your eyes tested by a qualified practitioner who will give you your lens prescription. You can then either buy your spectacles or contact lenses from that practitioner, or you can take the prescription to have your glasses or lenses made up at another dispensing optician. The costs of frames and lenses vary widely, but generally you should expect to pay £120 upwards for a pair of spectacles and around £85 upwards for contact lenses.

Eye tests are free if you are under 16, or under 19 and in full-time education; if you receive certain social security benefits or allowances; if you have diabetes or glaucoma; if you are aged 40 or over and have a close relative who has glaucoma; or if you are registered blind or partially sighted. If you are not entitled to free eye tests you will be seen as a private patient and the test will usually cost between £17 and £30.

General Optical Council: 41 Harley Street, London W1N 2DJ; ☎ 020-7580 3893; fax 020-7436 3525; www.optical.org.

SHOPPING

Like the rest of the UK, Scottish shopping centres are depressingly similar, all with the same selection of large chain stores. Although this means that shopping for the everyday things is perhaps much easier than it once was, it has become far harder to find the unique and individual 'shopping experience' – as the marketing men would like us to think of it. Small specialist shops cannot compete with the big stores, which can afford to pay premium rates for central properties and push up the rents, forcing the independent shopkeepers out of town or out of business. Local authorities are eager for the money the retail giants bring to their towns, and now even the smallest town seems to boast its antiseptic and anonymous indoor shopping mall. As well as dominating town centres, the retail giants are also to be found in the numerous out of town 'retail parks' which have sprung up across the country.

However, the shopping scene isn't all bad. Although there appear to be far fewer independents than there once were, good small shops still manage to survive – you just need to know where to look for them. Tourist towns and the quieter – and therefore less expensive – areas of cities are the best places to find more unusual shops. Glasgow has certainly managed to retain its local shops – every few streets, it seems, one finds yet another parade of small grocers, clothes shops, coffee bars and the like. They are clearly well-patronised by the local residents, or they wouldn't have survived against the out of town monsters.

Open-air and undercover markets have long been a feature of Scottish towns – the term 'burgh' which can be found in place names denotes a market town. Other towns, which don't contain the word in their names, are also historic Royal Burghs and many of them still have a market on at least one day a week. At these markets you can find versions of most of the things you would visit the large chain stores for, but generally at a cheaper price – although, be warned, the quality can be variable.

As a backlash against the over-corporatisation of shopping centres, there has in recent years been a great growth in Farmers' Markets where local food producers sell their wares direct to the public, cutting out the middle man and benefiting both seller and buyer in the process. These are the places to find superb quality meat, vegetables, dairy products and preserves, often organic, and always lovingly produced. However, if your main requirement of food is that it is cheap, you need to stick with the supermarkets, as their huge size allows them to negotiate rock-bottom prices with their suppliers – sometimes at not much above the cost of production – and pass these on to their customers. It is this process which has forced many a food producer to stop supplying the giants and head for the Farmer's Market.

If you're looking for bargain-priced good quality clothes, the so-called 'Designer Outlet Village' is the place. Despite the somewhat twee name, these are in fact shopping malls, where one can buy designer label 'seconds' – i.e. items which don't quite reach the standard required by the label, which may only be a little bit of uneven stitching which you wouldn't notice. You can save up to 50% on the full price of these clothes. You can find these listed on www.thesimplesaver.com.

In rural areas, many small communities have just one general store, and others have none at all, as they struggle – and sometimes fail – to compete with the shops in neighbouring towns, which are easily accessible now everybody has transport.

In these areas, there are still, however, some alternatives to travelling to the 'big city' for anything more than basic supplies. Companies selling household goods regularly set up in village halls for an all-day sale. Certain services are brought to your door in areas such as the Highlands and Islands, with butchers, fishmongers, banks and libraries travelling to remote communities on a set day and time each week.

Mail order and internet shopping have grown tremendously in recent years, now most people are connected to the world wide web. Just about everything you could choose to name can be bought on the phone or online, and delivered just a few days later. The latest growth area is online supermarket shopping. Tesco.com, the first in the UK field, is now being challenged by Asda and Sainsburys which have now both launched home shopping services. There are, however, still areas of Scotland – in the north-west Highlands in particular – where the supermarkets will not deliver.

Opening Hours. Traditionally, shops opened from around 9am to 5.30 pm, Monday to Saturday, sometimes closing for an hour at lunchtime, with half day closing on one day a week, normally Wednesday or Thursday. But this is rapidly becoming a thing of the past. The large stores don't close for lunch, nor do they have half day closing, so most smaller shops feel obliged to follow suit, ensuring they stay open while the shoppers are around.

Sunday opening, which was resisted for years by the retail trade, is now commonplace, and opening hours have been getting longer. Shops have recognised that many people prefer to shop after they return from work, so they stay open late into the evening. The ultimate extension of this, genuine 24 hour a day, seven day a week, opening is now a reality with more and more of the retail giants offering a 24/7 shopping experience.

Value Added Tax. VAT is charged on most consumer goods, at a rate of 17.5% on the retail price of the item. There are some exceptions to this. Food and books, notably, are still VAT free, as it is deemed politically unwise to increase the price of these commodities with tax.

Domestic gas and electricity is subject to VAT but at a lower rate of five per cent.

Service. Whether you choose to shop in the large multinational stores, the small independents, or markets, what you will almost certainly find is that you will be dealt with in a friendly and helpful manner. This characteristic of the Scots is very noticeable in shop assistants as it is elsewhere in daily life.

MEDIA

Television

Television can be received throughout Scotland and the Islands, but in mountainous areas, reception can be poor at times. It is possible to attach a booster to your home aerial to improve the sound and vision, but even then TV reception can be badly affected, or even non-existent, during bad weather, because of problems with transmitter masts situated in high, exposed areas. Many people in these areas have now switched to satellite TV reception which is far more reliable. In any event, analogue TV is going to be 'switched off' across the UK in the next few years, starting with southern Scotland in 2008, and with the rest of Scotland scheduled to follow by 2010, so it will be necessary for all homes to have digital TV by then.

The big five 'terrestrial' TV stations are BBC1 and BBC2, financed by licence fees, and three Independent channels, ITV1, Channel 4 and the youngest one, Channel 5 which was only introduced in 1997. These three get their revenue from advertising. In addition to these there are hundreds of other channels, available through satellite or cable connections.

In Scotland the British Broadcasting Corporation (BBC) channels are designated BBC Scotland on 1 and BBC Scotland on 2. Although programming is broadly the same across Britain, there are regional variations. BBC Scotland shows Gaelic programmes and Scottish news current affairs programmes. Independent Television (ITV) has regional companies across the UK which, in addition to showing UK-wide programmes, also have regionally specific transmissions. In Scotland there are three ITV companies: Border TV, covering the Borders region; Scottish TV, covering central Scotland; and Grampian TV, covering northern Scotland and the Islands.

Channel 5 is not yet available everywhere in Scotland and is unlikely to be transmitted to sparsely populated areas in the future. However, it can be received via satellite even in remote areas.

The main provider of satellite TV is Sky. In addition to its own channels, it also broadcasts a number of joint-venture channels and distributes other channels for third parties. Cable TV companies provide programming via underground cables, often in conjunction with telephone services. Subscribers to these services generally pay a monthly fee, but the Government has made a commitment to provide free to view TV via satellite, cable or broadband once the analogue signal is switched off, but it is likely that the householder will still have to pay for the satellite dish or broadband installation.

As far as the quality of TV is concerned, British television is still generally agreed to be the best in the world, but there are claims that the main channels are 'dumbing down' to attract market share from all the many competing channels now available. There has certainly been a glut of 'reality TV' shows over recent years, including an unbelievable number of programmes on buying, selling and renovating property. The BBC recently made a commitment to cut down on these cheap and unchallenging programmes. Alongside the pap, both the BBC and ITV do still produce high quality documentaries, drama serials and films, current affairs programmes and sports coverage.

Sadly, the vast majority of satellite and cable channels seem to be of poor quality, aside from some news programmes. Even the BBC and ITV digital channels, which run in addition to the terrestrial ones, generally seem to be very limited, showing the same few programmes with many repeats, and in effect previewing programmes which will eventually be run on the main BBC and ITV channels anyway.

There are controls and restrictions on the content of TV programmes and advertisements with programmes whose content is unsuitable for children only broadcast after the 9pm 'watershed'. The amount of advertising on commercial TV cannot exceed 7.5 minutes per hour during peak viewing times, between 6pm and 11pm.

Radio

UK domestic radio services are broadcast across three bands: FM (also called VHF); medium wave (or AM) and long wave. Radio reception can be patchy in mountainous areas of Scotland. Although booster aerials can improve reception, a satellite dish is the best solution.

The BBC has five nationwide stations. Radio 1 broadcasts pop music; Radio 2 provides a mix of easy listening music and relaxed discussion; Radio 3 is good for classical music and serious drama; Radio 4 broadcasts drama, documentaries, quiz shows and general interest programmes; Radio 5 broadcasts live sport and news. In addition, Scotland receives BBC Radio Scotland, and several local BBC stations including the BBC's Gaelic station.

The BBC World Service broadcasts across the world in 44 languages, including English.

The three main national commercial radio stations are Classic FM, TalkSport and Virgin 1215. In addition there are numerous local independent stations. In total, about forty domestic radio stations can be received in Scotland.

While the main stations can still be picked up on a traditional radio set, radio stations now transmit digitally and some can only be received through a digital set. Many can also be received through satellite, cable or the Internet.

Newspapers & Magazines

In Scotland there are around 160 national, regional and local daily and weekly newspapers available. In addition, in remote rural areas, which the regional papers tend not to cover in depth, there are many small local papers, often produced on a voluntary basis, usually weekly, fortnightly or monthly.

The Scottish national newspapers, the big two of which are The Scotsman and The Herald, tend to concentrate on events in Glasgow, Edinburgh and the Central Belt. Large regional papers such as the Press & Journal, produced in Aberdeen, do focus more on issues in their region of the country.

Scotland has both its own distinct newspapers and Scottish editions of some of the UK national newspapers. In the UK, Sunday newspapers are far more than just another edition of the daily papers. They are large and stuffed with supplements, often in colour, on all sorts of subjects, such as Lifestyle, Arts & Culture, Property, Sports, Business – so big they require a concerted effort to get through them in their entirety on Sunday!

There are thousands of magazines, on all sorts of subjects, for sale in the UK, but few specifically Scottish ones. These are available from newsagents or by subscription.

In most parts of the country newsagents will deliver newspapers and magazines to your door for a small weekly charge. Most are not available by subscription, but your local newsagent will order and reserve a regular copy for you to either collect or have delivered.

NEWSPAPERS IN SCOTLAND

Daily Papers

The Scotsman	The Herald
Daily Star of Scotland	Daily Telegraph (Scottish edition)
The Guardian (Scottish edition)	Scottish Daily Mail
Scottish Express	The Scottish Sun

Sunday Papers

Scotland on Sunday	The Sunday Herald
Sunday Post	The Independent on Sunday (Scottish edition)
Mail on Sunday in Scotland	The Observer (Scottish edition)
Scottish Sunday Express	Sunday Mail (Scottish edition)
Sunday Mirror (Scottish edition)	

Regional Papers

Courier and Advertiser (Dundee)	Daily Record (Glasgow)
Edinburgh Evening News	Evening Express (Aberdeen)

Evening Times (Glasgow)	Greenock Telegraph (Dunfermline)
Paisley Daily Express	Press and Journal (Aberdeen)
Scottish Magazines	
Scottish Field	Scottish Memories
The Scots Magazine	
Online Versions	
The Scotsman Online: www.scotsman.com.	
The Electronic Herald: www.theherald.co.uk.	
The Sunday Herald: www.sundayherald.com.	
Press & Journal: www.thisisnorthscotland.co.uk.	

CRIME

Levels of crime in Scotland vary widely, with the highest crime rates in cities, the lowest in rural, sparsely populated areas. Shetland, the Western Isles and Orkney report the lowest crimes rates of all.

In large areas of the Highlands and Islands there is almost no crime against property recorded, and as a result people feel safe leaving their houses and cars unlocked. This contrasts strongly with the perceived massively rising crime rates south of the border, even in previously quiet rural areas, where people feel less safe, and put stringent restrictions on their children, sometimes refusing to let them out alone, for fear of crime. In many areas even adults are starting to feel unsafe leaving home after dark. The low crime rate in the Highlands and Islands, and the consequent freedom children can experience, is a major reason for many incomers to relocate.

Even within the cities and towns, crime rates may vary dramatically between one area and the next. Certain districts will be locally known to be 'rough' and best avoided by those unfamiliar with the area. City centres, where large number of pubs, clubs and bars are found, may be perfectly respectable during the day, but at night can become places to avoid, as they are taken over by hordes of, generally young, people 'out on the town' and drinking heavily. This regularly leads to disorder and violence around 'chucking-out time' when these drinking venues close, anytime between 11.30 and the early hours of the morning.

As in the rest of the UK, drugs use is on the increase, in both urban and rural areas. The biggest problems are seen in the most deprived areas of Scotland's cities.

There are eight police forces in Scotland, each of which is divided into the uniformed 'bobbies on the beat' and traffic police, and the plain clothes Criminal Investigation Department (CID).

Most towns throughout Scotland will have its own police station, while cities will have several. In rural sparsely populated areas, one police station, with just one or two officers, will cover a large area.

LEARNING THE LANGUAGE

Perhaps the longest lasting legacy of British Imperialism is the belief among the British that everybody in the world does – or ought to – speak English. The other side of this coin is that foreign visitors will find that few Brits speak a foreign language with any great degree of competence. This tendency is one which has only been exacerbated by the growth of the internet, with English now the accepted online lingua franca. It is notable that, because this is overwhelmingly American English, many American forms are creeping into everyday British English. For example, most people now seem to be adopting the spelling 'program' over the correct British English form, 'programme'.

Although in Scotland the language spoken is officially British English, there is no guarantee that even a native English speaker will understand everything that is said or written. There are a large number of dialect words and grammatical usages which are very different from those used in England. Add to this the impenetrability of some dialects – notoriously, inner city Glaswegian and Aberdonian, for example – and one can feel as though one is in the midst of foreign language speakers. George Bernard Shaw's comment that 'England and America are two countries divided by a common language' holds just as true for England and Scotland!

Certain staff at the British Foreign Office clearly agree

In 2004 they rejected the visa application of a young Russian student who wished to study English in a Scottish university, on the grounds that: 'you cannot satisfactorily explain why you have chosen to attend an English course in Scotland rather than your other options of Oxford or Cambridge, where you should face less difficulty understanding a regional accent.' Needless to say, and quite rightly, the Scottish Nationalist Party were quick to condemn that type of discriminatory attitude in the Scottish Parliament.

There is certainly an argument for saying that, if you intend relocating to Scotland and are preparing yourself for the move, you should take English language courses in Scotland (rather than in England or even your home country) as this would help to avoid having to 're-learn' the language when you get to Scotland. There are a number of EFL (English as a Foreign language) courses available in various institutions throughout Scotland, the majority of these in the Central Belt.

Courses can be taken at various levels, from beginner to advanced, general to business or professional, and are available part time, full time or residential, with accommodation for the duration of the course in college residences, hotels or bed and breakfasts, or staying with an English (or Scottish!) speaking family. Intensive courses can be taken over a number of weeks, and allow the student to choose how many weeks, and how many hours per week, they wish to immerse themselves in the language. Some combine English tuition with a holiday – for instance, you can spend a holiday at Fort Augustus beside Loch Ness and learn the language at the same time.

Another option is a correspondence course, which allows you to study at home, in your own time at your own pace.

For the quickest results it is best to choose a course with one to one intensive tuition, where you are staying with a family. This is the way to maximise one's immersion in the language.

There are many courses advertised on the Internet. To be sure of quality, try to choose a course which is accredited by the British Council. This is a selection, but there are many others:

English in Britain: www.englishinbritain.co.uk. Has links to many accredited English courses.

ECS Scotland: 43-45 Circus Lane, Edinburgh EH3 6SU; ☎ 0141-226 5262; fax 0131-2265262; www.ecsscotland.co.uk. A small independent school specialising in one to one and small group courses.

Perth College: Creiff Road, Perth PH1 2NX; ☎ 01738-877000; www.perth.ac.uk. Year-round semi-intensive and intensive course (15 to 23 hours per week) with an annual Summer School during July and August.

InTuition Languages: Kingsmill, 4 Ravey Street, London EC2A 4QP; ☎ 020-7739 4411; fax 020-7729 0933; www.intuitionlang.com. On an InTuition programme, you live and study individual lessons in the home of a teacher who is qualified to teach English as a foreign language. One to one lessons (15, 20, 25 or 30 lessons per week) in a relaxed and friendly homestay atmosphere. There are InTuition teachers in Scottish locations.

Hawthorn–Edinburgh School of English: 271 Canongate, the Royal Mile, Edinburgh EH8 8BQ; ☎ 0131-557 9200; fax 0131-557 9192; www.hawthornenglish.com/ edinburgh. One of the first EFL schools in Scotland, with a wide range of courses focusing on small classes and quality teaching.

Glasgow School of English: 180 Hope Street, Glasgow G2 2UE; ☎ 0141-353 0033; fax 0141-332 8881; www.glasgowschoolofenglish.com. Claim to be the only school in the West of Scotland to be British Council Accredited. Courses suitable for students of all levels from the most basic of beginners to advanced level students. Choice of study on a short or long term basis, one to one or in a group.

English for Speakers of Other Languages (ESOL): Moray College, Moray Street, Elgin IV30 1JJ; ☎ 01343-576216; www.moray.ac.uk. ESOL courses available at 4 levels: English for Beginners; Cambridge Certificate English; Cambridge Advanced English, and Cambridge Proficiency in English. Courses are taken part time, during the day or as evening classes.

Business Training: Sevendale House, 7 Dale Street, Manchester M1 1JB; ☎ 0161-228 6753; fax 0161-236 6735; www.businesstrain.co.uk. Correspondence courses by post or email, teaching various levels of English, but concentrating on business English.

Loch Ness English: Inchnacardoch, Fort Augustus PH32 4BN; ☎/fax 01320-366376; www.lochnessenglish.com. A small school within the beautiful landscape of the Scottish Highlands with mountains, forests, rivers and the famous Loch Ness on the doorstep. Caters for small groups or private students.

Gaelic & Scots

Although English is the first language of just about everybody in Scotland, apart from immigrants, one has to mention Gaelic, found mainly in the Highlands and Islands, and Scots, spoken in the lowland areas.

In recent years there has been a movement to revive both languages. Gaelic is winning hands down at present. Children have the option of taking all their education in Gaelic, while official forms, and road signs in the north, include Gaelic as well as English. The 2004 Gaelic Language Bill puts in place the *Bòrd na Gàidhlig* which will prepare a national Gaelic language plan to promote the use and understanding of the Gaelic language, with the aim of increasing the number of persons able to use and understand Gaelic. This is a tall order, however. The language is spoken by a tiny proportion of the population. In the 2001 census, 58,333 people claimed to be Gaelic speakers, 1.19 per cent of the population.

There are various forms of 'Scots', including Lowland Scots, Lallans, and Doric, a dialect spoken in Aberdeen and the north-east. It is the language in which Robert Burns wrote his famous poems. Opinions are divided on whether Scots constitutes a genuine language, or is merely a collection of dialects of English. Although the European Charter for Minority and Regional Languages recognises Scots as a minority language, little official recognition or encouragement has yet been given to Scots by the UK Government. The Scottish Executive is being pressed to use the Scots tongue, as well as Gaelic, on public signs and official forms alongside English.

There are evening classes, usually local authority run, in various areas, mainly the Highlands and Islands, where Gaelic can be learned, but there don't seem to be any courses which teach Scots. In Glasgow at least, there is an informal group which gets together regularly to speak in Scots and generally celebrate the language. It is, actually, so similar to English in many of its words and grammatical structures that, once one's ears become acclimatised, it is reasonably easy for English speakers to understand.

A GLOSSARY OF SCOTTISH TERMS

English speakers moving to Scotland will rapidly come to realise that there are many unfamiliar words, phrases and grammatical structures in general use, some deriving from Scots dialect, some from Gaelic and yet others which can't really be traced to either.

Scottish	English translation
Ashet	Large serving plate (cf French 'assiette'.)
Bairn	Baby
Blether	Chat

Bonny	Pretty, splendid
Bourach	Mess, chaos
Burn	Stream
Carry-out	Take-away
	(e.g. fast food, or drink from an off licence)
Ceud Mile Failte	A hundred thousand welcomes
Dreich	Grey and dismal (of the weather)
Fasht	Troubled, worried
It needs done/signed etc.	It needs signing/doing etc.
Kirk	Church
Pished	Drunk
Squint	Lopsided
Stramash	A disturbance
Swithering	Undecided
The night/the day	Tonight/today
The river's well high	The river's very high
Timeously	Timely
Troc(k)	Rubbish, bric a brac
Wean	Child
Wee	Small
What like is he?	What is he like?
Where do you stay?	Where do you live?
Wifie	Woman (usually middle-aged to elderly)

Orkney & Shetland

Although, like everywhere else in Scotland, English is the common tongue in Orkney and Shetland, Gaelic is not spoken in these far northern isles. The two island groups share a dialect and vocabulary which has been heavily influenced by the old Norse settlers, and given an extra twist by the later introduction of English and Lallans, a southern Scots dialect. Given the huge importance of the land and weather to the local people living in often harsh northern conditions, these dialect words are particularly prevalent in relation to farming, fishing, weather conditions, natural features and wildlife. There are differences in the words used between the islands, with local variations of the same word used in Orkney and in Shetland, but it easy to see the close connection between them in the past.

It is often remarked as a curiosity that the Eskimos have numerous different words for snow. Well, the Shetland dialect has many different words for rain. Enough said!

For more fascinating information on the dialects of Orkney and Shetland, see the excellent book *Scottish Islands: Orkney & Shetland,* by Deborah Penrith (Vacation Work Publications).

SUMMARY OF HOUSING

House Prices

The first thing to be said is that property in the UK is expensive, compared with prices in many other countries. There are a number of reasons for this, among them the limited amount of land available in an island nation with a comparatively large population.

Another reason for rising prices is simply a matter of supply and demand. Currently there is something of a housing crisis, with it generally being recognised that not enough new building is taking place. Slow and outdated planning laws delay applications by developers and individuals who wish to build homes, with planning permissions taking many months, sometimes years, to come through. Even where planning permission is granted for a development, it seems increasingly to be the case that local residents near to the proposed development will object to the new building, often on environmental grounds. But too often it seems that this is just an excuse for their so-called 'nimbyism' – from the acronym NIMBY (Not In My Back Yard). This has reached such extreme levels over recent years, where it seems that any development is objected to on principle, despite the desperate need for new housing, that a new brand of nimbyism nicknamed BANANAS (Build Absolutely Nothing Anywhere Near Anything) has emerged!

A further factor in the demand for a limited housing stock is that property has long been seen in the UK as an excellent investment, and in recent years, with property values rising fast, many more people have preferred to put their money into bricks and mortar rather than the stock market or other financial investments.

Demographically too, there is an increasing demand for property, as there are growing numbers of single person households, as people delay getting married, or prefer the independence of living alone. Despite a declining population in Scotland, the number of people living alone has increased, with the total number of households rising by ten per cent since 1991.

There are big differences between average prices across the UK, and the average price of property is cheaper in Scotland than in England. However, as many regions in Scotland are more expensive than some regions in England, you need to pick your areas carefully if funds are limited.

The constant cry in connection with high house prices is that this prevents first time buyers from getting their foot on the first rung of the property-owning ladder. Often, wealthy incomers are blamed for pushing up prices in rural areas, meaning that local young people have to move away because they cannot afford to live in these places. It has to be said that there are some major flaws in this argument: far from blaming the over-generous incomers 'flashing their cash around' to pay well over the odds for rural properties, one must bear in mind that it is the greediness of the local sellers which is tempting them to ask high prices, rather than selling their house to a local family at a price they can afford. The Scottish system of asking for 'offers over' the asking price does, inevitably, have an inbuilt tendency for prices to become inflated over time. But no seller is forced to sell at the highest price – if sellers really wanted to pay more than lip service to providing homes for local families they could do so at a stroke.

Another point which is rarely made is that young people in the centre of Edinburgh or Glasgow, just as in London, also cannot afford to become first time buyers. It is not just a rural phenomenon.

The problem of affordability is particularly acute in the cities, with so-called 'key workers' such as police officers, teachers, doctors and nurses, fire crews, unable to afford to buy or rent property on the salary on offer in such public sector jobs, with the result that the organisations are having difficulty recruiting the numbers of staff they need.

In order to address these problems, the Scottish Executive has introduced a shared-ownership scheme for first time buyers on low incomes, whereby they can pay 60% to 80% of the cost of a mortgage, with the rest coming from the public purse via a housing association which would keep a share in the ownership of the house. The money owed would be recouped when the property was eventually sold on to a new owner.

There are similar schemes in various areas aimed at key workers. In Edinburgh, for example, new houses are being built which will be rented out at an affordable price, allowing public sector workers such as teachers, nurses and university staff to move to the capital to take up jobs. Anyone working in the public sector earning between £19,700 and £25,000 per year will be eligible.

Elsewhere across the country, local authorities are building affordable housing which is rented out, or made available on a shared ownership bias, to those on low incomes. New planning laws brought in early in 2005 stipulate that a quarter of homes in all new housing developments within areas identified as having affordable housing needs, should be provided for rent or low cost ownership.

The Scottish Executive also raised its three year target for new affordable housing from 18,000 homes to 21,500, as one step in their attempt to prevent an acute housing crisis in the years ahead.

As an additional measure to help first time buyers, who typically buy the cheapest properties, get into the housing market, in the 2004 Budget the UK Chancellor doubled the level at which stamp duty land tax becomes payable on the purchase of a property, from £60,000 to £120,000. As average house prices have risen over recent years, the £60,000 threshold had become far too low to affect more than a handful of property purchases. Effectively, the change in the tax level means a saving of £1,200 on the costs involved in buying a house costing £120,000, a great help to those stretching themselves to pay for a mortgage.

Level of Home Ownership

A sign of the increasing prosperity of the country is that home-ownership has been steadily rising over recent years. In 2004, around 65 per cent of Scots were owner-occupiers, a figure which continues to rise year on year. Of these, 28 per cent owned their properties outright, while 37 per cent were still paying off a mortgage or other loan on their home.

In comparison, only 27 per cent of households were renting from a social landlord, and six per cent from a private landlord.

Whether they own or rent has a significant effect on how people feel about the area in which they live: nearly two-thirds of outright owners and over half of those with a mortgage described their neighbourhood as a very good place to live. In contrast, only one third of those in the social rented sector did so.

Although overall accommodation accounts on average for around 20 per cent of a family's budget, it is comparatively more expensive to rent than buy. People in rented accommodation spend around 23 per cent of their income on housing costs, while mortgage payers spend only 15 per cent.

Regional Differences

There are large differences in prices of property across the country, affected by a wide range of factors. Property 'hot spots' occur in some very localised areas, with prices close by comparatively depressed. For this reason it is essential to research the area you wish to live in very carefully, because one flat in Glasgow, for example, may well be several thousand pounds – even tens of thousands – more expensive than a similar flat only a couple of streets away. This can be due to all sorts of factors, including the exclusivity of certain addresses; whether the area has been 'gentrified' or not, with old properties having been renovated to a high standard, or new properties developed for the professional market; the closeness to services; whether it falls into the catchment area of a desirable school and so on. A property on the edge of a newly gentrified area can be a very good investment, because that process of gentrification may continue outwards, pushing up the value of all property in the neighbouring streets.

Because of the transport infrastructure and the availability of jobs, it is not surprising that the top eight most expensive areas, based on average house prices, are in the Central Belt. The next highest priced area is Aberdeenshire, within commuting distance of the well-paying jobs connected with the oil industry in Aberdeen. Prices are comparatively high in the Highland region, where many properties are far away from well-paying jobs or easy transport links. Here, the value of property depends more on the desire of people to get away from the 'rat race' to live in a beautiful scenic and sparsely populated area.

Although generally the price of houses in coastal areas attracts a premium, because people love to live by the sea, rising sea levels associated with global warming could have a detrimental effect on the price of seaside properties. After severe storms in January, which eroded stretches of coastline in the Western Isles, it is estimated that some homes are as much as 50 metres nearer the sea than they were previously.

With such severe weather conditions increasingly likely, together with a general rise in sea levels, 94,000 Scottish homes are classed as 'at risk' of flooding because they are less than five metres above sea level. As well as homes in the islands, other residential areas identified include sections of northern Edinburgh and Leith, Helensburgh, Leven, Dumbarton, Saltcoats, Elgin, Monifieth and Gourock.

The dangers of flooding to these houses are such that new planning rules have been introduced that mean planning permission for new houses is unlikely to be granted in at risk areas. It will also be increasingly expensive – or impossible – to get insurance cover for houses in flood areas.

It is estimated that these factors could cause property prices in flood areas to fall by as much as 40 per cent.

Current State of the Housing Market

For decades the housing market in the UK has been characterised by periods of fast-rising prices when houses sell very quickly, followed by depressed prices leading to stagnation in the market. This cycle is termed 'boom and bust'. There was an unprecedented boom in the UK house market during the 1980s, partly fuelled by council house tenants for the first time having the right to buy their houses. At its peak, house prices rose by 30% during 1988. After this, the market slowed dramatically and by the mid-nineties house prices had fallen in real terms. Prices began to rise again at the end of the 1990s, and another boom occurred, reaching its peak in 2004.

Scottish property prices rose by 56% between 2001 and 2004. During 2004, the overall increase was over 22%, with the biggest regional increase seen in the Borders, at 36%. Hamilton and Kilmarnock, in the Glasgow commuter belt, were the towns with the highest rises, at 39%.

One reason for the boom had been a sustained period of low interest rates. Concerned that the housing market might get out of control, leading eventually to a damaging crash in prices, the Bank of England raised interest rates for several months in a row, and this succeeded in slowing the market.

At the time of writing in late 2005, it is clear that Scottish property prices are not continuing to rise at the same rate, but although the rate of increase has slowed, there is still a general upward price trend in most areas. In England, in contrast, prices have fallen slightly overall during the year. But figures released in October 2005 show that, after a loss of confidence among house-buyers earlier in the year, house prices across England and Wales were showing signs of rising for the first time in 18 months. This raises the question of whether prices will actually fall in Scotland at all. Although the normal pattern is for them to follow the trend in England and Wales, but with a time lag before the 'ripple effect' works north, the fact that prices further south are rising before they have begun to fall in Scotland, suggests that the country as a whole may not see falling prices but that they will continue to rise, albeit at a slower rate than during the boom years between 2001 and 2004.

Supporting this, Halifax, the UK's biggest mortgage lender, were predicting an overall fall in prices of two per cent across the UK, but a modest rise of three per cent in Scotland, while Nationwide predicted a UK rise of two per cent, with again a three per cent rise in Scotland.

BANK HOLIDAYS

Statutory public holidays are called 'bank holidays' for obvious reasons. Traditionally, other shops and services apart from banks were also closed on these days. In line with the general lengthening of shop opening hours over recent years, retail outlets now tend to stay open on bank holidays, because it is, of course, an ideal time to attract all those customers who would normally be at work. Nowadays, far from Christmas and Easter and other bank holidays being a time when shops are closed, they are more likely to be a time of seasonal special offers and sales in order to attract customers.

Post offices, schools, offices and workplaces, apart from essential services, are usually closed on bank holidays. Where people are obliged to work they are generally paid at a higher than normal rate for those days and are also entitled to time off on another day to compensate.

Bank holidays are normally on a Monday, although those associated with religious or secular occasions, such as Christmas and New Year may fall on different days of the week. The annual Scottish statutory public holidays are New Year, or Hogmanay, (two days), Good Friday, Easter Monday, May Day, Spring Bank Holiday, Summer Bank Holiday, Christmas Day and Boxing Day.

The May Day holiday is officially known as 'Early May Bank Holiday' and falls on the first Monday after 1st May; Spring Bank Holiday falls on the last Monday in May; and the Summer Bank Holiday falls on the last Monday in August.

Local Holidays

In addition to official bank holidays, in most parts of Scotland there are local and fair holidays, which vary from town to town. Dates of local holidays can be obtained from the local authority.

NATIONAL HOLIDAYS						
Public Holidays	**2005**	**2006**	**2007**	**2008**	**2009**	**2010**
New Year's Day	1 Jan					
New Year Bank Holiday	2 Jan					
Good Friday	25 Mar	14 Apr	6 Apr	21 Mar	10 Apr	2 Apr
Early May Bank Holiday	2 May	1 May	7 May	5 May	4 May	3 May
Spring Bank Holiday	30 May	29 May	28 May	26 May	25 May	31 May
Summer Bank Holiday	1 Aug	7 Aug	6 Aug	4 Aug	3 Aug	2Aug
Christmas Day	25 Dec					
Boxing Day	26 Dec					

LOCAL HOLIDAYS 2006 (DATES VARY EACH YEAR)

Glasgow Holidays

Spring	19 May
Glasgow Fair	15 July
Autumn	25 September

Edinburgh Holidays

Spring	10 April
Victoria Day	22 May
Trades Holiday	1 July
Autumn Holiday	18 September

Dundee Holidays

Spring	3 April
Victoria Day	29 May
Trades Holiday	25 July
Autumn	2 October

Aberdeen Holidays

Spring	17 April
Summer	10 July
Autumn	25 September

Inverness Holidays

6 February; 6 March; 3 April; 3 July; 2 October; 6 November

RESIDENCE & ENTRY

CHAPTER SUMMARY

O There are no border controls between England and Scotland. Anybody entitled to enter the UK may live in any UK country.

O The 'Fresh Talent' initiative encourages foreign students and professionals to live and work in Scotland.

O UK Immigration Rules are complex. Always get advice from an Immigration Advisor if you are uncertain of your status.

O EEA Nationals have an unrestricted right to live and work in Scotland.

O Nationals of most other countries must obtain entry clearance if they wish to settle, work or set up a business in Scotland.

O Most immigrants wishing to set up a business in Scotland must invest at least £200,000 in the business and employ at least two people.

O The Highly Skilled Migrant Programme (HSMP) encourages entry to the UK for successful people with sought-after skills.

O To come to Scotland as a retired person you must be at least 60 years old and have an income of at least £25,000 per year.

O You may apply for British Citizenship once you have been permanently resident in the UK for 12 months.

There are no border controls between England and Scotland, so anybody entitled to enter the UK may then reside in any UK country. In order to determine whether you qualify for immigration to Scotland, you need to consult the UK Immigration Rules. These can be found on the Immigration and Nationality Directorate website, www.ind.homeoffice.gov.uk/ind/en/home/html or there is a fuller discussion in *Live & Work in Scotland*, Vacation Work Publications.

The fact that, of necessity, immigration policy is uniform across the UK, has caused some problems for the Scottish Executive. They wish to encourage immigration to Scotland, and have put in a place the 'Fresh Talent' initiative aimed at attracting and keeping well-qualified students and professionals to Scotland, to live and work there. The Scottish Executive has put a large amount of funding into providing legal advice on immigration and asylum for those wishing to work or study in Scotland, and to give support to international students during their studies in Scotland and helping them make decisions about staying on in the country at the end of their studies.

The aim of the Fresh Talent initiative is to help halt the fall in the Scottish population at the same time as boosting the expertise within the workforce. However, England has a rising population, which puts great strain on public services, and there is also some resistance to immigration within the UK population, so it is in the interests of the Westminster government to keep a curb on immigration. These conflicting desires are difficult to reconcile, because although students may come to study in Scotland, there is nothing to stop them heading south for work after they are qualified, taking advantage of the education system in Scotland, but not putting anything back in once they are employed. Not surprisingly, this is somewhat irksome to the Scots.

The UK Immigration Rules are fairly complex, as there are many different categories of entry and rules regarding how long different people can stay in the country. However, the ease with which you can relocate to the UK depends ultimately on the country you come from. Firstly, those with the right of abode in the UK may live and work there without restriction. These include all British Citizens i.e. those entitled to a British passport.

Commonwealth citizens may also have the right of abode, if their parent, grandparent or partner were born in the UK. Depending on their particular circumstances, they may be restricted to a maximum stay of four years, but they have the right to apply for an extension to their stay. This application must be made before the initial agreed period of stay is ended.

Possession of a British Passport is all the proof needed that you have the right of abode. Any British citizens travelling on a foreign or commonwealth passport, and commonwealth citizens, need to apply for a Certificate of Entitlement via a British Embassy or Consulate.

Secondly, nationals of the European Economic Area (EEA) – i.e. the member states of the European Union plus Iceland, Norway and Liechtenstein – have an unrestricted right to live and work in the United Kingdom. In addition, Swiss nationals have the same rights as EEA residents. Although other EU countries put some bureaucratic obstacles in the way of Europeans wishing to live there, despite the agreed freedom of movement between member states, the UK puts few extra restrictions on EEA nationals wishing to relocate either temporarily or permanently. The main proviso is that, if they are not economically active while in the UK, they must be able to support themselves without recourse to UK public funds, such as social security benefits and the like.

Of the ten new states which joined the EU in 2004, nationals of Czech Republic, Poland, Lithuania, Estonia, Latvia, Slovenia, Slovakia and Hungary must register with the Home Office and obtain a workers registration certificate, but nationals from Malta and Cyprus have full free movement rights in line with other EEA nationals.

Visitors from other countries must generally obtain entry clearance in the form of a visa, a work permit or an entry certificate if they wish to settle, work or set up a business in the UK. Those with a criminal record or who are subject to a deportation order may be refused entry, and people may also be refused entry on medical grounds. Visitors to the UK are not entitled to free medical treatment and should make sure they have adequate medical insurance to cover their stay. It can take up to two to three months for a visa or work permit to be approved, so allow adequate time for your application..

There are regulations regarding the maximum length of stay granted under different categories. Each application is taken on its own merits, but, if you are coming here to work, for example, you may initially be granted a one year permission to stay, which you would then apply to renew before the end of that year.

Application for entry clearance should be made through the British Mission in the country in which the applicant is living, or through the Immigration & Nationality Directorate website: www.ind.homeoffice.gov.uk. Downloadable leaflets and application forms on all aspects of visa information are available on that site.

Family members of certain categories of entrants to the country may be entitled to stay, with the same rights of residence, but this is a complex area, with many provisos, so it is always wise to obtain the advice of an immigration specialist in your home country.

In order to attract students to the UK, there are special rules in place for them. Unless there are special circumstances, students may enter and remain in the UK for the full length of their studies, without the need to reapply annually to extend their studies. They can also work up to 20 hours per week during term time and full-time in vacations.

QUALIFICATIONS FOR ENTRY

If you are not an EEA national, and do not qualify for entry through reasons of Commonwealth ancestry, the general requirement for entry to live in the UK is that you either have a pre-arranged job to come to, or that you bring substantial funds with you which will be invested in the UK in some form or another. Within this overall policy, there are again specific rules relating to specific categories of immigrant.

Students

Can enter the UK for study or training of at least fifteen hours per week provided they can support themselves and pay for their studies without public funds. They will be given leave to enter and remain in the UK for the full length of their studies. If their course of study or training is longer than six months they can work up to 20 hours per week during term time and full-time in vacations, and where their studies include a period of work placements they do not need to obtain a work permit.

Employees

If you enter the UK intending to take up a post as an employee you will need to find and accept a job before you arrive. Certain categories of employee do not need a work permit, as follows:

- EEA nationals.
- Commonwealth citizens with a grandparent born in the UK and Islands.
- Working holidaymaker.
- Au pair.
- Minister of Religion.
- Missionary or a member of a religious order.
- The representative of a firm with no representative in the UK.
- A representative of a an overseas newspaper, news agency or broadcasting organisation on long term assignment to the UK.
- A member of the staff of a diplomatic or consular mission.
- A domestic worker in a private household.
- A teacher or language assistant coming to a UK school under an exchange scheme.
- A member of the operational ground staff of an overseas airline.
- A postgraduate doctor or dentist coming for training.
- A seasonal worker at an agricultural camp.

All other people entering as an employee need to obtain a work permit. This must be obtained on their behalf by their intended employer in the UK, before their new employee travels to the UK. Where they also need a visa, they can only apply for this once they have their work permit.

Self-Employed

You may only come to the UK permanently to run a business or be self-employed if you bring at least £200,000 of your own money to invest in the business and create at least two new jobs for people who are already settled in the UK.

As ever, there are a few exceptions to this requirement, as follows:.

- Writers, artists and composers. They must be able to support themselves by self-employment in their field once they have satisfied the immigration authorities that they have a proven track record in their field.
- Innovators. Defined as those with a new and innovative business idea, particularly in the areas of information technology and telecommunications, that will bring exceptional economic benefits to the UK. They must also have sufficient funding to establish the business; create employment for at least two people; have significant business experience; maintain at least a five per cent shareholding of the equity capital in the business.
- Citizens of Bulgaria, Czech Republic, Estonia, Hungary, Latvia, Lithuania, Poland, Romania, Slovakia, Slovenia may enter the UK to establish themselves in business under the 'EC Association Agreement'. To qualify under the agreement they need to be the owner, or have a controlling interest, in the business, and must be actively involved in trading or providing services in the

UK.

O Lawyers practising in non UK law are not subject to the above investment requirements.

Highly Skilled Migrants

A recently-introduced category, the Highly Skilled Migrant Programme (HSMP) encourages entry to the UK for successful people with sought-after skills. Points are awarded under various headings to assess an applicant's eligibility for an HSMP visa. A total of at least 65 points are required. For an at-a-glance explanation of the points system, see www.workpermit.com/uk/highly – skilled – migrant – program4.htm.

Points are awarded under the following headings:

O Young person assessment – extra points are awarded to those under 28 years of age when they apply.

O Qualifications – points awarded for bachelors degree, masters degree, doctoral degree, vocational & professional qualifications.

O Relevant work experience – points awarded for length of time spent in various levels of job, with weighting being given to those under 28.

O Earning power – points awarded for levels of earnings in your specific country of origin, with weighting given to those under 28.

O Achievements in your chosen field – points awarded for 'significant' and 'outstanding' achievements.

O Doctor entitled to practice as a GP in the UK – extra points awarded.

O Partner's achievements – points awarded for qualifications and work experience of the applicant's partner.

Investors

Must have documentary evidence to show that they have capital of at least £1 million and will invest not less than £750,000 in approved UK government bonds or companies. The UK must become their main home.

Retired Persons

Must be at least 60 years of age and have a close connection with the UK. They must have an annual income of at least £25,000 and be able to support and accommodate themselves and any dependants without working and without recourse to public funds.

RESIDENCE PERMITS

Under a fairly recent piece of European legislation, visitors to the UK who extend their stay or are intending to stay for longer than six months, are required to apply for a residence permit. The exceptions to this are EA nationals and visa nationals, who do not need one.

Under European Community law, EEA nationals have a right to live and work in the UK, known as a 'right of residence'. These people do not need to get a residence permit if they are staying here alone. However, they will need a residence permit if they have dependent family members who wish to apply for a residence document. It may also be useful to get a residence permit to prove your right to live and work in the UK. This can be invaluable when applying for bank accounts, mortgages and so forth.

Residence permits are issued by the Immigration and Nationality Directorate (IND) and are normally valid for five years. There is no charge for them. The IND website has downloadable application forms at www.ind.homeoffice.gov.uk.

Entry Clearance

An entry clearance is a visa or an entry certificate issued to a passenger prior to travel to the UK. A person who has an entry clearance will not be refused admission as long as there has not been a material change of circumstances since the entry clearance was obtained.

Fees

If you need entry clearance in the form of a visa, a work permit or an entry certificate, there are fees payable. There are also additional application fees payable for work permits. The level of these fees varies depending on the length of your proposed stay and the category under which you enter the UK. For a full list and latest fee schedule see www.skillclear.co.uk/services – pricing2.asp. Entry fees are payable in the local currency of the country in which you are currently residing.

Useful Addresses & Websites

For immigration, citizenship and nationality enquiries: *Immigration and Nationality Directorate:* Lunar House, 40 Wellesley Road, Croydon CR9 2BY; ☎ 0870-606 7766 (Mon-Fri 9am-4.30pm); www.ind.homeoffice.gov.uk/ind/en/home/html.

For advice on specific cases: *Immigration Advisory Service (IAS):* County House, 190 Great Dover Street, London SE1 4YB; ☎ 020-7967 1200; fax 020-7403 5875; www.iasuk.org.

To appeal against a decision to refuse entry to the UK: *Immigration Appellate Authority (IAA):* The Arnhem Support Centre, PO Box 6987, Leicester LE1 6ZX; ☎ 0845-6000 877; www.iaa.gov.uk.

There are British Consulates, Embassies and Missions around the globe. For a full list see www.fco.gov.uk and follow the link under Directory/UK Embassies Overseas or contact: *Foreign and Commonwealth Office:* Consular Division, King Charles Street, London SW1A 2AH; ☎ 020-7008 1500.

For advice and assistance on locating or relocating a business in the UK: *UK Trade & Investment Enquiry Service:* Kingsgate House, 66-74 Victoria Street, London, SW1E 6SW; ☎ 020-7215 8000; www.uktradeinvest.gov.uk/ukti/appmanager/ukti/home.

Detailed information and advice on UK immigration, visas and work permits: www.workpermit.com.

Immigration consultants can assist in all aspects of immigration. These are two which offer a comprehensive service and have very informative websites:

*Cooper Tuff Consultants:*146 Buckingham Palace Road, London SW1W 9TR; ☎ 0870-990 9480; fax 0870-990 9483; www.uk-immigration.co.uk.

*SkillClear Immigration, Work Permit & Visa Services:*Golden Cross House, 8 Duncannon Street, London WC2N 4JF; ☎ 0207-4845 070; www.skillclear.co.uk.

Part II

Location, Location...

WHERE TO FIND YOUR IDEAL HOME

REGIONS OF SCOTLAND, SOUTH TO NORTH

RETIREMENT

WHERE TO FIND YOUR IDEAL HOME

CHAPTER SUMMARY

- ◊ The scenery, climate and lifestyle vary greatly between different regions of Scotland, so try different areas before you decide where to settle.
- ◊ **Prices.** Average property prices vary tremendously, sometimes between quite small areas.
  - ◊ Remote rural properties tend to be cheaper, except in some areas such as the north west Highlands where there is a shortage of houses for sale.
  - ◊ The most expensive properties in Scotland are concentrated in Edinburgh and East Lothian.
  - ◊ Houses in the catchment areas of good schools can attract high prices.
  - ◊ The property market has been very volatile in recent years, with a pattern of fast rising prices followed by stagnation.
- ◊ **Location.** Good regional road, rail and air networks are important if you want your family and friends to visit.
  - ◊ If you are leaving family behind in England, the south of Scotland is a sensible choice – regular road and rail travel from the north is time-consuming and can become wearing.
  - ◊ Remote rural locations can lead to a sense of isolation.
- ◊ **Employment.** If you need to take a full-time job to support you and your family, it is advisable to live near an urban centre.
  - ◊ In rural areas, you may need to take several part-time jobs.
- ◊ **Retirement.** You can live in Scotland as a 'retired person of independent means' if you have an annual income of £25,000 or more.
  - ◊ Retirement pensions from many other countries can be paid to you in Scotland.
  - ◊ In Scotland, residential nursing care for the elderly is free.

OVERVIEW

So, you've decided Scotland is the place for you. But whereabouts in Scotland? That can be a harder decision to make. There are so many considerations to take into account: firstly, the basic practicalities of life, such as jobs, schools and shopping facilities; then the more aesthetic choices – do you prefer urban or rural, mainland or island, bustling cities, small intimate communities, or genuine isolation. Like Greta Garbo, do you want to be alone? And then, there are the financial considerations: can you afford the sort of property you would prefer in the area you like best?

And after deciding all these preferences, do you go with your heart or your head? Because although the idea of living in a remote island community is what really excites you, in practice this is not an easy move to make. You may find it much harder to adjust to such a change in lifestyle than you expect. In addition, these areas may have severe economic and/or social problems, with high unemployment, falling populations, lack of services and facilities, low educational and career prospects for young people and so on. The Government recognises this in its *Initiative At The Edge* scheme which helps to improve the future prospects of such fragile regions.

IOMAIRT AIG AN OIR/INITIATIVE AT THE EDGE

This scheme, funded by the Scottish Executive and a range of other partnership organisations, was launched in 1998 with the stated aim of concentrating attention and effort on tackling the problems faced by the most fragile rural areas of northern Scotland. Through the initiative, remote communities are helped to become more organised and better able to engage with key public services.

Forty-six such communities were originally identified. Of these, the following communities have benefited so far, some having now left the scheme after reaching certain standards, others which were admitted later and are still being helped, before being left to go it alone. Others will be admitted from time to time in coming years. www.initiative-at-the-edge.org.uk.

Argyll

Coll	Jura

Highland

Ardnamurchan	Arnisdale	Glenelg	North Sutherland
Southeast Caithness			

Western Isles

Barra	Bays of Harris	Bernera	Colonsay
Eriskay	Lochboisdale.	Lochs of Lewis	Uig
Vatersay			

Orkney

Eday	North Ronaldsay	Papa Westray	Sanday
Stronsay	Westray		

Shetland		
Fetlar	Northmavine (Mainland)	Unst
Yell		

If you are making the move from England or Wales, geographical distance from the family you leave behind could be a deciding factor. It has been said that moving to the Lowlands or the Central Belt from England is just moving north, whereas moving to the Highlands or Islands is far more like emigrating. However, even in those areas nearest to England, there are distinct differences in the way of life, the culture and the administrative organisation, which soon make you realise that this is another country, not just Scotland-shire. Amazingly, there are still UK residents (generally English, it has to be said), who think that Scotland is just a county of England. That sort of insularity and parochialism is something which is actually very foreign to the majority of Scots, whose history is run through with the notion of its residents moving about the world in search of work, adventure or fame and fortune.

For a relatively small country, Scotland has a wide variety in its various regions and in the lifestyle choices you could make. The following section looks at each region of Scotland in turn and gives a flavour of what life is like there.

Unlike other European countries such as France or Italy – or indeed unlike England – the choice of which regions to divide the country into is not easy. As far as environment and lifestyles are concerned, the basic topography of the country is an important consideration. Mainland Scotland is divided into three basic topographical regions: the southern uplands, the central lowlands, and the Highlands. In addition, there are the three major island groups, the Western Isles, Orkney, and Shetland. But these major divisions have within them a mixture of communities. The central belt, for example, takes in some very rural, fairly remote communities as well as the largest towns and cities of Scotland. The Highlands is a vast region, within which there is a distinct difference between the far more accessible, populous east and the relatively isolated north and west. Even the weather differs significantly between the two sides of the country.

Alongside the geographical divisions, administrative divisions also have an effect on life. Every few years, it seems, the administrative structure of the country is changed. Most notably, there was a re-drawing of local authority boundaries in 1975 and again in 1994, when Scotland's local government was divided into 32 'unitary authorities'. These replaced the previous two-tier system of nine regional and 53 district councils. In some cases, such as the Scottish Borders and the Highlands, the current unitary authorities are no different from the regional councils they replaced. In others, there are significant differences. As a result of these changes, one finds that the regions covered by other large public organisations do not necessarily follow the same regional boundaries. So, for example, the local councils, police forces, health boards and tourist board regions overlap each other in many places.

In the following sections, therefore, an attempt has been made to focus on common-sense divisions which take into account these variations. This means that in some cases the regions chosen follow the 1975 scheme, in others the region chosen is the current unitary authority area, in others just a section of the 'old' region, including a number of unitary authorities, has been chosen.

Details of the relevant local council or councils, police force, tourist board and so forth are given in each section. The local council websites are a very useful source of further information about living in the area, but these vary greatly from one area to another. Some concentrate solely on practical administrative subjects, listing services and so forth, while others have given themselves a much wider remit and contain far more information on the history and daily lifestyle of their region. The main towns, villages and islands are listed individually, to give a feel for specific communities. Local websites are another important source of information about the culture and lifestyle you could expect, and the best ones have been listed. However, it is always worth searching on the internet for other websites about specific areas – there is a wealth of information on the net, with updates and new websites regularly appearing. These are usually written by people actually living in the area, so you get the measure of the place from the horse's mouth, so to speak.

The history of Scotland, both ancient and modern, has been so turbulent, with many waves of invaders and settlers, and a constantly changing political relationship with England and Europe, that the different regions have distinctive variations, historically, culturally, socially and linguistically. These make Scotland a fascinating and diverse country.

Schooling. If you have children, there is the very important consideration of schooling to take into account. If you move to a rural area, you may find that the nearest school is some distance away, involving daily bus or car journeys, whereas in an urban area, the school may just be a short walk away from home. However, despite the extra travelling, the appeal of a small rural school with just a handful of pupils may outweigh the convenience of being minutes away from a large urban school with hundreds. Only you can decide which style of schooling would suit your child, and you, best. All state schools – which is the vast majority in Scotland – are administered locally and you will find information about them from the local authority.

Employment. How will you support yourself when living in Scotland? The answer to this question may determine where you choose to live. If you need to find a full-time job to support you and your family, your best chance of finding well-paid employment is to move to, or within commuting distance, of one of the cities. If, despite the need to find paid employment, you are determined to live in a remote rural area, you need to accept that you will be far less likely to find a conventional 'nine to five' job and may have to take a number of part-item or seasonal jobs to build up a reasonable income. In the north west Highlands, for example, most people do a number of different things: perhaps running their home as a bed and breakfast and augmenting this with a few hours a week serving in a local shop or behind the bar in the local shop, while taking on occasional work as a jobbing handyman.

Self-employment. If, however, you intend to run your own business, depending on the nature of that business, a remote location may have advantages. The Internet has allowed more and more people to work from home running information-based businesses. Now that Broadband is available throughout Scotland, and as long as you don't need good transport networks to deliver your goods quickly to your customers, you can base yourself on the most remote island. There are any number of freelance IT specialists, writers, editors, photographers, you name it, working in the furthest reaches of Scotland today.

You also need to consider whether, by setting up or moving your business to an urban area, you may find there is just too much competition to make a go of it. If you are the only hairdresser , plumber or website designer in a small community, you may find you can make a far better living than being just one amongst hundreds in a city.

Transport. Whether for work, leisure or visiting your wider family, transport networks are another important consideration. Would it matter to you if it was a two-hour drive including a ferry trip, to get to your nearest large town for your shopping or to visit your dentist? Or if you had to get in the car every time your child needed to go to the leisure centre for his/her swimming or football lesson, and wait around until it was time to take him/her home? Do you need quick access to an airport for business or pleasure trips? Are you happy with a once a day bus service to your nearest town or village? It goes without saying that the time – and money – involved in getting about if you live in the Highlands as opposed to a Central Belt location, is far greater.

Shopping. Are you a shopaholic? If retail therapy is essential to your well-being, you may not be happy to end up many miles from a good shopping centre – although, it has to be said, nowadays one can be just as addicted, and spend just as much money, shopping online!

Friends. If you are a gregarious individual, happiest when surrounded by people, noise and bustle, the thought of living in a small island community may not, at first sight, appeal to you. Paradoxically, perhaps, it is often far harder to gather a circle of friends and acquaintances around you in a town or city with a huge population, than it is in a community of a couple of hundred or less. It is generally the case that rural communities are more welcoming to newcomers simply because there are few people and you are therefore more noticeable when you move in. People are coming and going all the time in the cities, and it is therefore up to you to make a conscious and concerted effort to get involved in social activities, whereas in the rural areas your neighbours are likely to come knocking on your door to invite you to this or that club or coffee morning.

Healthcare. A final very important consideration is proximity to healthcare. If your state of health or your age makes easy access to doctors and hospital of vital importance, you need to factor this into your decision. There is a good network of local general practitioners in even the most rural areas, and you should always be able to get to see a doctor quickly if you have an emergency. Again, sometimes the provision in rural areas is better because of the smaller population and the distance to travel to the surgery. Doctors are more inclined to do house visits when necessary in rural areas, especially to the old, the very young, or those with chronic health problems. And if you can visit the surgery, you will almost certainly be more likely to get an appointment within 24 hours in a rural area than in the centre of a city.

As the days of the local 'cottage hospital' seem to have well and truly gone in the UK, if you need to visit a hospital, whether for routine or emergency treatment, you will need to travel to an urban area. The main hospital for the Highlands and Islands is Raigmore Hospital at Inverness, which may be two or more hours drive away. However, in life or death emergencies, rest assured that the air ambulance service will come to your aid and get you there in a fraction of the time.

MOST IMPORTANT AMENITIES FOR HOMEBUYERS

Halifax Estate Agents found that homebuyers put the following amenities at the top of their list of priorities when deciding where to live:

○ Close to countryside	28%
○ Close to shops, bars and restaurants	18%
○ Proximity to work	17%
○ Near good transport links	15%
○ Close to a good school	13%

Most people decide on these geographical factors first, before they go on to consider other factors such as budget, property specification and availability. In addition, about 24% of buyers investigate levels of anti-social behaviour, vandalism and theft in their new neighbourhood before making a bid on a property.

Caroline Deacon, who moved to Inverness, has this advice

It would be easy, I think, to be swayed by a lovely house or a lovely area into buying something you couldn't quite afford – but remember that if you are having to work then incomes up here are far lower than in the south, and you don't want to move and then have to slave away to finance your lifestyle. So keep your objectives in mind, and don't be panicked into buying something you can't really afford. You also need to have a clear list of what you need and stick to that too.

WHAT YOUR MONEY WILL BUY

The types of property available, the cost of buying property and, just as important a consideration, running that property, can vary considerably from one region to the next. Samples of the sort of prices to expect are given under each region. Council tax rates are also given for each of the 32 local councils. It should be stressed how important this can be when choosing a house. Council taxes are payable by all householders in the UK, and the rates are set individually by each local council. In a region such as Strathclyde, which covers no fewer than 11 local councils, variations between basic rates can be considerable. Within Strathclyde, Glasgow City Council has the highest council tax rates in the country, while South Lanarkshire has among the lowest.

The property market in Scotland (and the United Kingdom as a whole) has been notoriously volatile over the past few years, rising to an unprecedented high in 2003/4, followed by a stabilisation of prices as the Government used interest rate rises to put the brakes on the market before it ran out of control, pricing too many first time buyers and others on lower incomes out of the market. Prices are given here for actual properties advertised for sale in each region in October 2005.

It has long been a feature of the UK housing market that prices follow a cyclical trend, characterised by rising prices reaching a high, only to be followed by stagnation or falling prices. The various phases of this cycle work favourably at different times for house sellers, who obviously want to maximise their profits, and for buyers, who just as reasonably want to pay as little as possible. However, as most sellers will go on to buy another house, and because buyers (apart from first-time buyers) are often selling a house too, the overall advantages and disadvantages tend to be evened out.

Another feature of the UK market is the wide disparity in prices between different regions. Historically, the south east of England has enjoyed the highest property prices while Scotland has been comparatively cheaper. However, within Scotland there are large variations in price between the different regions, with Edinburgh, not surprisingly, commanding the highest prices. Glasgow, as the largest city in the country, also has high priced property, but when looking at average prices this is offset by some of the most disadvantaged areas of the country, generally in the south and east of the city, where property is of poor quality, neighbourhoods can be insalubrious, and prices are therefore low. This is feature of all cities in the country, but the difference between the 'good' areas and the 'bad' areas is at its most pronounced in Glasgow.

Where the house price cycle is on the up, it is invariably the south east of England which sees the highest price rises first, followed by the north and finally by Scotland. Equally, on the downward spiral, Scotland is generally the last place to see prices fall, sometimes continuing to rise while the further south prices are levelling off or even falling in real terms. During 2005, as the housing market cooled, house price growth in Scotland continued to outpace the UK average. In the year to July 2005, annual house price inflation rose by 12.5%, well above the UK average of 3.7%. However, in the last quarter of 2005, the rise in house prices in Scotland had slowed to just 1.4%

The Scottish town with the fastest increase during 2005 was Irvine, in North Ayrshire – a region whose position in the Glasgow commuter belt helped its high growth rate, with an increase of 20% during the year. The cheapest Scottish town in which to buy property was Fraserburgh in Aberdeenshire.

Average house prices continue to be the lowest of the countries of the UK, making it a desirable place for investors to buy in, but even here they succeeded in breaking the £100,00 house price average during 2005. However, there are still ten regions of the country where this level has not been reached.

The most expensive region of the country is now Edinburgh City, and the cheapest is Shetland.

AVERAGE UK PROPERTY PRICES, APRIL TO JUNE 2005

Region	Average price
England	£195,274
Wales	£138,329
Northern Ireland	£122,661
Scotland	£117,626

AVERAGE SCOTTISH PROPERTY PRICES

Area	Average price	Change in previous quarter	Change in previous year
Scotland	£117,626	2%	8.7%
Edinburgh City	£170,342	1.1%	4.9%
East Dunbartonshire	£162,962	0.1%	18.3%
East Renfrewshire	£161,278	-.0%	2.4%
East Lothian	£152,719	4.3%	9.7%
Stirling	£140,209	-3.0%	7.9%
Midlothian	£129,759	9.7%	15%
Argyll & Bute	£122,006	8.3%	20.4%
Perth & Kinross	£120,920	-8.0%	2.8%
South Ayrshire	£120,810	5.3%	20.7%
Glasgow City	£120,361	3.9%	9%
Aberdeenshire	£119,591	-1.9%	13.4%
Scottish Borders	£118,042	-0.7%	-0.6%
Highland	£111,693	3.1%	10.8%
Inverclyde	£111,620	6.6%	9.1%
South Lanarkshire	£107,157	0.4%	8.6%
West Lothian	£107,006	2.6%	6.3%
Aberdeen City	£106,813	3.1%	10.5%

Angus	£106,414	4.6%	19.3%
Dumfries & Galloway	£106,002	0.1%	5.4%
Moray	£103,263	12.1%	21.9%
Clackmannanshire	£102,730	11.8%	11.6%
Fife	£101,792	0.1%	8.8%
Renfrewshire	£99,131	4.8%	8.2%
Orkney Islands	£96,564	5.3%	28.7%
Falkirk	£96,210	4.3%	9.5%
North Lanarkshire	£93,936	7%	14.5%
West Dunbartonshire	£92,005	6.3%	13.8%
North Ayrshire	£90,712	4.6%	6.5%
Dundee City	£87,490	3.8%	17.9%
East Ayrshire	£86,398	4.3%	7.9%
Western Isles	£75,146	-2.8%	16%
Shetland Islands	£65,120	-13.1%	3.8%

Useful website

www.myhouseprice.com Contains a database with the exact price paid of every house sold in Scotland, England and Wales. There is a charge of £1 for each property searched for.

THE REGIONS OF SCOTLAND, SOUTH TO NORTH

DUMFRIES & GALLOWAY

GENERAL INFORMATION

Principal Town: Dumfries.

Local Authority: Dumfries & Galloway Council, Council Offices, English Street, Dumfries DG1 2DD; ☎: 01387-260000; fax: 01387-260034; www.dumgal.gov.uk.

Tourist Office: Dumfries & Galloway Tourist Board, 64 Whitesands, Dumfries DG1 2RS; ☎ 01387-253862; www.visit-dumfries-and-galloway.co.uk; email info@dgtb.visitscotland.com.

Police Force: Dumfries and Galloway Constabulary, HQ, Cornwall Mount, Dumfries DG1 1PZ; ☎ 01387-252112; fax 01387-262059; www.dumfriesandgalloway.police.uk.

Area: 6426 sq. km.

Population: 147,765

Population Density: 23 people per sq. km.

Airports: None.

National Scenic Areas: East Stewartry Coast; Fleet Valley; Nith Estuary.

National Nature Reserves: Silver Flowe, Cairnsmore of Fleet, Kirkconnell Flow, Caerlaverock.

Estate Agents: UK Property Shop, www.ukpropertyshop.co.uk/s/estate – agents – Dumfries – & – Galloway.shtml.

Dumfries & Galloway Solicitors Property Centre, www.dgspc.co.uk.

Your Move, www.your-move.co.uk.

Dumfries and Galloway, in the south western corner of Scotland, is its most southerly region and borders Cumbria in England to the south. It is one of the 32 unitary council regions of Scotland, and encompasses the old counties of Wigtownshire in the west, Kirkcudbrightshire in the centre, and Dumfriesshire to the east.

Largely rural, the region has a population density of only 60 people per square kilometre, compared with the Scottish average of 168. Dumfries, the principal town, has a population of 31,600, while the two other main towns are Stranraer, with a population of 10,800 and Annan, population 8,300.

Agriculture and forestry are very important to the economy of the region, with 70% of the land being used for agricultural purposes, while another 25% is covered with woodland. Much of this is in the three hundred square miles of Galloway Forest Park.

Tourism and a range of light industries are also important. In particular the chemical and plastics industries, and more recently digital telecommunications companies, make a significant contribution to the region's economy.

Unemployment in the region is higher than the national average, due in the main to its rural nature. In 2001 male unemployment stood at 7.6%, compared with the national rate of 6.2%.

Public transport is somewhat sparse within the region, with no commercial airports, but there is a railway line running along the coast as far as Stranraer.

BRITAIN'S BEST ROAD

A panel of racing drivers and motoring journalists voted a ten-mile stretch of road on the A708 between Moffat and Selkirk as the nation's best road, presumably for its scenic value as well as the pleasure of driving it. It runs beside St Mary's Loch and through beautiful rolling lowland landscape.

Geography & Climate

This area of Scotland is sometimes known as the highlands of the lowlands, with the Southern Uplands boasting large areas of mountains, moors, lochs and burns, scenery more usually associated with the north of Scotland. These wilder areas are counterpointed by fertile agricultural land, with 30% of Scotland's dairy cattle coming from Dumfries and Galloway.

This region has many dramatic rocky headlands and beautiful sandy coves along its extensive coastline, which borders the Solway Firth in the south and the Irish Sea to the west. It is the closest part of Scotland to Ireland, only 22 miles across the Irish Sea from Portpatrick to the coast of Ireland. The ferry crossings from Stranraer and Cairnryan are the main sea routes between Scotland and Ireland. The main rivers are the Annan, the Nith and the Esk.

The climate, along with all western areas of the mainland, is mild, thanks to the influence of the Gulf Stream. Palm trees can be seen flourishing in gardens near the coast. It is also wet, with above average rainfall for Scotland. The mild conditions mean that snow does not lie for long on the ground, although during January, February and March it will persist in mountainous regions such as Eskdalemuir.

WEATHER		
Annual averages	Dumfries & Galloway	Scotland
Rainfall (mm)	1400	1099
Sunshine (hours)	1268	1228
Temperature max (°C)	11.3	11.3
Temperature min (°C)	4.2	4.7

Towns & Villages of Note

Annan. This busy market town, with characteristic red sandstone buildings, was linked between 1869 and 1934 by a railway viaduct to Bowness on the English side of the Solway Firth, and before this by a dangerous route across the estuary at low tide. www.annan.org.uk.

Dumfries. The principal town of the region where the headquarters of the local authority, police force and tourist office are to be found. There are still some remnants of the medieval town to be seen, but it is probably more famous today for its association with Robert Burns, Scotland's national bard, who spent the last five years of his life here. www.dumfries-and-galloway.co.uk.

Gretna Green. World famous as the wedding capital of Scotland – maybe of the world. This came about because in 1754 marriage laws were tightened in England, preventing marriages under the age of 16 without parental consent. In Scotland all that was required was a simple declaration before a witness. So couples took to eloping over the border for quick marriages, and as Gretna Green was the first place they came to, an enterprising local blacksmith took it upon himself to help these couples by acting as a the required witness. www.gretna-area.co.uk.

Today, although laws have changed both sides of the border, it is still easier to

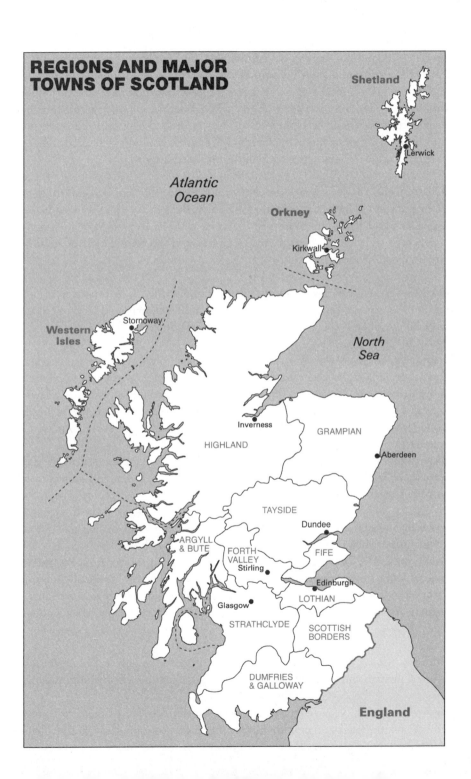

REGIONS AND MAJOR TOWNS OF SCOTLAND

Shetland

Lerwick

Atlantic
Ocean

Orkney

Kirkwall

Western
Isles

Stornoway

North
Sea

Inverness

GRAMPIAN

HIGHLAND

Aberdeen

TAYSIDE

Dundee

ARGYLL
& BUTE

FORTH
VALLEY

FIFE

Stirling

Edinburgh

Glasgow

LOTHIAN

STRATHCLYDE

SCOTTISH
BORDERS

DUMFRIES
& GALLOWAY

England

marry in Scotland, as there is no requirement for couples to have resided in the country for a minimum length of time before their marriage, as there is in England. It is also legal for a church minister to marry a couple anywhere in Scotland. This has encouraged a booming marriage industry throughout the country, with Scotophile couples travelling from the United States, Europe and elsewhere to be married in castles and beauty spots. Highland Country Weddings is an internet-based company arranging such marriages. www.highlandcountryweddings.co.uk

Kirkcudbright. An attractive town with exceptionally wide streets dating from the 18th Century, it has long been a centre for craft workers and artists, attracted here by the quality of the light. Full of history, the town centre is dominated by the ruins of MacLellan's Castle, dating from the 16th Century, and the market cross of 1610 still stands. www.kirkcudbright.co.uk.

Lockerbie. A small town which only became famous due to the events of 21st December 1988, when a Pan American jumbo jet was blown up in mid-air by a terrorist bomb, killing all on board as well as eleven Lockerbie residents.

Portpatrick. For many years Portpatrick was the main port for travellers from Ireland, via the short crossing to Donaghadee. In the past it therefore played the same role as Gretna Green for underage lovers from Ireland, which had the same marriage laws as England. Its picturesque old harbour is still busy with small trawlers and yachts, but it is no longer used as a ferry crossing because the sea here is so much stormier than Stranraer.

Very popular with holidaymakers since the 19th Century, it attracts walkers to the Southern Upland Way which starts here, sailors to the harbour, and golfers to the two golf courses. www.portpatrick.co.uk.

Stranraer. Shipping has always been important here, especially during the 18th and 19th centuries, when it was also a centre of shipbuilding. It was not used as a ferry crossing until 1872 because the crossing to Ireland was far shorter from Portpatrick. However, once steam powered vessels were common, the more sheltered conditions of Stranraer were favoured, and it is now the main ferry port with regular crossings to Northern Ireland through some of the world's busiest shipping lanes. www.stranraer. org.

Whithorn. Known as the 'Cradle of Scottish Christianity' because St. Ninian founded the first Christian church in Scotland here in the 4th Century. www.whithorn.com.

Wigtown. In recent years Wigtown has been named 'Scotland's book town' with a plethora of antiquarian and new bookshops, and plenty of spin-offs from that including literary festivals and the like. www.wigtown-booktown.co.uk.

REASONS TO BUY A HOUSE IN DUMFRIES & GALLOWAY

- 200 miles of unspoiled coastline.
- Southern Upland Way runs from Portpatrick to the east coast.
- Average house £11,600 below national average.
- A strong entrepreneurial spirit – around 300 small businesses start up each year.
- Low crime rate.
- Beautiful landscape – the 'highlands of the lowlands'.
- Renowned for its gardens.
- Within easy reach of England – Carlisle is the nearest urban centre.
- Schools achieve above average results.
- Historic towns and villages.
- Golf courses.
- Bookshops at Wigtown, Scotland's national book town.

Typical Properties for Sale

As a predominantly rural area, there are plenty of small traditional agricultural workers' cottages, in various states of repair, to be found. When these come onto the market they are quickly snapped up for holiday or second homes which tends to push up prices. There are over 1,000 second and holiday homes in the area already.

Almost 15% more people in the region live in detached houses than the national average. Towns such as Lockerbie are characterised by the red sandstone houses built in the Georgian and Victorian periods.

During the recent boom, the spa town of Moffat was one of Scotland's property hotspots, with prices rising at a faster rate than most other towns in the country. It has fine Georgian homes and traditional stone-built cottages, many painted in bright colours.

There is a demand for housing in the area generally, so property should be a reasonable investment in the long term. There are a number of new build developments currently underway.

Sample Properties For Sale, October 2005			
Location	**Type**	**Description**	**Price**
Twynholm	Mid-terrace	2 bed, with garage	Offers over £68,000
Duncow	Country cottage	3 bed, with gardens	Offers over £154,000
Dumfries	Ground floor flat	3 bed, with views of River Nith	Offers over £84,500

Dumfries	Terrace house	Listed building: 3 bed, with rear courtyard and gardens	Offers over £145,000
Carsluith	Detached house	4 bed, with p p. for a further 3 bed house	Offers over £274,995
Castle Douglas	Detached cottage	3 bed, with 2½ acres of land	Offers over £248,000
Port William	Former schoolhouse	Listed building; 3 bed.	Offers over £128,000
Stranrae	Farmhouse	3 bed, with 3 bed annexe, 25 acres land	Offers over £335,000
Castle Douglas	Building plot	P.p. for 2 storey house and garage	Offers over £45,000
Near Dumfries	2 building plots	Spacious, in rural position	Offers over £80,000
Kirkcudbright	Farm steading	For conversion to up to 5 houses	In the region of £225,000
Castle Douglas	Barns	With planning consent for conversion to 3 houses	Offers over £140,000

New Build Houses			
Location	**Type**	**Description**	**Price**
Dumfries	Split level villas & bungalows	Luxury,4 bed	From £305,000
Dumfries	Houses and bungalows	2, 3 & 4 bed	From £94,950
Lochmaben	Lochside family homes	4 & 5 bed	From £295,000
Lockerbie	Luxury homes	4 bed	From £210,000

COUNCIL TAX CHARGES 2005-2006 (FOR A HOUSEHOLD OF 2 ADULTS)		
Tax band	**Dumfries and Galloway**	**Scottish Average**
Band A	£658.67	£729.39
Band B	£768.44	£850.96
Band C	£878.22	£972.52
Band D	£988.00	£1,094.09
Band E	£1,207.56	£1,337.22
Band F	£1,427.11	£1,580.35

| Band G | £1,646.67 | £1,823.48 |
| Band H | £1,976.00 | £2,188.18 |

SCOTTISH BORDERS

GENERAL INFORMATION

Principal Town: Hawick

Local Authority: Scottish Borders Council, Council Headquarters, Newtown St Boswells, Melrose, Roxburghshire TD6 0SA; ☎ 01835-824000; fax 01835-825142; www.scotborders. gov.uk.

Tourist Office: Scottish Borders Tourist Board, Shepherds Mill, Whinfield Road, Selkirk TD7 5DT; 0870-608 0404; www.scot-borders.co.uk.

Police Force: Lothian and Borders Police, Police Headquarters, Fettes Avenue, Edinburgh EH4 1RB; ☎ 0131-311 3131; fax 0131-311 3038; www.lbp.police.uk.

Area: 4732 sq. km.

Population: 106,764

Population Density: 23 people per sq. km.

Airports: No commercial airports.

National Scenic Areas: Eildon & Leaderfoot; Upper Tweedale.

National Nature Reserves: St Abb's Head; Whitlaw Mosses; Cragbank Wood.

Estate Agents: Borders Solicitors' Property Centre, www.bspc.co.uk.

The Scottish Borders Property Centre, 7 Bank Street, Galashiels TD1 1EN; ☎ 01896-754842; www.johnsale.co.uk.

The Scottish Borders region is that portion of Southern Scotland which borders England along the northern boundary of Northumberland and the north western tip of Cumbria. The River Tweed runs through the centre of the region, from Galashiels to Berwick on Tweed. It is this river which, of course, gives its name to that most famous of Scottish textiles, tweed. Textile production is still important to the economy of the area today. The close proximity to northern England means that there are similarities between the accent of the English on the south and the Scots on the north side of the Border. The Scots spoken locally sounds to an English ear to be quite similar to Geordie, the dialect spoken in Northumbria.

The River Tweed also provides some of the best fishing in Scotland, and so adds to the tourism of the region. Agriculture is very important to the economy, with 80% of the land used for agricultural purposes. In addition to this, the land provides many more jobs, with countryside management, sports, tourism and maintenance employing some 4,250 people and bring in over £40 million per year.

The region is unusual in that it does not have a main regional centre. The largest town, however, is Hawick. The Borders is a good area if you are concerned about schooling, with the Borders claiming some of the best state schools in Scotland, providing performance in the majority of schools which is consistently better than the Scottish and UK average. In addition, a higher proportion of school leavers enter further and higher education than the Scottish national average.

On the downside, average earnings in the area are low with over a third of the population earning less than £250 per week. Many people who choose to live in the Borders commute to work in Edinburgh or elsewhere in the central belt, where higher salaries and higher profile jobs are available. The proximity of Edinburgh makes this feasible – as well, one suspects, as pushing down the earnings potential of those who work in the Borders region.

A major factor which discourages some companies from running their businesses from the Borders may well be the lack of good transport links. There are no railway stations and no commercial airports in the region. It was once connected to the Victorian railway system, but all the branch lines in the south were closed after the Second World War. There is currently a move to persuade the Scottish Parliament to introduce a commuter service south from Edinburgh to Melrose and perhaps Hawick, but this will be a major cost as an entire new railway system will need to be built. Whether it comes to pass will be down to the cost compared with the benefits to be brought by the new lines. It is estimated that new train services could cut the congestion in Edinburgh appreciably, which is a major argument in its favour.

Presently, the nearest railway stations are Ediburgh and Berwick-upon-Tweed. The nearest airports are at Edinburgh and Newcastle-upon-Tyne, both of which are international airports. Although there are several fast A roads through the region, there are no motorways crossing the border. Within the region are local bus services, but longer distance intercity coach services do not generally stop between Edinburgh and Newcastle. It is not even straightforward to get a bus or coach direct from Edinburgh or Glasgow to the region, as most journeys involve several time-consuming changes.

Rugby is very popular in the Borders, and most famous of all is the Melrose Sevens (seven-a-side rugby tournament.) There are six major sevens tournaments in the area: four in April (Gala, Melrose, Hawick, and Jedforest), and two in August/September (Selkirk and Kelso). All draw large and enthusiastic crowds from far and wide.

Geography & Climate

The River Tweed runs through the region from its source, west of Peebles, eastwards to the North Sea at Berwick on Tweed, just south of the Scottish Border. At times in its history, Berwick has actually been part of Scotland, so it has something of a 'mixed race' feel about it. To north and south, the ground is high, taking in the Moorfoot, Lammermuir, Tweedsmuir and Cheviot Hills. The central and eastern region is much flatter with just isolated groups of hills amongst the moorland and fertile agricultural plains. The high and rocky Berwickshire Coast is popular for its lovely beaches and attractive fishing villages.

St Mary's Loch in the centre is the region's largest body of water, but the whole area is watered by the Tweed and its many tributaries, making it very fertile. In consequence, as much as 80% of the land is used for agricultural purposes. It is a region characterised by small towns and villages, with no single large centre of population.

In common with most of the east of Scotland, it is relatively dry compared with the west.

WEATHER		
Annual averages	Scottish Borders	Scotland
Rainfall (mm)	656	1099
Sunshine (hours)	1523	1228
Temperature max (°C)	12.2	11.3
Temperature min (°C)	5.2	4.7

Towns & Villages of Note

Coldstream. This town, with a population of around 1,800, lies on the north bank of the River Tweed, where it forms a natural boundary between Scotland and England. An ancient ford at this point of the river is known to have been used to cross between the two countries by Edward I, Robert I, James IV and Montrose at various times before 1766, when the ford was replaced with a bridge.

Duns. The former country town of Berwickshire, Duns has a population of 2,600. The major attraction here is the Jim Clark Memorial Rally which is held on the first weekend in July each year. It is the only closed roads rally in mainland Britain and attracts up to 50,000 spectators. Jim Clark, the double World Motor Racing Champion, was born in the town.

The busy market town of Berwick-Upon-Tweed on the south of the border is only 15 miles away. www.duns.org.uk

Galashiels. A fairly large town with a population of 13,000, Galashiels owes its prominence and prosperity to the textile industry. The strength of the current in the Gala Water made it ideal for setting up mills for tweed and woollen manufacture. By the mid 19th century Galashiels was the main tweed-producing town in Scotland, and in 1909 the Scottish College of Textiles was established here. Only 33 miles from Edinburgh, it is within commuting distance of the city. www.galashiels.bordernet.co.uk.

Hawick. The largest of the Border towns, with a population of 15,000, Hawick is a centre for the Cashmere industry. It now has an international reputation for the quality of its fine woollens and big companies and smaller designers alike have their base here.

It is the home of one of the oldest Border Common Ridings (see below) which takes place in June each year and commemorates a band of local youths who waylaid a troop of English soldiers in 1514, capturing their banner, the 'Hexham Pennant'. www.teribus.com/hawick.htm.

It is also a rugby town, with Hawick Rugby Club having a reputation for producing fine players. www.hawickrfc.co.uk.

Jedburgh. Jedburgh was strategically the most important of the Border towns, due to its proximity to England. Being directly on their route north, it received the full force of the waves of invading English armies. As a result, it has many historic connections and this, together with the fact it is a very attractive town, makes it very popular with visitors.

Just ten miles from the English border, it lies on Jed Water on the northern edge of the Cheviot Hills and has a population of just 4,000. Worthy of comment is the fact that there are probably more alternative spellings of the town name than any other town in Scotland. Over 83 versions of the name have been recorded throughout the centuries, a sign of its antiquity with a version of the name first documented in 854AD. It claims to be the first established parish in Scotland. www.jedburgh-online.org.uk.

Kelso. The town lies at the point where the Tweed and the Teviot, the Borders' two main rivers, meet. It boasts the largest town square in Scotland. The cobbled French-style Kelso Square has some fine buildings on its perimeter, some with a distinctly French air about them, in keeping with the square itself. At the centre of the square is the Bull Ring, dating from the traditional market days in times past. Now Kelso square is home to many good quality specialist shops.

It has a population of about 6,000. Agriculture is very important to the local community, and Kelso is host to regular agricultural events including shows, livestock sales, steeple chasing and point to point races. The Scottish Championship Dog Show is also held in the town. www.kelso-online.co.uk.

Melrose. The Scottish Borders Council has its headquarters down the road from Melrose at Newtown St Boswells, whose 40 acre village green is said to be the largest in Scotland.

The town is popular with walkers, being dominated by the triple peaks of the Eildon Hills, which rise to a height of 422 metres (1385 feet). A marked route leads to the summit. The Southern Upland Way, which runs 212 miles (340 km) coast to coast, from Portpatrick on the south-west coast to Cockburnspath on the eastern seaboard, passes through Melrose. www.melrose.bordernet.co.uk.

The population of about 2,000 is swelled in April for the annual Melrose Sevens rugby tournament which attracts local and international teams:
www.melrose7s.com.

Peebles. The River Tweed rises close by and the town sits on the north bank of the river. With a population of 8,000 it is a popular tourist destination, especially for those interested in outdoor pursuits including walking and mountain biking.

It was made a Royal Burgh by David I and despite being further from the border than the other main towns of the region, it has seen its fair share of upheaval. In 1545 much of the town was burnt to the ground by Hertford's troops. It was again reduced to ashes – accidently this time – in 1607 and then in 1650 Cromwell garrisoned the town. www.discovertheborders.co.uk

Selkirk. To give it its full name, The Ancient and Royal Burgh of Selkirk is a town of around 6,000 souls. Its main claim to fame is the fact that Sir Walter Scott served as Sheriff here for 33 years.

In recognition of this, the town held in 2000 a pre-Christmas festival 'Scott's Selkirk'. It was such a popular success that it has been carried on ever since as an annual event.

Selkirk's Common Riding in June is another big annual event, when up to 500 riders saddle their horses at daybreak to ride the Marches. The Casting of the Colours commemorates the Battle of Flodden Field. Selkirk sent 80 men to fight with the Scottish King, but only one returned, bearing a blood-stained English flag. www.selkirk.bordernet.co.uk.

REASONS TO BUY A HOUSE IN THE SCOTTISH BORDERS

- Close to England.
- Average house pirces close to the national average.
- Close enough to Edinburgh to commute.
- New train link from Edinburgh promised.
- Over 1500 miles of dedicated walking paths.
- Golf courses.
- 100 miles of some of the world's best fishing on the River Tweed.
- Picturesque towns and villages.
- Historic Common Ridings, which make horse riding part of the culture.
- Rugby.
- Good state schools with above average results.
- Beautiful beaches.
- Lush moorland and rolling hills.
- Sir Walter Scott country.

Typical Properties for Sale

There is a wide range of property on offer in the Scottish Borders: large detached properties, old and new, with extensive grounds; small rural cottages; Victorian sandstone town houses; estates of modern semi-detached houses; modest terraced properties; and flats, both purpose-built and conversions of older buildings.

As a result, you should be able to find something to suit your pocket from the wide range of prices – in early 2004 a house in Galashiels sold for £250,000, while at the other end of the scale, another property in the town sold for just £38,000.

A popular tourist area, particularly with the northern English who don't have far to travel to reach the region, there are over 1,000 second or holiday homes in the Borders, and as suitable properties come onto the market they are likely to be bid for by incomers as well as local residents.

It does appear that the housing market has slowed quite significantly. Because of its accessibility to Edinburgh, when prices there rose dramatically, people looked to the Borders where they found they could get far more for their money, and still be within commuting distance. During 2004 and early 2005 prices in the Borders were well above the national average, but by the middle of 2005 they were only about £500 above the mean. At the time of writing, in Autumn 2005, there is a lot of property for sale, suggesting supply is currently out-stripping demand which suggests prices may fall further.

SAMPLE PROPERTIES FOR SALE, OCTOBER 2005			
Location	Type	Description	Price
Kelso	Georgian Villa	5 bed, B listed, in 0.6 acres of garden	Offers over £550,000
Jedburgh	Part 18th century house	4 bed, with coach house, paddock and residential p.p.	Offers over £485,000
Selkirk	Modern bungalow	3 bed, with 2 bed granny flat, stables and menage	Offers over £420,000
Kelso	Semi-detached house	4 bed, stone-built, refurbished.	Offers over £175,000
Melrose	Luxury converted flat	2 bed, in large Victorian property	Offers over £139, 500
Near Hawick	Rural lodge house	3 bed with garage and gardens, in need of modernisation	Offers over £139,500
Peebles	Detached bungalow	Modern, 2 bed, with garage and gardens	Offers over £149,000
Hawick	Flat	1 bed, ground floor	Offers over £36,000
Minto	Building plot	1/3 acre with p.p., panoramic views, planted borders and pond	Offers over £125,000
Eyemouth	Building plot	1/5 acres, in residential area	Offers over £42,000

New Build Houses			
Location	Type	Description	Price
Selkirk	Houses	3 & 4 bed	From £117,000
Lauder	Detached houses	4 & 5 bed	From £25,000
Hawick	Luxury apartments	3 bed	From £182,000
Kelso	Family homes	2 & 3 bed	From £109, 750
Coldstream	Villa	4 bed	£192,000

COUNCIL TAX CHARGES 2005-2006 (FOR A HOUSEHOLD OF 2 ADULTS)

Tax band	Scottish Borders	Scottish Average
Band A	£679.33	£729.39
Band B	£792.56	£850.96
Band C	£905.78	£972.52
Band D	£1,019.00	£1,094.09
Band E	£1245.44	£1,337.22
Band F	£1,471.89	£1,580.35
Band G	£1,698.33	£1,823.48
Band H	£2,038.00	£2,188.18

STRATHCLYDE

GENERAL INFORMATION

Main Town: Glasgow.

Local Authorities: East Ayrshire Council, Council Headquarters, London Road, Kilmarnock, Ayrshire KA3 7BU; ☎ 01563-576000; fax 01563-576500; www.east-ayrshire.gov.uk.

East Dunbartonshire Council, Tom Johnston House, Civic Way, Kirkintilloch, Glasgow G66 4TJ; ☎ 0141-578 8000; fax 0141-777 8576.

East Renfrewshire Council, Council Offices, Eastwood Park, Rouken Glen Road, Giffnock G46 6UG; ☎ 0141-577 3000; fax 0141-620 0884; www.eastrenfrewshire.gov.uk.

Glasgow City Council, City Chambers, George Square, Glasgow G2 1DU; ☎ 0141-287 2000; fax 0141-287 5666; www.glasgow.gov.uk.

Inverclyde Council, Municipal Buildings, Clyde Square, Greenock, Renfrewshire PA15 1LY; ☎ 01475-717171; fax 01475-712731; www.inverclyde.gov.uk.

North Ayrshire Council, Cunninghame House, Irvine, Ayrshire KA12 8EE; ☎ 01294-324100; fax 01294-324144; www.northayrshire.gov.uk.

North Lanarkshire Council, PO Box 14, Civic Centre, Motherwell, Lanarkshire ML1 1TW; ☎ 01698-302222; fax 01698-275125; www.northlan.gov.uk.

Renfrewshire Council, Council Headquarters, North Building, Cotton Street, Paisley PA1 1BU; ☎ 0141-842 5000; fax 0141-840 3335; www.renfrewshire.gov.uk.

South Ayrshire Council, County Buildings, Wellington Square, Ayr KA7 1DR; ☎ 01292-612000; fax 01292-612143; www.south-ayrshire.gov.uk.

South Lanarkshire Council, Council Offices, Almada Street, Hamilton, Lanarkshire ML3 0AA; ☎ 01698-454444; fax 01698-454275; www.southlanarkshire.gov.uk.

West Dunbartonshire Council, Garshake Road, Dumbarton G82 3PU; ☎ 01389-737000; fax 01389-737700; www.wdcweb.info.

Tourist Office(s): Greater Glasgow & Clyde Valley Tourist Board, 11 George Square, Glasgow G2 1DY; ☎ 0141-204 4480; fax 0141-204 4074; www.seeglasgow.com. Dumbarton Tourist Office, Milton G82 2TZ; ☎/fax 08707-200612; www. visitscottishheartlands.com.

Ayrshire & Arran Tourist Board, 15 Skye Road, Prestwick KA9 2TA; ☎ 0845-2255 121; www.ayrshire-arran.com.

Police Force: Strathclyde Police Headquarters, 173 Pitt Street, Glasgow G2 4JS; ☎ 0141-532 2000; fax 0141-532 2475; www.strathclyde.police.uk.

Area: 6,715 square kilometres.

Population: 2,875,135

Population Density: 670 people per square kilometre.

Airports: Glasgow Airport; Prestwick Airport.

World Heritage Sites: New Lanark.

National Nature Reserves: Clyde Valley Woodlands.

Estate Agents: Glasgow Solicitors' Property Centre, Kilpatrick House, 145/147 Queen Street, Glasgow G1 3BJ; ☎ 0345-229922; fax 0141-248 9055; www.gspc.co.uk. Your Move, 2A Righead Gate, East Kilbride G74 1LS; ☎ 01355-248133; fax 01355-248136; www.your-move.co.uk.

Your Move, 70 Cazdow Street, Hamilton ML3 6DS; ☎ 01698-891799; fax 01698-891895; www.your-move.co.uk.

UK Property Shop, www.ukpropertyshop.co.uk/s/estate_agents_Glasgow.shtml.

The most densely populated region in Scotland, Strathclyde nonetheless has plenty of green spaces. Glasgow, Scotland's largest city, is surrounded by easily accessible areas of beautiful scenery, both inland and along the Clyde coast. The city itself is not lacking in open spaces – it has over 70 parks and gardens, and handsome mature trees line many of the roads leading into the city centre.

All the local authority areas in this region (see above), with the exception of Glasgow City, have large areas of agricultural land, largely used for dairy farming and the production of beef and lamb. But each council area also has appreciable urban developments among the green fields. Although a good proportion of these residential developments are occupied by those who commute to work in Glasgow, there is also plenty of employment within the outlying districts.

With Glasgow and the Clyde area coming to prominence in previous centuries based on its shipbuilding and heavy industry, there has been a massive change in the last half century or so with a relatively rapid decline in these industries – only one shipyard remains today, in an area which was once one of the biggest shipbuilding centres in the world. Following periods of high unemployment in the mid to late 20th century, as the big industries closed down, Strathclyde has pulled itself up by its bootstraps in the last 15 years or so and attracted new hi-tech, service and retail industries, rebuilding itself as a vibrant commercial centre.

Glasgow in particular has been a great success story since it made the decision to cast off the partially deserved old image of the city as a rough, tough place of high unemployment, with a hard-drinking population occupying a cultural desert. By choosing to promote its exceptional architectural heritage, and its green areas, and to regenerate some of the worst areas of dereliction, it has now become a model of how to turn a city around. Although there are still deprived areas of Glasgow – mainly to the south of the river – where there are social problems and it is probably not advisable to walk after dark, the feeling throughout the city is that it is on the 'up' as the inexorable progress of the many regeneration, restoration and redevelopment schemes make their impressive mark on the city.

Strathclyde is in many ways the communications hub of Scotland. With two international airports within the region, at Glasgow and Prestwick, a network of motorways and main roads, good rail connections, and passenger and freight ferry terminals allowing access to Ireland and to the Highlands and Islands, this is the most accessible part of the country.

There is a healthy sense of competition between Glasgow and Edinburgh – while the capital city has much of the international cachet as far as its political, historical and cultural heritage is concerned, Glasgow presents itself as the more vibrant, chic, altogether younger and livelier, face of Scotland, than the somewhat staid, traditional image of Edinburgh.

The Glasgow accent has a reputation for being difficult to understand and for being a harsh version of Scots. This is true to an extent – the locals tend to speak very quickly and, in common with many urban accents elsewhere in the United Kingdom, it is not the most lilting or easiest on the ear. But as Glaswegian – the 'see you Jimmy' accent – is the one which most non-Scots think of as the 'normal' Scottish accent, it is perhaps more familiar to the ear than some other accents. For example, in more rural parts of Strathclyde, such as parts of Ayrshire, the accent can be even more impenetrable! But take comfort from the fact that, despite accents, dialect words and unusual grammatical constructions, at the end of the day, the language spoken is a form of English and your ear will soon adjust.

Geography & Climate

Around 60% of the land surrounding Glasgow is used for agriculture and many more acres are open countryside, whether in the form of country parks, moorland or sea and lochside areas. This feature, together with the extensive parks and trees throughout the city, particularly in the leafy West End, means that, despite Glasgow being the largest conurbation in Scotland, it doesn't have the built-up feel of many similar-sized cities. There is a genuine feeling that the countryside is literally on one's doorstep.

In addition to the green spaces, there is plenty of water in Strathclyde. With the Clyde and several other rivers crossing the region, and many reservoirs and lochs, including the southern end of Loch Lomond, which falls in West Dunbartonshire, in addition to the Firth of Clyde and the extensive coastline of Ayrshire, both the sea and fresh water have long been important to the region both for leisure and industry. The large island of Arran, plus the tiny pair of islands, Great Cumbrae and Little Cumbrae, are in North Ayrshire.

Although the region has its fair share of hills, there are few particularly high peaks. Despite this, there is the feeling as one travels north through the region that there is a change in the scenery and topography. As one nears the beginning of the highlands proper, it gets hillier, with more lochs and glens, more wide open spaces.

In common with the rest of the west, Strathclyde has higher than average rainfall, but it also has more than its share of sunshine. Snowfall is among the lowest in the country.

WEATHER		
Annual averages	Strathclyde	Scotland
Rainfall (mm)	1235	1099
Sunshine (hours)	1384	1228
Temperature max (°C)	12.4	11.3
Temperature min (°C)	4.8	4.7

Towns, Villages & an Island of Note

Arran. The largest island in the Firth of Clyde, lying off the mainland of North Ayrshire. It is 20 miles long and 11 miles wide and it has a resident population of 4,900. The main town is Brodick, with a population of just over 600. A popular holiday resort, its income comes mainly from tourism, crafts and whisky distilling. The island is mountainous to the north and gently undulating to the south.

The island has been inhabited since prehistoric times, with archaeological remains including stone circles and burial cists, an Iron Age fort and Bronze Age remains. www.visitarran.net.

Ayr. The administrative town of South Ayrshire, Ayr has a population of 46,400. It is a favourite holiday destination, thanks to its fine coastal setting and because of its historical links with both William Wallace and Robert Burns. The imposing Wallace Tower in the town commemorates his confrontation with the occupying English in

1297, when he set fire to their garrison. The first meeting of the Scottish parliament after his victory at Bannockburn took place at St John's Kirk in the town. Robert Burns was born in Alloway, on the southern outskirts of Ayr, and there are several tourist attractions in the town commemorating his life and works.

Situated among the historic relics dating back to the 1300s, there is a busy modern shopping centre. www.ayrshirescotland.com.

Bearsden. The town dates back to Roman times, when they built a fort and bathhouse here as part of the Antonine Wall defences. Originally called Kirktoune, it did not become of any size until the 19th century when it became popular with wealthy Glasgow merchants who moved to the countryside here to build their homes away from the growing newly industrialised city.

Today it has a population of around 28,000, having grown considerably in recent years. It is a desirable residential area with many Glasgow workers who commute into the city daily. www.scottielad.supanet.com/bearsdentoday/index.htm

Dumbarton. Now the administrative centre of West Dunbartonshire, Dumbarton was the capital of the Kingdom of Strathclyde in the eighth and ninth centuries. The town is dominated by Dumbarton Castle, described by King Henry VIII as 'the key to the realm'.

Starting in the 18th century, it was shipbuilding and marine engineering which provided the wealth of the town. The last shipyard closed down in 1963, and now whisky distilling and light engineering, along with council employment, are the mainstay of the town's economy. 25 years ago much of the town centre was demolished, its old buildings replaced with new civic and residential buildings, car parks and shopping centres. Its current population is 20,500. www.turningwood. fsnet.co.uk/dumbarton.html.

East Kilbride. East Kilbride, once a small village, became the first of Scotland's New Towns, constructed in the 1950s and 60s. Just nine miles from Glasgow, it was used to help solve Glasgow's housing shortage at the time. It is now Scotland's sixth largest town with a population of nearly 74,000. It is proud of its EK Centre, claimed to be Scotland's largest undercover shopping and leisure location. The original East Kilbride village, meanwhile, retains its old buildings and cobbled streets with specialist shops. www.eastkilbride.org.uk.

Glasgow. Scotland's largest city, with a population of 630,000, is affectionately known as the 'dear green place' – although opinion is divided as to whether this is the true derivation of the word 'Glasgow – in reference to its many parks, gardens and attractive tree-lined streets. Glasgow has reinvented itself in the past two decades, with startling success. Whatever the truth of the matter, and whatever the fiercely loyal residents of the city feel, the external reputation of the city for many years was not the best. The undeniably grim and deprived parts of the city, the ones which were the most prominent when approached by motorway, were taken to be the pattern for the whole, while the very desirable leafy West End and parks and museums and striking Victorian architecture, which were always there, were unpromoted to the outside world, certainly outside Scotland. Its image as a dirty and dangerous concrete jungle riddled with drunken football fans and drug addicts just kept tourists, businesses and potential workers and residents away.

Despite its shortcomings, Glasgow has always been a centre for commerce, which made it a wealthy place. Today it is the third most prosperous city in the UK, just behind Edinburgh, which is second only to London.

The rebirth of the city can be dated to the *Glasgow's Miles Better* campaign launched in 1983, which was so successful it won the International Film and Television of New York award an amazing four times between 1983 and 1987. But it wasn't just an advertising campaign – under the leadership of the then Lord Provost Michael Kelly, it was backed up with real investment, together with commitment, enthusiasm and downright determination to turn the fortunes of the city around. The flagship projects of the early years were the opening of the Burrell Collection gallery in Pollok Park in 1983; the opening of the Scottish Exhibition and Conference Centre (SECC) in 1985; and the Glasgow Garden Festival of 1988. All three attracted visitors in large numbers to Glasgow, and once there, they began to see that it had much more to offer.

WHY GLASGOW'S MILES BETTER

In recent years, Glasgow has been designated:

- European City of Culture 1990
- United Kingdom National City of Sport 1996-99
- United Kingdom City of Architecture & Design 1999
- European Capital of Sport 2003
- Host of the Special Olympics 2005 (for sports persons with learning disabilities)

Glasgow is home to Scotland's principal performing arts organisations:

- Scottish Opera
- Scottish Ballet
- Royal Scottish National Orchestra
- BBC Scottish Symphony Orchestra
- National Youth Orchestra of Scotland
- Scottish Youth Theatre

From its early days recognised as a powerful seat of learning, today Glasgow has a long list of educational establishments with more than 50,000 students in total:

- The University of Glasgow
- Strathclyde University

- Glasgow Caledonian University
- Royal Scottish Academy of Music & Drama
- Glasgow School of Art
- College of Commerce
- College of Building & Printing
- College of Food Technology
- Glasgow Hotel School
- Glasgow Nautical College

In a survey of UK graduates' satisfaction with their lives, graduates in Glasgow were at number nine, with a satisfaction score of 62 per cent.
Glasgow's cultural visitor attractions include:

- Burrell Collection
- Kelvingrove Art Gallery & Museum
- Hunterian Museum & Art Gallery
- Glasgow Transport Museum
- St Mungo's Museum of Religious Life & Art
- Gallery of Modern Art
- Scotland Street School Museum of Education
- Scottish Exhibition & Conference Centre
- House for an Art Lover (from a design by Charles Rennie Mackintosh)

The city's annual festivals and events include:

- Celtic Connections (late January-early February)
- International Comedy Festival (mid-March-early April)
- Guitarfest (April)
- Royal Scottish National Orchestra Proms (June)
- West End Festival (June)
- International Jazz Festival (July)
- World Pipe Band Championships (August)
- Glasgow Show (August)
- Glasgay! Gay & Lesbian Arts Festival (late October-early November)
- Shine on Glasgow Christmas Shopping Festival (November-December)
- Glasgow's Hogmanay (31 December)

In addition to all this, Glasgow has the reputation of being the friendliest city in the world, an accolade alluded to in its 2005 variation on the old slogan: *Glasgow Smiles Better*.

Alongside its cultural achievements, Glasgow is an important centre for business and finance. Glasgow has a long history as Scotland's industrial centre, but the traditional shipbuilding and heavy engineering have now made way for modern mixed economy with a particular expertise in knowledge-based industries including biological sciences, optoelectronics and e-commerce technology. Retail therapy is also important to the city, with Glasgow the second largest shopping centre in the United Kingdom, after London.

Over 20 years after the process started, regeneration of the city continues today. Derelict and neglected buildings in the city centre are being redeveloped as homes and businesses, pubs and clubs, theatres and entertainment venues, alongside brand new apartment buildings, making for a stunning and sympathetic mix of old and new architecture.

The waterfront is also being redeveloped, bringing the neglected Clydeside back to life. The ten year Glasgow Harbour regeneration project begun in 2001 aims to transform 120 acres of redundant shipyard and dockland, creating a brand new district incorporating residential, commercial, retail and leisure space.

To reflect the upmarket feel of these new developments, and stress its new image as a lively, cosmopolitan, sophisticated city, the latest municipal slogan is *Glasgow: Scotland with Style*. The increasing number of visitors to the city seem to agree.

Interesting Websites
www.footprintguides.com/Glasgow.
www.glasgowwestend.co.uk.
www.glasgowsurvival.co.uk.
www.scotguide.com/htm/links.htm.
www.glasgowmerchantcity.net.

Greenock. The administrative town of Inverclyde is Greenock, with a population of 45,400. It is an attractive town with many beautiful civic buildings, many of them with listed building status which will preserve them for the future. It was originally a small fishing village, and then during the Industrial revolution grew into a busy town dependent on industry and manufacturing connected with shipbuilding. Greenock is now one of the largest centres for high technology and communications media in Europe. The waterfront has been redeveloped for leisure and retail activities. It also has a large container and cruise ship terminal. The main *Caledonian Macbrayne* ferry terminal is in nearby Gourock. www.greenock.org.

Kirkintilloch. The administrative town of East Dunbartonshire, the town grew up on the site of a fort on the Antonine Wall. Once a coal mining centre, now it is little more than a dormitory town for Glasgow, with many of its 20,300 inhabitant commuting the six miles to the city for work.

THE DRY TOWN

Kirkintilloch's main claim to fame is that until recently it was a "dry" town with no licensed premises. This came about after the local miners' wives, fed up with their husbands spending all their wages on drink, got the licensing board to ban pubs. www.kirkintilloch-myhome.co.uk.

The folk group *The Corries* wrote a song about it, which claimed a more romantic reason for it:

In Kirkintilloch there are no pubs,
And I'm sure you wonder why,
My Brother and me, we went on a spree,
And we drank the pubs all dry, all dry,
We drank the pubs all dry.

Paisley. With a population of 74,000, Paisley is the largest town in Scotland outwith the five original cities. The two newest cities, Inverness and Stirling, are far smaller than Paisley. It was an important textile centre in the 19th century – the classic kashmiri-style 'paisley' fabric pattern is named after the town.

The town has a strong rivalry with its near neighbour, Glasgow. Many Paisley folk – who refer to themselves as 'Buddies' and won't thank you for calling them Glaswegians – feel keenly that the town should be accorded full city status. They argue that as they have both a cathedral and a university, as well as being the administrative centre of Renfrewshire, it is long overdue. Glasgow Airport, despite its name, is nearer to Paisley than to the city centre. www.paisley.org.uk.

History

Evidence of Stone Age fishing communities has been discovered in the Glasgow area. After that, little is known of local residents until the arrival of the Romans. Celtic druids were the earliest religious sect to live in the area, followed later by St Ninian who is known to have passed through the area.

However, Glasgow really dates its origins to the 6th Century when St Kentigern – later known locally as St Mungo, meaning 'dear one' – settled in the place then known as Glas Cu (derivations vary: possibly 'dear green place' or maybe 'grey blacksmith' or the 'grey hound ferry'. Take your pick.)

St Mungo is said to have performed four religious miracles in Glasgow, which are represented in the city's coat of arms and in this verse:

Here's the bird that never flew
Here's the tree that never grew
Here's the bell that never rang
Here's the fish that never swam

The bird: St Mungo restored life to the pet robin of his master St Serf, which had been killed by some of his fellow classmates.
The tree: St Mungo had been left in charge of a fire in Saint Serf's monastery. He fell asleep and the fire went out but Mungo succeeding in using a branch from a hazel tree to restart the fire.
The bell: Brought from Rome by Saint Mungo, it was used in services and to mourn the deceased.

The fish: The Queen of Cadzow was suspected of infidelity by her husband, who demanded to see her ring, which he believed she had given to her lover. Mungo ordered a messenger to catch a salmon in the river. The ring was miraculously found inside the fish, which allowed the Queen to clear her name and avoid execution.

REASONS TO BUY A HOUSE IN STRATHCLYDE

- Good mix of urban, semi-urban and rural.
- Glasgow, Scotland's largest city, at its centre.
- Condé Nast Traveller named Glasgow as the favourite UK destination outside London.
- Wide choice of communities and properties, all within easy reach of Glasgow.
- At the hub of Scotland's road network.
- Good public transport provision.
- Glasgow has Scotland's best shopping.
- Thriving café culture in Glasgow West End and City Centre.
- Within easy reach of the Highlands.
- Loch Lomond, Scotland's largest loch.
- Industrial heritage.
- Friendly suburban towns with affordable properties.
- Family-centred communities.
- Influential design and architecture.
- Charles Rennie Mackintosh country.
- Greatest concentration of universities and colleges.
- An area undergoing change, from its industrial past to a high-tech future.
- Riverfront areas being developed throughout the region with stunning new properties.
- Massive investment promises that the area will only improve in coming years.

Typical Properties for Sale

Glasgow. This is very much a region of contrasts, with areas of very expensive properties mixed in with others. Within Glasgow City Council area there is a dramatic difference in the social and economic make-up of different areas, some of them very small, encompassing only a few streets. The most expensive property in Glasgow, and the most desirable area to live, is without doubt the West End. Here the vast majority of properties are flats, with many beautiful old tenement buildings which have been renovated and finished to a high quality standard over recent years. In between these are modern apartment blocks which have in the main been designed to fit in with the traditional solid sandstone look of the area. Much of the West End is a conservation area, so developers have to stick to certain guidelines to get their plans through.

Tucked away between these are streets of substantial Victorian villas, some very large and imposing, which rarely come on the market, but when they do, sell for the best part of £1 million.

The City Centre, in particular the Merchant City, is an up and coming area. As traffic congestion grows and parking in the city becomes ever more difficult and expensive, people are moving back into the city centre, preferring the convenience and ease of being able to walk to work. Glasgow city centre as a whole is currently undergoing a rebirth, with renovation of old buildings and the building of brand new ones, to house good quality flats, offices and retail units, underway in the Merchant City area, moving towards Glasgow Green and the River Clyde. Further along the river, the Clyde waterfront is undergoing a massive face lift, with this previously derelict area being brought back to life with yet more conversions and new builds to provide accommodation, mainly in apartments. Planning permission has been granted for 770 new apartments at Glasgow Harbour.

At the time of writing in 2005, work is just starting on another 'forgotten corner' of north Glasgow, between Port Dundas and Maryhill, which is to be transformed into a canal quarter with over 400 new houses, offices, restaurant, bars and boat moorings. The project includes an ambitious plan to restore a missing link on the cannel, which will, 70 years on, re-link Port Dundas with the city centre. The entire project is envisaged to take 15 years, but the first houses should be available by 2007.

At the other end of the scale, the highest national levels of social deprivation are found in the city. Over 50% in the neighbourhoods in Glasgow City are defined as being in the most deprived 15% of neighbourhoods nationally. Notorious areas which you would want to avoid are Springburn, Baillieston, Shettleston and Easterhouse, all in the east of the city. For many years the Gorbals, south of the river, was the place everybody knew was rough. But in the last ten or fifteen years, the worst housing has been demolished and replaced with new development, and the City Council has tried to attract new residents by trying to give it an image makeover, so it is now called New Gorbals.

So you need to know your areas of Glasgow when house-hunting, although it's not difficult research to do: just look at the properties advertised for sale in various areas and the lower the price, the more deprived the area. Location is of crucial importance, so although you may find a nicely finished, reasonably good quality flat, within the city, a low price should make you find out more about the area. Having said which, there are areas which are 'on the up', and to buy at a cheap price in one of these improving areas can be an excellent investment as you can guarantee that prices will rise as the area improves.

As a broad rule of thumb, the most downmarket areas of Glasgow tend to be in the south and east of the city, but even here there are 'nice' areas scattered through the most socially deprived neighbourhoods.

And as part of the ongoing regeneration of the city, one of Glasgow's most deprived areas, the East End between Parkhead and Cambuslang, is to be transformed by

10,000 new homes and 20,000 new jobs. Substandard housing is to be demolished and replaced with modern housing, at the centre of which will be the tallest structure ever built in Scotland, a 42 storey skyscraper which will house leisure and shopping facilities, a hotel, and apartments. This is appropriate in the city which practically invented the tower block.

SCOTLAND'S FIRST GARDEN SUBURB

Drumchapel, on the north west outskirts of Glasgow, is due to become Scotland's first 'garden suburb' as a £100 million redevelopment of the area gets underway. It will include a revolutionary and pioneering scheme to build Scotland's first 'flat-pack' houses, provided by IKEA, the Swedish company long associated with furnishing our homes in a stylish, but inexpensive, fashion. Now they have branched out into producing the homes to put them in – and will include free furniture vouchers in the package for prospective buyers.

The homes will range in price from starter flats to £250,000 town houses, and will be built alongside shops, business premises, a civic centre and new roads, and will also incorporate a policy of providing substantial green spaces.

Surrounding Areas. Although there is currently a huge demand for inner city flats as people make the choice to move back into the city, the suburbs continue to be popular, in particular with families who look for good schools, and large houses with a front and back door and a garden. Although flat-dwelling is convenient and easy for young singletons and couples with no children, once those young people have families they find they want their own garden where the children can play safely

Within these areas also there are more and less desirable areas, which is reflected in the price of properties. Four of the local authorities in Strathclyde have areas where property prices are well above the average for the area as a whole. These are:

- Bearsden and Milngavie in East Dumbartonshire.
- Bridge of Weir in Renfrewshire.
- Newton Mearns and Clarkston in East Renfrewshire.
- Uddingston and Bothwell in South Lanarkshire.

These areas were built for the wealthy professional classes who made their fortunes in industrial Victorian Glasgow. Over the past century they have continued to attract wealthy people and the infrastructure that they demanded, including good quality shops, schools and amenities.

The good road and rail systems mean that even from these outlying areas, you can be in Glasgow in half an hour or less. Hamilton in Lanarkshire is sure to benefit from a new train line to Milngavie via Glasgow and this is likely to push prices up here.

To the south of the region, Ayrshire and Arran are predominantly rural, with attractive market towns and seaside resorts. Here you will find a mix of country cottages, detached and semi-detached houses with gardens, and terraced townhouses. Improvement of the road system from Glasgow to Ayrshire mean that travelling times have been cut and consequently people are finding it easier to live in the countryside and commute to Glasgow on a daily basis. This is likely to stimulate the housing market along the route of the A77/M77.

There are several amenable towns and villages along the firth of Clyde, including the traditional 'doon the watter' holiday favourites of the Glasgow workers, such as Port Glasgow, Gourock and Greenock in Inverclyde. These are still popular tourist areas and show their Victorian heritage in imposing houses, many in Scottish Baronial style.

Sample Properties For Sale, October 2005			
Location	Type	Description	Price
Greenock	Conversion on 2 floors	5 bed, 3 public rooms	Offers over £275,000
Glasgow City Centre	Flat	3 bed	Fixed price £175,000
Glasgow west end	Duplex conversion	3 bed	Fixed price £299,995
Glasgow Jordanhill	Mid-terrace	3 bed, with garage and garden	Offers over £249,00
Glasgow Harbour	Waterfront flat	1 bed	Fixed price £149,995
Brookfield, Renfrewshire	Detached house	3 bed, garden and integral garden	Offers over £325,000
Troon, South Ayrshire	Detached stone house	Stone, 5 bed	Offers over £285,000
Darvel, East Ayrshire	Cottage style terrace	Sandstone, 2 bed, needs modernisation.	Offers over £58,500
Lenzie, East Dunbartonshire	Victorian conversion	4 bed, upper duplex	Offers over £255,000
Milngavie, East Dunbartonshire	Semidetached bungalow	3 bed	Offers over £175,00
Coatbridge, North Lanarkshire	Modern semi-detached	3 bed	Fixed price £138,000
Drongan, East Ayrshire	Farmstead	With p.p. for conversion to 3 houses	Offers over £165,000

COUNCIL TAX CHARGES 2005-2006 (FOR A HOUSEHOLD OF TWO ADULTS)

Tax Band	East Ayrshire	East Dunbart-onshire	East Renfre-wshire	Glasgow City	Inver-clyde	North Ayrshire	North Lanark-shire	Renfrew-shire	South Ayrshire	South Lanark-shire	West Dunbart-onshire	Scottish Average
A	£744.18	£718.99	£702.00	£808.67	£784.00	£716.67	£694.00	£727.30	£708.54	£693.33	£742.00	£729.39
B	£868.21	£838.83	£819.00	£943.44	£914.67	£836.11	£809.67	£848.52	£826.63	£808.89	£856.67	£850.96
C	£992.24	£958.66	£936.00	£1078.22	£1045.33	£955.56	£925.33	£969.73	£944.22	£924.44	£989.33	£972.52
D	£1116.27	£1078.49	£1053.00	£1213.00	£1176.00	£1075.00	£1041.00	£1090.95	£1062.81	£1040.00	£1113.00	£1094.09
E	£1364.33	£1318.15	£1287.00	£1482.56	£1437.33	£1313.89	£1272.33	£1333.38	£1298.99	£1271.11	£1360.33	£1337.22
F	£1612.39	£1557.82	£1521.00	£1752.11	£1698.67	£1552.78	£1503.67	£1575.82	£1535.82	£1502.22	£1607.67	£1580.35
G	£1860.45	£1797.48	£1755.00	£2,021.67	£1960.00	£1791.67	£1735.00	£1818.25	£1771.35	£1733.33	£1855.00	£1823.48
H	£2232.54	£2156.98	£2106.00	£2426.00	£2352.00	£2150.00	£2082.00	£2181.90	£2125.62	£2080.00	£2226.00	£2188.18

New Build Homes			
Location	Type	Description	Price
Glasgow Merchant City	Conversion in B listed building	1 bed	Fixed price £189,000
Gourock, Inverclyde	Retirement apartments	1 bed	From £99,950
Gourock, Inverclyde	Detached homes	Large	From £322,950
Forth & Clyde Canal, Glasgow	Townhouses	1-4 bed	From £95,000
Milngavie, East Dunbartonshire	Luxury apartments	2 & 3 bed	From £212,000
Ayr, South Ayrshire	Detached houses	4 & 5 bed	From £360,000
Bearsden, East Dunbartonshire	Apartments	Classic Art Deco	From £169,000
Glasgow Harbour	Apartments	1, 2 & 3 bed	From £170,000

LOTHIAN

GENERAL INFORMATION

Main Town: Edinburgh.

Local Authorities:

City of Edinburgh Council, Wellington Court, 10 Waterloo Place, Edinburgh EH1 3EG; ☎ 0131-200 2000; fax 0131-529 7477; www.edinburgh.gov.uk.

East Lothian Council, John Muir House, Court Street, Haddington, East Lothian EH41 3HA; ☎ 01620-827827; fax 01620-827888; www.eastlothian.gov.uk.

Midlothian Council, Midlothian House, 40-46 Buccleuch Street, Dalkeith, Midlothian EH22 1DJ; ☎ 0131-271 7500; fax 0131-271 3050; www.midlothian.gov.uk.

West Lothian Council, West Lothian House, Almondvale Boulevard, Livingston, West Lothian EH54 6QC; ☎ 01506-777000; fax 01506-775099; www.wlonline.org.uk.

Tourist Office: Edinburgh & Lothians Tourist Board, 4 Rothesay Terrace, Edinburgh EH3 7RY; ☎ 0845-225121; fax 01506-832222; www.edinburgh.org.

Police Force: Lothian and Borders Police Headquarters, Fettes Avenue, Edinburgh EH4 1RB; ☎ 0131-311 3131; fax 0131-311 3038; www.lbp.police.uk. *Area:* 1,724 square kilometres.

Population: 778,367

Population Density: 608 people per square kilometre (includes City of Edinburgh at 1,699 pp sq.km.)

Airports: Edinburgh.

World Heritage Sites: Edinburgh Old & New Towns.

National Nature Reserves: Blawhorn Moss

Estate Agents: Your Move, 213 Gorgie Road, Edinburgh EH11 1TU; ☎ 0131-313 333; fax 0131-313 3344; www.your-move.co.uk.

Edinburgh Solicitors' Property Centre, 85 George Street, Edinburgh EH2 3ES; ☎ 0131-624 8000; fax 0131-624 8570; www.espc.co.uk.

UK Property Shop, www.ukpropertyshop.co.uk/s/estate – agents – East – Lothian.shtml.

The Lothian region includes the City of Edinburgh plus the three surrounding Local Authority areas, West Lothian, East Lothian and Midlothian. Although the region includes the capital city of Scotland, and much of it is therefore urban or semi-urban in nature, there is much agricultural and other scenic land in the areas immediately around the city. The region occupies only two per cent of Scotland's land area but has 15% of its population.

As the business capital of Scotland and the seat of the Scottish Parliament, the region is generally wealthy, although as with any city, there are poorer, more downmarket areas where unemployment is higher and average wages lower. In the city centre you will find the most expensive properties in the country. The three 'Lothian' counties are, not surprisingly, home to many people who commute into Edinburgh on a daily basis for work, and this has its effect on the house prices in certain parts of these areas too. East Lothian in particular owes its present size to its closeness to the capital, with its population growing from 52,000 to over 90,000 since 1951. It is perfectly feasible to have the best of both worlds, with a home in a rural area and a daily commute into Edinburgh of less than one hour.

Perhaps more than any other area of Scotland, Lothian has seen an upturn in its fortunes in recent years, fuelled by devolution and the new Scottish Parliament. Since 1996 around 21,000 new jobs have been created in Edinburgh and Lothian, 22 per cent of all new Scottish jobs. Various schemes to improve the infrastructure and regenerate neglected areas are either under way or at planning stage. The area around the infamous Holyrood parliament building has been redeveloped to provide residential, hotel and office accommodation, and a new visitor attraction 'Our Dynamic Earth', which together have brought employment and income to an area which was previously neglected and had higher than average unemployment rates for the city. Unemployment throughout the Lothian region has fallen significantly since devolution.

Transport links from Edinburgh are being upgraded and new ones are at planning stage. A tram network has been proposed, to run through the city, and there are plans to reinstate rail links between Edinburgh and the Borders, and between Airdrie and Bathgate. A new rail link is also planned to connect Edinburgh airport to main rail stations throughout Scotland, timed to be in place well before a second runway is built at the airport by 2020. Road links too are being upgraded – unfortunately with the inevitable roadworks having a detrimental effect on traffic flow through the city at busy times of day. The problem of congestion in the capital is so bad that a congestion charge, similar to that introduced in London a few years ago, was proposed for Edinburgh. However, a referendum came back with a resounding no from local residents in early 2005, so plans for the congestion charge have been dropped – for the time being at least.

The dropping of the congestion charge will have a knock-on effect on the transport scene in Edinburgh, as a proposed new tram system was to have been partially financed by income from the congestion charge. Originally, the first trams were to have started running in 2009, but this could be affected by the No vote, with only a core section of the system being built initially unless further funding can be found.

Edinburgh and Lothian are a world class centre for scientific study and production, focused on the Edinburgh Science Triangle, an alliance of seven science and technology parks within the region. All these development plans, although centred on Edinburgh, will inevitably have a knock-on effect on the East, West and Midlothian areas too.

The accent in Edinburgh is perhaps easier for an English person to understand than in any other area. Certainly among the higher classes in society, notably in the 'posh' Morningside area of the city, the accent appears to an English ear to be not far from so-called standard English (also known as Received Pronunciation' – what is somewhat anachronistically known as BBC English.)

Geography & Climate

Edinburgh city is dominated by the castle which sits on top of an extinct volcano with sheer drops on three sides. East Lothian too boasts significant volcanic outcrops at Berwick Law (187m/613 feet) and Traprain Law (224m/734 feet.) Edinburgh is in a coastal position on the south of the Firth of Forth and there are several fine sandy beaches nearby. Right in the centre of the city is the extensive Holyrood Park, covering 650 acres of natural unspoiled land. Its most famous feature is Arthur's Seat, a long extinct volcano.

East Lothian is characterised by its fertile farmland and sandy beaches, with some important areas of woodland, grassland and moorland – it has no fewer than 21 designated Sites of Scientific Interest. It has an extensive coastline, bordering the Firth of Forth to the north and the North Sea to the East. There are notable colonies of sea birds in its coastal cliff formations. To the south it is bordered by the Lammermuir Hills. Altogether an attractive place to live, with easy access to Edinburgh.

West Lothian has just a short stretch of coastline along the Firth of Forth to the west of Edinburgh. It rises from the lowlands in the north and east to the Pentland Hills in the south-east, with moorland in the south and west. Two-thirds of its land is agricultural, but there are significant urban developments in the region too, occupying ten per cent of the land.

Midlothian is a landlocked region sandwiched between West Lothian, Edinburgh and East Lothian to the north, the Scottish Borders to the south. It was once heavily dependent on coal mining but there are no operational mines now. The legacy of the industry can be seen at the Scottish Mining Museum at the Lady Victoria Colliery, Newtongrange. Today the area is a centre of light industry and residential areas within commuting distance of Edinburgh. Over 60% of the land is open countryside, with the North and South Esk rivers running through the region.

East Lothian in particular benefits from a mild climate with some of the lowest rainfall in Scotland, but the whole Lothian region is comparatively dry, being on the east side of the country. It is also sunnier than average, with temperatures above the national average, so overall one of the best climates in Scotland.

WEATHER		
Annual averages	**Lothian**	**Scotland**
Rainfall (mm)	590	1099
Sunshine (hours)	1351	1228
Temperature max (°C)	12.2	11.3
Temperature min (°C)	5.2	4.7

Towns & Villages of Note

Bathgate. An ancient town, dating from the 1100s, Bathgate has seen various waves of development during the centuries. A Sherrifdom in medieval times, it gained new importance during the 1700s as a staging post on the Glasgow – Edinburgh route. By 1800 the coaching inn has a nearby distillery, and coal, lime and ironstone extraction had begun in the surrounding area. In 1848 the world's first oil refinery was set up here, following James Young's success at extracting mineral oil from coal, thus inventing paraffin.

During the next century Bathgate was a centre of industry with steelworks and several coal mines in the area. Its recent history has been more mixed, with high levels of unemployment temporarily alleviated by manufacturing businesses such as Leyland Trucks and the Bathgate Chemical works which came and went. It is currently benefiting from the Silicon Glen industries in the area, although Motorola, one of the largest in the town, closed a few years ago. www.undiscoveredscotland. co.uk/bathgate.

Dalkeith. The administrative town of Midlothian, Dalkeith is six miles south east of Edinburgh, situated between the North and South Esk Rivers. It has a population of about 15,000 people. The town centre, like many in Scotland, is currently the subject of a regeneration strategy.

Dalkeith has an interesting history. It was made a Royal Burgh in 1540, allowing the town to run a market. By the 19th century it boasted the largest grain market in Scotland. Long before this it had set up its own Mint and was producing its own money. Dalkeith Castle, dating from medieval times, was the base for Oliver

Cromwell's government of Scotland in the 1650s.

Nearby Newbattle Abbey was established in 1146 by Cistercian Monks. By the 13th century, in an early example of diversification, they were involved in mining coal in the area. www.midlothian-online.com.

Edinburgh. With a population of under 450,000, the City of Edinburgh is not particularly large as capital cities go – it is only the second largest city in the country, with Glasgow being appreciably bigger. The historical nature of the city centre and the year-round foreign and domestic visitors make it feel far more like a tourist town than the centre of high finance which it is, being the UK's second largest financial services centre after London, and the fourth largest in Europe. It is also the home of the Scottish Parliament, which too adds to the tourist attractions in the city. Edinburgh Castle is the most visited tourist attraction in Scotland, with one million visitors a year, and the city accounts for 24% of income from Scottish tourism and 17% of tourism jobs. All these factors combine to make Edinburgh the most prosperous city in the UK outside London.

Edinburgh Old and New Towns were named UNESCO World Heritage Sites in 1995. These account for a large part of the city centre, taking in the medieval portions and the planned 'New Town' which was built between 1767 and 1810. At that time it was the world's largest planned city development. This means that development within that area is severely restricted and controlled by planning regulations

There are other areas of the city, however, where development is taking place. Notably at the Waterfront in the Granton area where derelict contaminated land is currently in the process of being reclaimed and developed to provide 7,500 new homes along with office, business and retail space as well as two new schools and a marina.

The central focus of Edinburgh is Princes Street, a wide thoroughfare, unfortunately with heavy traffic most of the time, with shops and hotels on one side, Princes Street Gardens along the other. The main Edinburgh train station Waverley, is here, and the castle dominates the skyline. www.timeout.com/travel/edinburgh.

Edinburgh Festivals. Edinburgh is the top tourist destination in Scotland, with year-round visitors from across the globe. But it is rightly famous more than anything for its festivals, most famously the Edinburgh International Festival, which has taken place every year since 1947, and its offspring Fringe Festival, which now overshadows its parent with over 1,600 shows in 300 venues in 2005. Both these take place in August, the peak month for festivals in the city. The Jazz and Blues Festival, the Book Festival, the Film Festival and the Edinburgh Military Tattoo also take place during the month. The city's population of 460,000 swells to one million during August, so don't come unless you have pre-booked accommodation! At the other end of the year is the famous Edinburgh Hogmanay (New Year) street party, the biggest in the world.

Websites

Edinburgh International Festival; www.eif.co.uk.
Edinburgh Fringe; www.edfringe.com.
All the Edinburgh Festivals; www.edinburghfestivals.co.uk.
Hogmanay Street party; www.edinburghshogmanay.org.
Edinburgh Tattoo; www.edintattoo.co.uk.

EDINBURGH VILLAGES

There are a number of self-contained communities within the city, each with its own distinctive character and village-like feel. Among these are:

Bruntsfield. Just 20 minutes walk from Princes Street, Bruntsfield is full of handsome Victorian sandstone tenement buildings, now upgraded to house desirable flats (apartments). There are inviting delicatessens and wine merchants, gift shops and florists. The Meadows is a lush green space in the heart of the city, with its own golf links.

Stockbridge. A good hunting ground for vintage clothes, art and jewellery, antiques and crafts. The Royal Botanical Gardens are here as are many bars and coffee shops.

Crostorphine. There are still remains of the original medieval settlement to be seen here. Today it is home to Edinburgh Zoo.

Dean Village. Lies beneath Thomas Telford's Dean Bridge over the Water of Leith. There is a quirky mix of interesting old buildings with modern architecture such as the Dean Gallery and the National Gallery of Modern Art.

Colinton. Fifteen minutes drive from the city centre, this does not feel as though it is part of the capital. It has a historic old church and churchyard which definitely give the village feel to this place.

Cramond. Four miles from Edinburgh centre, on the south shore of the Firth of Forth, where the River Almond runs into the Forth, Cramond is a very attractive and popular residential area. There are yachts moored in the harbour, and nearby are several golf courses. www. undiscoveredscotland.co.uk/edinburgh/cramond.

Leith. One of Edinburgh's fastest growing areas, Leith has seen major development in recent years and now has some good quality housing, shops and restaurants. Originally a busy port, its maritime heritage is seen in the seafood restaurants and the fact that is now home to the Royal Yacht Britannia, a major tourist attraction. www.undiscoveredscotland.co.uk/edinburgh/leith.

Livingston. Created as one of five New Towns in the 1960s, Livingston was originally built to ease overcrowding in Glasgow – despite the fact that it is far nearer to Edinburgh. It is now a thriving residential and business centre, thanks to the hi-tech Silicon Glen industries in the area. It is also the administrative centre of West Lothian. With a population of over 41,000 it is the largest Lothian town after Edinburgh, and the 13th largest in Scotland. Its status as an important and successful town is reflected in the fact that it was only just beaten by historic Stirling to become the Golden Jubilee city in 2002. www.livingstonalive.co.uk.

North Berwick. A place for golf fanatics, the proud claim of the self-styled North Berwick Golf Coast is that it has no fewer than 12 golf links. This, together with its attractive seaside setting, make North Berwick a popular holiday destination. www.north.berwick.co.uk.

History

The early geological history of Scotland can be seen at Edinburgh in the form of Castle Rock and Arthur's Seat, both of them volcanic in origin and dating from millions of years ago. The rock's defensive properties have been taken advantage of from Roman times, and it is believed there was a fortification substantial enough to deserve the title of castle as far back as the seventh century, when it was used as a defence against the Picts. The castle was added to over the years until the 18th century, when it was largely in the form we see today.

The town surrounding the castle began to grow in the 11th century, until in 1450 the first town wall was constructed, ringing the Old Town and Grassmarket. Much of the Old Town preserved today dates from these medieval times. It was in this era when Edinburgh was made Scotland's capital. The city became a focus for the country's political, cultural and intellectual aspects, and its population steadily grew, reaching 35,000 in the late 18th century. At this time it was the custom for the rich citizens to literally live on top of the poorer residents. The housing was in the form of multi-storey tenements, with the poor people living on the lower floors and the more well-off living above them on the middle and upper floors – literally the lower, middle and upper classes. However, this didn't suit many of the richer residents and they began to move from the city to London. In order to attract them back, a competition was launched to design a new town. The New Town, with a grid-like system of streets, was completed in 1810. Edinburgh soon became known as 'the Athens of the North' both because of its neo-classical architecture and because it was recognised as a centre of learning and culture.

REASONS TO BUY A HOUSE IN LOTHIAN

- ⭕ Easy access to Edinburgh, the capital.
- ⭕ Edinburgh one of the world's top tourist destinations.

- *Condé Nast Traveller* voted Edinburgh top Scottish city in terms of beauty, access to culture, cleanliness, accommodation, entertainment and safety.
- Edinburgh's many Festivals.
- One of the world's most distinctive and attractive capitals.
- Attractive to foreign nationals – 6.5% of its population were born overseas.
- Top financial sector in Scotland.
- Seat of the Scottish parliament.
- Great seaside holiday destinations in East Lothian.
- History and heritage.
- Edinburgh university ranked 11th best in the UK, 2nd best in Scotland.
- Top class properties in Edinburgh – over 26 £1 million-plus homes sold in 2005.
- Increasing number of international businesses opening offices in Edinburgh.
- The capital city surrounded by countryside and beautiful coastline.
- Historic towns and cities within commuting distance of the capital.
- Some of the country's top golf courses.

Typical Properties for Sale

Edinburgh. Lothian as a whole has by far the highest prices in the country, and not surprisingly, properties within the capital are among the most desirable in the country. Unlike the other Scottish cities, where record prices for the region tend be on their more rural outskirts, the best and most expensive properties are concentrated in Edinburgh itself with homes on the outskirts more affordable.

THE BEST ADDRESSES IN SCOTLAND

Of the most expensive properties sold in Scotland between May 2004-April 2005, 13 of the top 25 were in Lothian, 11 of them in Edinburgh itself. They all sold at well over £1 million with the top spot taken by a house in the Barnton area west of the city centre.

Merchiston, only two miles from Princes Street, near to the buzz of the city but not overrun with traffic and noise, has many imposing Victorian detached houses. It has been dubbed Writers' Block because top Scottish authors Ian Rankin, JK Rowling, Lin Anderson and Alexander McCall Smith all have homes here.

Morningside has long been the Edinburgh area with the highest cachet, although it is often characterised as somewhat snobbish. Grange, the New Town and Trinity are also included in the best areas of the city.

Colinton in the south west of the city has many large traditional sandstone houses which are popular with wealthy property buyers – the most expensive property sold during July 2005 was in Colinton, at a price of £1.85 million.

Waterfront development along the Firth of Forth, with luxury apartments and penthouses as well as more modest dwellings, has brought about an upsurge in property values to the north of the city, traditional a more downmarket area.

Outside the city, East Lothian has some of Scotland's most expensive property. The first £1 million house was sold in Inveresk back in 2000, and North Berwick broke through the £300,000 average price barrier in 2005.

Bruntsfield and Haymarket are near to the university and the railway station – Haymarket station is Scotland's oldest standing station building and its third busiest. The areas are popular with students, young professionals and families. There are no grand houses here, but there are plenty of handsome tenements and terraced houses. Prices here are far more affordable for both houses and flats, despite their close proximity to the city centre, with the exception of Edinburgh's famous 'Colonies' – tiny but charming former workers' cottages with picture postcard exteriors. Most have been upgraded and now sell for very high prices considering their size.

The suburban areas of Colinton, Barnton and Liberton are all popular with families, with more houses available than in the city centre where flats predominate.

Edinburgh is lagging behind Glasgow in regenerating its worst areas, but much improvement has been seen and there are many new developments at construction and planning stage in previously neglected city areas. Leith is one such area, which has reinvented itself as a modern waterfront district over the last decade or so. Originally industrial docklands, it now has new housing to suit a range of buyers, from luxury penthouses to entry level tenement flats

Despite efforts to address the issue, Edinburgh has a shortage of affordable housing, and its World Heritage status makes finding land for development a very difficult process. The City Council has proposed building 400 homes on the outskirts of the capital, but this has caused disquiet among many residents about building on the green belt ringing the city, which traditionally has been keep clear of development. However, prices in Edinburgh have risen so high that there is now a shortage of key workers such as nurses and teachers, who just cannot afford to live in the city.

University lecturers too are in short supply, and to address this, Edinburgh University, in August 2005, sold some of their land to the city council for the princely sum of £1, so that housing could be built, which would be rented out at an affordable level to newly qualified lecturers and researchers.

The pressure on prices in the capital is set to continue, as the £1 billion expansion of Edinburgh Airport attracts international property buyers, pushing up prices still further.

Like any other city, Edinburgh does have deprived areas, with Craigmillar in the south east, and Muirhouse in the north among the worst. However, compared with Glasgow, the social problems are concentrated in smaller areas. Of the 20 most deprived areas in Scotland, only one (Criagmillar, ranked fourth worst,) was in Edinburgh, whereas no fewer than 16 were in Glasgow.

Surrounding Areas. House prices are lower in these areas, so as prices in Edinburgh have climbed rapidly over recent years, people have been moving out of the city to where prices are more affordable but they can still commute easily.

Linlithgow in West Lothian is a popular tourist town with a rural feel. Here one finds attractive traditional detached and semi-detached houses as well as more modern homes. The town is particularly popular with families, as Linlithgow Academy is one of the country's top state secondary schools and parents who want their children to benefit from this will move to be in the school's catchment area. This became such a marked trend that in 2004 the council banned a housing developer from selling his properties in Linlithgow to buyers under the age of 50, because the school was oversubscribed. The academy is currently being upgraded and expanded.

East Lothian, bordering the southern edge of the Firth of Forth, is a popular holiday area, and it has a concentration of golf courses, which have attracted affluent communities between Gullane and North Berwick.

North Berwick currently holds the record for average house prices, at over £300,000. With two fine beaches and a yacht-filled harbour, a High School with a good reputation, and some fine, and large, Victorian houses, plus being within easy commuting distance of the capital, it has a lot going for it. The town is home to a high number of well-paid consultants working from home. Demand for housing here is strong, and the new Local Plan suggests the building of 500 new homes in the town.

More industrialised former mining areas, such as Cockenzie, Prestonpans and Tranent, have more affordable prices. Almost half of the working age residents of East Lothian commute to work, mostly to Edinburgh.

Recent extension of the A1 between Edinburgh and Dunbar has enticed people to move further away from the city, as the commuting time has become shorter. Hence, prices are now on the up in Dunbar and Haddington.

Sample Properties For Sale, October 2005			
Location	Type	Description	Price
Colinton, Edinburgh	House	With granny flat and indoor swimming pool	Offers over £1,250,000
Bathgate, W. Lothian	Detached house	4 bed, with 0.6 acre garden	Offers over £345,000
Barnton, Edinburgh	Semi-detached house	4 bed	Offers over £215,000
The Shore, Edinburgh	Flat	3 bed	Fixed price £199,995
Linlithgow, W. Lothian	Detached house	3 bed	Offers over £285,000
Dalkeith, Midlothian	Flat	4 bed, duplex	Fixed price £149,995

Gullane, E. Lothian	Lodge house	2 bed, B listed	Offers over £185,000
Prestopans, E. Lothian	Semi-detached house	3 bed	Fixed price £150,000
Barnton, Edinburgh	Retirement flat	2 bed	Offers over £110,000
West Calder, W. Lothian	Plot	Farmhouse courtyard plot with p.p.	Fixed price £195,000
Bilston, Midlothian	Plot	With p.p. for 4 bed house	Fixed price £125,000

New Build Homes			
Location	**Type**	**Description**	**Price**
Edinburgh City	Townhouses	3 bed	From £215,000
Leith	Apartments	1 & 2 bed	From £115,000
Athelstaneford, E. Lothian	Detached houses	5 bed	From £448,000
Cousland, Midlothian	Detached bungalow	3 bed	From £244,950
Bathgate, W. Lothian	Apartments	1930s style	From £244,950

COUNCIL TAX CHARGES 2005-2006 (FOR A HOUSEHOLD OF 2 ADULTS)

Tax band	City of Edinburgh	East Lothian	Mid-lothian	West Lothian	Scottish Average
A	£750.67	£712.62	£784.00	£716.00	£729.39
B	£875.78	£831.39	£914.67	£835.33	£850.96
C	£1,000.89	£950.16	£1,045.33	£954.67	£972.52
D	£1,126.00	£1,068.93	£1,176.00	£1,074.00	£1,094.09
E	£1,376.22	£1,306.47	£1,437.33	£1,312.67	£1,337.22
F	£1,626.44	£1,544.01	£1,698.67	£1,551.33	£1,580.35
G	£1,876.67	£1,781.86	£1,960.00	£1,790.00	£1,823.48
H	£2,252.00	£2,137.86	£2,352.00	£2,148.00	£2,188.18

FORTH VALLEY

```
┌─────────────────────────────────────────────────────────────────┐
│                      GENERAL INFORMATION                         │
└─────────────────────────────────────────────────────────────────┘
```

Main Towns: Alloa; Falkirk; Stirling.

Local Authorities: Clackmannanshire Council, Greenfield, Alloa, Clackmannanshire FK10 2AD; ☎ 01259-450000; fax 01259-452230; www.clacksweb.org.uk.
Falkirk Council, Municipal Buildings, West Bridge Street, Falkirk FK1 5RS; ☎ 01324-506070; fax 01324-506071; www.falkirk.gov.uk.
Stirling Council, Viewforth, Stirling FK8 2ET; ☎ 0845-277700; fax 01786-443078; www.stirling.gov.uk.

Tourist Office: Argyll, The Isles, Loch Lomond, Stirling & the Trossachs Tourist Board, 41 Dumbarton Road, Stirling FK8 2QQ; ☎ 08707-200620; fax 01786-450039; www.visitscotlandheartlands.com.

Police Force: Central Scotland Police, Headquarters, Randolphfield, Stirling FK8 2HD; ☎ 01786-456000; fax 01786-451177; www.centralscotland.police.uk.

Area: 2643 square kilometres.

Population: 279,320

Population Density: 277 people per square kilometre.

Airports: None.

National Parks: Loch Lomond & the Trossachs National Park

National Nature Reserves: Flanders Moss.

Estate Agents: Edinburgh Solicitors' Property Centre: 8 King Street, Stirling FK8 1BD; ☎ 01786-449201; fax 01786-449202; www.espc.co.uk.
Your Move: 4 Bank Street, Falkirk FK1 1NB; ☎ 01324-632266; fax 01324-612149; www.your-move.co.uk.

The Forth Valley region is made up of the three local authority areas, Stirling, Falkirk and Clackmannanshire. It lies in the hinterland between Edinburgh and Glasgow, and with Perth not far to the north, it could be expected to suffer economically, with money and influence being attracted to the surrounding cities. It is the unique position of Stirling in the nation's history which saves the area from this fate. In fact, historically Stirling was of supreme importance to Scotland, with its central position making it the centre of government on many occasions. Prior to the 17th century it was effectively the only accessible route between the central lowlands and the High-lands and north east of the country, due to the large area of bog which surrounded it. The huge outcrop of basaltic rock was the natural place to build the imposing Stirling Castle which still dominates the landscape as one travels on the A9, the present day major route from south to north. It is perhaps surprising that Stirling did not become the nation's capital in preference to Edinburgh. Its importance was finally given recog-nition as recently as 2002, when it became Scotland's newest city. It was granted city status as part of Queen Elizabeth's Golden Jubilee celebrations in that year.

A HOME IN

Scotland

Lochside cottages, Diabaig

Heriot Row, Edinburgh

Modern crofter's house, Loch Ewe

Mountain landscape in winter

House under construction, Dundonnell, by Little Loch Broom

Renovation project in the Highlands

City centre flats in converted Georgian building, Glasgow

Main street, Poolewe

Stirling's position put it at the centre of many decisive battles during the nation's history, and this ensures that it remains a vibrant and lively attraction to tourists. Its name derives from 'the striveling', meaning a place of strife. The building of Stirling University just outside the town in 1967 also gave it an economic boost. The university is well-respected, renowned for the quality of education, research and quality of life of the students, all of which have a beneficial effect on the Forth Valley region as a whole.

The second element of the region is Falkirk, another area with great historical importance, being the so-called 'buckle of the belt which girded Scotland' – that being the Antonine Wall, built by the Romans 2000 years ago to keep the barbarian northern tribes at bay.

Clackmannanshire, the third element, still prides itself on the title 'the wee coonty' dating from the fact that it was once Britain's smallest county, before local government reorganisation in 1975 lost it that crown.

The countryside in the region is delightful – rolling hills, broad fast rivers bordered by fertile plains, attractive towns, pretty villages and picture-book castles are the keynote. Not wild, not dramatic, not particularly adventurous. If your taste is for verdant and pretty, however, this is without doubt one of the most obviously attractive regions of Scotland.

Tourism, forestry and farming are the chief sources of income in the Stirling area, while Clackmannan and Falkirk's deposits of coal, clay and ironstone made this an important mining area in the past. This heritage is still evident in some of the traditional industries such as iron-founding and other heavy industries. Grangemouth is still Scotland's leading petrochemical complex and container port. However, today, as in many other areas, the traditional industries are being replaced by more hi-tech industries in addition to other light manufacturing including brewing and textiles. The industrial heritage of the area is being given a new lease of life, as mining areas and engineering feats such as the Falkirk Wheel are being reborn as tourist attractions.

Due to its central position, transport links to the region are fairly good, with international airports at both Glasgow and Edinburgh. It is near to the centre of the motorway network and the M9 runs just a couple of miles to the west of Stirling. The main line train route also runs through the city.

Geography & Climate

The countryside in the region is fertile and green, with towns and villages nestled in valleys amongst the gentle hills of the Campsie Fells to the south and the higher lands of the Trossachs to the west and the southern Highlands to the north. The bulk of Loch Lomond and the Trossachs National Park falls in the Stirling Council area. Flanders Moss, now a National Nature Reserve, is a relic of what once was one of the largest lowland areas of bogland in Britain. It is now a conservation area renowned for its sphagnum mosses and birdlife.

With the Rivers Forth and Tay both having their source in the region, it is a very fertile area, with excellent pasturage as well as a large acreage of cultivated land. A lot of fruit is grown in the area, mainly the soft fruits such as raspberries and strawberries Scotland is well-known for, but also more surprising fruits – one of the largest grapevines in Britain is near Stirling.

There are several lochs in the area, with Loch Lomond forming part of the western boundary. The highest peak in the region is Ben More, at 1174m (3852 feet).

Over 20% of the land is woodland or forest and around ten per cent is arable. Of the rest, just a small proportion is urban or rural settlements, with the remainder being pastureland, wetland or moorland.

Population within the region is concentrated in a few main centres, with Stirling and Falkirk being by far the largest. Overall, the feeling of the area is predominately rural – even the city of Stirling retains the feel of a country town.

Its position at the centre of the country fittingly means that weather conditions are pretty average, with few extremes of weather being seen.

WEATHER		
Annual averages	**Forth Valley**	**Scotland**
Rainfall (mm)	1120	1099
Sunshine (hours)	1300	1228
Temperature max (°C)	12.4	11.3
Temperature min (°C)	4.8	4.7

Towns & Villages of Note

Alloa. The country town of Clackmannanshire, with a population of around 20,000, Alloa sits on the north bank of the River Forth. It was once a seaport, an important trading port during the Middle Ages, but due to the silting up of the harbour and the growth of other forms of transport, the port eventually became redundant and the harbour was infilled in 1951. Today it has all the amenities of a modern town, from shopping centres to leisure facilities.

Its most notable feature is Alloa Tower, dating from the 14th century. It is the largest surviving tower house in Scotland, and had been allowed to fall into disrepair, until the National Trust for Scotland undertook an eight year renovation which was completed in 1997. www.clacksnet.org.uk.

Falkirk. Administrative centre of the local authority, Falkirk has a long and varied history thanks to its crucial strategic significance, due to its central position between Glasgow, Edinburgh and Stirling, and between the Forth and the Clyde. Its geographical location attracted the Romans, who built the Antonine Wall and its military road through the area in the second century, and was also crucial later when the Forth and Clyde Canal met the Union Canal in the town. Falkirk took great commercial advantage of this – at one time the Carron Ironworks in Falkirk was the largest factory in the world. The canal system fell into disuse, and the series of lock gates in Falkirk which once linked the two canals, were removed. Now, the Millennium Link project aims to re-open the 68 mile canal link between Glasgow and Edinburgh and as part of this the unique Falkirk Wheel was constructed. This is the largest revolving boat lift in the world, able to carry up to eight boats at one time, and is as important as a tourist attraction as it is for transporting boats from one canal to the other.

Second largest town in the region after Stirling, Falkirk has a population of 34,000 and is proud of its large shopping centre and its annual International Food Festival every July. One of its biggest claims to fame is that it is the birthplace of Scotland's second favourite drink (after whisky) the unique soft drink 'Irn Bru' – reputedly made from iron girders! – which has been made in the town by the family firm A.G. Barr for over 100 years. www.falkirk.net.

Stirling. With a population of 37,000, Stirling is the largest centre of population, and the only city, in the region. It is a pleasing mixture of old and new, with the well-preserved Old Town, dating back to the Middle Ages, close to the thriving modern shopping centre. Outside the town, the Wallace Monument commemorating William Wallace – now better known as Braveheart, thanks to Mel Gibson – represents the ancient aspect of the town, while the equally impressive Stirling University represents all that is modern and forward-looking.

The local authority, Stirling Council, has its headquarters here and is a big employer within the area. The university too is a significant employer and has had a dramatic effect on the town which, thanks to its student population, has a cosmopolitan feel with plenty of cafes and restaurants and cultural hotspots.

Dominating the town from its high vantage point is Stirling Castle, once the seat of Scottish kings. In recent years the Great Hall of the castle has been renovated to bring it back to its former glory. This, together with the Hollywood connection, has aroused new interest in the history of the area.

It is, there is no doubt, a popular place to live. During the height of the housing boom in 2004, Stirling was a property hotspot with prices rising faster than anywhere else in Scotland. Average incomes here are among the highest in Scotland. www.stirling.co.uk.

REASONS TO BUY A HOUSE IN THE FORTH VALLEY

- Verdant and pretty countryside.
- Loch Lomond & the Trossachs National Park.
- Stirling, Scotland's newest city.
- Stirling University – a friendly and attractive campus-based university.
- Close to Edinburgh but a far more rural feel.
- Castles and historic monuments.

- Close to good roads but not congested.
- Central position in country with easy access south and north.
- 40 minute drive to both Edinburgh and Glasgow.
- A thriving property market in Stirling.
- More affordable housing in Falkirk and Clackmannanshire.
- Reopening of passenger rail link linking Alloa with Stirling and Glasgow.
- Popular with walkers.

Typical Properties for Sale

Stirling was a property hotspot during 2004, as prices rose out of the reach of Edinburgh so they looked towards Stirling, the nearest city, which has far more affordable property. This pushed up prices in Stirling significantly. The property market there over the past few years has shown dramatic swings up and down, but always climbing faster then the national average. However, starting as they did from a far lower base than Edinburgh, prices here are still appreciably lower here than in much of the capital.

Stirling University, situated to the north of the city, close to Bridge of Allan, ensures that there is a constant demand for flats. However, there is a far lower proportion of flats to houses than in Glasgow and Edinburgh.

Clackmannanshire has seen rising house prices, helped by a new road between the county and neighbouring Stirling. There are also plans to put a second road bridge across the Forth at Kincardine which also will improve transport links. Dollar is a property hot spot, where the high educational reputation of Dollar Academy and the scenic rural setting encourage high prices.

The area as whole has a mixture of older houses, including solid Victorian villas, as well as more modern developments. There are a lot of new housing developments to cater for the demand for housing in this popular region. Despite the larger towns, this is essentially a rural areas so there are also farmhouses and workers cottages to be found very close to the urban centres.

Sample Properties For Sale, October 2005			
Location	**Type**	**Description**	**Price**
Drymen	Country home	4 bed, in 4 acres	Offers over £745,000
Stirling	Converted steading	5 bed, semi-rural	Offers over £498,000
Balquhidder	Detached house	2 bed, modern	Offers over £295,000
Dunblane	Mid terrace	3 bed	Offers over £105,000
Falkirk	Detached house	4 bed	Fixed price £144,995
Bonnybridge	Detached house	3 bed	Fixed price £130,000

Laurieston	Semi-detached cottage	2 bed, traditional	Offers over £90,000
Stirling	Flat	2 bed	Offers over £74,500
Alloa	Flat	2 bed	Offers over £59,000

New Build Homes			
Location	**Type**	**Description**	**Price**
Dollar	Apartments	1-4 bed	From £170,000
Tullibody	Detached houses	4 bed	£182,950-£199,950
Bo'ness	Semi-detached and terraced houses	2 & 3 bed	From £102,775
Bonnybridge	Detached houses	3 bed	From £132,995
Bannockburn	Detached houses	4 bed	From £176,995
Stirling	Townhouses	3 bed	£193,000

COUNCIL TAX CHARGES 2005-2006 (FOR A HOUSEHOLD OF 2 ADULTS)				
Tax band	**Clackmannanshire**	**Falkirk**	**Stirling**	Scottish Average
A	£716.00	£666.09	£766.00	£729.39
B	£835.33	£777.11	£893.67	£850.96
C	£954.67	£888.12	£1,021.33	£972.52
D	£1,074.00	£999.14	£1,149.00	£1,094.09
E	£1,312.67	£1221.17	£1,404.33	£1,337.22
F	£1,551.33	£1443.20	£1,659.67	£1,580.35
G	£1,790.00	£1665.23	£1,915.00	£1,823.48
H	£2,148.00	£1,998.28	£2,298.00	£2,188.18

ARGYLL & BUTE

GENERAL INFORMATION

Main Town: Oban.

Local Authority: Argyll & Bute Council, Kilmory, Lochgilphead, Argyll PA31 8RT; ☎ 01546-602127; fax 01546-604349; www.argyll-bute.gov.uk.

Tourist Offices: Argyll Square, Oban PA34 4AN; ☎ 08707-200630; fax 01631-564273.

Front Street, Inveraray PA32 8UY; ☎ 08707-200616; fax 01499-302269; www.visitscotlandheartlands.com.

Police Force: Strathclyde Police HQ, 173 Pitt Street, Glasgow G2 4JS; ☎ 0141-532 2000;

fax 0141-532 2475; www.strathclyde.police.uk.

Area: 7023 sq. km.

Population: 91,300.

Population Density: 13 people per sq. km.

Airports: Oban Airstrip (Currently no regular passenger services); Campbeltown; Islay; Tiree.

National Park: Loch Lomond & the Trossachs National Park.

National Scenic Areas: Island of Jura; Knapdale; Kyles of Bute; Loch Lomond; Loch na Keal, Isle of Mull; Lynn of Lorn; Scarba, Lunga and the Garvellachs.

National Nature Reserves: Glasdrum Wood, Staffa, Glen Nant, Ben Lui, Moine Mhor, Taynish, Loch Lomond.

Estate Agents: Oban Solicitors Property Group, ☎ 01631-566122; fax 01631-564764; email property@mackinnon-law.co.uk.

Stewart, Balfour & Sutherland, The Property Shop, 24-26 Longrow, Campbeltown, PA28 6AH; ☎ 01586-553737; www.sbslaw.co.uk.

Bute Property, 60 Montague Street, Rothesay, Isle of Bute, PA20 0BT; ☎ 01700-503168, fax 01700-503178; www.buteproperty.co.uk.

Although part of the old Strathclyde region, Argyll and Bute, a unitary authority in its own right, has a distinctively different character from the rest of the region, so for the purposes of deciding a location to make one's home, it makes sense to look at it separately from the more urban areas of Strathclyde.

Argyll and Bute is the second largest, in terms of geographical area, of the Scottish local authorities. However, its population is comparatively small, and has a low population density of just 13 people per square kilometre. This makes it an area where residents can have elbow room and a relaxed rural existence. The Lowlands meets the West Highlands within its boundaries, and so it has a great variety of terrain, from areas of forest and farmlands, to mountains, lochs and islands. The eastern boundary runs along the centre of Loch Lomond, the largest body of inland water in the United Kingdom and one of the most popular tourist destinations in the whole of Scotland. There are a significant number of Gaelic speakers in the region, nearly ten per cent of the population. These are concentrated on the islands and among the older generation.

The sea is very important to this region, as a result of its many peninsulas and islands. Fish farming, sailing and marine tourism all contribute to the economy. Whisky distilling is another speciality, with a dozen or so working distilleries altogether.

The largest employer in Argyll and Bute is the Ministry of Defence, thanks to the Clyde Naval Base at Faslane. Garelochhead is the nearest village to Faslane, and next to it is Garelochhead Training Camp, the largest military training establishment in Scotland.

With much of the Loch Lomond and the Trossachs National Park falling within its boundaries, in addition to numerous National Scenic Areas and National Nature Reserves, the scenery and wildlife of Argyll and Bute are second to none. Although nowhere so wild and untrammelled as much of the Highlands and Islands – this is tamer, more well-behaved Scottish scenery – there are no doubt many beautiful places to make your home, with the advantage that the Glasgow area is easily accessible by road from much of the region. It is very feasible to live in the region and commute to work in Glasgow, allowing the best of both worlds.

There is a railway line running from central Scotland to Oban, and there is a network of ferries to reach the islands.

Although the local authority has its home – in a castle, no less – in Lochgilphead, by virtue, one assumes, of its geographically central position within the region, the much larger town of Oban has more claim to being the principal town and is often termed the Capital of the West Highlands. With ferries to many of the west coast islands, it is also known as the Gateway to the Isles.

Although just one of the many islands within the region, Bute is named specifically by virtue of the fact that, prior to the 1975 reorganisation of local authorities, Bute and Argyll were separate counties.

Geography & Climate

Argyll and Bute has about 3,000 miles of coastline – longer than the entire coastline of France – and around 90 islands, of which 26 are inhabited.

Because of its topography, travelling by road is not always the quickest way to get about on mainland Argyll. Campbeltown on the Mull of Kintyre, for example, is one of Scotland's most remote mainland towns, being 134 miles by road from Glasgow. There are some ferries which cross between peninsulas on the mainland, including the ferry from Gourock (Strathclyde) to Dunoon (Cowal Peninsula), and another from Portavadie on Cowal for the ferry to Tarbert (Kintyre). This is certainly the most direct route from Glasgow to the Mull of Kintyre, cutting mileage – and probably journey times, as long as you research the ferry timetables in advance.

The Lowlands and the Highlands meet here, along the line of the Highland Boundary Fault. This starts at Lochranza on Arran, in Ayrshire, and runs south west to north east as far as Stonehaven in Aberdeenshire. Thus it cuts right through Argyll and Bute along the Firth of Clyde, via Helensburgh and Loch Lomond. It all but cuts the island of Bute in two, which makes for a dramatic contrast between the north and south of Bute, the high ground to the north rugged and rough, the south much lower-lying and gently undulating. Bute has been called 'the first island in the Scottish Highlands' in recognition of this fact.

Loch Lomond, the largest body of inland water in the United Kingdom, at 71.12 square kilometres (27.46 square miles), is here – at least, the western shore comes under the jurisdiction of Argyll and Bute. Ben Lomond is the region's highest mountain, at 974m (3193ft).

The climate of the region is mild and wet, and benefits from the effects of the Gulf

Stream. Bute has a favoured location in the Firth of Clyde, sheltered on all sides. The climate combined with the damp acid soil made it a favourite of Victorian, and more recent, plant collectors who found it ideally suited for the plants they brought back from many other regions of the world. There are a number of gardens in the region, on the mainland and the islands, where exotic plant species grow to enormous size.

WEATHER		
Annual averages	**Argyll & Bute**	**Scotland**
Rainfall (mm)	1473	1099
Sunshine (hours)	1400	1228
Temperature max (°C)	11.4	11.3
Temperature min (°C)	6.5	4.7

Towns & Villages of Note

Campbeltown. Situated at the head of Campbeltown Loch, the town was once a centre for whisky production, although today only one distillery remains in production. The two are brought together in the old music hall song:

Campbeltown Loch, I wish ye were whisky, Campbeltown Loch och aye.
Campbeltown Loch, I wish ye were whisky, I would drink ye dry.

It lies at the southern end of the Mull of Kintyre, making it the furthest point of Argyll from the central belt. A royal burgh, it is still an important fishing port although, like elsewhere in Scotland, its fishing fleet has been much depleted in recent years.

Campbeltown sticks out on a limb into the Atlantic, and this gives it a unique landscape. Flat for the most part, and exposed, it is often prey to cold thick sea mists which can cloak the town on an otherwise warm, sunny day. This exposed situation is now to be exploited by the development of a land-based wind farm in the area with the potential to be the most powerful in the UK. Depending on your stance on wind turbines and their effect on the environment, this is either a very good or a very bad thing.

It has a notable golf course at Machrihanish, voted by a leading golf magazine to have the finest first hole in the world. Also at Macrihanish there is a small airport, with regular flights from Glasgow.

It was near here that St Columba first landed on his mission to bring Christianity to Scotland from Ireland. www.argyllonline.co.uk

Dunoon. Dunoon is the Cowal Peninsula's only town. It bills itself as the Western Gateway to the Loch Lomond and the Trossachs National Park. It has been popular since Victorian times as a 'doon the watter' seaside escape from Glasgow for day trips and longer holidays. Paddle steamers would take visitors from Glasgow to admire the stunning scenery of the Firth of Clyde. The Waverley, the last ocean-going paddle steamer, still cruises from Glasgow to Dunoon and Rothesay on Bute.

An alternative route to the town from Glasgow is via the Gourock to Dunoon ferry, which avoids a long road journey around Loch Long. www.argyllonline.co.uk

The Cowal Gathering, held at the end of August each year, claims to be the world's largest and most spectacular Highland Games. It has been going for over 100 years, since the first gathering in 1894. www.cowalgathering.com

Helensburgh. This seaside town has a slightly old fashioned air, thanks to its predominantly Victorian architecture. It is set on a south facing slope overlooking the scenic Clyde Estuary. It was laid out by Sir James Colquhoun in 1777 as a new town and he named it after his wife, Lady Helen Sutherland. It got a boost in popularity in the 1800s when Henry Bell, pioneer of steam navigation, came to live in the town. By the time his steamship Comet was launched on the Clyde in 1812, it had become another popular watering place for Glaswegian day trippers.

The arrival of the railway in 1857 caused further expansion, as it was only 30 minutes from the city. It became popular with Glasgow merchants who took elegant houses in the town, away from the Glasgow grime. It soon became a rather exclusive suburb of the city with the late Victorian and Edwardian villas of upper Helensburgh reflecting the wealthy lifestyles and contemporary architectural tastes of their owners, resulting in one of the finest collection of buildings of their type in the West of Scotland. One of these was the publisher W.W.Blackie who commissioned Charles Rennie Mackintosh, one of Scotland's most famous architects, to design Hill House, a seminal example of his 'Glasgow style'.

Helensburgh was also the birthplace of John Logie Baird, television pioneer. www.helensburgh.co.uk

Inveraray. This town of whitewashed houses has been a Royal Burgh since 1683. It was rebuilt from 1753 onwards, one of several planned villages in Argyll with a regular grid pattern of streets. It is dominated by the French-inspired Inveraray Castle, seat of the Dukes of Argyll, which was rebuilt at the same time, with the renowned architects Vanbrugh and William Adam both having a hand in its design.

Apart from the castle, the town also boasts Inverary jail as a popular tourist attraction. Described as Scotland's 'living 19th century jail' it includes such delights as a 'Torture, Death and Damnation Exhibition'. www.inveraray-argyll.com.

Oban. A Gaelic name, meaning 'little bay', Oban's naturally sheltered position has made it popular with tourists and west coast residents alike. A busy but attractive town with a resident population of around 8,000, it is a centre for shopping, leisure and other services. The town is a key transport hub for the area. It has good road links north, east and south and is on the scenic West Highland line which connects Oban with Glasgow.

Ferries to Mull, Lismore, Kerrera, Barra, South Uist, Colonsay, Coll, Tiree, Islay, Iona and Staffa all start from the town. It also boasts an airstrip which, although it has no passenger services at present, could be developed at some time in the future to provide an airlink from the west coast.

Its importance to the surrounding communities, on the mainland and the islands, has earned it the title of the Capital of the West Highlands. www.oban.org.uk.

Main Islands

Bute. Once the island retreat of Scottish kings, the Isle of Bute lies in the Firth of Clyde, close to the mainland and only 15 miles long and five miles across. It is sometimes described as 'The Jewel of the Clyde'. It has a long and varied history, with its fortunes waxing and waning over the centuries. Following a period of stagnation and de-population since the 1950s, it is now on the up again, since a regeneration strategy incepted in the 1990s. The population now is 7,200, 5,000 of whom live in the principal town of Rothesay, the fourth largest town of all the Scottish islands.

Bute's economy depends on hospitality, agriculture, retail and construction. It has also embraced the opportunities provided by new technology with a large call centre and an electronics firm alongside more traditional industries such as food production and boat building.

Its sheltered position between Arran and the Cowal Peninsula together with the effect of the Gulf Stream mean it has a benign climate, creating favourable conditions for plant and wildlife. Apart from its magnificent gardens, the island is home to 100 species of birds and there are resident seal colonies in its waters. www.bute-gateway.org.

Coll. Lying around 2¾ hours from Oban by ferry, Coll is 12 miles long and a little over 3 miles wide. The main settlement on Coll is Arinagour, close to the island's pier. With only 150 living on the island, it would require a real pioneer sprit to make your home here. However, even such a small place as this has an eye to economic regeneration. Recent investment has seen improvements to the hotel, the Coll Business Centre and the village hall, and the island has its own development agency 'Development Coll'. www.isleofcoll.org.

Colonsay. Two and a half hours by ferry from Oban, Colonsay, like most of the Argyll islands, is warmed by the warm waters of the Gulf Stream resulting in favourable conditions for plants and animals alike. It is about ten miles long by two miles wide and its main settlement is Skalasaig. The adjacent island of Oronsay can be reached at low tide by walking across a tidal strand. Northern Ireland can be seen from the island on a clear day – and on a really, really clear day, you can even see Canada.

Gigha. Gigha is about six miles long and just over 1½ miles at the widest point. A fertile island, whose rich soil and mild climate are good for agriculture and horticulture, with the beautiful Achamore Gardens home to plants from around the world. Its main settlement is Ardminish and the island has a resident population of around 180, many of whom speak Gaelic. There is a ferry service to Tayinloan on Kintyre which takes 20 minutes and runs several times a day. The island has a private airstrip and anchorages. www.argyllonline.co.uk.

Iona. Lying off the south tip of Mull, Iona is the birthplace of Celtic Christianity. It is historically important for the monastery and ecclesiastical centre set up by Saint Columba in 563AD. Its Gaelic name, in fact, is *I Chaluim Cille* (Saint Columba's Island).

It is about 3.5 miles long and one mile wide and has a population of just 175. Its main settlement is Baile Mor, meaning Big Town. This, of course, is all relative, as it is anything but a big town! Iona is reached by ferry from Mull, but only residents' vehicles are allowed on the island. A low-lying island, it has beautiful sandy beaches.

Islay. Islay is definitely the place to go if whisky is your passion – with seven distilleries, including Lagavullin, Laphroaig and Bunnahabhain, for about 4,000 inhabitants, it is integral to the entire island economy and lifestyle.

For an enjoyable literary tour of Scotland's distilleries, read Raw Spirit by Iain Banks. Of his visit to Islay, he says:

The first signpost you see coming off the ferry at Port Ellen on Islay has only two words on it; it points right to ARDBEG and left to BOWMORE. Brilliant, I thought; a road sign that is made up of 100 per cent of distillery names; a proclamation that you are on an island where the making of whisky is absolutely integral to the place itself, where directions are defined by drink! (Arrow Books 2004).

Apart from this, Islay has other attractions. It is a low-lying, fertile island, with a ridge of hills along the east coast and spectacular beaches to the west. Bowmore is its main settlement. The most southern island of the Outer Hebrides, it is 25 miles long and 20 miles wide.

The ferry link to Kennacraig on Kintyre operates daily and has a journey time of around two hours. You can also fly from Glasgow and Prestwick, the flight taking around 40 minutes. www.islay.co.uk.

Jura. Lying to the north east of Islay, Jura is less fertile than its neighbour. It is 27 miles long and six miles wide. Far hillier than Islay, it is dominated by three conical peaks, the Paps of Jura, set in a wild mountainous region which attract climbers and hill walkers to the island. It is home to the Isle of Jura whisky distillery, producing its own distinctive island malt.

Lismore. This is another fertile, low-lying island, which lies between Loch Linnhe and the Lynn of Lorn. It is about ten miles long and 1.5 miles wide and has a population of about 180. There is a car ferry to Oban and a passenger ferry to Port Appin runs from the north of the island. The main settlement is Achnacroish, where there is a primary school. Sailing is important to the island, and there are several yacht anchorages. www.isleoflismore.com.

Mull. One of the largest Scottish islands, Mull is about 45 miles long by 25 miles wide, and has a population of around 3,000. Its capital, Tobermory, was planned and built in the 1780s by the British Fisheries Society and is now a conservation area. It is renowned for its brightly painted houses around the bay. These have received even greater prominence in recent years, as Tobermory has been reborn as Balamory in a young children's UK TV show.

There is a frequent ferry service from Oban, which takes 45 minutes. It is fairly mountainous, and boasts one Munro (a mountain over 3,000 feet high), Ben Mhore. It has deep sea lochs which penetrate deep into the centre of the island. Ferries run from Mull to Staffa and Iona and also to Ardnamurchan on the mainland.

Dervaig in the north of the island is famous for Mull Little Theatre, one of the world's smallest professional theatres. www.argyllonline.co.uk.

Tiree. The Gaelic name of Tiree, *Tir An Eorna*, translates as 'The Land Below the Waves', which refers to the low-lying nature of the island. It has a population of around 750 and covers an area of 30 square miles, with the main settlement at Scarinish. It is renowned for long hours of daylight and has the highest annual sunshine hours of anywhere in the United Kingdom.

It is also the windiest place in the UK and has some of the best windsurfing conditions in the world. It regularly hosts windsurfing and wavesailing championships. Apart from this, agriculture is the main activity on the island.

It can be reached by ferry from Oban, a trip of around 4 hours. There are also regular flights between Tiree and Glasgow, a trip which takes around 50 minutes. www.isleoftiree.com.

REASONS TO BUY A HOUSE IN ARGYLL & BUTE

- ○ 3,000 miles of coastline, and 26 inhabited islands.
- ○ Varied and stunning landscape and seascape – this is where the lowlands meet the highlands.
- ○ Superb sailing area.
- ○ Good transport links to Glasgow and Central Belt.
- ○ Good provision of ferries between the islands and mainland.
- ○ Popular tourist area.
- ○ High number of Gaelic speakers.
- ○ Low population density.
- ○ Whisky distilleries.
- ○ Oban, the capital of the West Highlands.

- Loch Lomond and the Trossachs National Park.
- Several stunning Victorian plant collectors' gardens.
- Bute, 'The Jewel of the Clyde'.
- Tobermory painted houses, now immortalised as Balamory.
- Opportunities on the smaller islands for real 'get away from it all' lifestyles.

Typical Properties for Sale

The picturesque loch and island landscape makes Argyll and Bute an extremely popular area with those wishing to relocate to a rural idyll. Inveraray in particular is a very popular area for second home buyers – city dwellers, the English and expatriates all have holiday homes here. It is also a popular retirement area.

One of the reasons for its popularity is the overall prettiness of the towns and villages, with a large proportion of the houses traditional-style white–painted cottages, often with dormers, sitting on the shores of tranquil lochs with mountains as a back drop, or looking out to the island-dotted sea. Much of the new houses built in the area are designed in this traditional style.

Tourism is extremely important for the whole region, and this has a significant effect on the property market. Argyll and Bute has the second highest number of holiday and second homes in Scotland, after the Highlands, with 5,158 at last count. This has the effect of pushing up prices meaning that many young people are now leaving the region, finding they cannot afford to buy a home, faced with competition from wealthy property buyers.

As an example of the exceptional prices some property sells for, in August 2005, a log cabin at Lochgoilhead went up for sale at offers over £250,000. If achieved, this would be a record price for an all-wooden house in Scotland. And the owner predicted that the property could sell for £100,000 over the asking price.

Another popular town is Lochgilphead, where the local council is based. Thanks largely to the employment provided by the council, there is a far lower percentage of holiday homes here than elsewhere in the region – three per cent, compared with over 15% in the region as a whole.

Although Bute lies close to the mainland, situated in the Clyde estuary, it has a genuine island feel. Rothesay has been neglected in the last thirty years, but in the last five years large investment has been made to renovate properties in the town, for both residential and commercial use.

A large proportion of the population lives in the traditional flats clustered around the harbour. Elsewhere on the island there are converted steadings and country cottages, as well as a number of substantial Victorian mansions, originally built for prosperous Clyde businessmen.

Sample Properties For Sale, October 2005			
Location	Type	Description	Price
Oban	Guesthouse	6 bed	Offers over £320,000

Ardfern	Detached house	4 bed	Offers over £230,000
Tobermory	Bungalow	3 bed	Offers over £320,000
Lochgilphead	Detached house	4 bed	Offers over £170,000
Mull	Cottage	Traditional stone, 2 bed	Offers over £170,000
Islay	Sem-detached house	4 bed	Offers over £88,000
Tiree	Cottage	Renovated, 1 bed	Offers over £140,000
Oban	Flat	Modern, 2 bed	Offers over £115,00
Crianlarich	Plot	0.3 acre with p.p. for 3 bed house	Fixed price £75,000
Lochgilphead	Plot	0.3 acre	Offers over £50,000

New Build Homes			
Location	**Type**	**Description**	**Price**
Cardross	Apartments	2 bed	From £143,000
Mull	Detached houses	4 bed	Offers over £175,000
Lochaweside	Detached house	4 bed	Offers over £230,000
Ardfern	Cottage	3 bed	Offers over £155,000
Ardrishaig	Semi-detached houses	3 bed	Fixed price £128,500

COUNCIL TAX CHARGES 2005-2006 (FOR A HOUSEHOLD OF 2 ADULTS)

Tax band	Argyll & Bute	Scottish Average
Band A	£744.67	£729.39
Band B	£868.78	£850.96
Band C	£992.89	£972.52
Band D	£1,117.00	£1,094.09
Band E	£1,365.22	£1,337.22
Band F	£1,613.44	£1,580.35
Band G	£1,861.67	£1,823.48
Band H	£2,234.00	£2,188.18

FIFE

GENERAL INFORMATION

Main Towns: Glenrothes, Dunfermline, St Andrews
Local Authority: Fife Council, Fife House, North Street, Glenrothes, Fife KY7 5LT; ☎ 01592-414141; fax 01592-414142; www.fife.gov.uk.
Tourist Office: Kingdom of Fife Tourist Board, Haig Business Park, Balgonie Road, Markinch KY7 6AQ; ☎ 01592-611180; fax 01334-472021; www.standrews.com
Police Force: Fife Constabulary, Detroit Road, Glenrothes, Fife KY6 2RJ; ☎ 01592-418888; fax 01592-418444; www.fife.police.uk.
Area: 1,325 sq. km.
Population: 349,429.
Population Density: 265 people per sq. km.
Airports: None.
National Nature Reserves: Tentsmuir; Isle of May.
Estate Agents: Fife & Kinross Solicitors' Property Centre, www.f-kspc.co.uk.
Your Move, 11 New Row, Dunfermline KY12 7EA; ☎ 01383-739729; fax 01383-620595; www.your-move.co.uk.
UK Property Shop, www.ukpropertyshop.co.uk/s/estate_agents_Fife

---

Although Fife was never a true Kingdom (unlike Strathclyde, say) residents of the region like to refer to it as 'The Kingdom of Fife', a title which stresses their feeling of independence, their sense that they are a place on their own. This is largely down to the fact that, with the sea on three sides, the area feels physically isolated, a feature reflected in the old saying *Bid farewell to Scotland and cross to Fife*.

The west of the region, between Dunfermline and Kirkcaldy, is where most of the industry and commerce is concentrated, while the east is a popular holiday area. This is a structural change as originally the eastern half of the county had the bulk of the population, but by the mid-twentieth century the population had trebled, with most of this growth in the urban centres of the west, which were centres of textile manufacture and, later, coal production. There was another boost to population in west Fife after 1964 when the Forth Road Bridge was opened, allowing quick and easy access to Edinburgh.

The Tay Bridge, constructed in the 19th century, allows direct access to Dundee, so the region as a whole is far less isolated than it once was.

St Andrews is one of the most ancient towns of Scotland, named after the country's patron saint. It was once the ecclesiastical capital of the country and, with the oldest university in Scotland, a seat of learning. It has gained the attention of the world in recent years as Prince William, heir to the British throne, has been attending St Andrew's University. Having graduated in 2005, the spotlight will presumably now be taken off the town.

Although the administrative town of Fife is Glenrothes – largely thanks to its central position within the region – Dunfermline was for many years far more important and was once the ancient capital of Scotland. St Andrews, however, is the most desirable area today, with the most expensive housing. The attractions of the town, whose main streets appear almost like a living museum thanks to the impressive medieval buildings, many now listed, plus the fact that it is the home of golf, with the most prestigious 'Royal and Ancient' golf club, attract wealthy residents.

Geography & Climate

Fife is located on a peninsula between the Firth of Forth to the south and the Firth of Tay to the north. It is surrounded by water on three sides and has a coastline of 115 miles. The majority of the region, due to its coastal setting, tends to be low lying and fertile. The highest land in the region occurs along the boundary between Fife and Perth & Kinross. Knock Hill rises to 1,189 feet.

The west of Fife is where the coal seams were found which led to a period of growth during the nineteenth to mid-twentieth centuries. Coal production ceased here in the 1960s, and now the west of Fife has become a commercial centre, as well as acting as a commuter belt for Edinburgh workers, since the opening of the Forth Road Bridge.

The two main rivers in the region are the River Eden, which flows eastward to the North Sea, and the River Leven which flows into the Firth of Forth. The Kingdom of Fife is an area of extensive natural beauty: Fife Regional Park occupies over 6,500 hectares of central Fife, and there are also 53 Sites of Special Scientific Interest, two National Nature Reserves, plus other local nature reserves and country parks.

Fife is one of the most productive farming regions of Scotland and it also has a bountiful climate with low rainfall and comparatively high temperatures.

WEATHER		
Annual averages	Fife	Scotland
Rainfall (mm)	653	1099
Sunshine (hours)	1415	1228
Temperature max (°C)	13.2	11.3
Temperature min (°C)	4.5	4.7

Towns & Villages of Note

Cowdenbeath. Originally a collection of farms, Cowdenbeath was reinvented in the late 19th century when it became the central town of the Fife coalfield. Both the town's facilities and its population grew rapidly, earning it the name 'The Chicago of Fife' at one time. When the coalfields declined in the mid-twentieth century, so too did the fortunes of the town. However, it is benefiting from the countrywide attempts at regeneration and now boasts that attractive housing, quality amenities and good infrastructure make Cowdenbeath a popular town, with properties in constant demand. www.fifedirect.org.uk/yourtown.

Dunfermline. With a population of nearly 40,000, this is the largest town and main shopping centre for west Fife. Dunfermline has a long and illustrious history. Dating back to medieval times, its importance during that era can still be seen in the Abbey and Palace which dominate the town. It is the final resting place of Robert the Bruce – minus his heart – and of other Kings and Queens of Scotland.

There are other impressive historic buildings in the town, including the French Gothic style City Chambers and the Old Sheriff Court. This is the town where the famous philanthropist Andrew Carnegie was born, in a humble weaver's cottage. www.fifedirect.org.uk/yourtown.

Glenrothes. Thanks to its central position in Fife, and with relatively easy access to Dundee, Perth and Edinburgh, Glenrothes is now the principal town of the region, with the local authority and the police both having their headquarters here. Its population of 38,600 make it the third largest town in the region and probably the newest. It was established in 1949, the second of Scotland's New Towns, intended to take the booming population from the opening of a new coal seam. Although the population never reached the predicted size, the town has managed to attract light industry and continues to thrive. It is known for its town art and – rather bizarrely – its excessive number of roundabouts.

20% of the local population are employed in engineering and manufacturing. The Kingdom Shopping Centre in Glenrothes, built in the 1960s and showing its age, is due for redevelopment which should make the centre of the town far more attractive. www.fifedirect.org.uk/yourtown.

Kirkcaldy. The largest town in Fife, with a population of nearly 47,000, it dates back at least to the 11th century. It is known as the 'lang toun' because it stretches in a wide sweeping arc along the north of the Firth of Forth. It grew around its harbour and developed during the 19th century through its textile, linoleum and coal industries.

Economist Adam Smith was born in the town, as was Sir Sandford Fleming who became chief engineer of the Canadian Pacific Railway and, more importantly, invented the Standard Time which came into international use from 1883.

The town centre, with numerous interesting historic buildings, was designated a Conservation Area in the 1980s. Other parts of the town are currently undergoing a regeneration strategy.

The Mercat Centre is the largest shopping centre in Fife, and the town also has a leisure centre, theatre, museum and art gallery. www.fifedirect.org.uk/yourtown.

St Andrews. This was the ancient ecclesiastical and university capital of Scotland. Its university is still one of the most prestigious in the country, especially since Prince William, heir to the British throne, chose to do his studies there. Its busy centre is full of historic buildings, including a cathedral and a castle, as well as many of the original university buildings still in use by the Faculties today, and the town has an appealing atmosphere.

An extremely photogenic town, it is a most attractive place to live and the atmosphere is friendly but with a cosmopolitan feel. There are many international students and tourists flock here from all over the world.

Today it is a golfers' mecca, with the most famous golf course and club in the country, if not the world – The Royal and Ancient. Its coastal setting makes it popular with other tourists too.
www.fifedirect.org.uk/yourtown.

REASONS TO BUY A HOUSE IN FIFE

- A region with a strong sense of individuality and independence due to its geographical position.
- Quick and easy access to Edinburgh across Forth Bridge.
- Similarly easy access to Dundee across Tay Bridge.
- Historic St Andrews with oldest university in Scotland.
- Probably the most famous golf course in the world – The Royal and Ancient at St Andrews.
- 115 miles of coastline.
- Area of great natural beauty with many environmental designations.
- Fertile and productive farming region.
- One of the best climates in Scotland.
- Popular tourist area.

Typical Properties For Sale

Property in St Andrews is among the most expensive in Scotland, with an average house price of over £242,000. A basic semi-detached former council house was valued at £170,000 in August 2005. Property continues to be in demand, with a significant proportion of it rented to students attending the university

In the centre of the town, the vast majority of the houses are old, some medieval, and many of them are listed.

St Andrews also attracts house buyers by its seaside setting – coastal properties throughout Scotland can always charge a premium.

Thanks to its fast rising property prices – in September 2005 they were rising three times faster in the town than anywhere else in Scotland – there is a serious problem of homelessness. Although you are unlikely to see people sleeping on the street, more than five percent – one in every 19 residents of the town – are officially homeless. These are often families, living long term in temporary accommodation such as hostels or bed and breakfast establishments. This compares with under one per cent of homeless people in Glasgow and just over one per cent in Edinburgh.

Kirkcaldy on the west coast of Fife has left its industrial past behind, when it was the largest producer of linoleum in the world. Now, the old industrial buildings, and the attractive harbour, once a busy port, are being redeveloped with new houses and apartments.

House prices in this part of Fife are lower than in the rest of the region. Kircaldy has a good stock of traditional Victorian properties and brownfield sites within the town are being redeveloped with modern apartments and houses. On the north east outskirts of the town there is a large development of new homes.

The East Neuk area is one of the most prosperous and desirable in Fife, where coastal properties are an average of £230,000.

Some of the most affordable houses in Fife are in the Cowdenbeath area, with an average price of just under £68,000. There are a significant proportion of council houses in the town.

Another affordable area is Glenrothes, with an average price of £89,000. Glenrothes is growing, with 2,450 new homes due to be built in the next few years.

Sample Properties For Sale, October 2005			
Location	Type	Description	Price
Aberdour	Traditional house	7 bed	Fixed price £595,000
Dunfermline	Detached houses	Modern, 4 bed	Offers over £400,000
Dalgety Bay	Detached house	Modern, 4 bed	Offers over £205,000
Cowdenbeath	Bungalow	4 bed	Offers over £195,000
Inverkeithing	Terraced house	3 bed	Fixed price £84,000
Kirkcaldy	Detached houses	3 bed	Offers over £440,000
St Andrews	Traditional townhouse	3 bed	Fixed price £385,000
Cupar	Converted steading	5 bed	Offers over £410,000
New Gilston	Rural cottage	5 bed	Offers over £410,000
Upper Largo	Building plot	0.3 acre, with p.p. for a house	Offers over £95,000

New Build Homes			
Location	Type	Description	Price
Kirkcaldy	Homes	2-4 bed	From £116,995
Kirkcaldy	Detached houses	4 bed	From £171,950

Dunfermline	Homes	4 & 5 bed	From £198,950
Cupar	Detached houses	4 bed	From £189,995
Glenrothes	Houses	3 & 4 bed	From £121,500
St Andrews	Retirement apartments	1 & 2 bed	From £175,880

COUNCIL TAX CHARGES 2005-2006 (FOR A HOUSEHOLD OF 2 ADULTS)

Tax band	Fife	Scottish Average
Band A	£700.00	£729.39
Band B	£816.67	£850.96
Band C	£933.33	£972.52
Band D	£1,050.00	£1,094.09
Band E	£1,283.33	£1,337.22
Band F	£1,516.67	£1,580.35
Band G	£1,750.00	£1,823.48
Band H	£2,100.00	£2,188.18

TAYSIDE

GENERAL INFORMATION

Main Town: Dundee.

Local Authorities: Dundee City Council, 21 City Square, Dundee DD1 3BY; ☎ 01382-434000; fax 01382-434666; www.dundeecity.gov.uk

Angus Council, The Cross, Forfar, Angus DD8 1BX; ☎ 01307-461460; fax 01307-461874; www.angus.gov.uk.

Perth & Kinross Council, 2 High Street, Perth PH1 5PH; ☎ 01738-475000; fax 01738-475710; www.pkc.gov.uk.

Tourist Office: Perthshire Tourist Board, Lower City Mills, West Mill Street, Perth PH3 1LQ; ☎ 01783-450600; fax 01783-444863; www.perthshire co.uk.

Police Force: Tayside Police Headquarters, PO Box 59, West Bell Street, Dundee DD1 9JU; ☎ 01382-223200; fax 01382-200449; www.tayside.police.uk.

Area: 7,528 sq. km.

Population: 389,012.

Population Density: 829 people per sq. km.

Airports: Dundee airport – flies only to and from London.

National Nature Reserves: Corrie Fee; Ben Lawers; Loch Leven.

Estate Agents: Perth Solicitors' Property Centre, 6 South St. John's Place, Perth PH1 5SU; ☎ 01738-635301; fax 01738-621168; www.pspc.co.uk.
Tayside Solicitors' Property Centre, 9 Whitehall Crescent, Dundee DD1 4AR; ☎ 01382-228770; fax 01382-228650; www.tspc.co.uk.
www.ukpropertyshop.co.uk/s/ estate – agents – Perth – & – Kinross.shtml
www.ukpropertyshop.co.uk/s/estate – agents – Angus.shtml.

Dundee, the principal settlement in Tayside, is the fourth largest city in Scotland. It was built on trade, being a port as far back as the 12th century. By the 16th century, textile manufacture was also very important to its economy, and it had become one of the first urban industrial areas in Scotland. In recent years it has, largely through its two universities, made an extremely successful foray into knowledge-based technologies. Ranging from the sublime to the ridiculous, it has become a world centre for life and science research and for the development of computer games.

Tayside is a diverse region with the city surrounded by the 'silvery Tay' to the south and the rural areas of Angus and Perth and Kinross to the north, east and west. Angus has some of the best agricultural land in Scotland and is renowned for its cattle, seed potatoes and raspberries. Perth and Kinross is the heartland of Scotland, the place where the Lowlands meet the Highlands. Although largely rural itself, its central position in relation to three of the four largest Scottish cities means that it is popular with commuters and businesses and thus has a relatively dense population. In fact, 90% of Scotland's population lives within one hour's drive of Perth.

Perth itself is often classed as a city, for historic reasons, although there is no official recognition of its city status. Scone Palace is the old home of the Stone of Destiny (although now it resides in Edinburgh Castle) and 42 of Scotland's kings were crowned here. There are therefore a lot of important national historic connections in the area.

The area is famous for its golf courses – there are over 100 courses within one hour's drive of Kinross, including the championship golf courses of Carnoustie and Gleneagles.

Its central position means that transport links, both road and rail, are very good here. The airports at Edinburgh and Glasgow are easily reachable, and there is also an airport at Dundee which has regular passenger flights to London City Airport. www.dundeecity.gov.uk/airport.

Geography & Climate

The city of Dundee rises steeply from the north shore of the River Tay, its houses terraced row above row. Dominating the cityscape is Dundee Law, an extinct volcano reaching a height of 174 metres (571 feet). Surrounding the city is lower ground, showing only gentle undulations and the occasional higher point. Angus, to the north and west of the city, rises from the North Sea coast in the south to over 900 metres (3000 feet) in the Braes of Angus which make up part of the eastern Grampian Mountains. Between these boundaries lies the fertile agricultural valley of Strathmore. All the most populous towns of Angus lie in the south of the region, with only small settlements in the Braes of Angus to the north.

Perth and Kinross straddles the boundary between the Lowlands and the Highlands. The River Tay running through is Scotland's longest river and one of the most important salmon fishing rivers in the country. There are some large lochs in the region, including Loch Tay, Loch Earn, Loch Rannoch and Loch Tummel.

The climate is generally favourable, with rainfall comparatively low and sunshine hours high compared with the country as a whole.

WEATHER		
Annual averages	**Tayside**	**Scotland**
Rainfall (mm)	720	1099
Sunshine (hours)	1404	1228
Temperature max (°C)	12.2	11.3
Temperature min (°C)	4.5	6.7

Towns & Villages of Note

Arbroath. The largest town in Angus with a population of 122,000, Arbroath is famous for its Abbey, where the historic signing of The Declaration of Arbroath took place in 1320. This attracts thousands of visitors each year to the Abbey and its Visitor Centre. Tourists also come here for its seaside setting, making this a popular holiday destination.

The town is also famous for its culinary delicacy, the Arbroath smokie, a smoked haddock unique to the town. Legal protection under European law means that to be called an Arbroath smokie it must be smoked in Arbroath itself. www.theshoppie.com.

Dundee. The City of Dundee is the smallest local authority in Scotland, but the fourth largest city, with a population of 145,600, after Glasgow, Edinburgh and Aberdeen. There has been a settlement here since ancient times – there was a Pictish fort on Dundee Law, originally known as Dun Daigh ('fortress of Daigh'), presumably some Pictish warrior, from which the town takes its name.

Dundee was long ago christened the city of the three Js – 'jute, jam and journalism', referring respectively to its important jute industry in the 19th century; to the famous Keiller's Dundee marmalade; and to the equally famous Dundee publishing house D.C Thomson which produces magazines, newspapers and, most loved of all, the Dandy and Beano children's comics.

Of the three Js, only D.C. Thompson still exists in Dundee. The city has, however, succeeded in re-inventing itself for modern times and is now an important centre of high-tech computer, scientific and bio-technology research and development. With reference to this, it styles itself Scotland's City of Discovery, taking its name from Captain Scott's polar exploration ship Discovery which is now a tourist attraction moored at Dundee. The City is home to one of the UK's largest scientific communities and is at the forefront of oncology research – it is widely expected that one day a cure for cancer will be found in the city. www.cityofdiscovery.com.

Perth. Known variously as 'The Fair City' and the 'Ancient Capital of Scotland' (a title which several towns like to lay claim to), modern Perth has a population of 43,500. The town's population has increased rapidly in recent years – in the 1990s, Perth and Kinross was one of the fastest growing areas of Scotland.

There has been a settlement here since Roman times when they built a fort where the rivers Tay and Almond join. The name is believed to derive from an old Celtic word for 'copse'. Whether or not it was ever the capital, Perth has always been an important centre of politics and commerce. Its harbour was used for overseas trade and by the 18th century the town was a major textile producing centre.

An attractive town, Perth has two large parks in the centre – the North and South Inches – in addition to many other gardens. These and its floral displays have made it a regular winner in the Britain in Bloom competitions.

It has been a Royal Burgh since the 13th century and has continued to be a busy and prosperous town through the centuries, re-inventing itself as necessary to take advantage of changing times. Its central position makes it popular with large businesses. Scottish and Southern Energy, Norwich Union and Bank of Scotland are all major employers, and Famous Grouse Whisky is also produced in the town.

Pitlochry. The resident population of 2,500 is swelled by the many visitors to this pretty town surrounded by mountains. It is one of the most popular destinations in Tayside, and has been for many years, since Queen Victoria commented favourably on the town after her stay at nearby Blair Castle in 1842. The railway reached here in 1863, making it then and now one of the premier mountain resorts in Scotland.

Despite its many hotels, camping and caravanning sites and other tourist facilities, it still manages to retain an air of individuality – although there are shops with the ubiquitous tartan and shortbread, this isn't just a tourist Mecca: the busy main street still provides services to a vibrant local community. www.scottish-towns.co.uk/perthshire/pitlochry.

REASONS TO BUY A HOUSE IN TAYSIDE

- Dundee's two universities, good reputation for IT development and life sciences.
- A diverse region.
- Perth most central town in Scotland.
- Over 100 golf courses within one hour's drive of Kinross.
- Road and rail links excellent.

> O Airports at Glasgow and Edinburgh easily reachable.
> O Flights to London from Dundee.
> O Fertile farming country.
> O Excellent for fishing.
> O A favourable climate.
> O Good employment prospects – many large companies in Perth.
> O Popular tourist area.

Typical Properties for Sale

For affordable city properties, Dundee cannot be beaten. It consistently has a significantly lower average property price than the other Scottish cities. However, as prices reached record levels in the other cities, Dundee's housing market picked up, as the property there was so much more affordable. By October 2005 Dundee was the fastest growing city in Scotland, so its fortunes were definitely on the up. Because prices are rising from a much lower starting point, Dundee is likely to be a good place for city bargains for some time to come.

With two universities, the need to house students in rented accommodation means that the buy to let market is good. Similar in its range of property to Glasgow and Edinburgh, there are a high number of tenement flats, both in old, renovated buildings, and in newer modern blocks. The student population of Dundee is not to be under-estimated – it has the highest proportion of full-time students aged 16-74 in Scotland, at 12.67%.

Just as in Glasgow and Edinburgh, there is large scale redevelopment of the waterfront in Dundee, with stylish apartments and penthouses attracting young professional residents.

On the outskirts of Dundee, Broughty Ferry is one of the most popular suburbs, with wide leafy streets and good housing stock, largely dating from the 1930s. Prices here have risen fast over recent years making it a property hot spot with houses selling very quickly.

Elsewhere in the region, the housing picture is somewhat different. In predominately rural Angus, there are ten per cent more people living in detached houses than the national average. Despite this, the average property price in Angus is over £10,000 below the national average.

Not surprisingly, the prestige of living in Carnoustie, home of four golf courses, one of them the famous Carnoustie course which has hosted the Open Championship six times in the past, makes this a property hot spot, with the average property here being far higher than in the rest of Angus.

For house-hunters, Perthshire has a great deal to recommend it. It has the thriving commercial town of Perth at its centre, with the A9, the main route north, running through its outskirts. Surrounding the county town are picturesque and peaceful rural villages with delightful country cottages and more substantial properties for sale. Add to this the stunning countryside, with the River Tay running through, and any number of outdoor pursuits available, including fishing and shooting, hill walking and skiing there's pretty much something for everyone. Not surprisingly then, the property market here is thriving, particularly at the upper end of the market, where large country homes are snapped up as soon as they come on the market.

Towns such as Dunkeld, Aberfeldy and Pitlochry are constantly popular with tourists, many of whom love the area so much they end up returning as permanent residents. However, there is a shortage of houses for sale in these towns, and also a shortage of new homes being built, partly because the local water supply cannot cope with increased demand, which inevitably pushes prices up. Scottish Water is investing money to address the water supply problem, so this should open the way for new development in the future.

Sample Properties For Sale, October 2005			
Location	Style	Description	Price
Dundee	Victorian stone house	6 bed	Offers over £395,000
Dundee	Apartments	3 bed	Offers over £175,000
Broughty Ferry	Apartments	In Victorian mansion, 4 bed	Offers over £215,000
Birnam	Converted stable block	4 bed	Offers over £295,00
Pitlochry	Country cottage	2 bed	Offers over £320,000
Perth	Apartments	2 bed	Fixed price £159,000
Perth	Detached house	Period refurbished, 4 bed	Offers over £425,000
Brechin	Traditional house	Riverside, 6 bed	Offers over £420,000
Comrie	Building plot	½ acre with p.p.	Offers over £250,000
Dundee	Building plot	With p.p. for 2 houses	Offers over £90,000

New Build Homes			
Location	Type	Description	Price
Broughty Ferry	Detached houses	4 & 5 bed	£225,995-£291,995
Perth	Detached houses	4 & 5 bed	£279,995-£389,995
Perth	Apartments	2 & 3 bed	£140,496-£175,495
Carnoustie	Detached houses	4 bed	From £199,995
Dundee	Conversions	1-4 bed	£130,000-£250,000

COUNCIL TAX CHARGES 2005-2006 (FOR A HOUSEHOLD OF 2 ADULTS)

Tax band	Angus	Dundee City	Perth & Kinross	Scottish Average
A	£691.33	£786.67	£725.33	£729.39
B	£806.56	£917.78	£846.22	£850.96
C	£921.78	£1,048.89	£967.11	£972.52
D	£1.037.00	£1,180.00	£1,088.00	£1,094.09
E	£1,267.44	£1,442.22	£1,329.78	£1,337.22
F	£1,497.89	£1,704.44	£1,571.56	£1,580.35
G	£1,728.33	£1,966.67	£1,813.33	£1,823.48
H	£2,074.00	£2,360.00	£2,176.00	£2,188.18

GRAMPIAN

GENERAL INFORMATION

Main Town: Aberdeen.

Local Authorities: Aberdeenshire Council, Woodhill House, Westburn Road, Aberdeen AB16 5GB; ☎ 01467-620981; fax 01224-665444; www.aberdeenshire.gov.uk.
Aberdeen City Council, Town House, Broad Street, Aberdeen AB10 1FY; ☎ 01224-522000; fax 01224-644346; www.aberdeencity.gov.uk.
Moray Council, Council Office, High Street, Elgin, Morayshire IV30 1BX; ☎ 01343-543451; fax 01343-540399; www.moray.org.

Tourist Office: Aberdeen & Grampian, Exchange House, 26-28 Exchange Street, Aberdeen AB10 1YL; ☎ 01224-288828; fax 01224-581367; www.agtb.org.

Police Force: Grampian Police, Headquarters, Queen Street, Aberdeen AB10 1ZA; ☎ 01224-386000; fax 01224-643366; www.grampian.police.uk.

Area: 8737 sq. km.

Population: 503,888.

Population Density: 401 people per sq. km.

Airports: Aberdeen Dyce International Airport.

National Nature Reserves: Forvie, Glen Tanar, St Cyrus.

Estate Agents: Your Move, 75 High Street, Elgin IV30 1EE; ☎ 01343-548861; fax 01343-549703; www.your-move.co.uk.
North East Solicitors' Property Centre, 31 Duff Street, Macduff AB44 1QL; ☎ 01261-832491; fax 01261-833444; www.nespc.com.
Solicitors' Property Centre Moray, 29/31 High Street, Elgin IV30 1EE; ☎ 01343-548755; fax 01343-550053; www.spcmoray.com.

Grampian is a diverse region, encompassing as it does the prosperous modern City of Aberdeen, the 'Oil Capital of Europe', and the rural hinterland of Aberdeenshire which, beyond the Aberdeen commuter belt, has areas where household incomes are well below the national average. Aberdeenshire, however, also includes the Balmoral Estate, famous as the Royal Family's holiday home. The third element of this region is Moray, another area reliant on income from traditional rural businesses, and which, to a certain extent, suffers from its proximity to Inverness, although the growth of the capital of the Highlands over recent years has undoubtedly contributed to rising house prices in areas of Moray within commuting distance of Inverness. The Cairngorm Mountain range is another element of its diversity, bringing income from tourism.

North Sea oil and gas has a tremendous effect on the area: in 2001 it directly accounted for 26,000 jobs, with another 244,000 being indirectly dependent on the industry. North east Scotland also produces around one third of Scotland's agricultural output, worth over £1 billion pounds per year.

Its position between Aberdeen and Inverness ensure that transport links to the region are good. There is an international airport at Aberdeen with flights to London and other UK destinations, plus flights to many International destinations including Europe and the USA. It is also well-served by the railway, which runs parallel to the coast from Aberdeen southward to Dundee and westward to Inverness.

Road travel is less well-provided for: there are no motorways in this part of Scotland, with only A class roads running from Aberdeen. But even on these major roads journey times can be slow because of the constant stream of traffic and lack of alternative routes. Most winters, these roads are affected by the sometimes severe weather, and reports of hold-ups and road closures due to snowdrifts are not uncommon.

Geography & Climate

Geographically, Grampian is a region of contrasts, from the imposing Cairngorms with some of Scotland's highest mountains – although Cairn Gorm itself is part of the Highland Council region – to the fertile lowland farm lands in the centre of the region, run through with some of Scotland's finest salmon rivers, to the small coastal fishing villages next to fine beaches or crags and cliffs, looking out over the expanse of the North Sea.

The income of the region is directly related to its geography. Historically, fishing, farming, textiles – in particular wool production – and whisky distilling have been at the centre of the local economy. Today, Peterhead is Europe's largest white fish port and Aberdeen is Scotland's primary fish processing centre, and the rich farmland ensures that agriculture will continue to be significant. However, another less immediately obvious geographical element has had a massive effect over recent years, that being the North Sea oilfields – not noticeable from the land, even in the form of oil rigs, which are situated 100 kilometres or more out to sea. But its economic effects have been immense, to the extent that over the last 20 years, Grampian has been the only part of the United Kingdom to have consistently outperformed the growth of the global economy.

It has turned Aberdeen into a thriving cosmopolitan city, with a higher employment rate and higher per capita income than either Edinburgh or Glasgow. This inevitably has led to a knock-effect in Aberdeenshire, where residents are looking to the 'big city' for employment. This, together with the countrywide downturn in demand for fishing and agriculture, has meant a decline in the traditional rural economy. There is a danger inherent in this, in that Aberdeen is now so heavily reliant on the oil and gas extraction industry, both directly and in all the infrastructure and research connected with the core industry, that when, as seems inevitable, the oil fields become less productive, the whole region will undoubtedly suffer economically.

Grampian has the harshest climate in mainland Scotland. In winter, in particular, the all but constant biting wind off the North Sea requires a high tolerance of low temperatures – or a heavy reliance on thermal underwear! Snowfall is high here, with snow lying for more days in the year than any other region. On the plus side, it is comparatively dry, with a lower than average annual rainfall.

WEATHER		
Annual averages	**Grampian**	**Scotland**
Rainfall (mm)	800	1099
Sunshine (hours)	1252	1228
Temperature max (°C)	10.5	11.3
Temperature min (°C)	3.5	6.7

Towns & Villages of Note

Aberdeen. Aberdeen lies in the angle between its two great rivers, the Dee and the Don, which both flow into the North Sea. The sea has always been important to Aberdeen, originally for its fishing and sea transport, more recently for North Sea oil. The city is known by several titles, including the Granite City, due to its imposing buildings constructed from the locally quarried rock; the Oil Capital of Europe, for its offshore riches; and the capital of the Grampian Highlands, because of its status as the main business and retail centre for the north east. With the most complete civic records of any place in Scotland, the historic buildings, and the ultra-modern hi-tech oil and gas industry centred on the city, Aberdeen is a true amalgam of ancient and modern. It succeeds in melding the two seamlessly, making it an interesting and vibrant city. Surveys have regularly shown that Aberdeen is one of the most desirable cities in the United Kingdom in which to live and work.

With a population of over 212,000, Aberdeen is the third largest Scottish city, after Glasgow and Edinburgh. It has two universities, the University of Aberdeen and Robert Gordon University. Because of the high number of foreign workers living in the Aberdeen area, connected with the oil industry, the city is better provided with international schools than anywhere else in the country. In a survey of UK graduates' satisfaction with their lives, graduates in Aberdeen were ranked eighth, with a satisfaction score of 64 per cent.

The prosperity of Aberdeen compared with Scotland as a whole is not in doubt: the average household income for Aberdeenshire (where many of the well-paid energy workers live) is well above the national average of £18,000 at £20,800. As a measure of its cosmopolitan nature, and an explanation of the high numbers of foreign workers in the city, one needs to look no further than the fact that there are over 400 internationally-owned companies operating in the city. In fact, Aberdeen has a higher employment rate than any of the English cities, and has the highest average earnings in the UK outside London.

Aberdonians, both by birth and by adoption, are fiercely proud of their town. It is indeed a handsome city, in a serious east coast way, and there is plenty in the way of cultural, social and retail activities to keep residents occupied. www.undiscoveredscotland.com/aberdeen/aberdeen.

Elgin. The administrative centre of Moray, Elgin is a busy market town. Dating back to the 13th century, much of the medieval town layout remains and the original cobbled market place is still in existence. More recently, military airbases have been established nearby at Kinloss and Lossiemouth. As a result, Elgin has a significant number of military personnel and their families among its residents.

Fraserburgh. Originally a village called Faithlie, it was developed into a port in the 1500s by the Fraser clan and it took their name after 1600. The lighthouse was once a castle, built in 1574 by Sir Alexander of Philorth. The importance of the town at this time is obvious, from the fact that in 1595 a university was founded in Fraserburgh. However, it closed down again in 1605 after its principal displeased James IV.

Known locally as 'the Broch', Fraserburgh today is an important fishing port. It is currently the largest shellfish port, and one of the largest whitefish ports, in Europe. At its harbour it has a dry-dock ship lift facility and the town also has a significant engineering presence, which specialises in refrigerated trailers amongst other products for the fishing industry. www.fraserburgh.org.uk.

Lossiemouth. This is a lively town which was established originally to provide a port for nearby Elgin when the original port at Loch Spynie silted up. Today, in addition to being a busy fishing port, it is home to RAF Lossiemouth, the largest fast jet base in the Royal Air Force, established in 1939. www.loscom.org.uk.

Peterhead. The most easterly town on the Scottish mainland, with a population of 18,000, Peterhead is the largest whitefish port in Europe and is the base for most of the Scottish fishing fleet. As a result, this is a thriving community with many businesses connected both with the fishing industry and with the oil extraction industry. It is particularly well-endowed with engineering firms of various types. www.peterhead.org.uk.

REASONS TO BUY A HOUSE IN GRAMPIAN

- A diverse region.
- Oil Capital of Europe.
- Aberdeen has highest per capita income in Scotland.
- Highest employment rate in the country.
- Two universities, good schools, including international schools.
- Fertile farming land.
- The Cairngorms for walking and skiing.
- Moray within commuting distance of Inverness.
- Good rail and air links.
- Salmon rivers.
- Attractive coastal fishing villages.
- Sea fishing.
- High snowfall, low rainfall.
- Peterhead an excellent seaside resort.

Typical Properties for Sale

Not for nothing is Aberdeen called 'the Granite City'. Both public buildings and houses have a solidity and sombreness due to the stone used in their construction. This, combined with the often harsh winds coming off the North Sea, gives the city a serious air, shared by many of its residents. This is contrasted, however, by the large student population which has a brought a lively night life to the city.

The most expensive area in Aberdeen City is prosperous West End, with leafy streets and imposing villas. Within the west End, Rubislaw Den is a particularly sought after address. With both St Margaret's Girls School and Robert Gordon's College in the city – both among the top ten private schools in the country – it attracts parents wanting the best education for their children.

On the western outskirts of Aberdeen, Cults is a very desirable suburb, partly due to the presence of Cults Academy, one of the country's top ten state schools. A classic leafy suburb with well-kept houses and good facilities, houses here sell quickly. The 15th most expensive house in Scotland during 2004-5 was sold in Cults, at £1.388 million.

Many of the well-paid oil workers of Aberdeen live in rural Aberdeenshire surrounding the city, which means rural properties are for sale at a premium. In August 2005, a former cowshed at Oldmeldrum, Aberdeenshire, with no roof and no services, went up for sale at offers over £70,000. And there was interest from many buyers, prepared to invest the additional £100,000 to £150,000 which would be required to turn the building into a home.

Banchory Academy in Aberdeenshire is another one of Scotland's top ten state schools, attracting families to the area and pushing prices up.

Moray is, in some respects, the poor relation of Grampian, with average property prices lower. Elgin, its administrative centre, is one of the more desirable areas, although, situated as it is halfway between Aberdeen and Inverness, with the notoriously slow A96 trunk road to contend with, it's not the most convenient place to live. However, it does have some strong plus points, one being its proximity to Scotland's most prestigious school, Gordonstoun, just five miles away. There are plenty of traditional stone houses, constructed in the neo-classical style of the 19th century, as well as new housing developments, in the town.

Typical rural and coastal properties are found elsewhere in Moray. Hopeman, on the Moray coast, is destined to double in size as 700 new homes are at the planning stage.

Sample Properties For Sale, October 2005			
Location	Type	Description	Price
Buckie	Semi-detached houses	Traditional, 3 bed	Offers over £140,000
Elgin	Detached house	Modern, 5 bed	Offers over £169,000
Aberdeen West End	Flat	2 bed	Offers over £225,000
Aberdeen	Semi-detached houses	2 bed	Offers over £109,000
Bridge of Don	Detached house	3 bed	Offers over £139,000
Cults	Former manse	5 bed	Offers over £450,000
Banchory	Converted steading	4 bed	Offers over £295,000
Fraserburgh	Flat	2 bed, requiring modernisation	Offers over £65,000
Inverurie	Farmhouse	Derelict, in 1/3 acre land	Offers over £70,000
Midmar	Building plot	With B listed church	Offers over £60,000

New Build Homes			
Location	Type	Description	Price
Aberdeen	Apartments	2 & 3 bed	From £138,995
Aberdeen	Detached houses	4 & 5 bed	£567,000
Ellon	Houses	4 bed	£210,950-£249,950
Balmedie	Detached houses	3 & 4 bed	From £186,995
Elgin	Houses	Executive	£260,000-£350,000
Dufftown	Houses	3 bed	£158,250-£178,500

COUNCIL TAX CHARGES 2005-2006 (FOR A HOUSEHOLD OF 2 ADULTS)

Tax band	Aberdeen City	Aberdeenshire	Moray	Scottish Average
A	£744.72	£710.00	£696.67	£729.39
B	£903.84	£828.33	£812.78	£850.96
C	£1,032.96	£946.67	£928.89	£972.52
D	£1,162.08	£1,065.00	£1,045.00	£1,094.09
E	£1,420.32	£1,301.67	£1,277.22	£1,337.22
F	£1,678.56	£,1538.33	£1,509.44	£1,580.35
G	£1,936.80	£1,775.00	£1,741.67	£1,823.48
H	£2,324.16	£2,130.00	£2,090.00	£2,188.18

HIGHLAND

GENERAL INFORMATION

Main Town: Inverness.

Local Authority: Highland Council, Glenurquhart Road, Inverness IV3 5NX; ☎ 01463-702000; fax 01463-702111; www.highland.gov.uk.

Tourist Office(s): Highlands of Scotland, Castle Wynd, Inverness IV2 3BJ; ☎ 01463-234353; fax 01463-710609; www.extranet.host.co.uk.

Police Force: Northern Constabulary, HQ, Old Perth Road, Inverness IV2 3SY; ☎ 01463-715555; fax 01463-230800; www.northern.police.uk.

Area: 25,659 sq. km.

Population: 208,920.

Population Density: 8 people per sq. km.

Airports: Inverness Airport; Wick Airport.

National Park: Cairngorms National Park.

National Nature Reserves: Loch a' Mhuilinn; Inchnadamph; Knockan Crag; Loch Fleet; Corrieshalloch Gorge; Ben Wyvis; Loch Maree Islands; Beinn Eighe; Rassal Ashwood; Glen Affric; Cragellachie; Abernethy Forest; Insh Marshes; Creag Meagaidh; Rum; Glen Roy; Claish Moss; Ariundle Oakwood; Glencripesdale.

Estate Agents: Your Move, 60 Academy Street, Inverness IV1 1LP; ☎ 01463-221166; fax 01463-710166; www.your-move.co.uk.

Your Move, 59 High Street, Dingwall IV15 9HL; ☎ 01349-864848; fax 01349-861479; www. your-move.co.uk.

Highland Solicitors' Property Centre, 30 Queensgate, Inverness IV1 1DA; ☎ 01463-231173; fax 01463-715292; www.hspc.co.uk.

With an area of nearly 10,000 square miles, Highland is a massive region, the largest of Scotland's local government areas. Despite its extent, the population is low, with just four per cent of the population of Scotland living there. This makes it the least populated region of Europe with an average population density of only eight people per square kilometre. The region includes Inverness, the fastest growing city in the UK, where nearly one fifth of the population resides – if this is taken out of the figures the average density plummets. The least populated areas of the Highlands are found in the north west where small crofting communities are the main form of settlement.

The mountains, lochs and glens of the Highlands are the image which says 'Scotland' to the rest of the world, making this the most desirable region of the country for incomers. The thing which prevents many more people making their lives here is its remoteness which inevitably means that making a living, at least in the traditional sense of 'getting a job' far more difficult. However, with the advent of the internet, this is far less of a bar than it once was – there has been over recent years an influx of professional people moving into the remote areas and running their businesses from their rural retreats. With Inverness becoming a more attractive place due to its current economic boom, more companies are considering it as a viable base, providing both good infrastructure for the business and an enviable quality of life for their staff. The recent transfer of Scottish Natural Heritage from Edinburgh to Inverness has raised the profile of the city as a centre for large organisations, and the Highland Council is concentrating effort on attracting other high status companies and organisations to the city.

As far as choosing wheareabouts in the Highlands to buy a home, there is a great difference in the way of life and access to services on the east and the west. However, as the west coast is so dependent on the towns and the transport infrastructure of the east, it makes little sense to talk about the north west in isolation from the rest of the region.

Although there are still many single track roads, especially in the north west, even here the road system has been upgraded in recent years, with large amounts of money being invested in improving transport links to the larger villages on the west coast, such as Ullapool, Gairloch and Lochcarron. The railway has never reached this far, with the mainline going to Inverness and then branch lines running all the way to the north coast at Wick. In a westerly direction it only reaches as far as Achnasheen, a good fifty miles from Gairloch on the west coast.

It is possible to travel south along the west coast, but the indented nature of the coastline, with numerous sea lochs, means that this is a beautiful route to drive, but not one to take if you are in a hurry. The fastest way to travel south from the north west is first to cut across country to Inverness and travel south on the A9, the main arterial route joining north and south.

There are buses connecting the main centres of population on the west with Inverness and, in some cases, with each other, but these are infrequent – generally no more than one a day in each direction, often less frequently.

Seven per cent of the Highland population speak Gaelic, although this is rarely as a first language, and then only among older people. Everybody also speaks English, and if you do come across people speaking Gaelic, in a shop, say, their natural politeness will show itself by their switching to English when you appear. Bilingual place-name signage has been introduced throughout the Highlands in recent years.

It is an interesting linguistic fact that the Highlands and Islands do not have Scots as an indigenous language. This is because the Gaelic language held sway here from early times, due to the influx of settlers from Ireland and other speakers of Celtic languages. Later, English was introduced from south of the border, through the English lairds and other people in positions of power, and it did not have the Scottish regional variations found further south. As a result, to English ears the accent in the Highlands and Islands is far easier to understand, gentler, more lilting than Glaswegian, for example, and with the accent being far more similar to the Irish accent.

The Highlands is potentially affected by the falling population of Scotland more than any other region, particularly outside the boom city of Inverness which is the only area of the Highlands which is growing substantially. To help to address this problem, Highlands and Islands Enterprise is aiming to create 20,000 new jobs, many of them homeworkers, in an attempt to increase the population to a more sustainable level in the next two decades.

Geography & Climate

The topography of the Highlands is varied. It is bisected by the Great Glen Fault, which runs along the line of the Caledonian canal and Loch Ness. To the north of the Great Glen, which all but splits the country in two, the west coast is deeply indented, making for spectacular scenery but difficult communications. As a result, small isolated communities have grown up over the centuries in this area. Historically, these communities were only accessible by sea, so they all cling to the coastline, although the length of many of the sea lochs means that the coastline does extend for quite some miles inland. As the west coast, thanks to the beneficent Gulf Stream, has a far kinder climate than the North Sea coast on the east of the country, the ancient invaders arriving from areas as diverse as Ireland and Scandinavia found this a viable and attractive area in which to settle, with the riches of the sea on their doorstep. The land was far less fertile, with the peaty moorland and mountains making agricultural production hard won. Livestock had to be hardy to survive here. Today less than 2.5% of the land, and this mostly in the less mountainous areas of Caithness and Sutherland, is used for arable farming. Unproductive heather moorland and peatland covers more than 26% of the Highlands.

Britain's highest mountain, Ben Nevis, is at the south end of the Great Glen Fault, while Loch Ness, its deepest and most famously mysterious body of inland water, runs along the fault line.

The natural unspoiled beauty of the region is unsurpassed, as is the chance of seeing a wide variety of wildlife in its natural element, and this is what attracts so many people to the area for holidays or for longer stays. The opportunities for outdoor activities are extensive, including climbing and walking, skiing (when the somewhat unreliable snowfall permits), stalking and shooting on highland estates, loch and sea fishing, watersports and golf.

There is a dramatic difference in climate between the west and east of the region, with the North Atlantic Drift, part of the Gulf Stream, having a significant effect, making the west far wetter and milder than the east. The Highland region sits on the edge of the land-mass of Europe, and lies between the stable Continental air and the Atlantic weather fronts to the west. These two weather systems – high pressure and low pressure, maritime and continental – meet over the Highlands and make the weather notoriously changeable. The weather is a constant topic of conversation here, even more than elsewhere in Britain. They do say, if you don't like the weather in the Highlands, wait half an hour. The topography of the west coast in particular, with a succession of sea lochs, all with their own peculiar characteristics, means that micro-climates develop around each loch: it can be sunny on one side of the loch, and raining or foggy on the other; or the communities round one loch can be having a dreich day, while the next loch along can be basking in sunshine.

Average climate figures for the Highlands, therefore, can only be a rough guide: bear in mind that rainfall can vary from 2,500mm in the west to less than 500mm in the east, while snowfall is far more frequent, and lies on the ground for longer, in the centre and the east than near the far milder west coast.

WEATHER		
Annual averages	**Highland**	**Scotland**
Rainfall (mm)	1192	1099
Sunshine (hours)	1169	1228
Temperature max (°C)	11.3	11.3
Temperature min (°C)	4.8	6.7

Towns & Villages & an Island of Note

Aviemore. Although there has been a settlement here since the 1600s, the town did not start to grow into the mountain resort it has now become until the railway reached here in 1862. It lies on the main line between Inverness and Perth, and is just off the A9, so access is easy. Its other attraction is its setting within the Cairngorms which, in the 1960s, was developed as a skiing centre. This began its present day position as one of Scotland's main tourist centres. In 2003 the Cairngorms National Park was established. Covering 3,800 square kilometres, it is the largest National Park in Britain.

Aviemore is now a year-round tourist centre, and has all the hotels, tourist shops, cafes and restaurants one expects. It is dominated by the grandeur of the Cairngorms, which can now be reached by skiers and non-skiers alike on the Cairngorm Mountain railway which has replaced the ski lifts. www.undiscoveredsotland.co.uk/aviemore.

Dingwall. An attractive town of 5,500, Dingwall shows its Viking ancestry in its name, which is derived from *Thing Vollr* – the Norse for 'meeting place'. In recent years, with the Highland Council introducing bi-lingual (English and Gaelic) signing throughout the region, the older Gaelic name *Inbhir Pheofharain* has been revived. This means 'the mouth of the River Peffery', which flows into Cromarty Firth at this point. The town grew up originally as a port, but it now lies inland, the original harbour now degenerated into mud flats.

Previously the county town of Ross & Cromarty, it is still the home to the offices of the Highland Council dealing with the Ross & Cromarty district. Despite being so close to Inverness, only 20 miles away, it remains a busy town, with a large agricultural market plus a reasonable shopping centre. www.dingwall.org.uk.

Fort William. Situated at the head of Loch Linnhe and the southern end of the Great Glen, Fort William is the largest town of the southern Highlands and an important population, retail and business centre. With a population of 9,300, it is the second largest town in the Highlands after Inverness. It is also a busy tourist centre, thanks to its closeness to Ben Nevis, the UK's tallest mountain and hence one of the major natural tourist attractions in Scotland. Being the major town for a large surrounding district, it has the full range of shops and services. The town is particularly popular as a base for outdoor enthusiasts.

At the hub of transport connections for the area, it is a starting point for some stunning road, rail and inland waterway journeys. The A830 – the Road to the Isles – begins here, while the train line between Fort William and Mallaig is one of the world's most scenic train journeys. If boats are your thing, the Caledonian Canal runs for 60 miles along the Great Glen, travelling from the west coast along Loch Linnhe, Loch Lochy and Loch Ness to Inverness on the east coast. www.undiscoveredscotland.co.uk/fortwilliam/fortwilliam.

Inverness. The Capital of the Highlands is experiencing a boom period at present, since being granted city status in March 2001. With a population of nearly 51,000 it is Scotland's smallest city, smaller than many towns in the central belt. However, when you consider the sparsity of population across the Highlands as a whole, this is a significant population, and the focus of economic, administrative and retail activity in the Highland region. The Census of 2001 recorded Inverness's population at 44,000, so there has been a significant growth in the last five years as new building, of housing and retail and business areas, continues on the outskirts of the city.

With the fledgling University of the Highlands and Islands growing in stature and the first Scottish Year of Highland culture, *Highland 2007*, being planned, which proposes amongst other events its own tattoo to rival the Edinburgh version, the city fathers are making a concerted effort to challenge the other cities of Scotland as a 'must-visit' place.

The city has a large retail and business park on its outskirts, providing all the daily necessities for the population of the mainland and the islands. Its setting at the head of Loch Ness makes Inverness popular with tourists too and in the summer months in particular the city centre is always busy. www.inverness-scotland.com.

Skye. This is the largest of the Hebridean Islands and the best known Scottish island of them all, thanks in the main to the connection with Bonnie Prince Charlie as immortalised in the *Skye Boat Song*. It is 50 miles (80km) long, and varies from 30 miles (48km) to 4 miles (6km) wide. There has long been a ferry making the short crossing from the mainland – at least since Bonnie Prince Charlie's day, seemingly – and since the opening of the controversial Skye Bridge in 1995 it is now even more accessible from the mainland. Consequently it attracts about ½ a million visitors a year.

Its population is around 12,000, of which about 2,500 live in its main town of Portree. The population of Portree doubles in the summer months with the influx of tourists. It is a picturesque town with a large harbour looking across to Raasay, the largest island of several surrounding Skye. www.skye.co.uk.

Thurso. Scotland's most northerly town, with a population of 7,800, Thurso shows its Nordic history in its name which means 'Thor's River'. The town is the setting off point for the Orkney Islands, which also looks more to Norway than to Scotland for its heritage.

Ullapool. Sitting on the shore of Loch Broom, Ullapool was built by the British Fisheries Society in 1788, in order to exploit the huge shoals of herring caught just offshore here. Although herring and fish stocks generally are far scantier now, Ullapool still has the remnants of a fishing industry. Its most noticeable – and notorious – connections with the industry used to be seen in the large factory trawlers, known as Klondykers, from Scandinavia and the Eastern Bloc, which would anchor in the sheltered waters of the loch for up to six months of the year, the foreign seamen spending shore leave in Ullapool. With the collapse of the Russian economy and the mackerel which the Klondykers caught and processed, they are a far rarer sight today.

Now the village is largely dependent on tourism. Numerous boats run trips to the Summer Isles or to view the extensive wildlife in the Minch, from seabirds to dolphins, porpoises and whales. There is plenty of holiday accommodation here, the provision of which is important to the local economy. Ullapool has become a centre for live traditional music thanks to the famous Ceilidh Place restaurant and music venue in the centre of the village.

Another attraction of Ullapool as a west coast residential area is that, with a fast road out of the village, Inverness can be reached in just under an hour, a short journey in Highland terms. www.ullapool.co.uk.

REASONS TO BUY A HOUSE IN THE HIGHLANDS

- Breathtaking scenery.
- North west Highlands least populated region of Europe.
- Inverness the fastest growing city in the UK.
- New job opportunities in Inverness area.
- Outdoor pursuits of all types.
- A real 'get away from it all' lifestyle possible.
- Popular tourist area.
- Slow pace of life.
- Lack of traffic congestion.
- Lack of pollution.
- Gaelic language and culture.
- University of the Highlands and Islands.
- Small, friendly communities.
- Low crime rate.
- Small schools.
- Great for children.
- Crofting.

Typical Properties for Sale

The traditional west Highlands house is a stone cottage, single storey, often with dormer windows in the roof, often white-painted. Many of the original ones had asbestos roofs, but these are now outlawed for health and safety reasons, so any which are renovated now must have the roof replaced. The modern alternative is plastic-coated corrugated metal, known as profile sheeting.

In the 1970s, there was a move to replace these old cottages, as they were substandard by modern requirements, being often damp and inadequately heated and insulted. Across the Highlands, the old cottages were abandoned while cheaply built wooden-framed kit houses, with white-rendered walls, were constructed in their place. Although warm and dry, many of these had little to recommend them aesthetically. Today, things have come full circle as the authorities try to encourage people to renovate old cottages rather than letting them fall into disrepair, and new houses tend to be designed in a far more traditional style, to echo the appearance of the original housing stock.

Highland Council planning regulations forbid the building of any two storey houses in crofting areas – all are either single storey or have the upstairs rooms set into the roof – classed as 1½ or 1¾ storey. They also normally require that the exterior of new houses should be painted white or off-white.

In the villages and towns, you will also find semi-detached and terraced houses and cottages, but again the more recent builds tend to be traditionally styled. On the east coast, older houses tend to be larger, stone townhouses, somewhat dour in appearance.

Flats are a rarity on the west coast, but there are a fair number in Inverness and some in the larger east coast towns such as Dingwall, Wick and Thurso. As elsewhere in Scotland these are a mixture of converted larger houses and more modern purpose-built flats. The central Scottish traditional tenement block is not seen this far north.

The population of Inverness has doubled in the last 30 years and is expected to double again in the next 30-50 years. Land will be needed to supply land for more than 10,000 houses by 2017, and these are most likely to be built along the A96 Inverness-Nairn road. A proposal was put forward in June 2005 to build a new town on the outskirts of the city at Tornagrain. In addition, a new village of 3,000 people has been proposed at the former Ardersier oil fabrication yard. However, after objections to the proposals, Highland Councillors back-pedalled somewhat to say that the new town was only one solution among several. Finding a solution to suit everybody is going to be a challenge for the future, there is no doubt.

Prices in Inverness have risen greatly over recent years, a direct result of its new city status. House-building has been going on apace in the Highland capital, and as luxury new homes on the outskirts of the city go up for sale at high prices, this has had a significant effect on average prices.

Elsewhere in the Highlands, prices have also risen fast. The increasing shortage of traditional properties on crofts, ideally beside a loch, means that when such properties do come on the market there is massive interest form buyers and they tend to sell for way over the asking price.

There have been well-publicised cases of 'silly money' being spent on some highland homes. Plockton, in particular, one of the prettiest villages on the west coast, has had a couple of recent cases where modest houses were sold for three times the 'offers over' prices, to people buying second homes. With 6,215 second or holiday homes in the Highlands, the highest total for any region of Scotland, and extremely high when seen in context of the resident population figures, this is an ongoing problem. Some communities have such a high proportion of such part-time homes, that outside the holiday season they become little more than ghost towns. This has grave implications for the continuing provision of local schools, where there are few resident families in the area, and local shops which find it uneconomic to stay open all year round.

As elsewhere in the country, this raises the same protests that local people are being priced out of the market, and the Highland Council are currently trying to address this by stepping up the building of affordable housing for rent or on shared ownership schemes.

In a reaction against the growing number of second or holiday homes in the Cairngorms National Park, at the time of writing, the national park authority is trying to restrict the sale of new-built housing to people who live, work or have family connections in the area. Final guidelines are to be drawn up in early 2007.

Sample Properties For Sale, October 2005

Location	Type	Description	Price
Craigellachie	Lodge house	10 bed, in 1.5 acres	Offers over £595,000
Tomich	Old brewery and cottage	Plus 2 building plots	Offers over £480,000
Newtonmore	Victorian house	4 bed with 1 bed annexe	Fixed price £350,000
Inverness	Detached house	Modern, 4 bed	Offers around £285,000
Inverness	Victorian conversion	3 bed	Offers over £159,000
Strathpeffer	Detached cottage	Modernised, 3 bed	Offers over £150,000
Skye	Cottage	3 bed	Offers over £120,000
Lochcarron	Semi-detached bungalow	3 bed	Offers over £85,000
Applecross	Croft house	Traditional, 2 bed	Offers over £128,000
Melvaig	Detached bungalow	In rural setting, 3 bed	Offers over £140,000
Lybster	Croft	With p.p. for a house	Offers over £30,000
Glenlivet	Former steading building	For conversion	Offers over £80,000

New Build Homes

Location	Type	Description	Price
Inverness	Houses	4 & 5 bed	From £210,995
Inverness	Retirement apartments	1 bed	From £98,450
Nairn	Houses	2-4 bed	From £130,995
Invergordon	Bungalows	2 bed	From £129,000
Muir of Ord	Houses	3 & 4 bed	From £189,000
Culloden	Semi-detached houses	2-4 bed	£137,950-£199,950

COUNCIL TAX CHARGES 2005-2006 (FOR A HOUSEHOLD OF 2 ADULTS)

Tax band	Highland	Scottish Average
Band A	£724.00	£729.39
Band B	£844.67	£850.96
Band C	£965.33	£972.52
Band D	£1,086.00	£1,094.09
Band E	£1,327.33	£1,337.22
Band F	£1,568.67	£1,580.35
Band G	£1,810.00	£1,823.48
Band H	£2,172.00	£2,188.18

WESTERN ISLES

GENERAL INFORMATION

Main Town: Stornoway.

Local Authority: Comhairle nan Eilean Siar/Western Isles Council, Council Offices, Sandwick Road, Stornoway, Isle of Lewis HS1 2BW; ☎ 01851-703773; fax 01851-705349; www.cne-siar.gov.uk.

Tourist Office: Western Isles, 26 Cromwell Street, Stornoway, Isle of Lewis HS1 2DD; ☎ 01851-703088; fax 01851-705244; www.witb.co.uk.

Police Force: Northern Constabulary, HQ, Old Perth Road, Inverness IV2 3SY; ☎ 01463-715555; fax 01463-230800; www.northern.police.uk.

Area: 3,071 sq. km.

Population: 26,502.

Population Density: 9 people per sq. km.

Airports: Stornoway Airport; Benbecula Airstrip; Barra Airstrip.

World Heritage Site: St. Kilda.

National Nature Reserves: Rona and Sula Sgeir; St Kilda; Monach Isles; Loch Druidibeg.

Estate Agents: Highland Solicitors' Property Centre, 30 Queensgate, Inverness IV1 1DA; ☎ 01463-231173; fax 01463-715292; www.hspc.co.uk.

The Western Isles is the current name for the Outer Hebrides, a 150 mile long chain of islands off the north western coast of Scotland. This is an area where the Gaelic language and culture is probably at its strongest, and in recognition of this fact, and to emphasise their traditional identity, the Western Isles Council now customarily uses its Gaelic name, *Comhairle nan Eilean Siar*. As many as 68% of the population of these islands speaks the Gaelic language, but this will nonetheless still be concentrated in the older age groups. English is also spoken by everybody, and this is the general language of daily communication.

There is a surprising mix of the traditional and the modern in the region – Stornoway on Lewis, the only large town in the region, is a busy modern town with all the amenities one would expect of a mainland town. The population of Stornoway and surrounding areas is 8,000, about 30% of the Western Isles population. The rest of the population lives in 280 communities scattered the length of the island chain.

The Western Isles are suffering a decline in population. The 2001 census figure of 26,502 people represents a fall of ten per cent since the previous census in 1991, when the population was 29,600. Although there is a general decline in the Scottish population, this is most marked in the Western Isles which has the fastest loss of population of all 32 council areas. This is a situation which is set to continue, as the region also has the oldest average age of population.

Transport around the islands is far easier than it once was, since European funds have allowed causeways and bridges to be built between various islands, meaning that Vatersay, Berneray, Scalpay and Eriskay are accessible by road and no longer dependent on ferry services. There are still ferry services operating to link all the islands, as well as ferries to the main islands from Oban, Ullapool and Skye. Flights from Glasgow, Edinburgh and Inverness land at Stornoway Airport. There are also tiny airports on Benbecula and Barra – famously, the only beach airport in the world with scheduled flights – which can be reached from Glasgow or via Stornoway.

Sunday observance is stronger in the Western Isles than in any other part of Scotland, so you will find that shops, pubs, restaurants and the like are closed on Sundays. There have been regular outcries over the years when it has been proposed to relax these laws, and to introduce Sunday ferry sailings and flights. Although there is now a restricted service on Sundays between some of the islands and the mainland, these are not universal so you always need to check if you are contemplating Sunday travel.

Geography & Climate

The Western Isles lie off the north-west coast at a distance from the mainland varying between 30 and 60 miles (48 and 97 km). In total, there are about 200 islands in the archipelago, but only 14 of these are inhabited. Because of its topography, the Outer Hebrides chain is sometimes known as 'the long island' despite the fact that there is a string of separate islands in the chain. The bridges and causeways now linking many of them, however, makes them feel far more like a single island than has ever been the case in the past. The aim eventually is to completely link all the islands in the chain in this way.

To confuse matters further, Harris and Lewis are actually a single island. Opinions are divided as to whether the convention of naming and treating them as separate land masses is because of a long-ago falling-out among the clans or simply topographical, due to the ridge of mountains which once made the southern end of the island (Harris) practically isolated from the larger northern end (Lewis).

Each island has its own distinct topography, and throughout the archipelago there is a range of landscapes, from mountainous areas to low-lying machair, glorious white sandy beaches along the Atlantic coast to the deeply indented coastline and myriad freshwater lochs of North Uist. 40 miles west of the main archipelago, the volcanic island of St Kilda, home only to wildlife and seabirds, has a dramatic and forbidding landscape.

The Western Isles are generally milder then the mainland western Highlands, their situation making them more strongly affected by the Gulf Stream and North Atlantic Drift. Their latitude means that they have long hours of summer daylight, with the sun setting after 11pm on the longest days of June.

Although they are not very wide, nonetheless the western coasts of the islands are appreciably wetter than the eastern coasts. Strong winds are normal with gales blowing on about 50 days per year. Snow occasionally falls but rarely lies for long.

WEATHER		
Annual averages	**Western Isles**	**Scotland**
Rainfall (mm)	1200	1099
Sunshine (hours)	1309	1228
Temperature max (°C)	13	11.3
Temperature min (°C)	5	6.7

Main Islands

Barra. At the southern end of the Western Isles, Barra is the smallest of the main islands, at just eight miles (13 km) long and four miles (6 km) wide. It has one road, about 12 miles long, which rings the island. From here one can reach the famous 'airport on the beach'. Its main town is Castlebay where most of the island's population of a little over 1,000 lives.

The greatest attraction of Barra is the island itself: tiny, remote and beautiful, its white sandy beaches, its grasslands – *machair* – with a huge variety of wildflowers, its seven trout lochs, all attract those in search of peace and quiet. www.isleofbarra.com.

Benbecula. Lying between North and South Uist, its name means 'mountain of the fords' in reference to the fords which originally linked it to the Uists. Today the fords have been replaced by road causeways. At only 409 feet (125m), Ruabhal, the island's single sizeable hill, isn't much of a mountain. The island, eight miles (13 km) west to east by five miles (7 km) north to south, is full of water features, including lochs and lochans surrounding small islands and inlets, shallow sandy bays and waterlogged *machair*.

Balivanich, the main settlement, is the most built-up area of the islands outside Stornoway. It is the administrative centre of the Uists. Benbecula, with a population of around 1,250, has an airport and a college which is now part of the University of the Highlands and Islands. www.undiscoveredscotland.co.uk/benbecula/benbecula.

Berneray. This tiny island, just three miles (5 km) long by 1 ½ miles (2 km) wide, has a population of around 140. It lies in the sound of Harris, from which island it can be reached by ferry, and there is a causeway linking it to North Uist. Having reached a population low in 1981, it has grown slightly since then, helped by the causeway which was opened in 1999.

The west side of the island is all but uninhabited, because of the large expanse of machair and a four mile long sweep of sand dunes rising to 50 feet high, edged by a stunning beach of white sands. www.isleofberberay.com.

Eriskay. North east of Barra, Eriskay's main claim to fame is that this is where, in 1941, the SS Politician sank, losing its cargo of whisky to the islanders which, a local legend immortalised in the Compton Mackenzie story, *Whisky Galore*. It is 2 ½ miles (4 km) by 1 ½ miles (2 km) and has a population of about 130.

Local industry consists of fishing, crofting and the characteristic local knitting which illustrates Eriskay's fishing lifestyle. Eriskay boasts its own ancient breed of pony, believed to be the last surviving remnant of the original native ponies of the Western Isles. By the 1970s there were only 20 left, but now, through a process of conservation, the worldwide population of Eriskays is around 300.

A causeway links the island to South Uist. There is also a ferry service to Barra. www.w-isles.gov.uk/eriskay/eriskay.htm.

Harris. In truth not a separate island, Harris occupies the southern end of the land-mass which has Lewis in its north. The land between the two 'islands' is deeply in-dented on the west by Loch Resort and on the east by Loch Seaforth. In between the two, there is a mountainous stretch which effectively separates Harris from Lewis, hence they are treated as two distinct island communities.

The population of Harris is just under 2,000 and its main settlement is Tarbert. Ferry services run from here to Uig in Skye and Lochmaddy in North Uist. It is a land of contrasts: the west has beautiful white beaches while the treeless and rugged east and north coast has been likened to a lunar landscape – although the numerous lochs rather weaken the comparison with the moon! www.undiscoveredscotland. co.uk/harris/harris.

Lewis. The largest of the Western Isles, Lewis occupies the northern two-thirds of the main landmass. It has a population of 18,000, with around 6,000 living in Storno-way, the main town. Its name comes from the Gaelic *leodhas* meaning marshy, very descriptive of this low-lying landscape. As a result, there are large areas of peat which the islanders traditionally used for fuel, and some still use it in this way today. It is as treeless as Harris, due to the original trees being cut down and burned generations ago. Trees have been replanted over recent years, and they are now becoming re-established in a number of areas.

Stornoway has the largest natural harbour in the Western Isles, which explains why this grew into the principal town of the region. The Western Isles council is based here, as is Stornoway Airport, which has regular flights to Inverness, Glasgow and Edinburgh as well as to Barra and Benbecula. A car ferry service links Lewis with the mainland at Ullapool.

The fishing industry has always been important to Stornoway, and it reached its height during the herring boom of the 1800s. But the harbour is still kept busy today with a fairly large fishing fleet, as well as leisure and ferry traffic. www.isle-of-lewis.com.

North Uist. This island is 12 miles long and 18 miles wide, with a population of 1,600. The main road, the A865, links together North Uist, Benbecula and South Uist, by means of causeways and bridges. The main village is Lochmaddy, where car ferries run to Tarbert in Harris and Uig in Skye.

There are many archaeological remains on the island and, in part due to the thousands of freshwater lochs which cover the island, it is also a great place for birdwatching. The Monach islands, which lie five miles (8 km) west of North Uist, have a huge seal colony where as many as 9,000 grey seal pups are born each year. www.undiscoveredscotland/northuist/northuist.

South Uist. The second largest of the Western Isles, South Uist is 22 miles (35 km) long and seven miles (11 km) wide and has a population of nearly 2,000. The west coast is stunning, with 20 miles of white shell beaches running the entire length. The *machair* and sand dunes running alongside are home to a vast array of wild flowers and wildlife including corncrakes and otters.

The traditional Hebridean lifestyle remains strong here, with peat cutting, wool dying and seaweed gathering still continuing today. Gaelic culture thrives here – the island has produced many famous pipers, in particular. The main town and ferry port for the island is Lochboisdale, which runs services to Oban on the mainland and Castlebay in Barra. Once a busy herring port, it now earns more from tourism.

The beautiful uninhabited island of Eriskay, of Whisky Galore fame, is accessible by a causeway from South Uist. www.undiscoveredscotland.co.uk/southuist/southuist.

History

The Hebrides have been inhabited way back to ancient times, and there are many archaeological remains throughout the islands. Of these, the most famous are the Neolithic 'Callanish Stones' in Lewis. These pre-date the Egyptian pyramids. Barra too has a wealth of archaeological remains, with evidence of occupation dating from the Neolithic period, through the Bronze and Iron Ages, the years of Viking occupation, the medieval period and up to the present day.

The Scandinavian influence in the islands can be seen in many of the place-names which derive from Old Norse.

As in the Highlands, the Outer Hebrides were greatly affected by the Clearances, where residents were forcibly removed off their land by greedy lairds, often from England, who found there would be a better return on their investment from sheep than people. Some of the islands which are now uninhabited once supported viable communities.

Despite, or perhaps because of this, great efforts are made today to ensue that the Gaelic culture and heritage is kept alive. It is seen here in its most undiluted form, and it is to be hoped that the islands' isolation from the mainland will help to keep the Gaidhealtachd viable in a living form, rather than being kept on artificial life support.

REASONS TO BUY A HOUSE IN THE WESTERN ISLES

- Quiet, peaceful island lifestyle.
- Beautiful wild landscape.
- Glorious white beaches.
- Sailing and other maritime pursuits.
- Wildlife.
- Crofting.
- Low population.
- Traditional way of life.
- Gaelic music and culture.
- Remoteness.
- Lack of pollution.
- Slow pace of life.
- Low crime rate.
- Low average house price.

Typical Properties for Sale

Housing in the Western Isles is very similar to that found in the western Highlands. The crofting lifestyle means that the same situation applies regarding traditional stone croft houses and the modern timber-framed replacements.

The housing, and general appearance of Stornoway, the capital of the Western Isles, is similar to a west coast town such as Ullapool, with a mixture of traditional and newer detached, semi-detached and terraced houses.

The islands' relative inaccessibility compared with mainland Highlands mean that the problem of homes being bought by incomers for holiday and second homes is less acute. The bigger problem is keeping the population of the smaller islands at a viable level. This has similar implications for communities here as for Highland communities with high levels of absentee property ownership, as the low permanent population makes local services including shops, schools and petrol stations uneconomic to run.

Sample Properties For Sale, October 2005

Location	Type	Description	Price
Lewis	Mansion house	In 4 acres of land	Offers over £375,000
Lewis	House	5 bed, with 1 bed flat	Offers over £125,000
Scalpay	Detached house	4 bed	Fixed price £128,00
Lewis	Detached house	3 bed	£115,000
South Uist	Bungalow	6 bed	£180,000
North Uist	Detached house	4 bed	Offers over £120,000
Harris	Detached house	4 bed	Offers over £110,000
Lewis	Bungalow	2 bed	Offers over £352,000
Harris	Building plot	¼ acre	Offers over £40,000
Lewis	Derelict cottage	On ¼ acre site	Offers over £25,000

NEW BUILD HOMES

Most new builds are 'one-offs' built for individual clients, so no prices are available.

COUNCIL TAX CHARGES 2005-2006 (FOR A HOUSEHOLD OF 2 ADULTS)

Tax band	Eilean Siar	Scottish Average
Band A	£637.33	£729.39
Band B	£743.56	£850.96
Band C	£849.78	£972.52
Band D	£956.00	£1,094.09
Band E	£1,168.44	£1,337.22
Band F	£1,380.89	£1,580.35
Band G	£1,593.33	£1,823.48
Band H	£1,912.00	£2,188.18

ORKNEY

GENERAL INFORMATION

Main Town: Kirkwall.

Local Authority: Orkney Islands Council, Council Offices, School Place, Kirkwall, Orkney KW15 1NY; ☎ 01856-873535; fax 01856-874615; www.orkney.com.

Tourist Office: 6 Broad Street, Kirkwell, Orkney KW15 1NX; ☎ 01856-872856; fax 01856-875056; www.visitorkney.com.

Police Force: Northern Constabulary, HQ, Old Perth Road, Inverness IV2 3SY; ☎ 01463-715555; fax 01463-230800; www.northern.police.uk.

Area: 990 sq. km.

Population: 19,245.

Population Density: 19 people per sq. km.

World Heritage Site: The Heart of Neolithic Orkney.

National Scenic Area: Bay of Skaill.

Airports: Kirkwall Airport; Airstrips at Eday, North Ronaldsay, Sanday, Stronsay, Westray, Papa Westray.

Estate Agents: Lows Orkney, 5 Broad Street, Kirkwall, Orkney, KW15 1DJ, 01856-873151; www.lowsorkney.co.uk.

Although the southernmost tip of the Orkney Islands lies only about six miles (10 km) off the north coast of Scotland, the residents do not generally think of themselves as Scottish; and although for many years the islands were owned by Norway, neither do they think of themselves as Scandinavian. Their mixture of cultures makes them in their eyes unique, and they prefer to class themselves as Orcadian above all else.

Depending on which source you go to, there are anywhere between 67 and 90 islands in the Orkneys – the larger number including, presumably, all the smallest islets to be found. Of these, only about 20 are inhabited. The islands are divided into three areas, the North Isles, the South Isles and, in the centre, the largest island called Mainland – another snub to Scotland, specifically not thought of as the mainland by the Orcadians! Mainland is itself divided into East Mainland and West Mainland.

There is a comprehensive network of ferries from the Scottish mainland and inter-island. There are also flights to Kirkwall Airport from Aberdeen, Edinburgh and Glasgow. Inter-island flights are operated by Loganair, who fly between Mainland, Eday, North Ronaldsay, Sanday, Stronsay, Westray and Papa Westray, including the shortest scheduled air route in the world, between Westray and Papa Westray, with a flight time of just 1.5 minutes when the wind is favourable.

Orkney is renowned for its history, ancient and modern, with 1,000 excavated archaeological sites and many more as yet unexplored, together with historic sites dating from the Second World War when Scapa Flow was used as a major naval base and Italian prisoners of war were set to work building causeways between the eastern isles. It is also notable for its wildlife, particularly its birds. Incredibly, one in six of all seabirds breeding in Britain nests in Orkney.

The population of Orkney is in decline – it fell by 1.87% between the census years of 1991 and 2001. However, this is a less severe fall than in Shetland (which has decreased by 2.37%) and the Western Isles (a fall of 10.47%.) In Orkney the overall figure disguises a 1.39% rise of population on Mainland, while all the smaller islands have shown population decline.

The dialect spoken in Orkney shows the influence of the old Norse settlers. There are many similarities with Norn, an ancient Scandinavian language, and these, together with other words introduced from southern Scots, have been absorbed into the day to day English spoken in the islands. Gaelic has never been one of the indigenous tongues of the islands.

Geography & Climate

Orkney lies at the confluence of the Atlantic Ocean and the North Sea. Nearer to the Arctic Circle than to London, the islands do truly feel remote. Due west of Orkney, the first land you would reach is Labrador in Canada, some 2,000 miles distant. There are a number of strong rip tides in the Pentland Firth, where the Atlantic and the North Sea meet, so sea travel to the islands can be bumpy.

The highest point of the Orkney Islands is Ward Hill on the Isle of Hoy, which reaches a height of 1,571 feet (479 m). More famous and impressive is the Old Man of Hoy, a rock pillar towering out of the sea up to 450 feet (137m).

Generally, the landscape of the islands comprises undulating hills with no true rivers, but many small burns, lochs and lochans. The islands are practically treeless, due to wholesale use of the indigenous trees for firewood many centuries ago. The strong winds from the west have prevented natural regeneration of the woodland, but trees are grown where protection is provided from the wind and grazing animals. The uplands are mainly heather moorland and extensive peatlands.

The weather is at least as changeable as the Highlands. As can be seen from the figures below, there is not a great deal of variation between summer and winter. Snow and frost are very rare.

WEATHER		
Annual averages	**Orkney**	**Scotland**
Rainfall (mm)	983	1099
Sunshine (hours)	1160	1228
Temperature max (°C)	10.4	11.3
Temperature min (°C)	4.8	6.7

Main Islands

Flotta. This island, whose self-descriptive name means 'flat', lies in the mouth of Scapa Flow, and is notable mostly for its industrial heritage rather than any intrinsic beauty. It came to prominence during the second world war when the Scapa Flow naval base was set up. It declined after the war, but came into its own again in 1974 when an oil terminal was constructed. This takes up much of the northern side of the island and about ten per cent of UK oil production is pumped into tankers here for transport across the world. It provides several hundred jobs.

Flotta's population has declined dramatically over the past decade – in 2001 it was 81, a fall of over 35 percent on the 1991 figure of 126. Most of the oil terminal employees commute from Mainland. www.undiscoveredscotland.co.uk/flotta/flotta.

Hoy. The second largest of the Orkney islands, Hoy is ten miles long and five miles wide. It has the highest, most rugged terrain of all the islands and thus is very popular with walkers. The Old Man of Hoy is Orkney's most famous landmark. It sits on the north-west coast near Rackwick, where it rises 450 feet out of the sea. It was first climbed as recently as 1966 and is now a challenge to experienced climbers. The 1000 ft (300 m) St John's Head, another natural feature of the island, was only climbed in 1970. Hoy has the highest point of the Orkneys, Ward Hill, which reaches 1,571 feet (479 m), hence its Norse name which means 'high island'.

The main settlement is on the east of the island at Lyness, where most of the 392 population live. This 2001 figure is again a significant decrease on the 1991 population of 477. The island was once home to many military personnel from Scapa Flow, and today many of the wartime buildings they left behind can still be seen. Tourism, centred on the Scapa Flow Visitor Centre, and the island's natural features, is very important for the economy of the island today. www.undiscoveredscotland.co.uk/hoy/hoy.

Mainland. The biggest island of the Orkneys, Mainland is sometimes known as Pomona. 26 miles long, it is divided by a narrow neck of land into West Mainland and East Mainland. It has a population of around 15,300, which shows an increase of 200 people on the 1991 figure.

Orkney's main town of Kirkwall lies at the centrepoint between East and West Mainland, and about half of the mainland population live here. It is a busy and attractive town in the main, particularly in the centre where most of its oldest buildings, some dating from the seventeenth century, are to be found. Ferries for the northern isles run from Kirkwall, while ferries for the southern isles and the mainland of Scotland run from Stromness on the south west of the island. This too retains much of its medieval heritage and has a maze of narrow passages and roads running off its main street, where pedestrians and car drivers carry on the local sport of dodging one another! Most of the houses along the shore have their own private wharves, demonstrating the importance of the sea to these island residents.

The sea has always been, and continues to be, the focus of life in Mainland. Its two main harbours are the lifeblood of the Orkneys, with regular ferries bringing supplies and transporting the people between the surrounding islands as well as to and from the Scottish mainland. As many as 70 cruise ships call into Kirkwall Harbour every year, bringing tourist money with them. www.orkneyjar.com.

North Ronaldsay. The northernmost of the Orkneys, its distance from Mainland has brought about a measure of cultural isolation on the island. At only four miles (6 km) long by two miles (3 km) wide, it now has a population of only around 70 hardy souls. Beyond the island there is open sea as far as Shetland and Norway . They were the last to give up their use of the Old Norse language, and today their dialect includes many words which are more intelligible to Scandinavians than to Scots. Another factor which has kept the island in its idiosyncratic cocoon is the fact that electricity was not available on the island until 1983.

Farming is the main activity, with beef cattle being kept on the crofts and the 2,000 sheep, outnumbering the inhabitants many times over, continue to be kept, as they have historically, on the beach. They are prevented by a high wall from coming inland except during the lambing season, so their diet is almost entirely of seaweed to which they have adapted over the centuries. These sheep are renowned for their fleeces which are spun into high quality yarn. www.visitorkney.com/island.htm.

Sanday. The largest of the northern Orkney isles, Sanday is about 16 miles (24 km) long and had, in 2001, a population of 478, a fall of over 10 per cent from a decade before. The main employment of the islanders is farming, in particular sheep and cattle production. One of Orkney's most fertile islands, settlers have been attracted here since prehistoric times. The archaeological record here is probably more impressive than any other of the islands, with literally hundreds of tombs and other sites to be investigated.

The island also boasts an airfield, a golf club and a light railway, in addition to a good range of shops and services. For detailed information on all aspects of Sanday you can't do better than browse the excellent website www.sanday.co.uk.

South Ronaldsay. This is the southernmost, and largest, of the chain of islands linked by the Churchill Barriers to the south of Mainland. It has a population of 854, a fall of over nine per cent in the last decade. Its main village is St Margaret's Hope, once a fishing station. It now has a ferry terminal for the one hour crossing to the Scottish mainland at Gills Bay near John o' Groats. www.undiscoveredscotland.co.uk/eastmainland/eastmainland.

Stronsay. Lying to the north east of Shapinsay, Stronsay is about seven miles (12 km) long by six miles (10 km) wide. It has a population of 358, compared with the 382 recorded on census night in 1991. Its deeply indented outline is caused by the three large bays which cut into it, St Catherine's Bay, the Bay of Holland and Mill Bay. It is surrounded by many small islets and has a dramatic rock arch, big enough for fishing boats to sail under, on its east coast. These all make for spectacular seaward views from the island.

Most employment is in agriculture and fishing, as well as local services. Work has also been provided by the ongoing construction of a new monastery on neighbouring Papa Stronsay, on the site of the most northerly early Christian monastery ever found, dating from 700 years ago. www.stronsay.co.uk.

Westray. Although not the largest of the north isles, at 12 miles (19km) long by four miles (6 km) wide, Westray has the largest population, 358 at last count (a drop of six per cent in a decade.) It can support this number of people through its beef cattle farming and its thriving fishing fleet. It has the largest white fish fleet in Orkney and there is also significant crab and lobster fishing.

Its largest settlement is Pierowall, which grew up around the harbour which the Vikings used as an anchorage. Archaeological evidence of their presence abounds here as elsewhere in the Orkney islands. Most of the population live around Pierowall, and the village has a school and a swimming pool as well as two shops and a post office. www.westraypapawestray.com.

History

The remarkable number of archaeological sites throughout the Orkneys has brought it the accolade of a World Heritage Site centred on West Mainland, with a collection of excavated and unexcavated monuments and other sites dating from 2000-3000 years BC. *The Heart of Neolithic Orkney*, as the World Heritage Site is named, is a recognition of the great importance of these sites as testimony to the remarkable cultural achievements of the Neolithic peoples of northern Europe.

Although Orkney seems a remote outpost of Europe today, 1,000 years ago, just as in prehistoric times, the sea was the easiest way of moving around the region, and the Orkney archipelago was at the centre of a Norse seafaring empire which linked Scandinavia, Iceland, Shetland, The Western Isles, Argyll, Ireland and the Isle of Man. Orkney lay at the geographical centre of all this, and Kirkwall was very important in that era. Thanks to the legacy of the Norse seafarers, there are common cultural elements to be discerned in all these regions.

Orkney was ruled by Norway from the ninth century, when the islands were first settled by the Norsemen. It wasn't until 1468 that James III annexed Orkney for Scotland in payment of a debt. To this day the Norwegians have never formally recognised Orkney as part of Scotland.

REASONS TO BUY A HOUSE ON ORKNEY

- Unique Orcadian culture.
- Historic and prehistoric sites.
- A World Heritage Site.
- Fishing and farming.
- Back to nature lifestyle.
- Isolation for those who want it.
- Small friendly communities.
- Bird watching.
- Unique wild landscape.
- Sailing.
- Very low crime rate.
- Relaxed way of life.
- Low average house price.

Typical Properties for Sale

There are two distinct styles of architecture in Orkney, not surprisingly stemming respectively from Scandinavia and the Highlands.

Towns such as Kirkwall and Stromness have a distinctly Scandinavian feel. Here one finds tall, often narrow, stone-built houses with two or three floors – bigger buildings such as the Stromness Hotel have four floors – with steeply pitched roofs. A characterises of this style of house is the stepped gable, often end-on to the street. Many of these houses retain the natural stone while others are brightly painted.

These houses line narrow, sometimes flagstoned, winding alleys, giving the town a somewhat crowded feeling, as if the houses huddle together against the sometime harsh conditions out to sea. This is both attractive and also distinctly unlike mainland Scotland.

Elsewhere, outside the towns, traditional style crofters' cottages dot the landscape, some renovated, others crying out for tender loving care. Converted steadings are as popular here as in the highlands. More modern houses follow the Highland style – white-painted, timber-framed, 1 ½ storey with dormers.

With comparative house prices on Orkney well below the natioanl average, there are still bargains to be had here, and there seems to be plenty of property to renovate and land for sale. However, alongside these are modernised, renovated and upgraded properties selling at high prices equivalent to those found on the mainland.

Sample Properties For Sale, October 2005

Location	Type	Description	Price
Kirkwall	Semi-detached houses	3 bed	£85,000
Westray	Small hotel	6 bed	Offers over £300,000
South Ronaldsay	Cottage	2 bed	Offers over £119,000
Birsay	Detached stone house	2 bed	Offers over £64,000
Kirkwall	Detached house	2 bed	Offers over £45,000
Stronsay	Cottage	2 bed	Offers over £69,000
St Margaret's Hope	Building land	7 acres	£250,000
Hoy	Plot	For building	Offers over £20,000

New Build Homes

Location	Type	Description	Price
Kirkwall	Bungalows	2 bed	From £39,500
Kirkwall	Houses	3 bed	£43,500

Most new builds are 'one-offs' built for individual clients, so few prices are available.

COUNCIL TAX CHARGES 2005-2006 (FOR A HOUSEHOLD OF 2 ADULTS)

Tax band	Orkney Islands	Scottish Average
Band A	£648.67	£729.39
Band B	£756.78	£850.96
Band C	£864.89	£972.52
Band D	£973.00	£1,094.09
Band E	£1,189.22	£1,337.22
Band F	£1,405.44	£1,580.35
Band G	£1,621.67	£1,823.48
Band H	£1,946.00	£2,188.18

SHETLAND

GENERAL INFORMATION

Main Town: Lerwick.

Local Authority: Shetland Islands Council, Town Hall, Hillhead, Lerwick, Shetland ZE1 0HB; ☎ 01595-693535; fax 01595-744509; www.shetland.gov.uk.

Tourist Office: Market Cross, Lerwick, Shetland ZE1 0LU; ☎ 01595-693434; fax 01595-695807; www.shetland-tourism.co.uk.

Police Force: Northern Constabulary, HQ, Old Perth Road, Inverness IV2 3SY; ☎ 01463-715555; fax 01463-230800; www.northern.police.uk.

Area: 1,466 sq. km.

Population: 21,988.

Population Density: 15 people per sq. km.

Airports: Lerwick/Tingwall Airport; Sumburgh Airport; Fair Isle Airport; Foula Airport.

National Nature Reserves: Hermaness; Keen of Hamar; Noss.

Estate Agents: Tait & Peterson, Bank of Scotland Buildings, Lerwick, Shetland, ZE1 0EB; ☎ 01595-693010; www.tait-peterson.co.uk.

More than the other island groups, Shetland is remote both geographically and culturally from the rest of Scotland. It lies about 95 miles (150 km) north east of the Scottish mainland, and 50 miles (80 km) north east of Orkney. Equidistant between Scotland, Norway and the Faroe Islands, it shows more cultural influence from the North Sea countries which originally colonised Shetland than from Scotland which only gained sovereignty over the archipelago in the 15th century.

Shetland, in the past sometimes known as Zetland (hence the 'ZE' postcodes and companies such as 'zetnet'), takes its name from the Norse name for the islands, Hjaltland.

As in Orkney, when Shetlanders refer to the Mainland, they mean the largest island of the group rather than the Scottish mainland. In total there are about 100 islands and islets in Shetland, only 14 of which are now inhabited, and with most of the 22,000 population living on Mainland.

The sea is, of course, of great importance to Shetland life and economy. The various waves of settlers, going back over 5,000 years, arrived by boat and fishing was essential to their survival. It is still important to the Shetland economy, but since the 1970s, another treasure of the North Sea, oil, has given the islands an economic boost. Much of the oil extracted from the sea bed is pumped to the Sullom Voe oil terminal on Mainland for transfer to tankers and thence across the world.

Transport links are good throughout Shetland, with an efficient system of ferries linking the islands with one another and with Aberdeen, Kirkwall, Faroe, Iceland and Scandinavia. Sumburgh Airport at the southern tip of Mainland has scheduled services to a wide number of destinations. The road network too is good, its fast, well-maintained roads running the length of the main islands with convenient ferry links making for efficient car travel from one end of the chain to the other.

The population of Shetland has fallen by 2.37 per cent between 1991 and 2001, and as with the rest of Scotland, the overall trend is for continued decline unless unforeseen circumstances reverse the trend.

The local dialect shows the strong influence of the ancient 'Norn' language of the North Sea countries including Norway, Denmark, Shetland, Faroe and Iceland. Shetland has its own versions of words heard in Orkney, plus others which are confined to these furthest northern isles. In particular, it perhaps should come as no surprise that the Shetlanders have a large array of words for describing different types of rain!

Geography & Climate

It is difficult to get a real 'feel' for just how far north Shetland is, because maps of Scotland nearly always show the islands re-sited in a box in the top right-hand corner. Lerwick, the main town, is actually as far north of London as Milan is south of the English capital. It is also further north than Moscow and southern Greenland, and nearer to Bergen in Norway than to Aberdeen. Little wonder then, that Shetlanders do not think of themselves as Scottish.

Shetland is a long straggling archipelago of over 100 islands and islets, over 70 miles (113 km) from Sumburgh Head at the southern tip of Mainland, to Muckle Flugga which is no more than a rock sitting to the north of Unst. The most northerly point of the British Isles, it was originally known as North Unst, but its name was changed to Muckle Flugga in 1964. It is the site of the most northerly lighthouse in Britain.

Shetland has a land area of 567 square miles (1466 sq km) and a coastline of 900 miles (1449 km). Characterised by long thin islands, lying generally south west to north east, nowhere on Shetland is more than three miles (5 km) from the sea. Another characteristic of the islands is that they are highly indented with inlets and bays – lots of 'crinkly bits' as Slartibartfast of Hitchhikers Guide to the Galaxy would say! The large fjord-like sea lochs which cut into the landmass are known by the Shetland term 'voes' – hence Sullom Voe, where the oil terminal is sited.

Shetland has no particularly high mountains – the highest point is Ronas Hill on North Mainland, which reaches 1,477 feet (450 m). It does, however, have some spectacular sea cliffs – Kame of Foula has a sheer drop to the sea of 1,220 feet (372 m) – in addition to a plethora of stacks and sea arches, caves and tunnels, all formed over the centuries by the might of the ocean at this meeting point of the North Sea, the Atlantic Ocean and the Norwegian Sea. In total there are about 400 km of cliffs, home to the most spectacular colonies of breeding seabirds in Europe, with more than one million birds of 22 different species.

Shetland is closer to the Arctic Circle than to Manchester, so it is not surprising that the climate is harsher than the rest of Scotland. However, the Gulf Stream does its important job of keeping the climate comparatively mild compared with, say, Moscow which is further south but far colder. Thanks to its northerly latitude, summer days are long – in June the sun sets for no more than five hours, and even then there is only a twilight rather than true darkness. It is, allegedly, possible to play golf at midnight at this time of year! Conversely, in December daylight hours get as short as six hours.

Shetland has more than its share of strong winds, and holds the UK record with a gust of 194 mph (312 km/h) in 1992.

WEATHER		
Annual averages	Shetland	Scotland
Rainfall (mm)	1177	1099
Sunshine (hours)	1056	1228
Temperature max (°C)	9.2	11.3
Temperature min (°C)	4.7	6.7

Main Islands

Bressay. This island sits opposite Lerwick, providing shelter for the harbour. It is seven miles (11 km) long by three miles (8 km) wide and has a population of 384, which is that rare thing, an increase in inhabitants of about nine per cent on the 1991 figure.

Bressay Sound has for centuries been a place of refuge for ships from bad weather. From the summit of Ward Hill, the highest point of the island, the whole of Shetland can be seen, weather permitting.

Much of the island can be explored by car on the single track roads, but to get to the remoter parts, you need to go on foot. Bressay is full of wildlife, from seabirds including puffins and skua, to seals and otters, through to the more mundane rabbits, hedgehogs and, of course, the ubiquitous sheep, introduced from the mainland. www.visitshetland.com/bressay.

Fair Isle. The southernmost of the Shetland Islands, Fair Isle is somewhat out on a limb, being 25 miles south of Sumburgh Head and midway between Orkney and Shetland. This makes it one of the most isolated inhabited islands in Britain. It has a population of 69, a tiny increase on that recorded a decade earlier. Interestingly, Fair Isle has the highest percentage of young residents of any of the Scottish islands apart from Vatersay in the Western Isles, with 29% of the population being under 16. One wonders if the isolation of the islanders has something to do with high breeding figures!

The name is known mainly in connection with knitting and the BBC Shipping Forecast, but it is important also for environmental reasons. The island is owned by the National Trust for Scotland and the community is involved in pioneering projects involving wildlife tourism, windpower and sustainable management of the environment. www.fairisle.org.uk.

Mainland. The largest island in Shetland, Mainland has a population of about 22,000. About 7,500 of the residents live in Lerwick, the capital, with nearly half the population living within ten miles of the town. The island is indented by long voes (inlets) making it distinctive and somewhat 'straggly' in shape.

Lerwick lies on the east coast, opposite Bressay which shelters the natural harbour which made Lerwick the historic focal point of Shetland. This was an important point on the Dutch and Scandinavian trading routes. The Norsemen are known to have gathered a large fleet here in the 13th century, and later the Dutch fishing fleet gathered in Bressay Sound outside the harbour, to catch herring, as this was on the migration route of the fish. Shetlanders would trade with the Dutch when they arrived, setting up a shanty town along the shore. This became an annual festival involving much drunkenness and misbehaviour.

Today Lerwick, the most northerly town in the British Isles, is a busy port and ferry terminal, as well as having all the other services expected of a much larger town elsewhere in Scotland. Alongside the working boats there are many yachts and other pleasure craft. The town also retains much of its historic charm with many buildings dating from the 18th century and earlier.

In the past, fishing and crofting were the main industries on Mainland, but today crofting is largely a part-time activity, as it is elsewhere in the Highlands. The oil terminal at Sullom Voe provides much employment, as does the provision of transport, including two airports, at Sumburgh and Lerwick, and numerous ferry services. Tourism is another important source of income and employment, as is the Shetland Islands Council which has its administrative centre in Lerwick. www.visitshetland.com/lerwick.

Muckle Roe. This island, whose name, despite its small size, means 'big red island', is situated in St Magnus bay on the west of Mainland, to which it is linked by a road bridge, built in 1905. The population is just over one hundred, most of whom are involved in crofting. www.visitshetland.com/west – mainland.

Papa Stour. Also to the west of Mainland, Papa Stour gets its name, meaning 'big island of priests' from the religious community of the Celtic Church who inhabited the island in the 6th and 7th centuries. Today it has a tiny population of about 24, who are mainly involved in crofting and tourism.

The island is now a Site of Special Scientific Interest because of its bird breeding grounds and its shoreline of numerous caves, tunnels, stacks and sea arches. It has no shop but does have a Post Office. The island only got mains electricity about ten years ago. reachedwww.users.zetnet.co.uk/papa-stour.

Unst. The most northerly of the inhabited islands, Unst is 12 miles (19 km) long by five miles (8 km) wide and supports a community of about 700, a fall from the 1,000 plus who lived there a decade ago. It boasts 'Britain's most northerly' in all sorts of areas, but the main claim to fame is probably that it has the most northerly brewery, whose name 'Valhalla Brewery' makes reference to the many Scandinavian connections and relics on this island.

The main settlement is Baltasound, where there is a harbour, shops, marina and also a leisure centre including a heated swimming pool. The island is noted for its Shetland ponies which run as free as they did in the past. Naturalists and geologists are attracted to the wealth of natural marvels on the island, as are scuba divers who dive the many wrecks which litter the seabed. www.unst.org.

Whalsay. To the east of Mainland, Whalsay means 'island of whales' so it's worth keeping a close look-out when crossing to the island. It is only five miles (8 km) by two miles (3 km) but has a healthy population of just over 1,000, a figure which has stayed static over the past decade, and has risen since the 1931 figure of 900. The island is at the centre of Shetland's fishing industry, which provides many jobs on the island.

The main settlement is Symbister, which is where the ferry from Laxo (near Lerwick) docks. This is the main port for some of the most modern fishing vessels in Europe. Fishing is a major earner for the island, and has made Whalsay home to most of Shetland's millionaires, apparently. Some of them can doubtless be found on the most northerly golf course in the British Isles which is on the island. http://www.visitshetland.com/whalsay.

Yell. The second largest island in Shetland, Yell is 17 miles (27 km) long and five miles (8 km) wide. It has, however, a smaller population than tiny Whalsay, at around 950. Much of the population is involved in fishing, crofting, tourism and wildlife-connected activities. Yell is known as the otter capital of Britain, because this is one of the best places to spot them. The island is also popular with birdwatchers and walkers. www.visitshetland.com/yell.

A POPULAR RETIREMENT PLACE

Shetland was voted seventh top retirement location by a UK magazine aimed at the over-fifties. It was the only Scottish location to make it into the top ten. It scored highly on a range of factors including houses prices, average hospital waiting times, crime rates, council tax, things to do, beauty spots, the landscape and the weather.

REASONS TO BUY A HOUSE IN SHETLAND

- Unique Shetland culture.
- The most northerly part of the UK.
- Remote island lifestyle.

- Exceptionally long summer days.
- Prehistoric sites.
- Transport links to Scandinavia, Faroe and Iceland.
- Nowhere more than three miles from the sea.
- Fishing and crofting.
- *Up Helly Aa* Viking Festival.
- Bird watching.
- Remoteness and isolation.
- Wildlife tourism.
- Low property prices.
- Low crime rate.

Typical Properties for Sale

Once known as 'Venice of the north', it is impossible to miss the importance of the sea to Lerwick.

The Lodberry, which originally described a flat rock that could be used as a natural landing place, became the foundation for the 18th century merchant's houses and stores along the waterfront at Lerwick, providing boats with access to unload directly into a merchant's courtyard. These buildings appear to be sitting in the water. The word has since become a generic term for this type of building. Lerwick's waterfront has changed in recent years, with much new building, but the Lodberry has remained virtually unscathed and is 'A' listed by Historic Scotland.

Lerwick Commercial Street is very attractive, with turreted buildings, fairytale castle style, which give it a Germanic more than a Scottish look. Similar to the architecture of Kirkwall, the traditional stone buildings of Lerwick are closely-packed tall houses with prominent gables.

In the more rural areas, the traditional houses are, in the main, stone built fishermen's and crofters cottages. There are larger houses here and there, often now operating as hotels and guest houses. There is also the normal mix of modern properties as found in the Highlands.

Sample Properties For Sale, October 2005			
Location	Type	Description	Price
Lerwick	Detached house	5 bed	Offers over £155,00
Lerwick	Flat	2 bed, modern	Offers over £90,000
Lerwick	Building plot	With derelict cottage	Offers over £150,000
Voe	Detached house	5 bed	Offers over £120,000
Gott	Detached cottage	2 bed	Offers over £70,000

Scalloway	Cottage	2 bed	Offers over £75,000
Sandwick	Stone cottage	Traditional, 2 bed	Offers over £350,000
Walls	Bakery	For conversion	Offers over £85,000

New Build Homes			
Location	**Type**	**Description**	**Price**
Scalloway	Detached houses	4 bed	£135,000-£147,000
East Voe	Detached houses	5 bed	£180,000
Scalloway	Semi-detached houses	2 bed	£85,000-£97,000

COUNCIL TAX CHARGES 2005-2006 (FOR A HOUSEHOLD OF 2 ADULTS)		
Tax band	**Shetland Islands**	**Scottish Average**
Band A	£654.00	£729.39
Band B	£763.00	£850.96
Band C	£872.00	£972.52
Band D	£981.00	£1,094.09
Band E	£1,199.00	£1,337.22
Band F	£1,417.00	£1,580.35
Band G	£1,635.00	£1,823.48
Band H	£1,962.00	£2,188.18

RETIREMENT

Location

Let's face it, nobody moves to Scotland for the weather. The image of people moving to warmer climes when they retire, for the sake of their health, doesn't apply to Scotland. But there are nonetheless a large number of people, generally from elsewhere in the UK, who do yearn to retire to Scotland, away from the noise, bustle and high crime rates of the towns and cities they have lived in all their lives.

For this reason, the rural areas of Scotland are the most popular destination for retired people. More often than not, after many years of holidaying in Scotland, they are finally free to move permanently, with the wherewithal to buy a nice property, having sold up further south.

Some incomers have planned their retirement for years, buying a second home in Scotland for their holidays many years before they retire, with the long-term plan of making it their main home once they have finished working for a living.

Sadly, some people find that, although their rural retreat was great for holidays while they were still fit and active, in their later years, when they may suffer from mobility and health problems, it is less than ideal. The very peace, quiet and slower pace of life which attracted them are accompanied by a number of disadvantages which can make life very difficult.

ADVANTAGES
O Beautiful scenery.
O Unhurried lifestyle.
O Quietness.
O Low crime rates.
O Neighbourliness.
O Good social network for the elderly.

DISADVANTAGES
O The weather.
O Isolation.
O Lack of services.
O Distance to hospitals.
O Distance to shops.
O Lack of public transport.
O Necessity of driving.
O Distance from family and friends.

Types of Property
Countryside. When buying a retirement home there are a number of factors to consider. As the purchase may be made several years before retirement age, while one is still hale and hearty, it is worth looking ahead to the worse case scenario. Although it may be depressing to think about our failing facilitates before we need to, it could end up even more depressing to find that the house you dreamed of retiring to for years turns out to be uncomfortable or completely unsuitable once old age catches up with you.

It is well worth considering the benefits of a single storey house. If you are retiring to the rural Highlands, the vast majority of houses there are detached and single storey, or at the most 1.5 stories (with the upstairs rooms fitted in under the roof.) This is because the planning laws in the Highland region generally restrict the height of buildings. This is both for aesthetic and practical reasons – with the extremely strong winds which can be experienced in the region, a low-built house in the lee of a hill is far more protected from damage to roofs and chimneys than one which stands high and exposed.

As you get older and less mobile, the lack of stairs or, in a 1.5 story building, having one's bedroom and bathroom on the ground floor, might well be a godsend. The upstairs rooms can then be reserved for more agile visitors!

Talking of visitors, consideration needs to be made as to how much and how often you wish to see your friends and family. If you intend them to come and stay regularly, don't underestimate the number of bedrooms you might need. Most Scottish houses have two or three bedrooms, but you may want to consider one with four, if you have a large family or circle of friends. Conversely, if one of your reasons for retiring such a distance away from your original home is to escape from constant incursions by visitors, you may want to downsize to two – or even one! – bedroom. Anybody who really wants to come and visit can always stay at a bed and breakfast or hotel down the road. Alternatively, a small house with a cottage or caravan in the garden can be a good solution in a rural area. This means that you can have visitors but they can have their own space. And when friends and family are not using the accommodation you can earn some useful extra income by letting it out to tourists.

Along with a rural property, of course, generally comes some land, ranging from a small garden to several acres of croftland. If you love gardening, this may be an absolute requirement. For others who hate it, the upkeep of your little patch of Scotland can become a burdensome chore. However, there are always jobbing gardeners around who will come in for a few hours a week to do your garden. And if you have a larger croft, rest assured that a local crofter would be delighted to be invited to graze his/her sheep on your land for a small rent.

Another consideration is the location of your new home. Although you may at present be attracted by the idea of living at the end of a rutted cart track, or where you have to park your vehicle some distance from your home – you may relish the isolation this provides – as you age this could become a big downside, as you become less agile. And the walk with your shopping which seems fine on a sunny day in summer, may lose its appeal in the middle of winter.

Urban. If you are moving to a town or city, the options are somewhat different. In town, the majority of houses will be either semi-detached or terraced, generally with a self-contained garden. In cities, the majority of central properties will be flats (apartments), while as you move out to the suburban areas, again semi-detached and terraced properties will become more common.

If you opt for a flat as a retirement home, it is very important to ensure that the one you choose is either on the ground floor or has a lift (elevator). Many apartment buildings, either older tenement-style or modern blocks, do not have a lift. Where a lift is provided, bear in mind that the management fees or factoring charges tend to be higher than those with only stairs, as the maintenance, upkeep and insurance costs of a lift can be substantial. Although these charges are shared amongst all the residents in the building, they can build up over the years, especially where a lift fails and wholesale repairs are required.

An advantage of a flat, if you are unable or unwilling to look after a garden, is that you would not have your own garden to upkeep. Sometimes there is a shared garden, where the upkeep is the responsibility of the tenants. This is fine if there are keen gardeners among the residents, but unfortunately this is often not the case. Informal – or even formal – agreements that each tenant plays their part in keeping the garden tidy may be unworkable in practice, if some residents are unwilling to do so. It may then end up both neglected and a matter of conflict between neighbours.

In some cases, particularly with more recently built complexes of flats, the surrounding grounds are landscaped and contract gardeners arrive once a week. The cost will be included in the management or factoring fees, but this is a price worth paying to ensure your surroundings are attractive and well-kept without the need to fall out with the neighbours!

If you or your partner should be, or become, infirm, it is well worth considering the advantages of buying a house in a so-called sheltered accommodation complex. Generally, these are small single storey dwellings, sometimes detached, sometimes apartment-style, which are close by a residential home for elderly people. The sheltered homes are designed for those folk who are still mobile and independent but need the reassurance of having people close by who can help in an emergency. The dwellings and the residents are looked after by wardens, and there is always somebody on hand night and day if a medical emergency should occur. The downside of this arrangement is that you will inevitably be surrounded by other elderly people, which does not suit everybody. You may prefer to live within a community with a more mixed age group. In this case, social services should ensure that any specific requirements you have regarding health checks, assistance in your home, or getting about, will be assessed and provided for.

Other Considerations

When buying a home for your retirement, you also need to consider the important practical details such as the ease of access to health care and other services, and the distance you will be from shops, garages, public transport and your nearest neighbours.

Do think about whether the Scottish climate is going to be the best for your health. The cold and damp conditions Scotland often suffers from are not ideal for arthritis sufferers, for example, whereas if you suffer from minor breathing difficulties, the clean air of rural Scotland could be just what you need.

If you have only visited Scotland for your summer holidays in the past, it is a good idea to find out what the weather and way of life is like in the winter. With the weather colder and wetter, the sun less in evidence and the towns and villages comparatively deserted with the summer visitors away, this can put a very different aspect on your favourite holiday spot. One advantage is that you won't be bothered by the dreaded midge outside the summer months of May to September!

Pensions

Retired persons with the right of abode in Scotland (as defined in *Residence & Entry* above) can claim all social security benefits they are entitled to just like other residents of the UK.

However, if you do not have an automatic right of abode, and are a non-economically active national of an EEA country, you can only live in the UK if you have sufficient funds to support yourself without recourse to UK public funds. This ruling applies also to dependent parents or grandparents of EEA nationals.

You may live in Scotland under the category 'a retired person of independent means'. To qualify, you must be at least 60 years of age and have a close connection to the UK. In addition, you must have an annual income of at least £25,000 which allows you to support yourself and any dependants indefinitely without working.

UK state retirement pensions are paid at a level depending on the cumulative National Insurance contributions which have been made during the course of one's working life. The pension currently becomes payable when men reach 65 and women reach 60, but this will change from 6th April 2010 when, to satisfy sex discrimination regulations, the pension for women will begin to be brought into line with men, and eventually all women will only be eligible for a state pension once they reach 65.

Some women may be entitled to receive a widow's pension on the basis of their late husband's pension entitlement.

Most pensioners do receive more than the basic state pension, through a variety of sources including occupational pensions and a range of social security benefits and allowances.

The UK has social security agreements with a number of countries which means pensions for residents from these countries are payable at the same level they would receive if they stayed in their home country. The countries involved may vary from time to time. See www.dwp.gov.uk for the latest information.

Where a retiree has made national insurance contributions both in the UK and another country, they may be eligible to a pension from both countries. If the insurance contributions are not at a high enough level in either country to entitle them to a pension, the two sets of contributions may be combined, which may then entitle them to a UK pension

Payments from company or private pension plans from another country vary depending on the details of the plan. In most cases, however, they should be payable directly to you if you move to Scotland.

Useful Address

For further information, contact The Pension Service at *International Pension Centre*: Tyneview Park, Newcastle Upon Tyne NE98 1BA: ☎ 0191-218 7777; fax 0191-218 7293.

Health

The National Health Service provides free prescriptions, eye tests and dental treatment for those over retirement age. In remote areas of the country, you may have to travel some distance to reach a treatment centre. If you prefer to visit a private doctor, you will need to be nearer to the centres of population as these are vary rare in rural areas. However, if you are an advocate of complementary therapies you may be better served – in recent years many alternative therapy practitioners have begun offering their services across the country, frequently in rural areas, as people involved in complementary therapies tend to seek out the 'back to nature' lifestyle to be found there.

If you are unlucky enough to need a serious or specialised operation, you may be unable to have the operation locally. Even a comparatively large hospital such as Raigmore Hospital in Inverness, even though it is the main hospital for a huge area of the Highlands, cannot offer all treatments. Patients are routinely sent to Aberdeen or to Edinburgh for some specialist procedures such as certain cancer treatments, or delicate surgery such as heart bypass operations. Once the patient's condition has stabilised, he/she would usually be brought back to Raigmore for recuperation. After discharge from the hospital, there may be a requirement to travel to Aberdeen or Edinburgh for follow-up appointments with your consultant.

Social Services

Elderly people in Scotland are encouraged to remain living in their own homes for as long as possible. A range of services is provided to make this as easy as possible, including domestic help, meals delivered to the elderly person's home, house alterations to aid mobility, emergency alarm systems, day and/or night attendants and laundry services. There may be charges made for these services, but if the person concerned has below a certain level of income or savings, these will be provided free of charge.

Elderly people may be entitled to a number of benefits and allowances, assessed on the basis of their financial circumstances, state of health and mobility. These include Attendance Allowance, Disability Living Allowance, Invalid Care allowance, Council Tax Benefit, Housing Benefit, Income Support, War Disablement Pension, Widow's Pension and War Widow's Pension.

Elderly people whose state of health deteriorates to a level where they or their carer can no longer cope in their own home, may be admitted to a residential home. Costs of care are free for all elderly people in Scotland, although additional charges may be made for accommodation and meals, depending on the financial circumstances of the individual.

Details of residential and nursing homes in Scotland can be found in the Yellow

Pages or can be obtained from the local council. Or see www.bettercaring.co.uk/ nursinghomes/scotland.

An Ageing Population

There is an ongoing debate in Scotland about the prospect for the future as the nation faces substantial falls in population over the coming years. The population is declining at a faster rate than anywhere else in Europe, due to a falling birth rate and younger people moving away. The elderly are the only group whose numbers are increasing. This is a trend which is set to continue.

It is predicted that Scotland's population will have fallen to 4.84 million by 2027, and it will lose half a million people, equivalent to ten per cent of its population, in the next forty years. Unless inward migration and/or the fertility rate increase, the gloomiest forecasts see Scotland with a population of just 3.47 million by 2101.

Even if the decline in population proves to be less dramatic, it is inevitable that the average age of the population will rise. By 2041, according to some forecasts, over 60 per cent of the population will be over 65. This will have serious consequences for the social infrastructure and services provision required over the country as a whole. There will be increased demand for pension provision and health care, while income tax revenues needed to pay for these will fall as the proportion of the population of working age decreases.

POPULAR REGIONS TO RETIRE TO

- Shetland.
- The Highlands & Islands.
- Argyll & Bute.
- Scottish Borders.
- Dumfries & Galloway.
- The Trossachs.

Part III

THE PURCHASING PROCEDURE

FINANCE

FINDING PROPERTIES FOR SALE

WHAT TYPE OF PROPERTY TO BUY

RENTING A HOME

PURCHASING, CONVEYANCING & FEES

FINANCE

CHAPTER SUMMARY

- **Banks.** Most banks and building societies in Great Britain have branches north and south of the border.
  - The banking system is the same as in England and Wales, so if you already have an account in those countries you do not have to open a new one when you move to Scotland.
  - To open an account you need proof of your identity, two proofs of your UK address, and proof of your previous address abroad if applicable.
  - There are many international banks with branches in the UK.
- **Currency.** Scotland has the same sterling currency as England, but issues its own banknotes. You can use English banknotes north of the border.
  - There is no limit on the amount of currency you can bring in or take out of the country.
- **Mortgages.** There are many types of mortgage available and a great deal of competition between lenders.
  - Mortgages are normally taken out for 25 years, but you can vary this.
  - The mortgage rate fluctuates as the Bank of England Base Rate changes.
  - Individuals can normally borrow up to three times their annual income; married couples can borrow 2.5 times their joint income.
- **Insurance.** Most lenders insist you have buildings insurance on your property.
  - If you buy a flat, buildings insurance will be included with your annual service charges.
  - Some mortgages require you to have life insurance to cover the loan in the event of your death.
- Most financial services in the UK are regulated by the Financial Services Authority.
- **Taxation.** The main taxes UK residents pay are income tax, VAT on purchases, and council tax.

> O There are a number of reliefs and allowances which reduce the income tax you pay.
> O If you are employed, your tax is deducted at source; self-employed people pay tax using a system of self-assessment.
> O **National Insurance.** Mandatory for most working people between 16 and 65. Your contributions entitle you to state benefits.
> O **Wills.** It is advisable to draw up a new will when you move to Scotland.

For people moving from elsewhere in the UK, there are few if any differences involved in the process of finding finance for a house purchase. There may be additional factors to bear in mind if, for example, you are looking for finance to buy a croft. In this case there may be extra criteria you have to satisfy before securing a mortgage. There are one or two building societies and banks which are still exclusively Scottish, so it is worth investigating these, but most financial institutions now have branches in both Scotland and England.

There are a number of different financial institutions which can provide you with a mortgage, the main ones being banks, building societies and insurance companies. In addition to the institutions with bricks and mortar branches in towns and cities across the UK, there are now many lenders who work exclusively via the telephone, through the post, and across the Internet.

The biggest problem the purchaser is likely to face is choosing which among all these companies to go with. As they are all competing with one another, and all are eager for your custom, it is well worth taking the time to compare a number of different lenders to ensure you achieve the best deal possible.

It is worth considering an online/telephone mortgage company: on the plus side, they will have lower overheads than the longer established high street mortgage lenders, so can offer loans at a competitive rate. However, on the downside, it is difficult sometimes to be sure of the calibre of these lenders. You need to be very careful before signing up with such a company – however tempting an offer may be, house purchase is too important and expensive a decision to entrust your money to a company which cannot in the end provide what it is promising, whether through lack of financial acumen, incompetence or sheer criminality. To remove as much risk as possible, always make sure that any company you use is an approved member of the relevant industry body (details below).

BANKING

Scotland does not have a separate banking system from the rest of Britain, so if you already have a bank account in Great Britain, there is no need to open a new one when you move to Scotland. Practically all UK financial institutions, including banks and building societies, have branches both north and south of the border. There are three apparently specifically 'Scottish' banks – the Royal Bank of Scotland, the Bank of Scotland and the Clydesdale Bank. The Royal Bank has long had branches south of the border, and now the Bank of Scotland (with branches in Scotland) has taken over the Halifax (with branches in England and Wales) you can operate your account from branches of either. The Clydesdale was the last to spread southwards, but it is now increasing the number of branches in England.

Choosing a Bank

If you will be living in a small rural community in Scotland, you should check which banks have a local branch. Many will have only one, or maybe none at all. Generally, the Royal Bank of Scotland and the Bank of Scotland are the best ones to choose as they cover these areas better than others, as well as having mobile banks which visit areas without branches on a weekly basis.

This is far less of a problem than it once was, however, as most banks now have telephone and internet banking facilities available to their customers, so you can check your balance and carry out transactions without needing to visit a branch.

You can apply to open an account online or by visiting a branch. If you apply online, however, you will need to visit a branch to present your identification documents. Once your account is set up, you can carry out transactions by visiting any branch of the bank or by using their telephone or online banking service.

ATMs are available in even the remotest places nowadays, so generally cash withdrawal is not a problem. However, some ATMs do charge quite high fees for taking out cash, while others are free. There is a legal requirement for these machines to indicate what fees, if any, are payable, so do be wary.

Some banks also have arrangements with the Post Office so that you can carry out bank transactions such as paying in and withdrawing money, or paying bills, via the Post Office if you have no local bank branch.

Although all banks offer similar accounts, each has their own special features so it is worth shopping around for the one which suits you best. Things to consider are:

- What interest rates do they pay?
- Do they have telephone and Internet banking?
- Is there a branch or ATM close to your home?
- Can you use the Post Office for transactions?
- What level of bank charges do they make?
- Is a service charge payable?
- Can you get instant access to your money?
- How much do they charge for overdraft facilities?
- What interest rate do they charge on loans and mortgages?
- How helpful and efficient are they, and what are their charges, when it comes to sending and receiving money overseas?

Building Societies & Banks

These are some of the largest lending institutions active in Scotland, but there are many smaller ones. A full list is available from *the Council of Mortgage Lenders:* 3 Savile Row, London W1S 3PB; ☎ 020-7437 0075; www.cml.org.uk.

A full list of members of the *Building Societies Association* can be obtained from them at the same address: ☎ 020-7437 0655; fax 020-7734 6416; www.bsa.org.uk.

Addresses and phone numbers of local bank and building society branches can be found in local Phone Books or Business Pages or via their websites.

Abbey: www.abbey.com..
Alliance & Leicester: www.alliance-leicester.co.uk..
Bank of Scotland: www.bankofscotland.co.uk..
Barclays Bank: www.barclays.co.uk.
Clydesdale Bank: www.cbonline.co.uk.
HSBC Bank: www.hsbc.com.
Lloyds TSB Bank: www.lloydstsb.com.
National Westminster Bank: www.natwest.com.
Northern Rock: www.northernrock.co.uk.
Royal Bank of Scotland: www.rbs.co.uk.
Scottish Building Society: www.scottishbldgsoc.co.uk.
Woolwich: www.woolwich.co.uk..

Post Office Accounts

Giro Bank, run by the Post Office, offers both current and savings accounts. Just as with other banks, cash can be withdrawn at post office branches or via ATMs.

Also administered by the Post Office, National Savings and Investments offers an easy access savings account and an investment account. Both pay interest on a sliding scale depending on the balance, and the investment account requires one month's notice of withdrawals..

Post Office: www.postoffice.co.uk..
National Savings & Investments: www.nsandi.com..

Postal and Internet Banks

Some banks operate without High Street branches, conducting their business through the post and through the internet. As they have lower overheads they may offer competitive rates for savers and borrowers, and they are worth investigating.

Egg: www.egg.com.
Smile: www.smile.co.uk.

Loans

Banks, building societies and credit card companies offer both personal and business loans. There are also direct loans companies springing up, who provide loans via telephone and internet services. Before deciding on a loan source, do check their interest rates and terms and conditions carefully as these can vary greatly. Some of the direct loan companies in particular may offer unsecured loans to people who have difficulty getting funds from more conventional sources, but interest rates can be punitive, sometimes leading to borrowers' financial difficulties worsening as a result of taking out the loan. The Citizens Advice Bureau can advise in such circumstances.

CREDIT & DEBIT CARDS

Debit Cards. These take the money from your account electronically at point of sale, but there must be funds to cover the full amount in the account. The service is free for the customer and no interest is payable. The main debit cards you will come across are Maestro, Solo and Delta. Maestro and Delta cards can be used internationally.

Security on debit cards has been improved, allegedly, with the introduction of the 'chip and pin' system. This involve keying in one's personal identification number ('pin') at the point of sale, removing the need to sign a paper receipt to prove you are the owner of the card. The onus is on the owner to keep their pin number and card secure.

Mail order companies take debit card payments and many shops allow customers to obtain up to £50 in cash, known as 'cash-back', when paying a bill with a Maestro card, useful in areas where there is no bank cashpoint machine.

Credit Cards. These are accepted just about everywhere in the UK, apart from some very small shops and businesses. Payments made using the card are itemised on a statement once a month, and there is a minimum amount you are obliged to pay off each month. You pay interest on the balance owing, so if you pay off all outstanding balances at the end of each month, no interest is payable. Interest rates vary from card to card: some cards charge an additional annual fee, while others with no annual fee may charge a higher rate of interest. You should read the small print of any cards you are considering as some can be misleading in their advertising.

Different credit levels are available on cards, depending on your income and the scheme you choose. Those with a higher credit level may be termed gold or platinum cards, and they may have extra benefits included in the package.

There is a vast range of choice when it comes to credit cards. Most financial institutions issue their own as do a range of other organisations including chain stores and charities. If you want to give something back from your spending, a charity card could be a good choice as a certain percentage of their profits is used for charitable works.

The main credit cards in Britain are Visa and Maestro (once known as Mastercard). Although your card may be issued by a bank or other company, it will be linked to a Visa or Maestro or other credit card service, so there is the guarantee of sound financial backing to the service.

Store cards, issued by companies such as Marks & Spencer, often carry a higher than average rate of interest and are mainly used for purchases in that store. Incentives such as discounts on purchases are available to card holders.

As you can use the main credit cards internationally, and can also get cash from ATMs using your card, in the short term you may find no need to open a bank account in the UK.

Credit cards are being upgraded to include chip and pin, but if your card does not have this facility, a signature is required. You need to use a personal identification umber (PIN) to withdraw cash from an ATM.

American Express: www.americanexpress.co.uk.

Mastercard: www.mastercard.com/uk.

Visa: www.visaeurope.com.

Charge Cards. The most well-known of these are American Express and Diners Club, but they have proved far less popular in Britain than in other countries. On a charge card you must pay off the total outstanding balance every month, otherwise a penalty must be paid. American Express introduced a credit card in 1995 especially aimed at the British market.

Diners Card: www.dinerscard.co.uk.

CURRENCY

Scottish currency is sterling, the basic unit of which is the pound (£) of 100 pence (100p). Coins are in denominations of 1p, 2p, 5p, 10p, 20p, 50p, £1, £2. Notes are in denominations of £5, £10, £20, £50 and £100.

All these are acceptable throughout the United Kingdom. In addition to coins issued by the Royal Mint and banknotes by the Bank of England, there are three banks in Scotland allowed to issue their own banknotes. These are the Bank of Scotland, the Royal Bank of Scotland and the Clydesdale Bank. Due to historical anomaly, Scottish banknotes are not technically classed as legal tender (although the Scottish Parliament is currently trying to change their status.) However, they are 'authorised' currency and should be accepted in the same way as Bank of England notes. You may find you have occasional problems using Scottish notes south of the border. You can ask any bank to exchange them for English notes.

Avoid taking Scottish notes abroad, as you may receive a lower exchange rate than for Bank of England notes.

Foreign Currency

Britain has no limits on how much currency you can take out or bring into the country. Foreign bank notes (not coins) can be exchanged for sterling at banks. Generally, the rate of exchange for travellers' cheques is better than for bank notes.

Shop around for the best exchange rates at banks, bureaux de change, building societies and post offices. Commission charged on the transaction will be around one or two per cent with a minimum charge of £2.50. Building societies and larger post offices will also buy and sell foreign currency. You will need your passport if buying or selling foreign currency.

The Euro

Britain has not yet joined the Euro, the single European currency. Before the decision is made whether to join or not, the UK Government has said they will see how the Euro performs. Once certain 'economic tests' have been met (determined by the Treasury) a referendum will be held for the UK people to decide whether to join the Euro zone or not. No referendum will occur before 2006, and it may be some years later. If there was a 'yes' vote it would take several years after that before the Euro was in use in the UK.

However, some businesses which trade within the Euro zone find it convenient to carry out their business using the Euro, and some large High Street shops, including Marks & Spencer, will accept Euros for purchases. You would be given any change in sterling.

The following websites give more information on the Euro in the United Kingdom.

http://europa.eu.int.

www.euro.gov.uk.

www.hm-treasury.gov.uk.

MORTGAGES

The UK Mortgage Market

There is a huge amount of competition to provide mortages, with many different institutions getting in on the act since financial services regulations were relaxed a few years ago. They are available from banks, building societies, specialised loans and mortgage companies.

They offer a wide range of mortgages to those buying houses in Scotland, designed to suit a wide range of people in different circumstances – and also designed to get your custom through the offer of apparently good terms compared with their competitors. If you look closely, you may find that there is not, at the end of the day, a vast amount of difference between similar products from different companies as far as the mortgage itself is concerned, but if you are canny you may be able to make good savings on the one-off fees charged in relation to setting up your mortgage.

It is wise to get good independent advice before choosing a mortgage. Mortgage lenders are required by law to advise you responsibly, but you should remember that they receive commission for every mortgage they sell, and there may be an incentive for them to sell one type of mortgage over another. There have been well-publicised cases of 'mis-selling' – i.e.where they sell a customer a mortgage which is not the best one for them – so you must examine all the alternatives carefully.

There are many independent mortgage brokers and advisers who should act to advise you on the best mortgage for your purposes and find one from a range of mortgage lenders which suits you.

It is wise to ensure that anybody you borrow or take advice from is a member or associate member of the Council of Mortgage Lenders. Any complaints you have regarding the advice or service you are given can then be reported to them for investigation. There is a directory of their members on their website www.cml.org. uk.

Find Financial Directory has listings of financial services and advice providers of all types at www.find.co.uk.

Types of Mortgage

Despite the huge number of mortgages available, there are actually only two main types of mortgage available – repayment and interest-only. The normal period for a mortgage is 25 years, but this can be shorter or longer depending on your individual circumstances and requirements.

Repayment Mortgage

Sometimes called a Capital & Interest Loan. Both the interest on the loan and the capital are repaid over a period of years. Each monthly payment includes an amount which pays off a little of the underlying debt, as well as interest on the loan. By the end of the mortgage period, as long as you have made all the scheduled payments, the loan is fully paid off.

During the course of the mortgage, the proportion of interest and capital paid off varies, with mostly interest paid off in the early years, a greater capital element in the later years. The amount of interest paid fluctuates in line with the interest rate.

There is no protection should the mortgage payer die before it is paid off, and the debt would be passed to his/her heirs. It is advisable to take out a mortgage protection policy which would pay off the loan in this eventuality.

Interest-only Mortgage

Only the interest on the loan is paid, and another payment is made into some sort of investment plan which is used to repay the capital amount at the end of the mortgage period. Interest payments vary in line with rising and falling interest rates.

There are three main types of interest only mortgage:

Endowment Mortgage. A life insurance endowment policy is taken out with an insurance company. Premiums are calculated to ensure that the accumulated investment funds produce a lump sum sufficient to pay off the loan at the end of the mortgage period. Depending on how well the investments perform, you may end up with a shortfall or a surplus. The insurance company should monitor the policy and send an annual statement of the estimated shortfall or surplus. They may increase the monthly premiums payable to avert a predicted shortfall. At the end of the mortgage period, you must pay a lump sum to cover any shortfall. If there is a surplus, it is paid to you as a lump sum at the end of the mortgage period.

Around five per cent of the monthly premiums go to provide life insurance cover. This means that the mortgage is paid off if the mortgagee should die. Where a couple take out a joint mortgage, and both lives are insured, the mortgage is paid off on the death of either party, so the surviving mortgagee then owns the property outright.

These sort of mortgages were sold heavily in the 1980s, but the returns have proved not to reach forecasts, and now millions of borrowers face the prospect that their endowments will not pay off their mortgages at the end of the term, although originally they were guaranteed to do so. As result, they have lost favour, and now only seven per cent of new mortgages are being taken out with an endowment policy.

Pension Mortgage. Premiums are paid into a personal pension plan. When you re-tire, you receive a tax-free lump sum as well as a monthly pension. At the end of the mortgage period, the lump sum is used to pay off the loan. This sort of mortgage may be attractive because payments into a pension plan qualify for tax relief. However, there are disadvantages: life insurance is not included; you cannot take any of the money before age 50 or 55; there will be less money for your pension if you use the lump sum to pay off the mortgage.

ISA Mortgage. The loan is linked to an Individual Savings Account (ISA) which al-lows you to invest tax-free in a wide range of investments including bank, building society and National Savings & Investments accounts; insurance plans; stocks and shares. At the end of the mortgage plan, your accrued savings provide a capital lump sum to pay off the loan.

This is a very flexible form of saving, as you can invest as and when you please – although there is a ceiling of £7,000 you can invest in any one year – and profits can be taken from the ISA at any time. However, if the stock market is performing badly the value of the ISA may be depressed when repayment of the loan comes due. In addition life insurance is not included, and it is up to the individual to ensure that sufficient payments are made into the ISA to cover the capital cost of the loan at the end of the period.

Specialised Mortgages
Foreign Currency Mortgage. If your circumstances are right, you may want to con-sider taking out a mortgage in a currency other than sterling. In this case, a bank lends you a sum in US dollars, for example. You sell the dollars for sterling and use this to buy your house. However, your debt remains in US dollars and you pay dollar interest rates.

If you, or your financial adviser, are clever, by shifting your mortgage between a variety of currencies you may be able to make large savings, but it is a risky business as currency swings can also go against you.

These sort of mortgages are generally only available to very high earners and for a maximum of 60% of a property's value.

Euro Mortgage. If you are an EU resident, it is possible to take out a mortgage from another European country. At present only about one per cent of Europeans do so, mostly second home owners or people living in border regions. The European Commission is keen to encourage this and would like to see a single European market for home loans, which would allow cross-border competition. They argue that this could increase choice and reduce costs for buyers. Language, legal barriers and different rules from country to country are seen as barriers to a single mortgage market. To get over these problems, the Commission is considering the possibility of introducing a euromortgage – a Europe-wide mortgage deed.

Buy to Let Mortgage. If you wish to buy a residential property to let out, it is worth considering a tailor-made buy to let mortgage. Although they are more expensive than mortgages for buying your own home, the lender will take into account the expected rental income on the property when assessing how much they will lend you.

Flexible Mortgage. Allows the borrower to pay off varying amounts during the period of the loan. When your financial circumstances are good, you can elect to pay increased monthly payments. Then later on you can choose to take a break from repayments, reduce them, or borrow back any money you have previously overpaid. You can also choose to overpay each month, and thus pay off your mortgage more quickly and cheaply.

Self-Build Mortgage. For those borrowers building their own houses or contracting a builder to build one for them. In order to manage cash flow during the course of the build, stage payments are made at each stage of the build. Typical stage payments are made in advance of purchase of the land, laying of foundations, erection of the walls or timber frame, putting the roof on, having the walls plastered, and final completion.

These mortgages can be used for both traditional and timber frame builds, as well as for renovation and conversion projects.

Large Mortgages. If you want to borrow a large amount of money – typically over £200,000 – mortage lenders may deal with the application in a specialist department, and they may offer you lower rates of interest and competitive fees. There are some companies which specialise in this sort of mortgage, and claim to arrange you the best deal. See www.moneyquest.co.uk/123 – mortgages.asp.

Offshore Mortgages. Again generally aimed at those who want to borrow large amounts, and are high earners, you can arrange a mortgage which takes advantage of the financial advantages of accounts in tax havens such as Jersey, Guernsey and the Isle of Man, as well as Switzerland, Liechtenstein and Luxembourg. You need to speak to a specialist adviser for this sort of mortgage. One company specialising in these is Singer & Friedlander. See their website at www.sfbank.co.uk/private/offshore-mort.htm.

Mortgage interest rates

These are set by individual lenders at a figure based on the current Bank of England base rate, which applies to the whole of the UK. This is reviewed by the Bank of England every month, when they may decide to raise it, lower it, or leave it unchanged.

As a broad rule of thumb, mortgage providers usually set their standard variable rate at around two to three per cent above base rate. Depending on the conditions of the particular mortgage, you may find the rate you are charged is higher or lower than this.

When the mortgage rate is changed, there may be a time-lag on the part of the lender before it is applied, which means that you won't benefit from the reduced rates immediately. This may, of course, balance out with occasions when rates rise – although mortgage lenders may well be quicker at applying the change when it is to their benefit!

ILLUSTRATION OF BASE RATE CHANGE AFFECTING MORTGAGE RATE.

In August 2005, the Bank of England cut the Base Rate by 0.25%, from 4.75% to 4.5%. The Royal Bank of Scotland cut its Standard Mortgage Rate by 0.2%; their new rates, effective from September 2005, were:

100% Mortgage Rate	7.09%
Standard Variable Rate	6.59%
Flexible Choice Rate	5.84%
Managed Rate	5.4%

Interest rates are one of the biggest factors affecting the housing market in the UK. There was a boom in the market between 2000 and 2004, with rapid house price inflation, significantly during a long period of low and falling interest rates. The rate bottomed out at 3.5 per cent in July 2003, when the market, according to analysts, had become over-heated, with prices rising at an unprecedented rate. The Bank of England began to calm the market down by a series of small rate rises during the first half of 2004. By August, the base rate was at 4.75 per cent, and there had been a corresponding slowdown in the UK property market as people became more wary about taking out a mortgage as the cost of borrowing became higher, with no guarantee that they would not rise further. After staying at this rate for a full year, the rate dropped to 4.5% in August 2005 which almost immediately encouraged a slight rise in property rpices.

There is a certain amount of flexibility in interest rates applied to your mortgage, whether you opt for a repayment or interest-only package.

Variable Rate. Your mortgage provider sets a Standard Variable Rate with reference to the Bank of England base rate. The interest payments you make on your mortgage will fluctuate as base rate, and therefore mortgage rates, move up and down.

Fixed Rate. As its name suggests, here the interest rate is fixed for a number of years at the start of the mortgage term, after which the standard variable rate is paid. The longer the fixed rate period, the lower the interest rate offered. There are pros and cons to take into account here: on the one hand, you know exactly what your repayments will be every month during the fixed rate period; on the downside, if interest rates fall during that period, you would end up paying more. Equally, if interest rates rise appreciably in that period, you would save money.

Discounted Rate. Here you pay a special low rate of interest in the early years of the loan. You must read the small print on such deals because sometimes the discount may not be all it seems – you could find that the interest saved during the discounted period is simply added to the outstanding loan.

Capped Rate. This is a variable rate which has an agreed 'interest rate collar' so it will not rise or fall outside a certain range. The capped rate operates for a fixed period of the loan, after which standard variable rate is paid.

Tracker mortgages. Here the interest rate 'tracks' the Bank of England base rate. They may:

- Track the base rate for the duration of the loan
- Operate at an agreed differential to the base rate for a set period, then revert to the standard variable rate
- Keep a margin between the base rate and the mortgage interest rate which does not go beyond a set level.

Obtaining a Mortgage

You can apply for a mortgage by going into a branch of your chosen lender or, in many cases now, online. Unless there are unusual circumstances, you may be able to get an agreement in principle immediately, but it can take a lot longer – a month or six weeks sometimes – to get the mortgage offer completed and the money available for your purchase. So you do need to allow yourself enough time to complete. This is important if you need to agree a possession date for your new property.

The application form asks for your personal details, including your income, and your partner's income if you are making a joint application. Mortgages usually allow borrowers up to 95% of the value of a property, termed the 'maximum loan to value' (LTV). Some 100% mortgages are available, but will usually be at a higher rate of interest.

With a self build mortgage you may usually borrow up to 95% of land purchase price, up to 95% of the building costs and up to 95% of the end value.

If you have savings or other sources of funds, you may decide to take out a mortgage for just a portion of the house value. For example, you may buy a property costing £200,000, where you have £100,000 savings, or equity from your previous house, so you would apply for a mortgage for £100,000 to make up the shortfall.

You will normally be allowed to borrow up to three times your annual salary, or 2.5 times the joint income of a married couple.

HOW MUCH CAN I BORROW?

Example 1 – Single person mortgage

Property cost	£200,000
Maximum LTV 95%	£190,000
Shortfall	£10,000
Earnings	£60,000 per year
Maximum borrowing	£60,000 x 3=£180,000
Additional funds needed	£20,000

Example 2 – Joint mortgage

Property cost	£200,000
Maximum LTV 90%	£180,000
Equity from previous house	£40,000
Earnings of partner1	£55,000 per year
Earnings of partner 2	£20,000 per year
Maximum borrowing	£55,000 + £20,000 x 2.5 = £187,500
Amount borrowed	£160,000

You may be able to persuade your lender to lend you more than three times your salary, but this is a risky move. If prices rise this could leave you with a monthly debt you cannot afford and your house may be repossessed. Note that a mortgage lender is committing an offence if he encourages you to overstate your income in order to obtain a larger mortgage.

If you have bad credit ratings or an uncertain income you may find it difficult to obtain a standard mortgage. It is estimated that as many as one in four British people have this problem. Self-employed people may have problems obtaining a mortgage, and will need to produce at least three years' accounts so a lender can determine the level of risk they pose.

There are lenders who offer specialised mortgages designed for people with an adverse credit history including such things as mortgage or rent arrears or bankruptcy.

These mortgages are known by a number of names:

- O Adverse credit mortgage.
- O Bad credit mortgage.
- O Sub prime mortgage.
- O Non standard mortgage.
- O Poor credit mortgage.
- O Credit impaired mortgage.

The lender makes an assessment of the risk you pose, and will almost certainly charge higher interest rates than on a standard mortgage and may impose large penalties if you fall into arrears. However, if you keep up your mortgage payments without default for three years this will improve your credit history and you could then switch your mortgage to a high street lender and get improved terms and interest rates for the remainder of the mortgage period.

Self-employed people or those with a fluctuating income may not need to go this route. They may be able instead to obtain a 'self-certification mortgage' where you simply state your income without the need to support it with payslips, bank statements or accounts. The interest rate you have to pay will probably be higher than normal. It is always worth trying to demonstrate to a mortgage lender that you are a good credit risk by showing them evidence of paid bills and invoices, direct debit agreements which you have never defaulted on, and so forth.

DOCUMENTS NEEDED TO APPLY FOR A MORTGAGE

Before your mortgage is agreed you will need to produce certain documentation. Requirements vary between lenders, but typically you will need to provide some or all of these:

- O Payslips.
- O Bank statements (for the last three months).
- O Birth certificate.
- O Driving licence.
- O Utility bills.
- O Savings statements.
- O Existing mortgage statement (if applicable).
- O Business accounts if you are self-employed (for the last three years if possible).

Charges

Valuation Fee. Before lenders agree to give you a mortgage, they have the property valued to ensure it is worth at least as much as they lend you. The fee for this valuation varies depending on the lender and the value of the property. Generally you will pay about £10-15 for each £10,000 value of the house, with a minimum fee of between

£50-200. Your lender may also add an administration charge for the valuation.

Arrangement Fee. May also be called an application or acceptance fee, this is charged by a lender for arranging a mortgage. Normally it is about £250 to £300. You need to read the small print on each mortgage, however, as the fee will vary between lenders and even between different mortgages from the same company. Some, as an incentive, charge no fee.

Lender's Legal Fees. Legal fees charged by your lender's solicitor are payable by the borrower. If the same solicitor acts for both lender and borrower the fees may be lower.

Redemption Charges. If you wish to pay off your mortgage early or switch to a different mortgage a redemption charge may be levied. The earlier you repay the loan, the higher the charges. High redemption charges are most common with fixed rate or discounted mortgages.

Some lenders advertise mortgages with no redemption fees. Do look carefully at the other costs: you may find you have to pay a higher arrangement fee than if you take another type of mortgage which does have a redemption fee.

CHAPS Fee. This is an administration fee charged when the loan proceeds are issued to the solicitor, generally deducted up front from the amount sent.

BARGAIN FOR A BETTER DEAL

Take advantage of the competition within the mortgage market to try to get the best deal from your lender. Shop around and compare fees with different lenders and different mortgages. Most lenders are open to negotiation on different elements of the fees charged, if they know that you know you can get a better deal elsewhere. They may be prepared, for example, to waive the arrangement fee in order to persuade you not to go to another lender who has no arrangement fee.

If you already have a mortgage, you may be tempted by a better deal from another lender and consider switching your mortgage to them. But it can be very expensive to switch lenders, once you add the cost of valuation fees, legal fees and redemption fees. It can amount to as much as £1,000. In this case, ask your lender if he can match the cheaper deal. If you are a good customer they may be prepared to look again at your existing loan and offer you some form of discount to tempt you to stay.

It is, however, up to you to approach your lender with these requests – they won't offer discounts without being asked. Be cheeky – it often works!

Non-Mortgageable Properties

There are certain types of properties which you cannot get a loan on. The lender has to be satisfied that their money is safe so will not offer on sub-standard properties.

For instance, they may be reluctant to lend money on a derelict property you wish to renovate, especially if it is not of approved construction or includes substances such as asbestos which must be removed in an approved – and expensive – way.

You may find that another lender is prepared to give you a mortgage on the same property, but there may be conditions attached to ensure that the sub-standard elements are brought up to scratch.

If not, one alternative is to take out another sort of loan which is not dependent on the property as security – maybe by taking out a second mortgage on your existing house. Or, of course, pay cash.

Other Sources of Funding for Property

If you can't get a mortgage for any reason but still need a source of funds, there may be alternatives. If you have bought, or are a tenant of, a croft you may be able to access various grants and loans from the Crofters Commission. These are available for both domestic and business/agricultural buildings. There is a wider range of grants available to tenant crofters than to owner/occupiers. As the schemes and the rules of eligibility change from time to time, contact the Crofters Commission for full details of what is currently available.

A variety of grant and loan schemes open to non-crofters are run by Scottish Enterprise in the south of Scotland, and Highlands and Islands Enterprise in the north. These are administered through their subsidiary Local Enterprise Companies (LECs). If you wish to build, renovate or extend a property to run a business from, or to use part of your house for business purposes, you may be eligible.

Both the Crofters Commission and LECs may be able to assist with funding towards ancillary elements of a house build, such as fencing, the provision of access to a property and so forth.

Your local council may also be able to assist with funding towards a business, via their economic development department. However, this is unlikely to be available for the bricks and mortar – they may agree to help with funding for equipment and other aspects of running the business.

Useful Addresses

Crofters Commission: 4-6 Castle Wynd, Inverness IV2 3EQ; ☎ 01463-663450; fax 01463-711820; www.crofterscommission.org.uk..

Scottish Enterprise: Atlantic Quay, 150 Broomielaw, Glasgow G2 8LU; ☎ 0141-248 2700; fax 0141-221 3217; www.scotent.co.uk.

Highland and Islands Enterprise: Cowan House, Inverness Retail and Business Park, Inverness IV2 7GF; ☎ 01463-234171; fax 01463-244469; www.hie.co.uk.

See contact details for all Scottish local councils in *Where to Find Your Ideal Home.*.

Insurance

Buildings Insurance. Most mortgage lenders insist that you have buildings insurance which covers damage to the structure of the property from severe weather; theft and vandalism; fire, smoke and explosions; subsidence; burst pipes; civil commotion; water or oil leakage; impact from vehicles, falling trees, aircraft, masts, aerials.

The amount guaranteed by the policy must cover reinstatement – i.e. the cost of rebuilding the house. Your house survey will recommend the level of buildings insurance to be taken out. There is no legal requirement to take out contents insurance on the movable objects inside your house.

Rented Properties. Most standard residential insurance policies do not cover rented property – they are unlikely to cover for damage or theft occurring while your house is let to a tenant. There are special 'landlords' policies' for long term lets, and other policies designed for self-catering holiday properties which are empty for parts of the year.

Flats. Buildings insurance for flats is included in any management charges (often called factoring charges in Scotland). The factor (usually a firm of solicitors) will arrange insurance for the whole building and tenants pay a proportion of the premiums as part of their annual charges.

Life Insurance. Some mortgages require you to take out a life assurance policy which will pay off the loan in the event of your death. If your mortgage does not insist on this, it is wise to consider some form of insurance cover which will pay for your repayments in the event of difficulty. Mortgage protection insurance covers mortgage repayments for a period, usually of up to a year, in the event of the mortgagee becoming unemployed, ill or injured.

Association of British Insurers: 51 Gresham Street, London EC2V 7HQ; ☎ 020-7600 3333; fax 020-7696 8999; www.abi.org.uk.

Protection for Borrowers

From 31st October 2004 the Financial Services Authority took over regulation of mortgages, and most polices taken out on or after this date are subject to their scrutiny. To protect borrowers they ensure that:

lenders give you clear information about mortgages and mortgage services in a standard format called 'Keyfacts' (see below). This makes it easier for you to compare mortgages and services from different lenders.

- Price information, including the annual percentage rate (APR) in any mortgage advertising and marketing material must be clear.
- When you receive advice from a firm they must make sure that they recommend a suitable mortgage based on your needs and circumstances.
- Charges are not excessive.
- There are new standards offering greater protection should you get into arrears with your mortgage.

Keyfacts

A Keyfacts Illustration Document (KFI) summarises the important features of the mortgage and must be clear, fair and not misleading. It is presented in a standard way adhered to by all lenders and brokers, so you can easily check the cost and terms of the mortgage and compare it with other mortgages.

A mortgage lender or broker must give you a KFI whenever you ask for one, whenever they recommend a particular mortgage for you, and before you apply for a mortgage. That information will be tailored to your particular circumstances and the amount you want to borrow. This does not apply, however, to buy to let mortgages.

Once the lender has assessed your application by checking your identity, that you can afford the mortgage, and they value the property, you will then be sent a mortgage offer pack which will include an updated version of the KFI. You should compare this with the original document, and check that you are happy with the all the terms and conditions of the mortgage. If anything is not clear, or if there are differences from the original KFI ask your lender to explain. Only once you have read and understood the document should you sign up for a mortgage.

Complaints

If you have a complaint about certain aspects of your mortgage, you should first contact your lender to see if the matter can be sorted out. If you are still not happy you should contact the Financial Services Authority or The Financial Ombudsman Service.

The sort of problems you can complain about include:

- Unexpected or excessive charges.
- Losing money because of a firm's slow administration.
- A dispute over who is at fault if money is stolen from an account.
- Incorrect or misleading information about a product.
- A firm's failure to adequately warn about the risks of a product.
- A firm's failure to draw attention to a particularly strict condition in the contract.
- A firm's failure to carry out your instructions.
- Unfairly being offered worse terms than other customers.
- Not being given adequate notice about changes to a contract.

BEST BUY MORTGAGES IN SEPTEMBER 2005.

The following are the terms of the three best available for each category at the time:

VARIABLE RATE

Rate	Period	Max LTV	Fee	Redemption Penalty
4.75%	for term	95%	£549	none
4.89%	for term	80%	none	none
4.90%	for term	95%	£349	none

FIXED RATE				
Rate	Period	Max LTV	Fee	Redemption Penalty
4.20%	to 31/10/07	95%	£499	to 31/10/07
4.29%	to 31/10/07	95%	£499	to 31/10/07
4.35%	to 31/12/08	95%	£399	to 31/12/08

100% MORTGAGES				
Rate	Period	Reverts to	Fee	Redemption Penalty
5.25%	to 1/12/07	6.59%	none	to 1/12/07
5.55%	to 30/11/07	6.59%	£195	to 1/12/07
5.59%	to 30/11/07	6.59%	none	none

SELF CERTIFICATION				
Rate	Period	Max LTV	Fee	Redemption Penalty
4.64%	for 2 years	75%	£399	1st 2 years
4.99%	for 2 years	85%	£405	1st 2 years
5.04%	to 31/10/07	85%	£399	to 31/10/07

BUY TO LET					
Rate	Type	Period	Max LTV	Fee	Redemption Penalty
4.99%	discount	to 31/1/09	75%	£499	to 31/1/09
4.54%	fixed	to 30/11/08	75%	£595	to 30/11/08
4.94%	discount	for 3 years	80%	£449	1st 3 years

Sources of Information

High Street banks and building societies have free leaflets outlining the mortgages they have to offer. The same information is also explained on their websites.

Houseweb (www.houseweb.co.uk.) is a very useful website. It has information, advice and current facts and figures on all aspects of house-buying, including current mortgage rates and links to other useful sites.

The Times and Sunday Times, plus most other weekend papers, publish lists of the best mortgages of various types. The Electronic Telegraph publishes them at www.telegraph.co.uk in their 'money' section. www.aboutmortgages.co.uk has tables of the best value mortgages currently available.

For mortgage advice and links to relevant websites including online mortgages: www.100-mortgages.gbr.ru.com.

For more information about mortgages and their regulation see the Financial Services Authority website: www.fsa.gov.uk/consumer. You can also search on the website for companies which come under FSA regulation: http://www.fsa.gov.uk/register.

The Council of Mortgage Lenders represents about 98 per cent of residential mortgage lenders in the UK. There is a directory of their members on their website: www.cml.org.uk.

There are some useful online mortgage calculators which will show you what repayments you would make for certain levels of borrowing and interest rates.

http://money.msn.co.uk/mortgages/calculate/Tools/mortgagecalc/default.asp..
www.bbc.co.uk/homes/property/mortgagecalculator.shtml..

PROPERTY TAXES

Council Tax

Scottish residents are charged council tax to pay for local services including education, road maintenance, police and refuse collection. Each council fixes its own tax rate and there is quite a variation between different council areas. In 2005-2006, the lowest rates were in Eilean Siar (Western Isles) and the highest in Glasgow City, where residents were paying around 21% more than in the Western Isles. See *Where to Find Your Ideal Home* for the rates charged by each local council in 2005-2006.

The amount payable is based on the value of your home as rated by your council, which puts each property into a valuation band. This is not necessarily current market value as the valuation bands currently in use were set according to open market value on 1st April 1991. As property prices have risen greatly since that time, there are plans to revalue all properties throughout Britain. This has already taken place in Wales, and some people saw their properties being rebanded resulting in council tax rises of up to 70%. It has not yet been decided whether a similar exercise will soon be carried out in Scotland, but as it is a bit of a political 'hot potato', guaranteed to upset many householders, revaluation may be postponed. There are, at the time of writing, signs that England are back-pedalling on their stated intention to revalue and reband properties for council tax, and there are indications that the process may be delayed.

PROPERTY VALUATION BANDS	
Band	**Property Value (£)**
A	27,000 or under
B	27,000 to 35,000
C	35,000 to 45,000
D	45,000 to 58,000
E	58,000 to 80,000
F	80,000 to 106,000
G	106,000 to 212,000
H	over 212,000

When you move into a property you should contact the local council to arrange to pay your council tax. In rented accommodation it is the tenant who is liable to pay council tax on their own behalf and it is therefore not included in the rental.

Council tax is payable by weekly or monthly instalments or a lump sum. It can be paid by standing order or direct debit through your bank account, by cheque or postal order through the post, at post offices or in person at council offices.

People with low earnings or those living alone may be entitled to a discount on the level of council tax they pay. Owners of second homes and long-term empty properties, or those undergoing renovation which means they are currently uninhabitable, may be eligible for discounts of up to 50%. Contact your local council about this.

Capital Gains Tax

This is charged on profits made from selling land, property or businesses other than your personal residence. The level of capital gains tax (CGT) payable is calculated on the basis of the increase in an asset's value since you acquired it.

At current rates, the first £8,500 of any profit made on the transaction is tax free. The remainder of the profit is added onto your income and then tax charged in line with income tax rates. If profits made from the disposal of the asset are re-invested in another allowable business, you may be able to receive 'roll-over' relief, so CGT is not payable until such time as a business asset is finally disposed of without profits being re-invested in a business. The tax-free allowance on CGT is increased most years.

The rules on which sorts of assets or businesses are allowed for roll-over relief and which are not are fairly complicated and not always logical – for example, you can claim roll-over relief if you buy and let a property for holidays, but not if you let it out long-term to a tenant. You should always check with the Inland Revenue regarding what is allowable before you decide what to re-invest your profits in.

Where a property has been let, either long term or as holiday accommodation, capital gains tax will probably be due when the property is sold. If you have two homes and live for part of the year in one, part in the other, you must nominate your 'main residence'. The sensible course here is to nominate the one with the highest value.

Husbands and wives each have an annual CGT exemption, which usually increases in the Budget each year. So if the house is jointly owned, both these exemptions will be taken into account. For example, in 2005-2006 the exemption was £8,500 per person, so on a jointly owned property CGT would not be charged on the first £17,000 of profit when it was sold.

If you are resident or ordinarily resident in the UK, you may be liable to capital gains tax on the disposal of assets situated anywhere in the world, unless you are a resident of a country with a double taxation agreement with the UK.

OTHER TAXES

Value Added Tax

VAT is paid on most goods and services at a standard rate of 17.5%. Domestic fuels for heating and lighting carry VAT at a reduced rate of five per cent. Children's clothes and footwear, books, magazines and newspapers, and most foods, are zero-rated. Sales and lettings of land and buildings, insurance, the provision of credit, and the services of doctors, dentists and opticians are exempt.

A business with a turnover in any one year of at least £60,000 must be registered for VAT, while those with a lower turnover may choose to be – in some cases this may be advantageous, but generally it is advisable to remain unregistered if you are allowed to, because it does involve a lot of paperwork and associated cost. A business which supplies only VAT exempt items cannot register for VAT, but one making or supplying zero-rated items can. The VAT charged on goods and services used in your business can usually be reclaimed.

It is important to understand the VAT regulations if you have a business, as there are high penalties for failing to register for VAT or making a false declaration.

Corporation Tax

This is payable on company profits of over £10,000 per year. The rates vary on a sliding scale depending on the amount of profit made. In the 2005-2006 tax year the small companies' rate was 19% on taxable profits between £50,000 and £300,000. Marginal rate relief can be claimed if your profits are between £10,000 and £50,000.

Large companies with profits over £300,000 pay tax at the full rate of 30%, although marginal relief may be claimed by companies with profits between £300,000 and £1,500,000.

Income Tax and Further Information

Information on all these matters, in more detail, is given on HM Revenue & Customs website: www.hmrc.gov.uk. This is a fairly new government department, which combines the previous Inland Revenue and Customs and Excise. For contact details regarding specific matters, see the website.

There are a number of downloadable leaflets on the site. The following are particularly useful for those moving to and buying property in Scotland. IR20 Residents and non-residents – Liability to tax in the United Kingdom; IR90 Tax allowances and reliefs; and IR139 Income from abroad? A guide to UK tax on overseas income.

If you have any queries on your tax position, you can contact your local Tax Office. The address will be listed in the phone book under 'Inland Revenue'. Alternatively, there is a national telephone helpline to deal with queries about National Insurance, tax or VAT, ☎ 0845-900 0444. They will ask for your NI number when you call.

If you wish to consult a tax advisor, they should be a member of *The Chartered Institute of Taxation (CIOT):* 12 Upper Belgrave Street, London SW1X 8BB; ☎: 020 7235 9381 fax: 020 7235 2562; www.tax.org.uk. *Institute of Chartered Accountants of Scotland:* CA House, 21 Haymarket Yards, Edinburgh, EH12 5BH; ☎ 0131-347 0100; fax 0131-347 0105; www.icas.org.uk.

Association of Chartered Certified Accountants: 2 Central Quay, 89 Hydepark Street, Glasgow G3 8BW; ☎: 0141 582 2000; fax: +44 (0)141 582 2222; www.accaglobal.com.

Directgov: www.direct.gov.uk A useful site with simple guides to all areas of UK tax.

WILLS & INHERITANCE LAW

If you move to Scotland from elsewhere, and that includes elsewhere in Britain, you should consider making a new will due to differences in Scottish law. If you ask your bank or solicitor to draw up your will they will charge around £50-£120. If you have straightforward disposal instructions it is far cheaper to do it yourself – you can purchase a will form 'according to Scottish law' from stationers and post offices for around £5. It is advisable if your instructions are at all complex to pay to have a solicitor draw it up for you.

Alternatively you can complete an interactive will form online, which you simply download then print off and sign it. This service costs £35. www.scotwills.co.uk

When somebody dies it is necessary for an executor to be appointed to 'wind up their estate'. This is usually a friend or relative – often one or more of the beneficiaries of the estate – but solicitors, banks or building societies will act as executor. The executor may be named in the deceased person's will, but if none is named, or if there is no will, an executor will be appointed by the local sheriff court. This may be a close relative or friend, or a solicitor.

Foreign nationals can specify that their will should be interpreted under the law of another country, otherwise Scottish law will apply. If you are domiciled in another country you will not be subject to UK inheritance laws and tax.

In Scotland, only a proportion of the deceased's estate can be freely disposed of because members of their family have certain legal rights which must be satisfied – it is not possible to 'cut them out of the will'. Any debts, inheritance tax (see above) and legal fees are payable out of the whole estate before any division.

The remaining portion is divided as follows:

- The spouse is entitled to one-third of the estate if there are children or other descendants, one-half of it if there are none.
- Children are entitled to one-third of the estate if there is a surviving spouse, one-half of it if there is not.
- Where there are no surviving spouse or children, half of the estate is taken by the parents and half by the brothers or sisters of the deceased person.
- Legacies and bequests are paid from the remainder.
- Where somebody dies without making a will, the spouse automatically inherits the matrimonial home up to a value of £300,000, or one matrimonial home if there is more than one; the furnishings and contents of that home up to the value of £24,000; cash or bank accounts, shares or other estate to the value of £42,000 if the deceased left children or other descendants, £75,000 if not.

The remaining portion of the estate is then divided between the surviving spouse and children as specified above.

FINDING PROPERTIES FOR SALE

CHAPTER SUMMARY

- In Scotland, solicitors can also act as property agents.
- Most houses and land are sold through estate agents and solicitors, but they may be sold privately.
- Estate Agents and Solicitors charge a percentage of the sale price of all properties they sell.
- There are dozens of property websites on which vendors can advertise. Practically all estate agents and solicitors now have their own websites.
- New build properties are usually sold directly by the builders.
- Property and land is advertised for sale in local, regional and national newspapers.
- Relocation Agents can help you find a home.
- Making local contacts can help you find land and houses for sale.
- A small proportion of properties are sold at auction.
- Property schedules produced by estate agents and solicitors must abide by the Trade Descriptions Act.

There are several different ways of finding property or building plots for sale in Scotland. Although most property and land in Scotland is sold through estate agents or solicitors it is perfectly possible to have a private sale. A vendor can choose to advertise his/her property for sale in newspapers, on the internet, on notice boards in shops, by putting a 'for sale' sign outside the house, by word of mouth, or a mixture of these, without the need for any professional assistance. This can work out to the advantage of both buyer and seller, because the seller will not have extra fees to pay to the selling agent. As this can be as much as two per cent of the purchase price it can be an appreciable amount and buyer and seller would normally agree to 'split the difference' of this saving.

It is only once the sale has been agreed and the conveyancing process begins that it is essential for both buyer and seller to engage a solicitor. Note that they cannot both use the same solicitor, as this would be classed as a conflict of interests.

ESTATE AGENTS

In the UK, estate agents are often characterised as 'joke' professionals. Their public image is not as bad as it once was, because some regulation has been introduced into the house-selling business, whereby descriptions of property and land for sale do have to comply with the Trades Description Act. However, there is some basis in fact for the distrust some estate agents are held in. Anybody can set themselves up as a estate agent, and they are not required by law to have any legal or professional qualifications nor be a member of any professional body. As far as you can, try to satisfy yourself that they are trustworthy before doing business with them. There are some very large chains of estate agents in Scotland, and if you choose a branch of one of these, you can be fairly confident the service will be of a reasonable standard.

In most cases, an estate agent charges a percentage of the sale price they achieve for the property, which is paid by the vendor out of the funds they receive for the house. It is therefore in the estate agents' interest to inflate the price of houses. However, this can be counter-productive, putting off prospective purchasers. This can result in properties sitting on the market for some time, with the advertised price being reduced finally in order to generate some interest from buyers.

If an estate agent does not succeed in selling your house, there should be no fee charged. If they do ask for an upfront fee, look for another estate agent who doesn't! There is nothing to stop you advertising your house for sale with more than one estate agent at a time. And if you succeed in selling your house from a private advert, while you have it advertised with an estate agent, you should keep evidence to show that it was not sold through the offices of the estate agent and therefore you should not have to pay them a selling fee.

Details of properties they have for sale will be displayed in their offices, and if you request it, they will mail you properties matching your requirements. Most of them also have their own websites with details of their properties, and very often you can print off the full schedule of details from your home computer.

If you tell them about the sort of property and the area you are interested in, estate agencies will keep you updated with details of suitable properties as they come onto their books. This service, plus house-viewings, are free to the prospective purchaser.

SOLICITORS

One area where Scottish law differs from English law is that many Scottish solicitors also act as estate agents. Although this might seem odd to buyers from south of the border, familiar with a demarcation of interests between the legal side of house purchase and the sales side, the Scottish system seems to work fine. The purchaser must choose a solicitor who is not acting in any way for the vendor, so conflict of interests is avoided.

The estate agency side of a solicitor's business – which is often run from a separate department within the firm – operates in much the same way as a dedicated estate agency. They advertise properties and building plots for sale, arrange viewings and charge fees to the vendor, generally on a percentage basis. Check their charges before engaging one to act for you as these can vary.

Scottish solicitors acting as estate agents often (but not always) belong to their local 'Solicitors' Property Centre' (SPC) which will generally have town centre premises, a regular free newspaper listing properties for sale by all their members, and a website. At their central office they generally have a duty solicitor available who will advise you on buying a property in Scotland. The SPC acts as a central advertising agency for member firms, and there may be a charge for vendors to have their property displayed in the SPC offices and newspaper, in addition to the fee charged for their solicitor's services.

Each solicitor, whether a member of an SPC or not, acts on its vendors' behalf in the sale of their properties. As a buyer, once you have identified a property to buy, you must engage the services of a different solicitor to complete the purchase.

Those solicitors who do not belong to their local SPC advertise their properties in their offices, in local newspapers and on their own websites.

THE INTERNET

Estate agents and solicitors have found their business hit in recent years by the phenomenon of property websites where vendors can advertise their properties or land for sale, often for free, or sometimes for a small charge.

In addition, vendors can create their own websites to advertise their house for sale. These can be an effective and cheap way of advertising, with the advantage that it is accessible from all over all world, 24 hours a day, seven days a week.

It is this threat which has encouraged solicitors and estate agents to advertise their properties on the internet too, so it is possible now to find suitable properties, download full details, and arrange viewings, in the comfort of your own home, from anywhere in the world.

BUILDERS

New properties are usually sold directly by the builders, although you may find details of them advertised in local estate agencies. Most new build developments are undertaken by large, nationwide, companies, which have developments in various parts of the country. You can contact them direct for details of properties currently available or under construction.

Smaller regional or local builders may also have small developments or individual houses for sale, under construction or completed. Details of these can be found in local and regional newspapers, or in the Yellow Pages classified telephone directory. You could also try searching on their website, www.yell.com which lists categories of companies by region.

Some local builders may have house sites for sale in their area. Although they would usually prefer you to buy a site and have them build you a house on it, they may agree to sell you a site on which you then find another contractor to build you a house, or arrange to build one yourself.

ADVERTISEMENTS

Local and national newspapers usually have a property page or section containing advertisements of property and plots currently for sale. In daily or evening newspapers this will usually appear on one day a week, so check which day this is. Local newspapers in particular are a good place to find properties which are being sold privately. Often estate agents or solicitors will advertise a selection of the properties on their books, so this is a good place to find the addresses of local firms.

You will find very expensive 'upmarket' properties – large country estates and castles, for example – advertised for sale in glossy magazines such as *Scottish Field* and in the quality national daily or Sunday newspapers.

There are also some magazines dedicated to new housebuilding, including *New Home Locations*, and *Scotland's New Homebuyer* and these carry adverts for housing developments throughout Scotland.

If you have chosen a specific area in Scotland to relocate to, it is always worth driving round the area, searching out 'for sale' boards outside houses, and looking in local shops at advertising noticeboards – you may find private adverts for properties or building plots for sale which you will find advertised nowhere else. Small local shops have always had free advertising boards as a service to local residents, and now supermarkets in large and small towns have taken up this idea.

AUCTIONS

Property auctions in Scotland account for only a small proportion of properties for sale. However, it is a way that you may be able to buy a property at a bargain price. The other advantage is that, as the property becomes yours the moment the hammer falls, it avoids the often long drawn out process of house-buying. It does mean that you have to do a certain amount of work in advance, and ensure that you have ten per cent of the money available immediately and the other 90% within 28 days.

In theory, any property can be sold at auction, but in practice the main sort of properties you will find for sale in this way are on the market for one of the following reasons:

- Repossession, bankruptcy or because the seller needs to clear their debts.
- The owner has died and the property has been left empty.
- They are in need of renovation work – it is rare for properties in 'move in' condition to be sold at auction.
- They are very unusual and difficult to value.
- They are likely to generate a great deal of interest.

There are few property auction houses in Scotland, but nationwide firms based in England may have Scottish properties for sale from time to time. You can find their addresses on the internet or in the phone book.

Most auction houses hold regular sales with a catalogue printed weeks in advance. Contact the auction house(s) and request their catalogue, or subscribe to their catalogue mailing list. The auction house will make an appointment for you to view any properties you are interested in.

Auction houses charge a commission in the form of a percentage of the sale price. Generally this is around 2.5% charged to the seller. Some auctioneers also charge a buyers' premium of around 1.5% of the sale. There is usually an administration fee of around £150 plus 17.5% VAT, either instead of or in addition to the buyers' premium.

RELOCATION AGENCIES

It can be difficult to find the right property or building site from a distance. This is especially the case in remote rural areas. Some vendors seem to think they can sell their property without advertising it beyond their local area. Houses or crofts for sale may only be advertised in small local newspapers, in the local shop or by word of mouth. It is useful to have a contact in the area who can find these for you. Relocation Agencies will act for you in this way, for a fee.

Generally they will search for properties matching your requirements and charge a finder's fee. Some require you to register with them and charge an up-front fee, others charge depending on the services you require. They may agree to view properties on your behalf, and send you a detailed report plus pictures or a video/DVD of those which interest you. This can save a lot of time and money by allowing you to discount properties which prove to be unsuitable without the need for you to visit them in person.

WORD OF MOUTH

Finally, don't overlook the gems you might find by staying in your chosen area for a while and asking around amongst the local residents about houses and building plots which may be for sale. Not only could you track down elusive properties which are currently for sale but not widely advertised, you might even be able to get an offer in before a property officially goes on the market, maybe saving yourself money and certainly avoiding competition from other prospective buyers.

If you're really lucky, and in the right place at the right time, you might be pointed in the direction of somebody who has an empty property, or a patch of land, which they hadn't intended to put up for sale. And you might be able to make the owner an offer they can't refuse and persuade them to sell it to you. As they say, everything and everybody has their price!

DIRECTORY OF PROPERTY FOR SALE

Estate Agents & Solicitors

Aberdeen & Northern (estates) Ltd: Thainstone Centre, Inverurie AB51 5PW; ☎ 01467 623800; www.goanm.co.uk/estates.

Aberdeen Solicitors' Property Centre: 40 Chapel Street, Aberdeen AB10 1SP; ☎ 01224-632949; www.aspc.co.uk.

Action Property Sales: 450 High Street, Cowdenbeath, Fife KY4 8LR; ☎ 01383-512512; www.mozolowskiwyse.co.uk.

Alan J Baillie: 37, Union St, Dundee Angus DD1 4BS; ☎ 01382-202444; www.alan-j-baillie.co.uk.

Alex Mitchell & Sons: 21 Eskside West, Musselburgh, Midlothian EH21 6PW; ☎ 0131-665 2468; www.amslegal.com.

Allan Grant: Millers House, 8 Shillinghill, Alloa, Clackmannanshire FK10 1JT; ☎ 01259-723201; www.allangrant.co.uk.

Allen & Harris: 18 Parkhouse Street, Ayr KA7 2HH; ☎ 01292-267248; www.sequencehome.co.uk.

Al Property Ltd: 64 Drysdale Street, Alloa, Clackmannanshire FK10 1JL; ☎ 01259-720242; www.alproperty.co.uk.

Baird & Co: 2 Park Place, Kirkcaldy, Fife KY1 1XL; ☎ 01592-268608; www.bairdonline.co.uk.

Bell Russell Property Services: 111a Graham Street, Airdrie, Lanarkshire ML6 6DE; ☎ 01236-770100; www.gspc.co.uk.

Bennetts: 52 Crossgate, Cupar, Fife KY15 5JX; ☎ 01334-655150; www.rben.net.

Bensons Estate Agency: Elizabeth Court 4 Stuart Street, East Kilbride, Glasgow, Strathclyde G74 4NG; ☎ 01355-907771; www.bensonsestateagents.com.

Blackadders: 30/34 Reform Street, Dundee DD1 1RJ; ☎ 01382-29222; www.blackadders.co.uk.

Blackadder & McMonagle: 41 High Street, Falkirk, Stirlingshire FK1 1EN; ☎ 01324-12999; www.blackandmac.com.

Borders Solicitors' Property Centre: www.bspc.co.uk.

Bowman: 27, Bank St, Dundee Angus DD1 1RP; ☎ 01382-22267; www.bowman-solicitors.co.uk. /property/general/propservices.htm.

Bradburne & Company: 139 South Street, St. Andrews, Fife KY16 9UN; ☎ 01334-79479; www.bradburne.co.uk.

Braxfield Estate Agents: 18 Bloomgate, Lanark, Lanarkshire ML11 9ET; ☎ 01555-66990; www.teamprop.co.uk.

Bruce & Partners: 23-25 Chapel Street, Aberdeen, Aberdeenshire AB10 1SQ; ☎ 01224-50600; www.bruce-and-partners.co.uk.

Caesar & Howie: 29 Upper Newmarket Street, Falkirk, Stirlingshire FK1 1JH; ☎ 01324-28332; www.caesar-howie.co.uk.

Castlehead Properties: Unit 33 The Paisley Centre 23 High Street, Paisley, Renfrewshire PA1 2AQ; ☎ 0141-848 1856; www.rightmove.co.uk.

Cluny Estate Agents: 5, Thunderton Place, Elgin, Morayshire IV30 1BG; ☎ 01343-548505; www.clunyestateagents.com.

Clyde Property: 145 Byres Road West End, Glasgow, Lanarkshire G12 9TT; ☎ 0141-576 1777; www.clydeproperty.co.uk.

Condies: 77 George Street, Perth, Perthshire PH1 5LF; ☎ 01738-441124; www.condies.co.uk.

Corum Estate Agents: 4 Canniesburn Toll, Bearsden G61 2QU; ☎ 0141-942 5888; www.corumproperty.co.uk.

Countrywide: Kilmarnock, 45 John Finnie Street, Kilmarnock, Ayrshire KA1 1BL; ☎ 01563-528165; www.countrywidenorth.co.uk.

Dewar & Co: 52 Overhaugh Street, Galashiels, Selkirkshire TD1 1DP; ☎ 01896 758081; www.dewarandco.co.uk.

Drever & *Heddle:* 56a Albert Street, Kirkwall, Orkney KW15 1HQ; ☎ 01856-872216; www.drever-heddle.co.uk.

Drummond Miller Ws: 64 South Bridge Street, Bathgate, West Lothian EH48 1TL; ☎ 01506-656645; www.drummondmiller.co.uk.

Dumfries & Galloway Solicitors' Property Centre: 14 Queensberry Street, Dumfries DG1 1EX; ☎ 01387-252684; www.dgspc.co.uk.

Erskine Estate Agency: 12 Bridgewater Shopping Centre, Erskine, Renfrewshire PA8 7AA; ☎ 0141-812 6060; www.erskineestateagency.co.uk.

Edinburgh Solicitors' Property Centre: 85 George Street, Edinburgh EH2 3ES; ☎ 0131-624 8000; www.espc.co.uk.

Ferguson & *Will:* 24 Swan Street, Brechin, Angus DD9 6EJ; ☎ 01356 622289/62; www.fergusonandwill.com.

Falkirk For Sale: Grangemouth Enterprise Centre, Falkirk Road, Grangemouth, Falkirk FK3 8XS; ☎ 0845-147 0007; www.falkirkforsale.co.uk.

Fife & Kinross Solicitors' Property Centre: PO Box 10034, Dundee DD3 8WA; ☎ 01334-880593; www.f-kspc.co.uk.

Finlayson Hughes: 31 Barossa Place, Perth, Perthshire PH1 5HH; ☎ 01738-451111; www.perth.skdfh.co.uk.

Goodfellows Estate Agents: 11a West Portland Street, Troon, Ayrshire KA10 6AB; ☎ 01292-313519; www.goodfellow-ayrshire.co.uk.

Gorrie & *Davidson:* 26 Viewfield Terrace, Dunfermline, Fife KY12 7LB; ☎ 01383 723618; www.gorriedavidson.co.uk.

GSPC: 145-147 Queen Street, Glasgow, Lanarkshire G1 3BJ; ☎ 0141-572 2400, www.gspc.co.uk.

Hewats: 63 King Street, Castle Douglas, Kirkcudbrightshire DG7 1AG; ☎ 01556-502946; www.hewats.co.uk.

Highland Solicitors' Property Centre: 30 Queensgate, Inverness IV1 1DA; ☎ 01463-231173; www.hspc.co.uk.

Inverclyde Solicitors: 120 West Blackhall Street, Greenock, Renfrewshire PA15 1XR;

☎ 01475-726424; www.isea-greenock.co.uk.

Jardine Donaldson: 18-22 Bank Street, Alloa, Clackmannanshire FK10 1HP; ☎ 01259-724411; www.jardinedonaldson.co.uk.

J L Anderson: 40 High Street, Kinross, Kinross-Shire KY13 8AN; ☎ 01577-862405; www.jlanderson.co.uk.

Murray Donald & Caithness: 17 Bell Street, St Andrews, Fife KY16 9UR; ☎ 01334-474455; www.md-c.co.uk.

North East Solicitors' Property Centre: 31 Duff Street, Macduff AB44 1QL; ☎ 01261-832491; www.nespc.com.

Pagan Osborne: 106, South St, St. Andrews, Fife KY16 9QD; ☎ 01334 475001; www.paganproperty.co.uk.

Perthshire Solicitors Property Centre: 6 South St Johns Place, Perth, Perthshire PH1 5SU; ☎ 01738-635301; www.pspc.co.uk.

Remax – Livingston: Remax House, Fairbairn Road, Livingston EH54 6TS; ☎ 01506-418555;

Slater Hogg & Howison: Head Office, City Wall House, 32 Eastwood Avenue, Shawlands, Glasgow, Lanarkshire G41 3NS; ☎ 0141-632 3300; www.slaterhogg. co.uk.

Solicitors' Property Centre Moray: 29/31 High Street, Elgin IV30 1EE; ☎ 01343-548755; www.spcmoray.com.

Stewart Property Services: 1 Great Western Road Trinity, Aberdeen AB10 6PZ; ☎ 01224-582830; www.sol.co.uk.

Strutt & Parker: Edinburgh Office, Edinburgh, Midlothian EH3 7HR; ☎ 0131 2262500; www.struttandparker.co.uk.

Tayside Solicitors' Property Centre: 9 Whitehall Crescent, Dundee DD1 4AR; ☎ 01382-228770; www.tspc.co.uk.

Thomas Purdom & Sons: 10 Oliver Place, Hawick, Roxburghshire TD9 9BG; ☎ 01450-375567; www.bannermanburke.co.uk.

T P & J L Low: 5 Broad Street, Kirkwall, Orkney KW15 1DJ; ☎ 01856 873151; www.lowsorkney.co.uk.

Watts Solicitors: 55 High Street, Montrose, Angus DD10 8LR; ☎ 01674-673444; www.wattssolicitors.com.

Winchesters: 71 Station Road, Ellon, Aberdeenshire AB41 9AR; ☎ 01358-724252; www.winchesters-law.co.uk.

Wink & Mackenzie: 87 High Street, Elgin, Morayshire IV30 1EA; ☎ 01343-542623; www.wink.co.uk.

Your Move: 213 Gorgie Road, Edinburgh EH11 1TU; ☎ 0131-313 333; www.your-move.co.uk.

Internet Property Sites

Property Live: www.propertylive.co.uk.

The Property Market: www.propertymarket.co.uk.

Property Window: www.propertywindow.com.
UK Homes For Sale: www.homes-uk.co.uk.
Asserta Home: www.assertahome/com.
Property Finder: www.propertyfinder.co.uk.
The House Hunter: www.thehousehunter.co.uk.
Home Hunter: www.homehunter.co.uk.
S1 Homes: www.s1homes.com.

Newspapers & Magazines
National Newspapers
The Scotsman: www.scotsman.com.
The Herald: www.theherald.co.uk.
Scotland on Sunday: www.scotlandonsunday.scotsman.com.
The Sunday Herald: www.sundayherald.com.
Sunday Post: www.dcthomson.co.uk/mags/post/news.htm.

Regional Newspapers
Courier (Dundee): www.courier.co.uk.
Daily Record (Glasgow): www.dailyrecord.co.uk.
Edinburgh Evening News: http://edinburghnews.scotsman.com.
Evening Express (Aberdeen): www.thisisaberdeen.co.uk.
Evening Times (Glasgow): www.eveningtimes.co.uk.
Greenock Telegraph: www.greenocktelegraph.co.uk.
Paisley Daily Express: http://icrenfrewshire.icnetwork.co.uk.
Press and Journal (Aberdeen): www.thisisnorthscotland.co.uk.

Magazines
Scottish Field: www.scottishfield.co.uk.
The Countryman: www.countrymanmagazine.co.uk.
Country Life: www.countrylife.co.uk.
New Home Locations Scotland: Adaptive House, Quarrywood Court, Livingston EH54 6AX; www.new-home-locations.net. A quarterly publication available by subscription though the website. It contains details of new developments around the country in addition to articles on all aspects of buying a new house.
Scotland's New Homebuyer: Pinpoint Scotland Ltd, 9 Gayfield Square, Edinburgh EH1 3NT; ☎ 0131-556 9702; www.snhb.co.uk. Another quarterly publication, available free from estate agents and SPC offices.
Homebuilding & Renovating Magazine and sister publication *Plotfinder* are available via newsagents or by subscription. ☎ 01527-834406; www.homebuilding. co.uk. The website includes a self-build directory which lists products, suppliers and services. It also has a database of building plots for sale throughout the

country.

Build It: Inside Communications Ltd, 19th Floor, 1 Canada Square, Canary Wharf, London E14 5AP; ☎ 020-7770 8300; www.self-build.co.uk. Available through newsagents or by subscription. 12 issues around £40.

Auctions

Directory of UK Property Auctions: www.wheresmyproperty.com.

SVA Property Auctions: www.sva-auctions.co.uk.

Relocation Agencies

Location Highland (Inverness): ☎ 01463-234422; www.locationhighland.co.uk.

Compass Relocation: 19A Ruisaurie, Beauly, Inverness-shire IV4 7AJ; ☎/fax ☎ 01463-783242; www.compass-reloc.co.uk.

Scott's Relocation: 23 Queen's Avenue, Edinburgh EH4 2DG; ☎ 0131-539 5367; www.scottsrelocation.co.uk.

Rural Relocation: (Covers Perthshire, Angus, Fife & Kinross.) Main Street, Dalguise, Dunkeld, Perthshire PH8 0JU; ☎ 01795-2970388; www.ruralrelocation.com.

The Association of Relocation Agents (ARA): PO Box 189, Diss IP22 1PE; ☎ 08700-737475; www.relocationagents.com.

Builders – New Build & Land for Sale

There are a large number of building companies with new developments throughout Scotland. Some of the largest are listed below, but there are smaller companies operating regionally. Contact details of these can be found in local phone books or on www.yell.co.uk.

Barratt Construction: Golf Road, Ellon, AB41 9AT; ☎ 01358-724174; fax 01358-724043; www.barratthomes.co.uk.

Bett Homes: Argyle House, The Castle Business Park, Stirling FK9 4TT; ☎ 01786-477777; fax 01786-477666; www.betthomes.co.uk.

Alfred McAlpine Homes: Linnaird House, 1 Pall Mall East, London SW1Y 5AZ; ☎ 020-7930 6255; www.alfred-mcalpineplc.com.

Redrow Homes: Redrow House, 3 Central Park Avenue, Larbert, Falkirk FK5 4RX; ☎ 01324-555536; fax 01324-574890; www.redrow.co.uk.

For a full list of current developments with contact details see *New Home Locations Scotland* and *Scotland's New Homebuyer* (details above.)

Castles, Listed Buildings & Luxury Properties

Pavilions of Splendour Ltd: 22 Mount View Road, London N4 4HX; ☎ 020-8348 1234; fax 030-8341 9790; www.heritage.co.uk. Specialises in the buying and selling of listed buildings.

Castles for Sale: www.castles-for-sale.com.

Castles of the World: www.castles.org.

International Castles for Sale: http://castles.glo-con.com.

Frank Knight Estate Agents: www.knightfrank.com/Webui/uk. Specialists in luxury properties.

Buildings at Risk Register for Scotland: www.buildingsatrisk.org.uk. Buildings of historic importance which need rescuing.

INTERPRETING PROPERTY ADS

Estate agents and solicitors produce a schedule containing photographs and reasonably detailed particulars of each property they have for sale. Some schedules are more detailed than other, but generally they will include dimensions and description of the salient features of each room in the property, plus any outside space and what is included there.

These descriptions have to be truthful, as they are governed by the Trades Descriptions Act, but they give themselves a legal get-out by hedging the schedule around with provisos and exemption clauses such as:

- While these particulars are believed to be correct, they cannot be guaranteed and prospective purchasers are asked to satisfy themselves with regard thereto. No liability will be accepted for any deviations.

- Measurements are approximate and are given for general guidance only.

- Any photographs used are purely illustrative and may demonstrate only the surrounds, they are not therefore to be taken as indicative of the extent of the property, or that the photographs are taken from within the boundaries of the property, or of what is included with the sale.

So the bottom line is, *caveat emptor!*

Advertisements for properties for sale privately or through websites do not have to comply with any legal requirements, so you must find out exactly what it is the vendor is offering for sale before you submit a formal offer. Your solicitor, during the process of conveyancing, should carry out searches regarding the exact extent and alignment of boundaries and so forth, to ensure that the vendor is actually the owner of, and entitled to sell, what he is offering you.

Property auction houses publish a catalogue of the lots for sale in each auction sale. This may be available online, from the auction house, or through the mail. Generally the details of each lot will not be as detailed as those provided for properties for sale conventionally via an estate agent or solicitor.

GLOSSARY OF PROPERTY TERMS

Types of Property

amenity land	an area of land which may be designated for other purposes than housing. It may not be possible to get planning permission for a dwelling house on the site.
building site/plot	an area of land usually with planning permission for a dwelling house.
bungalow	single storey house.
chalet (holiday)	a small house intended for holiday use, usually wooden.
conversion	a newly designed and constructed flat within an old building.
cottage	small house usually in a rural area.
croft (house)	a house situated on a croft (see below).
detached	an individual house not physically connected to any other.
duplex flat	a flat on two stories.
end terrace	house on the end of a terrace so it has one outside wall.
flat	apartment (NB: see INTERIOR (below) for meaning of *apartment*).
garden flat	basement flat with direct access to a (usually communal) garden.
granny flat	part of a house, or an annex to a house, set up as a small self-contained flat.
loft style flat	an open-plan modern-style flat.
main door flat	a flat which is entered through the main front door of the building, rather than having an internal front door off a hallway.
mews	a terrace of small houses, or an individual house, in a courtyard or set in the back garden(s) behind larger houses.
penthouse flat	top floor flat, usually large, luxurious and expensive.
retirement home/flat	a small house or flat designed for retired people, often with an on-site warden.
semi-detached	joined by a party wall to one other house only.
tenement	a traditional apartment building, usually in a Scottish city.
terraced house	one of a connected row of houses.
town house	a terraced house within a town, usually larger in size or more modern than a traditional terrace.
villa	a house of more than one storey (a term only used by property agents).

Interior

apartment	main room, not including kitchen and bathroom (e.g. a 5 apartment flat might have 3 bedrooms and 2 reception rooms).
breakfast room	a casual eating area separate from the dining room.

dining hall	a central hall large enough to dine in, usually in traditional tenement-style flats.
dining kitchen	kitchen with space for a dining table and chairs.
drawing room	in larger houses, a formal sitting room.
dressing room	a room leading directly from a bedroom for the storage of clothes.
cloakroom	for outdoor clothing and footwear.
en-suite	a bath or shower room leading directly from a bedroom.
entrance vestibule	small internal hall by outside door.
extension	room or rooms added on to a house to make it larger.
lounge/diner	open plan main room with a comfortable seating area and a dining area.
lounge; living room; or sitting room	interchangeable terms for the main communal room with comfortable seating, TV, fireplace etc.
master bedroom	main bedroom of the property.
study	office.
reception room	a communal main room such as a lounge.
utility room	room housing sink, washing machine, freezer etc.
videophone; audiophone	electronic systems allowing a flat-owner to hear or see and speak to a visitor at the external door to the building, before unlocking the door by remote control.
coombed ceiling	where the walls of a room extend into the roof and the ceiling is therfore partially sloping.
Velux window	a skylight window set into a roof.

Exterior

decking	outside seating area on a wooden platform.
outbuildings	non-residential buildings set in the grounds of a property.
private mooring	boat mooring sold with house.
shared access	road or driveway to house also used by neighbouring residents.
steading	agricultural outbuilding(s), usually stone-built.

Other

croft	small area of land in the Highlands and Islands administered via the Crofters Commission.
croft tenancy	the right to use croftland in return for rent.
factor	agent managing an estate or a block of flats.
factoring fees/charges	annual charges paid by residents in a block of flats, including buildings insurance.
feu hold	freehold (i.e.owned outright).
owner-occupied	residential property lived in by the owner, or a croft which the occupier has bought from the estate.

WHAT TYPE OF
PROPERTY TO BUY

CHAPTER SUMMARY

- Two thirds of Scots live in houses, one third in flats.
- In the southern cities there are many Victorian tenement flats.
- Parking can be a problem if buying in a city area.
- Many of the houses in the Highlands, Islands and Argyll & Bute, are croft houses.
- There is specific legislation relating to the purchase of crofts.
- City living is very popular at present and there are many new housing developments on inner city sites.
- In rural areas it is common to buy a plot of land and build your own house.
- There are islands, mansions, estates and castles for sale in Scotland, sometimes surprisingly cheaply.
- If you buy a listed building you have to abide by strict planning regulations regarding any work you do on it.

Although on bald figures two out of three Scots live in houses, the other third in flats (apartments), this doesn't give a particularly useful picture of the housing market as the pattern of housing varies quite significantly across the country. In the city centres the majority are flat dwellers, while in the towns and suburban areas there is more of a balance between flat and house dwellers. In rural areas, flats are few and far between, with most people living in houses.

In the north of Scotland and the Islands, the pattern of land ownership is different from elsewhere. The land is divided into privately-owned large estates, areas of which are divided into crofts of around five hectares (12 acres) and rented out to tenant crofters. Tenant crofters have the right to build a house on their croft and can, if they wish, become owner-occupiers by buying their croft from the estate.

Many rural dwellers prefer to build their own houses, or commission a builder to build one for them. In the more populous areas, if you want a brand new house, you are more likely to have to buy one on a development of several such houses. If you buy 'off-plan' you may be able to specify your own particular requirements before the house is built.

Houses are detached (free-standing in their own gardens}; semi-detached (two houses connected by a shared party wall); or terraced (a row of connected houses.) Modern new-build developments are usually a mixture of detached and semi-detached houses. Terraced houses tend to be small and cheaper than other types of houses and are usually found within towns.

Flats are of various types. The traditional high-density accommodation in the cities – particularly Edinburgh, Glasgow and Dundee – was tenements, sandstone or granite apartment buildings dating from the Victorian era. By the mid 20th century many of these had deteriorated to the point where they were condemned as slums, being completely inadequate as far as modern standards of hygiene and other facilities were concerned. Many were demolished at that time, but in recent years the preference has been to renovate and upgrade them into desirable apartments.

There are also many more-recently constructed purpose-built blocks of flats in towns and cities. A third alternative is where large old houses have been sub-divided into flats of various sizes.

MODERN V OLDER

Generally house-buyers will have a distinct preference regarding the age of the home they wish to look for. Many people are looking for an old building with plenty of character and original features, while others want the ease of maintenance and 'mod cons' of a house built in the last couple of decades. Properties built between the 1960s and the 1980s, say, can seem to have the worst of both worlds, lacking the attractive architectural features of an older house, and although they may have fitted kitchens and bathrooms, central heating systems and double glazing, unless they have been renovated already these will be old and tired and ready to be replaced. However, a property from this era which does need work to improve and update might be available at a bargain price compared with others, so they should not be overlooked.

There are of course advantages and disadvantages with both types. Properties dating from the first half of the 20th century or before tend to be built more substantially than some of the more recently built property. The tendency in Scotland is for modern houses to be built with a wooden frame, which is then enclosed with concrete blocks and plasterboard. These are sometimes called 'kit houses' because the wooden frame is constructed in sections off site and then brought to the house-plot for erection. There are plenty of these to be found in the Highlands where, in the 1970s, many crofters were tempted by cheap grants and loans to replace their old stone-built croft houses with wooden framed kit houses, some of which proved to be cheaply and sometimes shoddily built. You should always get a good quality survey done of a house of this type.

Many old stone crofts have been rescued and renovated (often by incomers) to make charming homes, and you will see others still standing in a ruinous state. However, as many crofters are reluctant to sell them, preferring to use them as barns or storage sheds rather than selling them on to a family to live in, those which do come on the market are becoming rarer than hen's teeth and the price they attract is often well over their intrinsic worth. For more on the subject of crofts, see below.

It might seem self-evident to say this, but the history of a town or city determines the kind of property you will find in different areas. Historic cities such as Glasgow and Edinburgh have, in the more central areas, plenty of substantial old properties, Victorian or earlier, with all the architectural features you could hope for. In many cases these were originally built as tenements – apartment blocks – while other large individual houses have been divided into flats more recently. When a still intact house of this type comes onto the market nowadays it is likely to sell for well in excess of half a million pounds.

In the last twenty years many old-style flats have been upgraded and now can reach a premium price in desirable areas of cities. In other, less wealthy areas, where unemployment and social problems are more evident, it is often the case that the older tenements, built far more cheaply than those in the wealthier areas, were demolished and replaced with modern tower blocks and other cheap housing some decades ago. These now have also deteriorated, and there are large swathes of Glasgow and Edinburgh where they in their turn are being demolished and replaced with new housing.

On the outskirts of the cities, as they spread with the growth of population during the 20th century, 'housing estates' were built, with construction being particularly extensive in the 1930s and the 1960s. In the city centres, the last two decades have seen a concerted effort to regenerate some of the dilapidated areas with so-called 'brown-field development' where new modern blocks of flats and townhouses were built to 'fill in the gaps' where older property had been demolished, or where owners of large houses sold off their surrounding gardens to developers.

The centres of the long-established cities of Scotland, with Glasgow leading the way – at the time of writing a huge £3 billion of private money is being invested in new housing, offices and retail premises throughout Glasgow – are seeing a renaissance with the Scottish Executive determined to make its mark on the country, and upgrade living conditions for its people, since devolution. Wholesale renovation of old buildings, plus construction of brand new ones, is taking place, with the long-neglected waterfronts in Glasgow, Edinburgh and Dundee being brought back to life with luxury flats and other new developments.

Inverness, as the second newest Scottish city and also the fastest-growing city in Europe, is belatedly following trends seen in other Scottish cities a century ago, with new housing being built all around the outskirts of the city, generally on estates of houses near to new retail parks.

WELL-PRESENTED PROPERTIES

Whichever type of property you choose to look for, you will find that the extent to which it has been 'prepared for sale' will have an effect on the asking price. The days when people accepted that any home they bought would need work done on it, from modernisation of fixtures and fittings to redecoration, seem to be numbered. In recent years there have been numerous TV programmes where property developers and estate agents take house-vendors in hand and show them how to maximise the profit from their house sale by spending several thousand pounds to redecorate their homes in a bland style, and 'dress' them for sale by putting in expensive modern furniture and soft furnishings (sometimes rented for the purpose) and clearing away all the clutter of day to day life. Sometimes they even suggest that vendors banish their children and pets to stay with a relative while they have their house for sale, in order to attract buyers who like their purchase to look like a brand new show home. Despite the fact that those sumptuous furnishing are rarely for sale with the house, estate agents insist that they do help to sell houses at maximum prices.

If you are willing and able to do some redecorating once you have purchased your property, try to look past the dubious taste of the previous owners, and visualise what you could make of it to suit your own style, you should be able to get a property at a more reasonable price. And always remember, that even the best dressed, blandest house you can buy, is unlikely to be exactly what you want, so you will probably end up redecorating sooner or later anyway, to suit your own taste. Is it really worth spending the extra simply for a 'well-presented' house?

HOUSES

Houses of various types are the most popular of dwellings for Scots to live in. In urban areas, these will be a mix of detached, semi-detached and terraced houses, on one or more floors. In the Highlands it is rare to find houses of two full stories or more, as the planning rules in the region generally restrict property to a maximum of 1.5 stories, where the upstairs rooms extend into the roof and will therefore have partially sloping or 'coombed' ceilings. The traditional style houses have characteristic, usually very attractive, 'dormer windows' which extend upwards from the roof on the outside with their own pitched 'mini-roofs' over. Some modern houses retain the normal roofline and instead provide light to the upstairs rooms through skylight windows set flush to the slope of the roof. The main company providing such windows is Velux and the term velux window is often used as a general term for any roof window.

Single storey bungalows are common throughout Scotland. They are often thought to be the preserve of the more elderly, as the lack of stairs make them ideal for anybody with mobility problems. However, bungalows are becoming more popular with young families, which is reflected in the fact that over the past decade bungalows have recorded the highest price growth of any sort of property, with values increasing 119% during the period.

Detached houses, whether one or more stories high, are generally the most desirable properties with families, and is reflected in their prices. They provide the ultimate in privacy, with a garden and other outside space running around all four sides of the building. The increased demand for bungalows is partially an indication of the popularity and high prices of a larger detached property – bungalows tend to be smaller and cheaper and therefore more affordable for a young family. Other factors could be that families tend to be smaller now, so a large detached house with four or more bedrooms is not required. It could also be that in the booming house market, people are thinking that there is scope to buy a bungalow and build on to it to increase the value of their home. If this is so, it suggests that many of them may not remain as bungalows, as owners convert the loft (attic) into extra rooms, thus creating a 1.5 storey house.

Semi-detached and terraced properties are generally not the first choice for buyers, if money is no object, but they are cheaper to buy and therefore the market is always strong, particularly with first time buyers and with older people who are downsizing after their children have left home.

Gardening is very popular with many Scots, as can be seen from the number of garden centres in the country, and the plethora of television programmes on the subject. One of the main reasons buyers choose houses over flats is that they have their own little bit – or much larger bit – of outside space where they can create a garden and stamp their personality on their surroundings.

Despite – or maybe because of – the indifferent summer weather sometimes experienced in Scotland, people do like to be able to get outside as much as possible when the weather allows. They like to be able to use their outside space as an extra 'room' with an area where they can sit and eat outside, perhaps with a barbecue in situ. Wooden decking areas are currently very fashionable for the purpose, and garden centres and DIY stores all have decking of various types for sale.

Having your own outside area means that in nearly all cases you will have space to park one or more vehicles. There may also be a garage, or space for one, within the grounds. Detached or semi-detached houses will almost certainly have parking space. Terraced houses, however, which often front on to a street, with very little or no garden area in front of the house, may have no off-street parking. You may be able to get a residents' permit to park in front of your house, but this will depend on local council by-laws. Many terraces have a lane running along the back, allowing access for residents to back yards or gardens. There may be space to park here, either in the lane or within your own grounds.

If you will need some income to help pay for a mortgage, or to help with daily living expenses, it is worth considering the idea of looking for a house which has one or more cottages in the grounds. These come up for sale reasonably frequently, particularly in rural areas which attract plenty of tourists. In Scotland, it is not necessary to pay a massive amount for a large estate with a big country house in order to find cottages in the gourds. In the Highlands in particular there are many average-sized modern family homes in a large, but not excessive garden, which has the original cottage in the garden, with potential for letting it out either long term or for short term holiday lets.

> **Pam & Bernard Clarke wanted a house in Argyll big enough for their family plus friends and relatives who came to visit**
> *Because we couldn't find just what we wanted, we ended up buying a three bedroom house with a small cottage in the grounds. It proved to be an excellent decision. Not only could we put our friends and family up in comfort when they visited, we also earned useful extra income from letting out the cottage to tourists during the summer season.*

Another alternative is to look for a house which is divided internally into two flats – usually one upstairs, one downstairs – allowing you to live in one flat and let out the other, again either on a long let or short let basis.

THE RISE OF THE ONE MILLION POUND HOUSE

In March 2000, a house in East Lothian sold for over one million pounds, the first time this price had been achieved in Scotland. Since then there have been 221 properties sold which have broken the million pound barrier and the market at this top end seems to be booming, despite a slowdown generally. In 2005 estate agents were reporting that there was a far healthier market for properties worth over one million than for those in the £500,000 to £750,000 bracket.

Part of the reason for this is that property is comparatively cheap, compared with prices paid for equivalent properties in London and the South East and abroad. Edinburgh has the largest number of very expensive properties, although there are a lot in rural areas, plus a handful in Glasgow and Perth. An equivalent London property to one selling for one to two million pounds in Edinburgh could well achieve up to £20 million. This fact is encouraging wealthy investors to buy in Scotland, buying into the better quality of life and better standard of living they can afford compared with living in London.

In May 2005, a detached, six bedroomed, stone built Victorian villa in Edinburgh, with walled garden, conservatory and orangery, went on the market at offers over £975,000. It had attracted 60 serious bidders within four weeks of going on the market and sold for well in excess of one million pounds.

There is a shortage of such 'top-end' properties in Scotland, with an estimated 850 homes worth seven figures. This compares with 33,000 in London alone. As a result, demand for them is predicted to remain strong amongst wealthy buyers and investors for years to come.

FLATS

Thirty-eight per cent of the Scottish population live in flats, compared to 20% in the UK as a whole. If you are intending to look for property to buy in a town or city centre, you will undoubtedly find that there are far more flats for sale than houses, and that houses, because they are far less common in such areas, are comparatively expensive.

The wholesale building of tenements to house the rapid growth in population brought about by the Industrial Revolution means that flat-dwelling is seen as the normal way of living in Scottish cities. What is also noticeable, largely as a result of this historical form of town planning, is that there is far less demarcation between residential and business or shopping areas in Scottish cities than is commonly the case in the English cities.

Although in the past tenements had a very bad name, because by the mid 20th century they had, on the whole, been neglected and had deteriorated to such an extent that many were condemned as slums, today renovated flats within sandstone tenement buildings are for sale at a premium, and far more desirable than many more recently built flats. It has to be said that where tenements, built of so-called blonde or red sandstone, or of granite, have had the black grime of centuries removed and been brought back to their original state, they are extremely attractive and architecturally striking buildings. Large areas of Glasgow's desirable West End, and areas of other cities, are filled with these buildings, and are now designated conservation areas in recognition of their historical importance. The flats inside them are often stunning too, with large rooms and high ceilings, full of attractive original features such as stone fireplaces and plaster cornices. The stairwells and hallways within these buildings can be just as striking, with the original brightly coloured ceramic tiles on the walls and floors. In 2005, a well-presented large flat in one of these tenements in a desirable road in the West End will sell for in excess of £300,000.

WHAT IS A TENEMENT?.

In common parlance, as well as in estate agents' details, the term tenement relates to traditional sandstone or granite properties. However, its definition under Scottish law is far broader: A tenement is a building comprising two or more related flats that are owned or designed to be owned separately and which are divided from one another horizontally. Thus all of the following are legally defined as tenements:

- Modern blocks of flats.
- Large houses that have been converted into flats.
- Other buildings which have been converted into flats.
- High-rise blocks.
- Four-in-a-block.
- Blocks of flats with commercial properties in them, such as ground floor shops.
- Office buildings if they have two or more flats in them.

There are also many more modern flats, generally built in the last twenty years, to choose from, and these tend to sell more cheaply than the older-style flats. There are advantages with regard to the amount and costs of maintenance required on an old building. The price you pay for a modern apartment depends on the quality of the building, the area in which it is situated, and whether the flat has been recently upgraded, with kitchen, bathrooms and the like replaced. As there was a boom in building such blocks in the 1980s, many are now over 20 years old, and consequently look tired and old-fashioned. When an untouched one of these comes onto the market, it is likely to be bought by a private buyer looking for a relatively cheap property, who will then upgrade the flat as money permits; or in many cases, it will be bought by a property developer who will gut the flat, put in a new kitchen and bathroom(s), maybe put down fashionable wooden flooring, and generally upgrade the entire unit. Then it will go back on the market to be sold at a much higher price.

There is a new phase of city flat building in progress currently, especially in Glasgow, with whole areas of the city being regenerated. The city centre and the harbour and riverfront in particular are currently full of new developments in various stages of completion. Luxury flats commanding high prices are particularly in demand as Glasgow becomes an increasingly attractive and desirable place for the wealthy to find a home.

Aside from the maintenance aspects, one of the big advantages of going for a new or more modern flat is parking. Most modern flats were built, and are being built, with residents' parking spaces and/or garages, either outside the building or underground. This is an important consideration, because most of the gorgeous old-style flats in stunning sandstone buildings only have on-street parking, Some are in areas which have parking restrictions on them, which may mean that you cannot park there between certain hours each day (8am-6pm is usual). In some cases you may be able to purchase a residents' parking permit which will allow you to park outside or near your flat, but this is by no means always the case. There are constant grumbles by residents in the local papers about the difficulty of finding a parking space, complaining that workers and shoppers fill all available spaces. But, of course, they do need to park too, so it's an insoluble problem in most cities. So it is well worth deciding how important having a readily accessible personal parking space is before you decide whether to go for an old or new flat.

Derek Taylor bought a flat in the West End of Glasgow

Originally my wife and I intended to buy a two bedroom flat in a Victorian sandstone tenement. We looked at some truly beautiful flats, with large rooms full of original features. But the more we looked at, the more we began to realise just what a problem parking was in many areas. Sometimes we would have to park several streets away from a flat we were going to view, and we wondered how often the flat-owners managed to park outside their own front door. So in the end we decided to buy a modern flat which included a private parking place in the price. Since we moved here, the parking restrictions in he area have been extended so we are even more glad we decided on practicality and convenience, at the cost of a little architectural heritage!

If you like the look of the centuries old buildings, but prefer a more modern style flat, it is possible to get the best of both worlds. There are many old buildings, often originally built for business purposes by large companies, which have been gutted and transformed inside into modern flats, sometimes with facilities such as residents' gyms within the building. In Glasgow city centre, for example, this has been done with the old GPO (General Post Office) building, and another imposing old building once belonging to the Co-operative Society.

Another important consideration is whether the building has a lift (elevator). By no means all of them do, so if you are looking at a top floor flat in a building without a lift, you do need to be sure this isn't going to be or become a problem for you or your visitors.

The lack of one's own private garden is either an advantage or a disadvantage, depending on your attitude to gardening! Blocks of flats or tenements often have communal gardens, responsibility for the upkeep of which will vary depending on local agreements. In some cases, residents are left to work it out for themselves, in which case, unless there are keen gardeners living in the building prepared to take control, the garden may end up a sorry, neglected plot of land. In other cases the gardens are looked after by a specialist company, and residents will each pay a share of the cost.

The problem of noisy neighbours cannot be ignored when thinking of buying a flat, especially if you have not lived in one previously so know what levels of noise to expect. Even everyday noises of footsteps, music, vacuum cleaners and the like can be an irritation if you are particularly sensitive to noise or the building is not well-insulated between flats. The current trend for wooden and laminate flooring in homes has had a significant effect on the levels of complaints about noise from flat-dwellers living below flats with wooden floors, to the extent that the government commissioned a report into the problem. The study found that walking on a carpet is 22 decibels quieter than walking on a wooden floor – a noise reduction equivalent to wearing earplugs. If you have complaints from your downstairs neighbours, rugs can substantially cut down on the noise from footsteps on wooden floors. Siting loudspeakers from music systems on the wall, or standing them on special insulated blocks, can also make a big difference. It is worth considering a top floor flat as these have the advantage over others that one has no overhead noise to contend with.

A licensing scheme has been introduced for flats which are rented out to students or other groups of adults. Landlords of Houses in Multiple Occupation (HMOs) have to register these properties, which means that it is now possible to carry out a search to discover whether a property you are thinking of buying is next door to, and close by, any HMOs. It has been predicted that the introduction of this scheme, in 2005, will depress the value of flats in tenements where there are HMOs. This remains to be seen. But as a buyer, if the thought of potential noisy neighbours is a really important factor in your choice of a flat, it might be worth paying the fee to a solicitor to carry out the search.

At the end of the day, you have to accept that flat dwelling will almost certainly involve living with noises from other flats, and tolerance of others is needed. However, if noise is genuinely excessive and unreasonable, there are legal solutions – contact the local council or the police if you have problems with noisy neighbours and you cannot reach an amicable agreement with them to moderate their noise.

When buying a flat it is important to enquire about any additional service charges on top of your council tax you will need to pay. In Scotland, most blocks of flats and tenements are 'factored' which means a factor or property manager is assigned to look after the building as a whole. Nowadays, the factor is usually a company of solicitors, estate agents or surveyors, rather than an individual. The residents will each be charged an annual factoring fee, assessed on the basis of the size of their particular flat, which covers buildings insurance and ongoing maintenance of the buildings and grounds. Any one-off costs for repair work or similar may be charged for in addition.

The level of fees can vary quite substantially depending on the buildings and the services provided. Some provide a weekly cleaning service, where an outside firm of cleaners comes in to spruce up the communal areas; some provide gardeners; having a lift in the building can add to the factoring fees because they are expensive things to maintain and insure; if there is a residents' gym this is another expense; underground car parks and garages all need maintaining. And don't forget that the older a building is, the more likely it is to need, at some time or even at regular intervals, expensive maintenance,

As a broad guide, you should expect to pay between £500 to £800 extra per annum for factoring fees on a flat in a good quality area of Glasgow. Bear in mind that this includes buildings insurance for your flat, and if you buy a house your mandatory annual buildings insurance will probably be well over £100.

Whether your flat is factored or not, the owners of flats in Scotland have certain legal responsibilities for maintaining and repairing the common parts of the building. These are explained simply but in detail in a Scottish Consumer Council publication *Common Repair, Common Sense – A Homeowner's Guide to the Management & Maintenance of Common Property.* This can be downloaded from www.homepoint. communitiesscotland.gov.uk.

NEW BUILD

There are about 20,000 new homes built in Scotland each year, including all types of housing built for private purchase and for social housing such as Housing Association properties. Around 60% of new houses in Scotland are constructed using brick and block cavity walls, 40% being of timber frame construction. This does not include blocks of flats which are generally built around a metal frame, which is then blocked around. Some go for a more traditional look, and may be faced with brick, while others make a virtue of modernity and use lots of glass, concrete, metal and hi-tech materials.

There are a number of advantages in buying a new house:

o Built to higher standards than many older houses.
o Have thermal insulation, double glazing, modern central heating, adequate

ventilation.
- Sold complete with fitted kitchens, bathrooms and bedrooms, usually with kitchen appliances such as fridges, freezers, dishwashers, washing machines etc.
- Maintenance-free living.
- If you buy 'off-plan' you may have a certain degree of personal choice in the layout, décor or fittings
- No repair work or decoration required when you first move in.
- If the builder is registered with the National House-Building Council (NHBC) they have a ten year warranty and insurance cover for major defects.

However, there are potential disadvantages to bear in mind. New houses are usually built in communal 'estates' or 'developments' of a handful up to scores of similar houses. This may be a disadvantage if you prefer more individuality in the design of your home, and if you like to live at a distance from your nearest neighbours.

The dream of moving into a maintenance and problem-free house or flat may prove to be just that – a dream. Many new owners find that their properties have many minor so-called 'snagging' faults, including such things as leaky showers, ill-fitting windows, broken or chipped tiles, scratched wooden floors and overall shoddy workmanship, often carried out by sub-contracted tradesmen such as plumbers, joiners and electricians. Although most new homes have a ten year warranty, this only covers major defects and not these minor faults – even though there may be a long list of them in your property (some people have reported hundreds of minor snags in their new homes).

If you are buying a property from a previous owner, your surveyor and solicitor should ensure that any minor defects are brought to your attention, and anyway, minor wear and tear is to be expected in a property which has been previously lived in. With a new property, the purchaser deals direct with the builder, and although he should have checked that the workmanship was up to scratch, very often these problems can be overlooked.

It is therefore very important when you decide to purchase a new home that you enquire about the arrangements for fixing snagging faults. NHBC rules state that you have two years in which to discover and report any minor defects to the builder, who should then put them right. But some builders may try to get you to report such defects within seven days and imply you have no comeback after that time. Make sure you insist on your rights if this affects you and contact NHBC or your local Trading Standards Authority if you do not get satisfaction.

Local authority building inspectors must inspect and pass new homes as safe and fit for habitation before they can be sold, but they are not looking for minor defects. This problem is so worrying to some home-buyers that they are seeking the services of professional snagging inspection companies which charge up to £400 to look for and identify faults they may not have spotted in their initial viewing of the property. As this can identify faults which may cost hundreds or thousands of pounds to put right, if the property has a particularly long list of problems, some new house-owners think it is money well-spent.

National House-Building Council: www.nhbc.co.uk..

SELF-BUILD

Building your own house is a popular option, especially if you are looking to buy a croft. Crofters have the right to build a house on their croft, and can also 'decroft' one or more building plots on their croft. These may be sold with or without a house built on them. As a result of this system, you will find in the Highlands in particular that new houses tend to be built as individual properties rather than developments of several houses.

If you do not plan to buy a croft, but still fancy the challenge of self-building, you can find building sites for sale through estate agents, local builders or by approaching local land-owners.

The term 'self-build' is a bit of a misnomer, which can put some people off this option. You do not have to physically design and construct the house yourself – most self-builders hire a builder to undertake the work. Alternatively you may prefer to act as the main contractor yourself, and hire tradesmen and craftsmen to do various parts of the project. If you have the skills to carry out certain parts of the work, such as the electrical work or the plumbing, say, you may decide to do this. Or you may hire professional tradesmen to do the skilled work, up to the stage where the house is habitable, then finish off the inside yourself, maybe doing the decoration, and/or fitting the kitchen and bathrooms yourself.

This 'piecemeal' approach is possible even where you decide to hire a building contractor to do the bulk of the work. You can agree with him that he will build as much or as little of the house as you wish, maybe just as far as it is watertight – windows in and roof on, say.

However you decide to allocate the work, you do have overall control of the build from start to finish. Another advantage is that you will work with an architect and/or builder to produce exactly the house you want, to suit your own specific requirements. Your house will be unique, which may well mean that it is worth far more than neighbouring houses if and when you come to sell it. However, if you do think you might want to re-sell it one day, it may not be a good idea to make it too quirky – this could put off prospective purchasers who do not have the same eccentricities as you!

An advantage of building a new house rather than buying an existing small house and converting or extending it is that there is no value added tax (VAT) charged on the building of a new house, while 17.5% VAT is charged on extending, improving and repairs to an existing house. With a self-build property, you can claim back all the VAT paid on materials on completion of the project, without having to register as a VAT trader.

However, self-build is not necessarily a cheaper option. By the time you have bought a site, paid for planning permission, the cost of the build and for the installation of electricity, water and sewerage on site, it might cost you more than buying an existing house, or buying a completed new house from a builder. If you can do parts of the contracting and the building work yourself, you should be able to bring the price down. But you should always keep a contingency fund for any unforeseen costs that may arise. Planning regulations may require you to abide by stringent specifications in regard to domestic sewerage and drainage arrangements, especially where you are not on mains sewerage, and these can work out very expensive, sometimes adding thousands of pounds onto the cost.

However, on average the re-sale value of a self-built house is at least 25% greater than the cost of the land and the build. You must occupy the house for at least a year before selling on for it to be classed as your principle residence – in this case you will not have to pay any capital gains tax on the profits from the sale.

A word of warning: most people who undertake a self-build project find it a very stressful process. as well as having the vagaries of the weather and unreliable tradesmen to contend with, both of which can make the build far longer than anticipated, most builds also run over budget, so there may be money worries to deal with. And while the build is going on you need to pay the cost, and put up with the inconvenience, of living in some form of temporary accommodation. So it is a choice to be considered very carefully before you take the plunge. Make sure the relationship with your partner or family is strong enough to withstand all the potential stresses and strains!

> **Peter and Mandy Allengame** *lived in a static caravan, with their young daughter and Mandy's mother, on their croft for nearly two years before they had everything in place to start building their house. It was a great relief once the foundations went in, because the end was then in sight, but it was several months before the house was completed. The stress of living in cramped, uncomfortable conditions, for such a long period, during which there were the worst winter storms in the area for decades, made it an experience they wouldn't want to repeat in a hurry.*

CROFTS

If you wish to move to the Highlands or Islands, and are looking for a house with a reasonable amount of land attached, you are more than likely going to be looking at a croft. Crofts, with and without habitable houses on them, regularly come up for sale and can be found advertised alongside other land and houses in estate agents' and solicitors' advertisements.

First, a brief explanation of crofting, as the laws relating to it are specific and you must be aware of them before pursuing the purchase of a croft or a croft house.

A croft is a small agricultural unit situated in one of the former counties of Caithness, Sutherland, Ross-shire, Inverness-shire (all now in Highland Region) and Shetland, Orkney & Argyll. A crofter was, and still is in many cases, the tenant of a croft, and pays rent to the landlord of the croft. However, since 1976 it has been legally possible for a crofter to acquire title to his croft, thus becoming an owner-occupier. He must live on the croft, otherwise he is classed an 'absentee crofter' and is obliged, in theory if not always in practice, to himself take a tenant who will pay rent to him, as the owner, for use of the croft.

Crofts, whether owned by the estate landlord or by an owner-occupier, are administered according to the Crofting Acts, first passed in 1886 in order to give security of tenure to crofters, protecting them from forced removal from the land, as happened on a massive scale during the Highland Clearances in the 18th and 19th centuries. This, plus legislation added or amended over the years, was amalgamated into the Act of 1993. A new Crofting Act is proposed as part of the Scottish Executive's Land Reform Programme. The Crofters' Commission is the government body which deals with all matters regarding crofting.

Crofts are found in areas where large estates are owned by a landlord – sometimes private individuals, but increasingly today estates are owned by companies, often foreign. Areas of the estate may be divided into numerous small crofts, which together make up crofting townships. There may be several townships on an estate, and crofting decisions are taken for the township as a whole by the local Common Grazings Committee, whose members are elected from among the township crofters. A croft has an average size of around five hectares, plus a share in hill grazing, held in common with other crofters in a township. This average figure disguises the fact that crofts can vary greatly in size, from only 0.5 hectares to some which may be as large as 50 hectares (although it is rare for one this size to come up for sale.)

The rent paid by the crofter is for the bare land of the croft only, while the houses and any agricultural buildings and infrastructure are provided by the crofter himself. There are, however, grants and cheap loans available to assist crofters to build such infrastructure on their croft. Owner-occupiers also have access to some grants and loans, but generally not to such an extent as a tenant, and the amount of money they are eligible to is means-tested.

Annual rents for a croft are very low – £15 to £30 is not uncommon for a small croft – which (along with the loss of access to certain grants and loans) is why most crofters are reluctant to become owner-occupiers. A tenant crofter has the right to buy his croft for just 15 times the annual rent, a price way below market price. It is only once the croft is sold on the open market that normal market prices come into play. Although in theory anybody can buy their croft, they do have to formally apply to buy it, and the sale has to be agreed by the Crofters' Commission who will seek the views of neighbouring crofters who may feel they should not be allowed to buy the croft. The Crofters' Commission will adjudicate any objections and make a final decision.

Changes in tenancy also have to be agreed by the local township, represented by the Common Grazings Committee and, ultimately, the Crofters' Commission.

Although the official definition of a croft implies agricultural use, today there are few if any crofters who can get a full-time living from purely agricultural pursuits

– croftland is generally not particularly fertile; add to that the costs of transporting animal or vegetable produce from the far north and west of Scotland to the population centres further south, and the profit margins become very tight on straightforward agricultural produce. Crofters are increasingly diversifying into forestry, woodlands, renewable energy and tourist-related ventures. In addition, most of them also have a 'proper job', supplementing the relatively small income from the croft with local work as builders, postmen, working in hotels and shops, even running a high tech business from home.

Crofters have the right to build a house on their croft, so in almost all cases planning permission will be granted to build one, and maybe two houses, on the land. You will see as you travel around crofting areas that many old crofters' cottages, some one hundred years old or more, still stand. Some have been modernised and are lived in today, others have been turned into holiday accommodation, but many have been left derelict, or pressed into service as barns and sheds.

What you will generally see alongside the old stone cottage is a timber-framed 'kit house', the modern version of the crofter's cottage, which began to spring up in the 1970s when crofters were given generous grants and loans to build these to replace the old, usually sub-standard, cottages. At the time this was seen as the way to go, rather than investing money into renovating the traditional cottages and bringing them up to standard. It has finally been recognised at government level that it was a short-sighted policy and the Scottish Executive is introducing initiatives to bring these older properties back into the housing market.

Another means crofters have of raising capital is to de-croft plots of land, generally between a quarter and half an acre, which they then sell on to outside purchasers to build a house on. This is not necessarily an easy thing to do. It requires the consent of the township and the landlord and the crofters commission and, increasingly, if profit is made on it, some form of clawback might be applied.

CHECKLIST FOR BUYING A CROFT

There is much red tape involved in buying a croft, and some traps for the unwary. It is essential that you employ a solicitor well-versed in crofting law if you take this route. When making initial enquiries about a particular croft for sale, satisfy yourself regarding the following:

- **Is the croft owner-occupied?** If so, does the owner live there himself or does he have a tenant? If there is an existing tenant, you may find you buy the croft but that the tenant has the right to continue to work the land. If the owner has only recently bought the croft, there may be a 'clawback' clause which means he has to pay a proportion of his profit on the sale to the estate owner. In this case, he may wish to sell you the house initially and complete the sale of the land some years later so he can get round the clawback.

- **Is the croft tenancy advertised for sale?** In this case, the croft is not owner-occupied, and although you would probably own any house on the land, you would only be the tenant of the croft itself, paying rent to the landlord. You may find that the croft has been sub-let to another tenant and again you might find your legal right to use the croft is in question. However, if you take on a croft tenancy, you may then be eligible to buy the croft at a bargain price.

○ **Do you satisfy Crofter's Commission criteria?** Anybody buying a croft has to formally be approved by the Crofters' Commission as a suitable person to have a croft. You have to satisfy them that you will be living on and working the croft in some way. You must explain what productive use you will make of the croft: this may be raising livestock, growing vegetables, planting trees, developing renewable energy, running a tourism business such as holiday accommodation, or even running a small business unconnected with the land directly, as long as you can demonstrate that it will be of community benefit and ideally employ local people.

○ **Is planning permission to build, renovate or extend a house included in the sale?** If outline planning permission exists, this will increase the price asked for the croft. If there is no p.p. you should check with the planning department that it would be granted. If there is an existing house on the Croft, or has been in the past, even if it is a complete ruin, you will almost certainly be granted permission to build a new house on that site. Check whether you could build a house with a larger 'footprint' than the existing site, and also look into whether the planning department and Crofters' Commission would look kindly on building another house elsewhere on the croft.

○ **Are there services such as electricity, water and sewage disposal already on site?** If you have to bring these services to the site, this can add a large cost to your build. Sewage disposal is almost certainly going to be in the form of a septic tank – few crofts are on mains sewage – and there are stringent criteria for the type and efficiency of septic tank you use. This alone could cost you thousands.

○ **Are there any problems regarding access to the croft?** Some crofts are situated in inaccessible positions – halfway up a hillside, for example. If there is no existing access road, the cost of constructing one may be prohibitive, so it is worth getting an estimate of cost before making an offer on the croft. In some cases you will find there is shared access to the croft. If this is the case you must ensure you get your solicitor to check that any agreement with your neighbours is set in stone, or you could find some time down the line that they withdraw your permission to reach your croft via their access point. It is always desirable, if at all possible, to construct your own personal access, to avoid potential problems in the future.

CASTLES, ESTATES & ISLANDS

Scotland also has some more unusual and unique properties on offer. Fancy living in an ancient castle? Or being the laird of your own estate? Or how about buying your own private island? Although you might expect such a unique bit of real estate to come with a price tag to match, Scottish castles are relatively cheap, compared to prices elsewhere.

Cheap castles may be a thing of the past now, however, as international buyers have recognised the bargains that are on offer. Now, multi-million pound castles and mansions are being snapped up abroad, and by English buyers, for several times the asking price on the Scottish market. For example, a stately home in Midlothian was advertised for sale at £2.25 million in 2003, and in 2005 a Texas-based estate agent was advertising it to international buyers through the internet at £13.5 million. Similarly, Seton Castle in East Lothian was sold at offers over £1.3 million in 2003, and was advertised at £15 million two years later. But even at these prices, they are seen to be cheap for a unique bit of history – when you consider than a fairly ordinary house in the centre of London can sell for up to £20 million, it puts it into context.

Estates can also come with an affordable price tag. Lyricist Tim Rice bought a 33,000 acre estate in the Highlands for just £2 million in 2001, while a 3,000 acre estate near Inverness is up for sale, in September 2005, at offers over £850,000. This includes a period farmhouse, forestry, salmon and trout fishing and deer stalking plus its own island in the River Beauly.

If you fancy a more remote island, there is one at the time of writing up for sale off the Argyll coast at just £10,000 – a fraction of the price of a one bedroom flat in Glasgow or Edinburgh.

PREMIER PROPERTIES FOR SALE, SEPTEMBER 2005

Property	What you get	Asking price
Eilean Tornal, Argyll	12 acre private island with existing timber building and planning consent for a 6 apartment house	Offers over £10,000
Castle for restoration, Scottish Borders	Category B listed 7th century castle in need of complete restoration	Offers over £250,000
Small Perthshire Estate	50 acre estate with family house, a range of buildings with planning permission for development, good rough shooting, pastureland and woodland	Offers over £700,000
Small farm, Stirlingshire	Modern farmhouse with 2 reception rooms, 5 bedrooms, 3 bathrooms and space to extend into loft, modern farm buildings and 89 acres of land	Offers over £700,000
Insch Castle, Aberdeenshire	15th century castle with substantial Victorian additions, potential for development and restoration, listed courtyard with planning for 5 houses, outbuildings. Additional estate land also available	Guide price £1,000,000

| Mansion, Fifeshire | castellated, listed mansion, extensively renovated, with gardens and parkland, arboretum, staff apartments and gardeners' cottage, outbuildings, swimming pool, tennis court, stables | Offers over £2,500,000 |
| Little Cumbrae, Ayrshire | 684 acre island off the Ayrshire coast, including 12 bedroom Victorian mansion house; Gertrude Jekyll designed gardens; 2 cottages and studio flat; 13th century castle keep and other monuments; former lighthouse complex with 3 houses; steadings and modern workshop; boathouse and jetty | Offers over £3,000,000 |

LISTED BUILDINGS

If you decide to look for an unusual property of historical importance, you will probably find it is 'listed' by Historic Scotland. Buildings assessed as being of special architectural or historic interest are assigned a category, A, B or C, according to their importance.

Controls are placed on the alterations which can be made to listed buildings and their immediate surroundings, and the higher the listing category, the more stringent are the conditions. You must contact the planning authorities before doing any work on a listed building because it is a criminal offence to undertake unauthorised works to demolish, significantly alter or extend such a building.

There are obligations on the owner to keep the building in a reasonable state of preservation. Grants towards the repair, maintenance or sympathetic improvement of listed buildings may be available through central or local government. If you are granted permission to undertake any work, conditions are likely to be attached: you may be obliged to use materials and techniques identical or sympathetic to those used at the time of original construction. You may also be restricted to using tradesmen from a list of approved specialists provided by the planning department.

For further information about the regulations relating to listed buildings, see the Historic Scotland website at www.historic-scotland.gov.uk/index/historicbuildings.htm.

The Buildings at Risk register for Scotland lists all those properties deemed by Historic Scotland to be worthy of conservation. These vary from historically important cottages to churches to castles. There is a searchable database of these properties on their website, but by no means all of the properties are for sale, nor is it always obvious who the owner is, so if you consider going this route, don't expect it to be an easy way of finding a derelict property to renovate. www.buildingsatrisk.org.uk.

RENTING A HOME IN SCOTLAND

CHAPTER SUMMARY

○ It is a good idea to rent a property in Scotland before deciding to buy a house.
○ It is advisable to sell your existing house before buying in Scotland, to avoid any difficulties with your house sale falling through.
○ There are far more rental properties in urban than in rural areas.
○ In holiday areas you may be able to rent holiday accommodation on a long term basis.
○ Short term accommodation is available in hostels, hotels, guest houses and bed & breakfasts.
○ Rental properties are advertised by estate agents, lettings agencies and in newspapers.
○ When you rent a home you should sign a tenancy agreement.
○ You must pay a deposit which will be returned at the end of the tenancy period, minus the cost of any damage.
○ Tenants pay council tax, contents insurance, gas, electricity, water rates and telephone bills in addition to the rental.

WHY RENT?

It is a good idea to consider renting before you buy in Scotland, for a variety of reasons. In the first place, it gives you the opportunity to decide whether living in Scotland long-term is really for you. If you spend a couple of weeks there each year on holiday, probably during the summer months, you will have a one-dimensional view of what it is really like. Spending a month or more during the winter, when the weather is bad and the days are short, might make you change your mind altogether!

Renting for a period gives you the chance to have a good look at the properties available to buy, and wait for the right one to come up. Such a big purchase is not one to be rushed into. If you are already settled on a particular area, then you can spend time getting to know the various towns and villages to find your ideal spot.

If you not committed to a particular area by work or preference, it is worth taking the time to explore as many areas of the country as you can. The various regions of the country are so different in feel that you may find your ideas change. Your dream of a remote rural Highland retreat might pall once you have spent several weeks in a hideaway, miles from your nearest neighbours. You may find the pull of the town is too strong, and you decide that a home nearer to urban facilities is going to be a far happier choice for you.

If you have to move to Scotland by a fixed date, to take up employment, for example, you may find that you have not been able to conclude the sale on the house you are moving from. The lack of funds might well prevent you from buying immediately in Scotland, although an option is to rent out your other house and use the rental income to pay for mortgage payments on your new Scottish home.

It must be stressed that the house-buying system in Scotland works under different rules from those south of the border (see *Purchasing & Conveyancing*, below.) Once you have made an offer in Scotland, and it has been accepted, in most cases that offer is binding, and you may find it very difficult, or face financial penalties, if you find you have to pull out of a deal at this stage, for instance if your house-sale in England falls through. For this reason it is strongly advised that you do not make a firm offer on a Scottish house before you have signed contracts on the sale of a house elsewhere. It is wise, therefore, to rent accommodation until the deal on your other house is completed.

If you are setting up a new business in Scotland, and you need a mortgage to purchase a property, you may find lenders will not give you a loan until they are certain that you would be able to keep up the repayments on a mortgage. Self-employed people will usually be asked to produce the last three years' accounts before they can apply for a mortgage. If you can obtain a mortgage, using for example, a self-certification mortgage (see above), you will be charged a higher rate of interest than normal. In these circumstances, renting could be the better option until such time as you have three years accounts to produce and can get a better deal.

It is financially sensible in the longer term to buy rather than rent a property. It is estimated that if you are in rented accommodation you will spend around 23% of your income on housing costs, whereas if you have a mortgage, housing costs account for only 15% of your household budget. Historically, property is one of the best investments you can make in Scotland, and this is unlikely to change in the future, despite current uncertainties about the housing market. If you choose the area where you buy wisely, and can identify an area which is 'on the up' socially, you could make a substantial profit if you sell after a few years.

THE RENTAL SCENE

About 65% of homes in Scotland are owner-occupied, but of the 35% rented, around three-quarters are social housing, rented from local authorities or housing associations. Short term rentals, which account for only about six per cent of the total rentable properties available, are almost certain to be let by private landlords,.

As a result there has been a shortage of properties to rent in many areas, particularly larger homes which you may be looking for if moving with your family. One or two bedroom flats or one-room studios are more common. Your biggest choice of rentable property will be in towns or cities. It is far harder to find rentable accommodation in rural areas.

However, buy-to-let is currently a popular form of investment, which suggests that the amount of private rented accommodation is on the increase. With the recent housing market boom, many potential first time buyers have been priced out of the market, which means they are more likely to be looking for rented accommodation, so the market is likely to match this increased demand with increased supply. Nonetheless, the majority of new properties coming into the private rented sector will inevitably be in urban areas.

This phenomenon has been evident in Edinburgh during 2005, with the cost of renting property in the capital city increasing ten per cent from the previous year. This follows a ten year static period in the rental market. With property prices reaching heights which many workers coming to the city cannot afford, the demand for rented property has risen dramatically. As a result, rents have been increased for the first time in three years. This is not just the fault of the housing market – the buoyant economy has caused an upsurge in jobs, particularly in the IT sector, with a resultant influx of new Edinburgh workers and residents.

Rented accommodation is available both furnished and unfurnished, although the majority is furnished. Furnished accommodation is more expensive, and if you have your own furniture already, this may need to go into storage, which is an additional cost. The problem you may find with furnished property is that, unless you are looking at the luxury end of the market, the furnishings may not be of a very high standard. Unfurnished properties normally include carpets, curtains and kitchen appliances such as a cooker and a fridge.

Monthly rental varies widely, and is dependent on a variety of factors including the size of a property, its condition and its location. Rents are highest in desirable city areas, lowest in rural areas, and you can assume that the more remote a property is, the lower the rent is likely to be. Bear in mind, however, that although you may save on rent in the countryside, fuel costs and the price of food in local shops will be higher.

Social Housing

Low cost rented accommodation is provided by local authorities and housing associations. In most areas there is a shortage of such housing, and the Scottish Executive is currently putting a lot of money into schemes to allow local authorities to build more affordable housing, usually through housing associations.

To qualify for such housing you would have to show that you are eligible to benefit from public resources – certain categories of immigrants are disbarred from doing so. (See Residence & Entry above.)

If eligible, you would then have to formally apply for accommodation. Your need for housing would be assessed on the basis of a number of criteria, including whether you are currently homeless, the standard of the housing you are currently in, whether you have children living with you, whether you are employed and what your income is, and so forth. In nearly all cases you would have to go on a waiting list for a property, because there is a shortage and in some areas waiting lists are long.

You may be offered a property which is available in an area, or in a type of housing, which isn't your first choice. It is worth considering whether it is sensible to accept this as if you refuse too many times, your application may move further down the waiting list. Once you are in a property, you can then apply to be transferred to another area when a property comes vacant.

Once you are in social housing, you may be eligible to apply to buy the property under the 'right to buy' legislation. Some housing association properties are available under shared ownership schemes where part rental/part mortgage is paid until such time as the tenant has paid the full value of the property, and this can be a good way to get to own your own home if money is a little tight at first.

For Council Housing, contact your local authority. Addresses are listed under the relevant regions in *Where To Find Your Ideal Home* (above).

Communities Scotland: Thistle House, 91 Haymarket Terrace, Edinburgh EH12 5HE; ☎ 0131-313 0044; fax 0131-313 2680; www.scot-homes.gov.uk.

Scottish Federation of Housing Associations: 38 York Place, Edinburgh, EH1 3HU; ☎ 0131-556 5777; fax 0131-557 6028; www.sfha.co.uk.

WHERE TO STAY WHILE HOUSE-HUNTING

Most rented accommodation is available for a minimum six months lease, although some places might insist on a year minimum. Some landlords will agree a shorter rental period, but they may ask for a higher monthly rental in this case. Once you have stayed for the minimum six months, it may be possible to extend your tenancy for a month at a time, rather than signing up for a full six months.

Although six months may seem a long time, the housebuying system as it currently operates is often not a quick process. It is likely to take several months to identify a suitable property to buy, have a survey done and an offer accepted, and for the entire purchasing and conveyancing process to be concluded.

If you need a shorter rental period – say if you have already had an offer accepted on a house, or are waiting for your mutually agreed moving-in date on a house you have bought – you may find that hotel or guest house accommodation, or taking a vacation rental property, might work out the cheapest option. Although the monthly rental may work out higher, it gives you far more flexibility as you can rent for a week at a time. Also take into account the fact that as a tenant you pay your own council tax and utility bills on top of the rental, whereas the owner pays the council tax on holiday accommodation. Costs of electricity and other services may be included in the weekly rental, or may be charged for separately. Check if there are any additional costs such as these if you do take holiday accommodation.

Serviced Apartments

An alternative is to take a serviced apartment, mainly found in Glasgow, Edinburgh and Aberdeen, which strike a balance between a hotel and a flat. They are available in various sizes, from studios to three bedrooms or larger, and are fully self-contained, with well-equipped kitchens and bathrooms and well-furnished living areas and bedrooms. Maid service is usually provided, so the flat is cleaned and bed linen changed on a daily basis. These can work out expensive, but they provide top quality hassle-free accommodation which is available from one night to monthly contracts. Generally, the longer you stay, the cheaper the price is pro rata.

Large corporations often use this kind of accommodation for their staff if they are staying in the country on business for a an extended period, so good quality accommodation and service is pretty much guaranteed.

Glasgow: www.whitehouse-apartments.com.

Edinburgh: www.fountaincourtapartments.com.

Aberdeen: www.deepblue-apartments.com/scotland/aberdeen/aberdeen-apartments.
  html.

Hotels, Guest Houses, Bed & Breakfasts

If you are undecided whereabouts in Scotland would be best for you, you might be better not committing yourself to a long-term rental, which is likely to be for minimum of six months. If you wish to travel around the country, exploring different areas for your perfect house, you might be better treating it as an extended holiday, and staying in hotels, guest houses and B&Bs as you travel about.

These are available at different standards throughout Scotland. Most of them are graded through one tourism scheme or another which will give you a guide to the facilities you can expect, but the safest guide is price. The cheaper it is, the more basic it will be.

Generally, for equivalent standard, the cost of staying in hotels will be more expensive, followed by guest houses (which are, in effect small hotels), followed by bed & breakfast in a private home.

The VisitScotland (Scottish Tourist Board) website is a good place to give an idea of the range of facilities and prices available across Scotland for all forms of holiday accommodation: www.visitscotland.com.

Holiday Cottages

As discussed above, there is a shortage of rented accommodation in rural locations. It is worth enquiring whether there is any self-catering holiday accommodation available for long term let. It may be possible to come to an agreement with the owner to stay in a holiday cottage during the winter months, and maybe during the summer as well. Generally, the price charged for short term holiday accommodation is too high to make this an affordable prospect for longer than a couple of weeks, so try to negotiate a reduced price for a longer stay.

As the majority of cottage owners now advertise their holiday lets on the internet, it is a far easier matter to identify possible properties from a distance and contact the owners by email to see if they would be prepared to let you stay there for an extended period at a lower rent. In some areas of the Highlands, in particular, there is an oversupply of holiday cottages, and full occupancy, other than in the busiest weeks of the year in the height of summer, is unlikely. An owner might well be tempted by the prospect of letting their property for months rather than the occasional week here and there.

Caravans

If you're hardy, a static caravan (also called a mobile home) is a cheap option for temporary accommodation. These are available to rent in most holiday areas, and the owners are generally open to negotiating a reduced rental for a longer stay. They can, of course, be rather cold and damp, especially if you are staying over the winter months, so do check what heating and cooking facilities are included before committing yourself.

Brenda and Terry Stopford and their two boys opted to stay temporarily in a static caravan while their house purchase was going through

We needed to be in Scotland, ideally close to our new home – but it proved to be difficult to find a temporary let. We settled for the relatively easy, relatively uncomfortable and inconvenient option, by moving to a friend's static caravan at Lairg, 100 miles from the house and cottage we were buying in Wester Ross. October to December in a caravan in the Highlands, with two large, lively boys, isn't to be recommended. Of course, we had no idea it would be two months – we'd been assured, once we'd put in our offer (as soon as our house was definitely sold) that it would take no more than three weeks. As the date we'd agreed to leave Lancashire coincided with a two week school holiday in the Highlands, we'd decided there was no need to put the boys to school until we reached our permanent home. But as it became apparent that the time would drag on, for legal and educational reasons, not to mention the boys' boredom threshold and our sanity threshold, we sent them temporarily to the local school. This was an unsatisfactory situation – it would have been far preferable to put them through only one change of school, but without knowing anyone in the area to advise us we could find no way of fixing up a short let near to the house we were buying. Once we finally moved into our house and got to know the local situation, we realised that winter lets were available – but by then it was too late. Thankfully we'd got through our two months of purgatory – all in one piece, if not in the most desirable of situations.

Hostels

Youth and backpackers' hostels are found throughout Scotland. This is cheap and cheerful accommodation, but if you are prepared to rough it for a while, it can be a good value option – and possibly more comfortable than a caravan! You may even be able to negotiate a reduced rate for an extended stay in off-season months.

Scottish Youth Hostels Association: www.syha.org.uk.

Independent Backpackers' Hostels: www.hostel-scotland.co.uk.

Home Exchanges

A home swap is a way of arranging rent-free living for a period while you house-hunt. It is an idea which is only just catching on in Scotland, but it is one which is likely to become more popular in coming years. There has recently been a television programme on national television which looks at UK families and their experiences of home-swapping, which is a sure sign that it is a growing market.

The downside is that you have to find somebody in the right area of Scotland who wants to stay in your house, wherever that may be. However, as Scotland is such a small country, if you can find yourself a base somewhere in the centre, you will be within reasonably easy travelling distance of all areas of the country.

Global Home Exchange: www.4homex.com/europehomeexchange.htm.

HomeExchange.com: www.homeexchange.com.

Sources of Rental Properties

Properties available to rent are advertised in all the same places as properties to buy. Most estate agents, although fewer solicitors, have rental properties on their books. Some have specialised rental departments or offices. In addition, there are Letting Agencies and lettings websites which solely deal with rental property, so these may be the best place to start.

Local papers (rather than national ones,) are a good place to look for privately-advertised properties, as are 'Free-ads' papers, where individuals advertise property for sale and rent free of charge.

If you are having difficulty finding any property to rent in a specific area, a relocation agent with contacts in the area may be able to help you track one down.

See *Finding Properties for Sale* (above) for contact details of estate agents and relocation agents throughout Scotland.

Scot Ads: ☎ 08457-434343; www.scot-ads.com.

Letting Web: www.lettingweb.co.uk. Properties to let via lettings agents across Scotland.

Better Renting Scotland: www.betterrentingscotland.com. Advice and information on all aspects of renting property, for both landlords and tenants.

Pastures New: Contains an exhaustive list of letting agents in Scotland. www.pastures-new.co.uk/agents/scotland.

FORMALITIES OF RENTING

Renting a property is a far less complex process than buying one, so it should only take between two to four weeks to arrange. Once you have decided on a property you wish to rent, both you and the landlord must sign a tenancy agreement. This is a legal contract, and if either landlord or tenant fails to abide by the conditions of the agreement, the other party can take legal action against them. Read the tenancy agreement carefully and consult a solicitor if there is anything you are not clear about or feel is too onerous a condition.

Before the landlord decides to let the property to you, he may ask for references from people who can vouch for your suitability as a tenant, maybe from a previous landlord. In addition, he may carry out a credit check on you to see whether you have a bad credit history, in which case he may refuse to accept you as a tenant.

If there is any doubt as to whether you will be able to keep up the rental payments, you may be asked to provide a guarantor who will undertake to cover any payments if you should default on your rent. Obviously, somebody putting themself in this position will need to know you well and find you trustworthy because the implications for them could be serious – and expensive.

You are far more likely to be asked for these forms of security if the tenancy is being arranged via a lettings agency rather than directly with a private landlord.

On accepting the terms of the tenancy agreement, you will be required to pay a deposit, generally equivalent to around four to six weeks rent. This money should be kept in an interest-bearing account by the landlord or letting agent until the end of the tenancy, when it may be used to cover the costs of any damage to the property or rental arrears. Any balance, including interest, is returned to the tenant. Ensure that the tenancy agreement states these conditions, as it can help to ensure that, if the landlord or letting agent should go bankrupt, you do not lose your deposit.

Ensure you get an inventory when you take the property which lists the items provided and describes the state of the property at that time, so you do not get charged for damage or loss which was not caused by you.

Rental is normally payable in advance, so at the time of paying your deposit you will be asked for the first rental payment. This would normally be for one month at a time, although in some cases you may be asked to pay three months at a time. It may be a condition of the agreement that you use a UK bank account to make the payments.

The tenancy agreement will state the length of time you have contracted to take the property – normally a minimum of six months – and you are obliged to pay rent for the whole of this period even if you leave early, at least until a new tenant for the property is found.

You should be issued with a rent book in which all rental payments you make are recorded. If the landlord does not give you a rent book, it is sensible only to pay by cheque and insist on a receipt, then you have evidence of what you paid and when, if there is any dispute on the matter.

As the tenant, you are responsible for paying, in addition to the rental, council tax, contents insurance, gas, electricity, water rates and telephone bills. Buildings insurance should be paid by the owner.

Both tenant and landlord are required to give a period of notice, usually a month, if they wish to terminate the agreement.

Letting Agents

If the property is let through a letting agent, they carry out all the administrative tasks involved in setting up the rental agreement, including following up references, credit checks and so forth. They also collect deposit and rental payments and pass these on to the landlord. They usually ask for a reservation fee, deductible from the deposit when you sign a rental agreement. They may in addition charge a non-refundable fee, typically of up to £100, to acquire references and carry out credit checks.

If you do rent a property through a letting agency, make sure you only deal with a member of the Association of Residential Letting Agents (ARLA). This will help to safeguard you against any problems with them. If you have any complaints, first take them up with the letting agent, and if you do not receive satisfaction, contact ARLA as they may be able to provide advice and assistance. They have a code of practice which their members should abide by. Their website includes a list of their registered members plus other useful advice. www.arla.co.uk

Property Management Companies

Some properties, in particular buildings containing a number of flats, are run by property management companies (often called 'factors' in Scotland). The flat-owners pass over to them responsibility for the day to day maintenance of the building. In some cases they may also be involved in the collecting of rents from tenants which they pass on to the owners. The management company levies service charges on owners and tenants for maintenance and repairs to the building.

Assured Tenancies

Most properties let by private landlords must legally be 'assured tenancies', which give legal protection and greater rights to a tenant. A landlord cannot evict his tenant if he observes the terms of the tenancy agreement. If the landlord feels he has a case to evict the tenant, he must apply for a court order on the basis of certain matters specified in the Act, which include unpaid rent, damage or otherwise breaking the contract with the landlord. Assured tenancies do not apply where the landlord lives on the premises.

However, if the landlord offers you alternative, similar, property, needs the property for himself, or wishes to sell the property, a court may send you a written order to quit.

Where there is no written tenancy agreement, the tenant has the same rights as under an assured tenancy.

Short Assured Tenancies

Where your agreement with the landlord is for a fixed period of time, of not less than six months, your tenancy would then be a short assured tenancy, and you must be given a written notice stating this. In this case, the landlord has the right to regain possession on giving notice to the tenant, whether or not the tenant has observed the terms of the tenancy agreement.

Other Forms of Rental Agreement

If you make an informal agreement with somebody to rent their property – for instance, if you take a holiday cottage for an extended period – these contractual agreements do not apply and you are far less protected in law. So you must ensure that the agreement you make with the owner is one which you are happy with. Although in normal circumstances you would not pay council tax while staying in a holiday cottage, if you are living there for an extended period and it is your only home, you would be required by the local authority to pay council tax on your own account.

More Information

There is detailed information about the legal niceties of renting in Scotland on the *Pastures New* website: www.pastures-new.co.uk/info/basics/legalsscot.

SAMPLE PRIVATE PROPERTIES TO RENT OCTOBER 2005

Area	Type	Cost per Month
Peebles, Scottish Borders	unfurnished 4 bed town house	£650
Bonshaw Tower, Dumfries & Galloway	6 bed historic tower	£1,300
Braids, Argyll & Bute	4 bed flat on 2 floors	£895
Kilbirnie, N.Ayrshire	furnished 2 bed cottage in rural area	£550
Kirkintilloch, E.Dunbartonshire	unfurnished 5 bed Victorian detached house	£900
Glasgow West End	furnished 1 bed flat	£495
Glasgow Merchant City	furnished 2 bed flat with parking	£650
Leith, nr Edinburgh	furnished 2 bed flat with parking	£675
Edinburgh Old Town	furnished 2 bed flat	£600
Dundee City waterfront	furnished 2 bed flat	£710
Auchterarder, Perth & Kinross	unfurnished 4 bed terraced house	£650
Aberdeen City	furnished studio flat	£325
Footdee, nr Aberdeen	furnished B listed 2 bed terraced cottage	£650
Kintore, Aberdeenshire	5 bed detached house with garden	£850
Inverness City	2 bed flat with parking	£450
Kingussie, Highlands	3 bed family house	£650
Lochinver, Highlands	traditional 2 bed cottage	£500

PURCHASING, CONVEYANCING & FEES

CHAPTER SUMMARY

- The housebuying system in Scotland is quite different from that in England and Wales.
- You are strongly advised to wait until contracts have been exchanged on a property sale south of the border before you make an offer on a property in Scotland.
- Most property and land is advertised for sale at 'offers over £X'.
- If more than one person wants to buy a property, a closing date is set and all interested parties must submit a sealed bid.
- Vendors have no obligation to accept the highest, or any, offer.
- Potential buyers normally have a survey done before they submit an offer.
- Only qualified Scottish solicitors can carry out conveyancing in Scotland.
- Solicitors exchange a series of letters called 'missives' when negotiating a sale, which should ensure that all potential pitfalls are avoided.
- The offer, acceptance and missives together form the legal contract between buyer and seller.
- There are additional legal requirements in connection with buying croftland.
- There are substantial extra costs and fees to take into account when buying a house or land.

HOW TO BUY PROPERTY IN SCOTLAND

The most important thing to be aware of is that Scotland has its own distinctive legal system and that the property purchase and conveyancing process is different in many respects from that in other parts of the United Kingdom.

MAIN DIFFERENCES OF SCOTTISH SYSTEM

- Asking price normally in the form of **Offers over £X**. This is the lowest price the vendor expects to get for the property.
- You should **Note your interest** with the selling agent if you are still interested in the property after viewing it.
- Normally you would commission a **Survey** on the property before making an offer. The surveyor will give an estimate of the value of the property, which will help to guide you when deciding the level of offer to make.
- If you wish to **Make a formal offer** on the property you should employ a solicitor.
- **Conveyancing** must be carried out by a solicitor qualified in Scottish Law. You cannot undertake self-conveyancing in Scotland.
- If there are several parties noting their interest in a property, the selling agent may set a **Closing date** for offers.
- Everybody wishing to make an offer on the property should ask their solicitor to send a **Sealed bid** before the closing date, stating the amount they offer and any other relevant details or conditions of their offer.
- Once an offer is made and accepted, this forms a **Legal contract** binding on both parties.
- Negotiation about the specific terms and conditions of the sale is carried out by the buyer's and seller's solicitors through the exchange of a series of letters called **Missives.**
- Once the missives are concluded satisfactorily, the vendor(s) sign a **Disposition** which formally records the passing of title in the property from them to the new owner(s).

Asking Price

When you start house-hunting in Scotland, you will find that most property is advertised for sale at 'offers over £X'. This is the lowest price which the vendor expects to get for the property. The trick for the buyer is to gauge what is a reasonable price for that particular property in that particular area, and to make an offer which is likely to be acceptable to the vendor.

The percentage over the asking price you need to offer to secure the property depends on many factors in which both geography and time play a great part. Geographical factors include the desirability of property in that area; the availability of similar property nearby; the desirability of specific schools within the catchment area; any development, either forthcoming or in progress in the locality – depending on what type of development this is, it may either inflate or depress the price you would need to pay to secure the property.

Time factors include the general level of prices nationally (within both Scotland and the UK as a whole) and locally at the time you are house-hunting; the rate of inflation, or stagnation, in the housing market; the current state of the economy generally, and the effect this has and is likely to have on interest rates.

The estate agent selling the property will be happy to advise you on the percentage over the asking price expected on properties in the area you are looking at, but be wary. As they are working on behalf of the vendor, and they earn commission based on the price at which they sell the property, it is in their interests to inflate the price. It is not unusual, in desirable areas and at a time of rising prices, for estate agents to quote expected levels of as much as fifty per cent over the offers over price.

Your own solicitor might suggest a more reasonable premium – twenty per cent is the historical average they tend to quote, but this will vary according to demand and other factors.

A third source of information will come from a survey of the property. Any surveyor's report will give an estimation of the market value of the property, which is a good starting point. If you need a 100% mortgage, of course, this is the maximum you should offer, as a mortgage lender will not agree to lend more than that valuation.

Some properties are offered for sale at a fixed price, similar to the system in England and Wales. The advantage of this is that, although the asking price may appear higher than a similar property advertised at an offers over price, you know at the outset just what the vendor would be happy to accept.

The 'offers over' system works for the benefit of the seller rather than the buyer, and is designed to encourage the highest possible bids. However, there is no reason why you should not make a lower offer, if that is all you can afford, or all you think the property is worth to you. Many properties are sold at less than the offers over price – although selling agents don't like to advertise this fact. In a falling or static house market, the buyer has the upper bargaining hand, so find out from the selling agent how long the property has been on the market. If it has remained unsold for some months, you can assume that there is little current interest in the property so it is unlikely to go to a closing date anytime soon. In such a case, the seller may be becoming eager, or even desperate, to sell and you may be able to get it at a lower price.

MOVE TOWARDS FIXED PRICE

There are strong signs that the offer over system is losing some favour in Scotland, as more properties are advertised for sale at a fixed price. In 2005 about a quarter of all properties for sale quoted a fixed price, and in some areas it was far higher. In the first three months of the year, three-quarters of properties for sale in south Edinburgh were offered at a fixed price.

Buyers too, aware that in a competitive market the temptation is to offer more than they can comfortably afford, are less inclined to offer substantially over an offers over price to secure a sale. A survey in mid 2005 found that one in five Scots were in favour of replacing the system with one similar to that in England and Wales.

Noting Your Interest

If, having viewed a property, you are still interested in it, you should 'note your interest' with the vendor's solicitor or estate agent. Even if you haven't had a chance to view the property, due to time constraints, you may wish to note your interest anyway. This does not commit you to buy, so it is worth doing even if you think you may not eventually make an offer on the property. This ensures that you will be kept informed of matters such as a change in the asking price, withdrawal of the property from the market, or the fixing of a closing date for offers

Asking that your interest in a property be noted is one of the few aspects of house-buying that you can do yourself without employing a solicitor. However, if you have already got yourself a solicitor, they will undertake this notification of interest on your behalf.

Surveys

Under the Scottish system, a prospective buyer should generally have a survey done on the property before making an offer, as this can affect the amount of the offer. The surveyor's report will state any repairs or other work which should be carried out on the property to bring it up to an acceptable standard, and will give his/her assessment of the market value of the property in its current state.

If you are applying for a mortgage to buy the property, you must get this valuation done before the mortgage lender will decide whether to offer you a loan or not.

If you are in a hurry to secure a property, you may choose to make an offer before having a survey of the property carried out by a qualified surveyor, in which case the offer would be made 'subject to a satisfactory survey'. But you would have to assess the price you were willing to pay, without the guidance of the surveyor as to its market value. Remember though, that this is only his/her opinion, and there is nothing legally binding about it.

As the law stands at present, each prospective buyer of a property should have their own survey carried out. This means that if there are several people bidding on a property, there will be numerous surveys carried out, which does little more than make money for surveyors, as only one of those people can be successful. This also means that if your offer is unsuccessful and you then go on to make an offer on another property, you will have to stand the cost of two surveys. And if second or subsequent bids are unsuccessful, you could find yourself paying out hundreds of pounds on surveys, only to find you still haven't managed to buy a house. This is a very compelling reason, if you are in a position to do so, to make your offer subject to a satisfactory survey.

In order to cut down on these unnecessary surveys, the Scottish executive is committed to introducing a single survey scheme – probably from 2007, but as this is legislation which has to be debated and passed by the Scottish Parliament, the form and timing of the law may change. When it is introduced, this scheme will make it the responsibility of the seller of a property to commission a survey which will be made available to all prospective buyers. The details of the scheme have yet to be finalised, but it is likely that other information relating to the property, such as local authority searches (see below) is included in a comprehensive 'Property Information Pack' (PIP).

The surveyor may note in the survey details of any alterations or extensions which have taken place to the building. Your solicitor should, after your offer has been accepted, ensure that the seller confirms the existence of, and passes over, any building warrants, planning permissions and completion certificates legally required in respect of these past works.

There is currently no legal requirement for the vendor to inform prospective buyers of any defects in a property, although this will change when a mandatory single survey scheme is introduced. It is, therefore, advisable to obtain a survey on a property you contemplate buying, however there is no legal requirement to do so.

If a mortgage lender requires a valuation, they instruct their own surveyor to carry this out, at the mortgage applicants' cost. You must pay this even if the mortgage is later refused, or the sale does not go through for any other reason. If you want a more detailed survey, you can either employ your own surveyor or ask the lender's surveyor to include it with their valuation report. This may reduce the overall costs.

TYPES OF SURVEY

- **Valuation Survey:** Carried out for the lender and required in all cases where you are applying for a mortgage to buy the property. It is an assessment of the value of the property, and gives no guarantee that the property is structurally sound.
  Cost: Typically around £10-15 for each £10,000 value of the property, minimum fee of £50-200.
- **Homebuyer Report:** A more detailed survey on the condition of a property, together with a valuation. Major defects will be listed, such as whether there are signs of subsidence, dampness, rot or woodworm. Recommendations for remedial work may be made.
  Cost: Typically between £300-500 depending on the value of the property.
- **Building Survey:** A full structural survey, advisable for older or unusual properties. The surveyor will inspect everything that is accessible including examining the roof space and pulling up carpets to examine floorboards.
  Cost: Most expensive, can vary considerably depending on age, type and value of property. Generally upwards of £700. Make sure you get several quotations to choose the best deal.
- **Specialist Survey:** If you or your surveyor have special cause for concern in specific areas, or if it is an especially unique, old or important building such a listed building, you may choose to have a highly detailed specialist survey.
  Cost: Likely to be very expensive, over £1,000.

If your survey indicates that a property is in poor condition or has structural faults, use this as a bargaining tool. Find out the estimated cost of any remedial work required and try to negotiate a reduction in your offer price to take account of this. However, if a property is particularly poor, or does not conform to certain standards of construction, you may be refused a mortgage on it.

If you purchase the house and find it has faults which were not identified in the survey and should have been, you may be able to sue the surveyor for damages. You do need to read the small print on your survey before deciding whether it's worth trying – they often include 'escape clauses' designed to reduce your rights to claim against the surveyor.

Any survey should be carried out by a qualified surveyor who is a member of the Royal Institution of Chartered Surveyors in Scotland (RICS): 9 Manor Place, Edinburgh EH3 7DN; ☎ 0131-225 7078; fax 0131-240 0830; www.rics-scotland. org.uk.

Making An Offer

Scottish law does not allow you to do your own conveyancing on a property. This process must be carried out by a Scottish solicitor who is a member of the Law Society of Scotland.

Prior to making a 'formal offer' you may wish to contact the vendor or their agent to sound them out on the level of offer which may be acceptable to them. Often an informal approach, especially if you're not making an unreasonably low offer, may get a positive response. This is particularly worth trying if you are a cash buyer and are not involved in a property chain and can therefore conclude any deal quickly. But it is imperative if you take this approach that you stress it is an informal offer only.

If you then decide to make a formal offer, this should be done by a solicitor as a formal offer is a long and complex document which contains various conditions and requirements for the seller to disclose certain facts about the property and the title deeds. It also states an entry date, the date on which you wish to take possession of the property if your offer is accepted and all the conditions are agreed to the satisfaction of both parties.

If you have not already secured the services of a Scottish solicitor, this is the time to do so. Note that you cannot use a solicitor from any other country to do the conveyancing on your Scottish property.

Once the formal offer has been made, and accepted, this is a legally binding contract. You should be given a copy of the formal offer for future reference. Unlike under the English system, if you do back out of the agreement after this stage, you may be subject to financial penalties and legal costs.

However, it isn't quite as black and white as this, because your solicitor can make the offer subject to certain (reasonable) conditions. If these conditions are not satisfied by the seller you are no longer committed to the sale and could back out without any penalties.

To find a solicitor qualified in Scottish law, look in your phone book or contact *The Law Society of Scotland*, 26 Drumsheugh Gardens, Edinburgh EH3 7YR; ☎ 0131-226 7411; fax 0131-225 2934; www.lawscot.org.uk. They will provide with a list of all their members. They also produce a free booklet *called Your Solicitor and House Purchase and Sale*, available from them, through the Citizens Advice Bureau in Scotland, or from individual solicitors.

Closing Date

Where there is interest noted by more than one prospective buyer, the vendor may decide to set a closing date for offers. All prospective purchasers who still wish to pursue the property have to make a formal offer via their solicitor by the date set. This is done in the form of 'sealed bids' from solicitors acting for prospective purchasers, to the vendor's solicitor which states the price offered and any other factors which may be relevant e.g. how quickly you could conclude the deal.

Your solicitor may be able to advise you on a sensible offer to make, on the basis of his local knowledge, knowledge of the housing market, and the valuation given by the surveyor. There are also certain other 'tricks' that can be used which may help you in the competition against other bidders. One of these is to offer a small amount above a 'round' figure – e.g. £220,101 instead of £220,000 – in the hopes that this is just a little higher than your nearest bidder.

If you can move quickly, and want to avoid getting into a sealed bids situation, you can try to speed up the process by making an offer before a closing date is set. This then shifts the pressure from purchaser to vendor and he may be tempted, especially if you are making a generous offer. The vendor may decide your offer is acceptable, and choose not to go to a closing date as long as you submit a formal offer quickly. If they show signs of preferring to go to a closing date, and you are prepared to pay a little more in order to secure the property, you could try coming to an agreement with the seller that you will add a premium of a few hundred – or even thousand – pounds on your offer if they agree to take it off the market immediately. However, this does demand a high level of trust between buyer and seller.

> **Helen Walsh agreed to sell to a prospective buyer without going to a closing date**
>
> *He told me he would pay an extra £5,000 on top of his offer price if I took it off the market immediately. This I did, but a couple of weeks later the buyer let me down by saying he couldn't raise the purchase price we had agreed. I then had to go to the expense and inconvenience of putting the house back on the market again. My advice is to make sure your solicitor ties any prospector purchaser down firmly if you are faced with a similar situation.*

Sealed bids will be received by the seller's solicitor up until a specified time on the closing date. At this time the seller and his/her solicitor will open all the bids and the seller will decide which one to accept.

The vendor is not obliged to accept the highest offer they receive, although obviously in most cases this would be the one they would favour. However, there may be other factors which encourage them to accept a lower offer. For example, the highest offer may be from somebody who is caught in a property chain, where their buying of the property is dependent on selling their own first. One of the lower bidders may have no property to sell and can therefore move far more quickly. It is always worth using these factors as a bargaining chip if you are in a position to do so.

Your solicitor will contact you shortly after an offer has been accepted to tell you whether you were the successful bidder.

Missives

If an offer is accepted, it is initially termed a 'qualified acceptance' in reference to the fact that the formal offer includes various conditions, or qualifications. This might include such negotiable things as the settlement date (i.e. when the money, and therefore the property, actually changes hands); what fixtures and fittings are included in the sale; or whether there is an extra cost if the buyers wished the vendor to include certain things – washing machine or curtains, for example.

These are not usually matters which would threaten the sale finally going through, although in certain cases – such as where a condition is that the Crofters' Commission accepts the buyer as eligible to take over a croft – if the condition cannot be satisfied it may be that the whole sale becomes invalid, and the property would then need to go back on the market and the whole process start again.

The subsequent negotiations between the buyer's and seller's solicitors will often take the form of 'bargaining' about these various qualifications – e.g if the vendors agree to pay for agreed repairs to be done after the buyers take possession, the settlement date will be brought forward. These negotiations take place through the exchange of letters known as 'missives'.

In addition to unique items relating to one particular sale, the missives also include many standard legal items which need to be clarified before the sale goes through. This includes such things as the condition of the property, where the vendor has to indicate if there has been any history of such things as wet rot or woodworm infestation, and if it has been treated for such things in the past, they should hand over certificates to indicate when this was done and showing the date of any guarantees still in force. It also includes such matters as whether the roadway leading to the property is maintained by the Local Authority or if it is a private road which must be maintained by the householder. Planning permission and building warrants relating to the property should also be produced by the vendor and this is another matter dealt with through the missives.

In the past, these missives were produced separately for each purchase, but it was recognised some years ago that they were becoming over-complex, causing consumers to suffer delays, with transactions sometimes falling through as a result. This led to solicitors in geographical areas drawing up a Standard Missive, a pre-agreed contract to help speed the process. There is still leeway for buyers and sellers to vary certain items on the Standard Missive, but most of the items on it are non-contentious so it does streamline the process. Currently, there are Standard Missives in Edinburgh, Dundee, the Highlands and other areas. Experts agree that it is only a matter of time before a Scotland-wide Standard Missive is produced.

Your solicitor should keep you informed of the progress of these negotiations. The offer, acceptance and missives together go to form the legal contract between buyer and seller. When all matters have been agreed to the satisfaction of both parties, a final acceptance is issued. At this point the bargain is concluded and a binding contract exists between vendor and purchaser. This may occur at any time before settlement date, but in practice, solicitors being notoriously slow in many cases, the deal often goes right down to the wire, with documents for signing being sent out just hours before the agreed date and time of entry.

To finalise the sale, the vendors sign a disposition in the presence of a witness, which then becomes part of the title deeds. The seller does not have to sign anything.

Sharon Blackie found the whole Scottish system somewhat bizarre

I was particularly astonished to receive a letter from my solicitor one day telling me I now owned the house. I told her I couldn't see how I possibly could, as I hadn't signed any contract! I have to admit that I was fairly horrified to discover that this isn't required in Scotland; the letters exchanged by solicitors on behalf of the purchaser and the vendor represent the contract. I never did see any of those letters before the purchase was completed. Moral: you really need to be able to trust your solicitor, or insist on seeing the letters to make sure everything is clear before you send the money!

Local Authority Search

As part of the conveyancing process, your solicitor will carry out a local authority search, designed to discover if there are plans afoot which may affect the value or desirability of your new property in the future. The search looks for planning proposals for things such as:

- New roads.
- Changes to road layout.
- Building developments in the vicinity.
- Alterations to land use or public rights of way.
- Changing the status of the land – e.g. putting your home into a conservation area or National Park.

There will be a charge made by the local authority for this search, and by your solicitor for carrying it out.

Title Deeds

Every property should have title deeds, naming its owner and any previous owners, describing its exact extent and including any conditions relating to the property. These might include such things as restrictions on business use, or an agreement for drainage from the property to cross a neighbour's land.

During the conveyancing process, your solicitor will examine the title deeds to ensure that:

O The vendor is the legal owner of the property.

O There are no restrictions on the vendor's right to sell it.

O The property and the land upon which it stands are precisely what you think you are buying.

O Any conditions in the title are acceptable to you. If there are unnecessary or unfair restrictions, you may be able to have those conditions amended or removed.

The new disposition, drawn up by the seller's solicitor, names the new owner and is signed by the vendor in the presence of witnesses. Once the sale is concluded this disposition becomes part of the deeds. The deeds on some very old properties are a fascinating record of the history of the building.

It is not uncommon for some old properties, particularly in the Highlands and Islands, to have no deeds. In such a case the vendor should have some drawn up, at his expense.

Settlement

This refers to the payment of the purchase price plus any other legal costs relating to the sale. Your solicitor will give you a statement detailing how much you need to pay. This will be more than the purchase price of the property: it will also include your solicitors' fees and various other fees which they will disburse on you behalf. (For a fuller description of costs and fees, see below.)

You must ensure that you have cleared funds in place with your solicitor in good time before the date of settlement. If you are paying by cheque, you need to get this to your solicitor a full week before settlement, to allow the funds to be cleared. It is preferable to arrange an electronic CHAPS transfer from your bank account to the solicitor's client account. You need to allow 24 hours for the transfer to take place, but there is no need to wait for these funds to clear.

If for any reason the cleared funds are not available at the stated time, the sale cannot go through and you will not be given the keys until all the money has been paid. You may also be charged a financial penalty, in the form of interest at so much per day for each day late. This will be clearly stated in the missives.

What Happens Next?

Once the property has changed hands and any outstanding matters and payments are completed, the new owner's solicitor forwards the title deeds for registration in the Land Register of Scotland. On their return, the solicitor forwards them to you or your mortgage lender. If you have taken out a loan or a mortgage to buy the property, the deeds will normally be lodged with the lender until such time as you have paid off the loan. If you have bought the property outright, the deeds remain in your possession. Alternatively you may instruct your solicitor to lodge them securely in their offices. Do ensure that your title deeds are kept safe, as they are essential when you come to sell the property on, or if it is passed on to your heirs.

Buying a Flat

There is little difference in the procedure for buying a flat from buying a house. When you are sent the deeds by your solicitor, check them carefully to see what responsibilities owners of flats within the building have for maintaining the common areas, including any garden or landscaped areas outside the building. You should also ascertain if the building is factored or run by a property manager, and if so what level of annual costs you will be required to pay. If there is not a factor, bear in mind that any costs of repairs or maintenance will have to be shared between the owners of the flats, and without an outside agency to insist on such payments, difficulties or disputes between neighbours may arise. It can be well worthwhile paying the extra charges of a factor in order to avoid such potential problems.

You will almost certainly be required to pay an initial charge for factoring fees – usually called a 'float' – at the time of settlement, so the amount you pay will be the cost of the flat, plus legal fees and the factor's float.

Buying a New Build Property

There is unlikely to be a closing date set for a new build property, which are usually offered for sale at a fixed price. You may be able to negotiate a discount on the asking price – sometimes there will be a note 'Incentives Available' so it always worth haggling a little on the price.

Once you have agreed to buy a new property, and agreed on the price, you will probably be asked to pay a reservation fee of between £100-1,000 to secure the property. In effect, this is a non-refundable deposit, the amount of which will be subtracted from the price payable on settlement date. However, if you do pull out of the deal, you will forfeit your reservation fee.

Buying Land

Conveyancing procedures for buying land are broadly similar to those for buying bricks and mortar. However, you may find you cannot get a mortgage to buy a piece of land, unless you are also applying for the loan to pay for the building of a house. In this case, you would need to look for a self-build mortgage (see *Finance* above for further details.)

In most cases, a building site will already have outline or full planning permission granted on it to build a house. You would expect to pay much more for a site with P.P. than one without, because there is no guarantee that the planning permission would be granted. If you are contemplating buying land which does not already have P.P. it is strongly advised that you talk with the local planning officer to discover the likelihood of permission being granted for a house if you were to apply. This is important because some land is categorised as being in areas where residential building is not allowed.

Even if they indicate that, in principle, it is likely to be granted, the other thing they would have to be satisfied with is that the land is suitable for sewage drainage . Where the land is on or near to mains sewage, this is no problem. But there are many rural areas which have no mains sewage, in which case you would have to install a septic tank. In some places, particularly in the Highlands, the land is such that a basic septic tank is not suitable and you may be granted planning permission with the condition that you install a specialised septic tank, which may cost as much as £5,000, so it is sensible to factor this cost into your budget from the outset.

If the site already has planning permission, ensure that it is not about to expire. Normally, planning permission remains in force for three years from the date when it was granted, and you can apply for renewal of the permission before the expiry of that three years. This is generally a formality, and renewal would be granted without any problem. However, if something dramatic has changed in local circumstances – for instance if the area has become a National Park and therefore subject to far more stringent planning laws – you may find renewal of the planning permission is not granted. Therefore, do ensure that any planning permission in force on the land has a long enough period of time to run to allow you to begin your build before it expires. Once the foundations are laid, even if the house isn't completed within the three years, the planning permission remains valid and cannot be rescinded. Where planning permission has expired, the owner can apply to have it re-granted, as long as he does so within five years of the date the original permission was granted.

All these matters should be looked into by your solicitor during the conveyancing process, and if public bodies such as the planning department are involved, this can slow things down tremendously as they are notorious for the snail's pace at which they work.

Buying a Croft

The purchasing and conveyancing procedures for buying croftland are broadly similar to buying any other property or land. However, it is subject to additional laws – for good reason, a croft is often defined as 'a small piece of land surrounded by red tape'! It is therefore essential to determine, when house-hunting in crofting areas, whether the land or property you are interested in is croft land or not. This is not always made clear in the details of the property for sale, so if you are in any doubt, make further enquires with the selling agent.

Some houses in these areas have been built on land which has been officially decrofted, which means it is not subject to crofting law. These are the most straightforward purchases to make – the property and land is freehold and there are no requirements to use, or not use, the land in certain ways, beyond those listed in the standard local missives. However, as crofters generally only get permission to decroft quarter to half an acre of land for a house site, you would not get much land with it. If you want several acres, you would almost certainly only find this in the form of a croft. Unless, of course, you can afford to buy a whole estate.

The status of a house standing on a croft varies. If you are buying an owned croft, all the land, the house and the garden around it, belongs to you, so there should be no legal problems. However, if you are buying a house plus a croft tenancy, the legal situation is less clear-cut. In some cases you may find that a house on a tenanted croft stands on decrofted land, but the garden or land surrounding it and apparently being sold with it has not been decrofted, which could put you in a difficult legal situation. In yet other cases, a house on a tenanted croft may stand on land which is still owned by the estate, a situation you should avoid.

You also need to be aware that if the croft has recently been bought by the crofter, he may be reluctant to complete the deal quickly, as the estate may be able to claim some of the profits from the sale

---

When Sharon Blackie bought a croft in Wester Ross she negotiated her way round this situation

The croft at the time I offered to buy it was still part of Dundonnell estate, and rented by the crofter from whom I was to purchase it. To do this, it was necessary that he purchase the croft from the estate, thus becoming an 'owner-occupier' of the croft. (Crofting law grants any crofter the right to buy their croft from the landlord at what is usually a tiny, token amount). At that point I could purchase it from him and in turn become the 'owner-occupier'. However, if a crofter buys his land from the estate and then sells it on to someone else within five years, there is a provision that 20% of the proceeds is payable back to the estate. This provision applies only to land, not to property on the croft. For that reason we split the purchase so that I bought the ruined croft-house and a small piece of garden at once, and the rest of the land purchase is to be completed five years later.

If you find yourself in a similar situation, you must be absolutely certain that the crofter is trustworthy – and even if you are, make sure you back up these promises with a legal agreement, so he cannot refuse to honour the arrangement after the five years have passed.

If it is croft land, you or your solicitor should discover the identity of the landlord and of the assigned crofting tenant. If it is a tenanted croft, it will be owned by the local estate, whereas if it is an owned croft, it will be owned by a private individual. However, even if it is has been bought from the estate previously, and is therefore an owned croft, it is still possible for the crofting tenure to be assigned to another individual. In such a case, you may find that, although you can buy the croft from the owner, the crofting tenant retains the legal right to continue to use the land for his own purposes.

And it may not just be a tenant who has rights over the land: croftland may be subject to official sub-lets, unofficial sub-lets or occasional grazing rights. Because of the legal protection afforded to crofters, you may find that the removal of a neighbouring crofter's habitual rights of access to that croft could be challenged in court. Even if things do not go that far, you may find that said neighbours are distinctly cool, or downright hostile, towards you if you don't treat them in a sympathetic manner. A friendly visit to them with a bottle of whisky can be a good way of starting the thawing process!

If you do buy a croft, you should be aware that each crofter is entitled to a share in the township's common grazing lands. These are areas of land, in some cases extensive, which are shared proportionately between the active crofters in the township. An annual peppercorn rent (of £1 or so) asserts your right to use this land for specific agricultural purposes. A crofter can apply to the common grazings committee to fence off his 'apportionment' – i.e. an area of the common grazings equivalent to his proportionate holding. If this is agreed, that apportionment is then reserved for the sole use of that crofter.

Don't assume that this will be explained to you by your local common grazings clerk when you arrive as new crofter! Land and access to it is jealously guarded, and they will be happy to leave you unaware of your entitlement to a share in the common grazings. It is wise to ask your solicitor to include in the missives a requirement that you receive your share of the common grazings, and also to enquire whether there is any apportionment connected with the croft you are purchasing.

When buying a house site in a crofting area you must ensure that it is officially decrofted before you buy it, and it is wise to ensure that it has outline or full planning permission to build a residential dwelling on it which is still current. If you buy the land and find afterwards that these matters have not been attended to, you may find yourself the bemused owner of a piece of land you cannot build on, while your neighbour continues to have the right to graze his sheep on it!

Crofting law allows tenanted crofts to be passed on through families with the minimum of legal niceties, so it is rare for tenanted crofts to be available on the open market to incomers. The majority of crofts for sale will be owner-occupied, where the land has been bought from the estate. You must still be aware of your rights and responsibilities if becoming an owner-occupying crofter. Crofting law states that the Crofters Commission have to ensure that any croft, owned or tenanted, is occupied by a 'suitable' person. You are not allowed to buy a croft and just treat the land as a garden or entertaining space, as you can with a house in town. You must demonstrate that you will use the croft in a productive way, as defined by the Crofters Commission. If you buy a croft before the Crofters Commission have made an assessment of your plans, they may decide you do not satisfy their requirements to be classed as a crofter, in which case they have the right to give the tenancy of your croft to another person to use it in an approved way. It is essential that you sort out these issues before committing yourself to buy. If time is an issue, you would be best advised to put in an offer for the croft, with an attached condition that you are accepted as suitable by the Crofters Commission. This would allow you to withdraw your offer without financial penalty.

All this sounds quite frightening and off-putting, but in practice, nowadays the Crofters Commission are keen to get new blood into crofting areas and to widen the uses to which crofts are put, largely because the old-style crofter is finding it increasingly hard to make a productive return from his croft. In the past, the range of activities you could carry out under the heading of 'crofting' was limited to agricultural activities, which in practice tended to come down to keeping sheep and cattle. Today they are eager to encourage more environmentally friendly activities, such as planting trees and growing organic produce. There are now grants available to help crofters set up these and other such businesses, while subsidies given for keeping livestock are being eroded. In addition, the Crofters Commission look seriously at plans which include tourism activities and the catch-all phrase 'any activity which is of community benefit.' However, it's always a good idea to ensure at least some element of your plan is related directly to the soil – but if you are contemplating buying a croft, that is sure to be a central part of your Highlands dream!

Crofting legislation is a specialist area and advice should always be sought from a solicitor well-versed in crofting law, preferably based in a crofting area themselves – Glasgow and Edinburgh solicitors will not necessarily be the best choice, although some firms will have one partner who specialises in this area.

Further Information

Crofters Commission (Ughdarras Nan Croitearan): 4/6 Castle Wynd, Inverness IV2 3EQ; ☎ 01463-663450; fax 01463-711820; www.crofterscommission.org.uk.

Scottish Crofters Union: Old Mill, Harapool, Broadford, Isle of Skye IV49 9AQ; ☎ 01471-822529; fax 01471-822799; e-mail crofters.union@talk21.com; www.scu.co.uk.

PUBLICATIONS.

- ○ *Purchasing Your Croft*
- ○ *Owner-Occupied Croft Land*
- ○ *Becoming a Crofter*
- ○ *Decrofting*
- ○ *Crofting Counties Agricultural Grants Scheme: Guidance Notes*
- ○ *Scottish Agriculture: Guide to Grants and Services*
- ○ *Biodiversity on Croftland & Common Grazings*

These and other publications are available from the Crofters Commission.

Time Scale

Whether you buy property or land, a flat or a house, a croft or freehold property, under the current system it is rare that you can conclude the deal in less than eight weeks of making your offer. In some cases, where problems arise regarding the title to the land, the extent of its boundaries, or issues which involve public bodies such as planning departments or the Scottish Environmental Protection Agency (SEPA) the procedure could take a great deal longer.

HOW TO BUY A HOUSE IN FIFTEEN MINUTES

A new scheme has been introduced by four legal firms and an estate agent, who joined forces to form The Conveyancing Hub, where properties can be bought and sold almost instantly, using the power of the internet. E-conveyancing can cut the transaction time from an average of eight weeks to as little as 15 minutes! They have already concluded 150 deals and predict that by Spring 2006 more than 1,000 property transactions per month will take place at the click of a mouse.

The ability to do this will increase as elements of the house purchasing system become automated and standardised over coming years. Solicitors and estate agents are making increasing use of the internet to speed transactions. More than 50% of title deeds are already registered with the Scottish Land Registry, and eventually all properties should be on the Register. This cuts out the need for solicitors to examine bundles of ageing title deeds – one document, the Land Certificate, is kept on an electronic system and is all the conveyancer needs to check. From 2007 the Land Registry is introducing Automated Registration of Title to Land (ARTL) which will speed up the processing of property transactions even more.

Property Information Packs (PIPs) due to be introduced in 2007, mean that surveys and searches will have to be obtained by the vendor before he even puts the property on the market. And when Standard Missives are introduced throughout Scotland, this will simplify property transactions further.

Doubtless there will always be properties which are not suitable to be sold so quickly, but where there are no special circumstances involved, there seems no reason why this should not be the normal pattern for transactions in the future.

It is also whispered that this should bring down the costs involved with buying and selling property. But whether solicitors and estate agents pass these savings on to the customer in full, remains to be seen.

Further information: www.theconveyancinghub.co.uk.

Buying at Auction

If you are buying from a property auction, the property becomes yours the moment the hammer falls. Although this can avoid the often long drawn out process of house-buying, you should not buy the property 'blind': employ a solicitor to do a certain amount of work beforehand, such as carrying out local authority searches to discover if there are any local planning proposals in the offing which may affect the property.

Many auction properties require extensive work doing on them, which is often the reason why they are marketed in this way, so it is sensible to have the building surveyed before the auction, to give you an idea of the work that would be involved. You can then get an estimate for the cost of this work which will allow you to devise a reasonable budget for the whole project and decide the maximum amount you can afford to pay for the basic property. Remember to include the amount of buyer's commission and auction fees you have to pay on top. These vary between auction houses, so contact them in advance to find out their terms.

You must ensure that you have ten per cent of the money available immediately; the other 90% must be paid within 28 days. It is advisable to engage a solicitor before the auction.

POTENTIAL PITFALLS

At the risk of being alarmist, it is wise to be aware of the sort of problems you, your solicitor, or your surveyor may discover during the process of conveyancing. Your solicitor should have made your offer in terms that allow you to withdraw without penalty from the sale if material matters are brought to your attention in these areas. Even if you don't think the problems are big enough to cause you to halt the purchase, you may be able to use them as a bargaining chip to reduce the price you pay – if, for example, the survey shows the property needs remedial work to the value of several thousand pounds. Alternatively, you may agree that the vendor has the work done at his own cost, with an amount of money being held back by your solicitor at the time of the sale, and only paid over to the vendor once the work has been done. This is a way of allowing you to move in before the work is done, happy in the knowledge that it will soon be carried out at the vendor's cost.

Septic Tanks

If you are trying to buy land or a house in a rural area, you may find that it is not on the mains sewage system. In such a case, sewage and waste water would be disposed of via a septic tank. In recent years, EU and other regulations regarding the quality of any discharge from a septic tank have been tightened greatly, in the interests of environmental safety. The Scottish Environmental Protection Agency (SEPA) is the body charged with policing these matters and any planning application will be passed to them for comment on the environmental aspects of the application, as a matter of course. They may require specific, and sometimes fairly stringent, conditions to be applied to any house built on the site.

If there is an existing septic tank at the property, it may need to be tested to ensure it is working properly. If it is not, or if the distillate (i.e. the water which runs off once it has been processed) does not reach a specified standard, you may be required to upgrade the tank.

Before planning permission is granted to build a house on a specific plot of land, the applicant will be obliged to do a 'percolation test' which involves digging specified holes in the land to determine whether ground water drains away quickly enough. If these do not meet the standard required, planning will only be granted on the basis of you using a form of septic tank which produces a far more purified distillate.

There are some hi-tech tanks which have a processing unit within them, which means the distillate is far purer than from a standard septic tank. Another system which might work, if the land permits, is a 'reed-bed system'.

REED BED SEWAGE SYSTEMS

A reed bed is an artificially created wetland planted with specially selected species of reed that have the ability to absorb oxygen from the air and release it through their roots. This creates ideal conditions for the development of huge numbers of micro-organisms which are able to break down any soluble material present.

A reed bed system has many benefits:

O Efficient and cheap to run.
O Relies on biological processes.
O Returns solid matter to the soil.
O Recycles liquids in the form of purified water.
O Produces reeds which can be harvested for compost.
O Avoids the need for chemical treatment.

There are strict controls on how far from a water course a septic tank should be. Where distillate is permitted to be run off into a loch, it must only enter the loch at beyond low water mark and must satisfy quality standards.

Many stretches of coastal water, and lochs, around the Scottish coastline are now designated as shellfish producing waters. In some cases this means that SEPA will no longer allow any further discharge, of any kind, into the water. In other cases, they may set such a high standard of purity of any discharge that only a new breed of very hi tech and carefully controlled septic tanks can produce distillate of such quality. These do not come cheap – they will probably cost you £5,000 or more.

If you are contemplating building your own house in such areas you will need to investigate these requirements closely, and should in any event allow several thousand pounds in your budget to cover the potential costs of waste water drainage.

Further information on these matters is available from SEPA Corporate Office, Erskine Court, Castle Business Park, Stirling FK9 4TR; ☎ 01786 457700; fax 01786 446885; www.sepa.org.uk.

Asbestos

If the property you are buying contains any asbestos – for instance, in the form of a roof, as some old croft cottages do – you will be required to have this safely removed and disposed of by an approved disposal firm.

Structural Faults

Even the most basic survey should indicate whether there are any potential structural faults in a building, such as subsidence, woodworm, damp, dry rot or wet rot. If the surveyor suspects any of these are present, you may be required to have further investigations, and remedial work carried out, to put the problem right. If subsidence is particularly bad, you may be unable to obtain a mortgage on it at all.

Where there is evidence that such problems have existed in the past, and remedial work has been carried out, the vendor is obliged to hand over to the new owner any certificates indicating approved work which has been done, with dates, and noting any warranties on the work.

Planning Permission

Where major alterations or extensions to a property have been made in the past, the vendor will be required to produce evidence that planning permission was granted for the work and that a completion certificate was issued at the end of the work. Where evidence of this is not forthcoming, you need to ensure that the local planning department is contacted to give their comments on the situation. If works were done without permission at any time in the past, they are entitled to insist the building is put back exactly as it was prior to the work. If they feel, however, that the works are acceptable, and permission would have been granted if sought, they may issue retrospective planning permission, or a so-called 'letter of comfort' which covers the new owner from suffering any orders to dismantle, or re-do to an approved standard, any unauthorised building work which was done. Any cost incurred in such investigations, or for work done, should be paid for by the vendor.

It cannot be stressed too strongly, that if you have no evidence of planning permission being granted, and if the vendor is reluctant to approach the planning department on the issue, your best move would be to withdraw from the deal forthwith, unless you feel the property is worth taking a risk on. But do be aware that there are potentially large additional costs or, in the worst case scenario, that you may have to dismantle a large part of the house you have bought!

Where an extension has been built by the vendor, this may have an effect on the council tax banding. You should be aware that, at the time of compilation, the house is not normally reassessed for council tax, which the householder continues to pay at the existing banding. But when the property changes hands, the property will then be reassessed for council tax, a move which will not occur until the new owner is in the house and sends his details to the council tax office. If you have bought a house on the understanding it is Band D, and then it is reassessed to take in the increase in size of the property since the extension was added, you might find it moves up one or more bands, to Band E or F, which can make a substantial difference to the council tax payments you will make.

Building Warrants

Smaller alterations, usually internal, to a property, often require a building warrant to be issued by the local council, which indicates that the work is approved and will be done to a required standard and in line with building regulations. Again, where building warrants are not forthcoming from the vendor, it is wise to seek a letter of comfort from the building control department at the local authority. This is unlikely to be refused if the works were minor and do not transgress any building regulations.

Planning Issues

Local authority searches in relation to the property should show up any planning issues that may affect the property, such as if there are any new roads or building development planned in the vicinity in the near future. These may not have a detrimental effect on the property – in fact, some development of the area may actually increase the value of existing homes.

Environmental Designations

You should ascertain whether the land or property falls into an area with an environmental designation on it, or whether this is planned for the future. Such designations can put restrictions on any development you can make to your property, or any business you could run. Anything of this nature you wanted to do would almost certainly have to be approved by another body – such as Scottish Natural Heritage or a National Park Authority – as well as the planning department.

Access

Access to your property can sometimes prove to be a contentious issue where, for instance, there is a long-standing agreement to share access with a neighbour. If the neighbour chooses to be difficult when a new owner moves in, or if that neighbouring property changes hands, you may find that your access is taken away. Even if the law shows that you are entitled to continue using it, you may find this makes living in the community uncomfortable. If at all possible, investigate the costs of providing your own access – it can be money well spent in the long run.

Disabled Access

There are now very specific requirements to provide disabled access to a new build house, even if you intend to have no disabled people either living or visiting the property. This must be provided, and if it cannot be provided within your proposed house plans, they will have to be modified, even to the extent of re-positioning the house on the site if this is the only way to provide it.

Parking

The local authority roads department is always asked for their comments on road access to and the provision of car parking outside a new build property, and they have powers to insist that your plans conform to their regulations.

COSTS & FEES

In addition to the purchase price of your property, you need to budget for a number of other costs, fees and tax which together can increase the overall bill substantially. All these costs are generally dependent on the selling price of the property – the more expensive the property, the higher the additional fees you will have to pay.

Solicitors

Solicitors charge fees to cover:

- Perusal of the deeds.
- The preparation of legal documentation.
- Administration charge for local authority searches.
- Exchange of missives with the seller's solicitor.
- Arranging for stamp duty to be paid.
- Administration charges connected with setting up a mortgage.
- Passing monies to the mortgage lender.

Fees charged are usually between one and 1.5% of the purchase price, plus 17.5% VAT, with costs relating to disbursements to other agencies (such as stamp duty, land registry, lender's legal fees) on top of this. It is worth getting quotes from several solicitors as their charges may vary.

Estate Agents

As a buyer, you should not have to pay anything to the estate agent or solicitor who is selling the property. They charge fees only to the vendor, of about 1.5 to 2% of the selling price.

Stamp Duty Land Tax

This is a government tax levied on the buyers of residential land and buildings. It is payable at the stated rate on the whole cost of the property – so if you buy a house for £120,000 you pay no stamp duty; if you pay £120,001 for it you owe stamp duty of £1,200. At the top end of the scale, if you buy a property for £500,000 you pay £15,000 stamp duty, compared to the £20,040 you pay on a property at £501,000. It is therefore sensible to offer just under rather than just over the level at which each new rate applies.

Tax rate	Cost of property
Nil	£0-£120,000
1%	£120,001 – £250,000
3%	£250,001-£500,000
4%	Over £500,000

Land Register

The details of the new owner are recorded in the Land Register of Scotland once the sale has gone through. There is a fee payable, calculated on a sliding scale.

Cost of property	Fee
Up to £10,000	£22
£15,000	£33
£20,000	£44
£25,000	£55
£30,000	£66
£35,000	£77
£40,000	£88
Fees increase by £11 for every £5,000 until:	
£200,000	£440
£300,000	£500
£400,000	£550
£500,000	£600
£600,000	£650
£700,000	£700
£800,000	£800
£1,000,000	£900
£1,500,000	£1,500
£2,000,000	£2,000
£3,000,000	£3,000
£5,000,000	£5,000
Over £5,000,000	£7,5000

Survey Fee

The fees payable for a house survey can vary considerably, as there are several variables to take into account:

- O Fees are generally based on the value of the property – the more expensive it is, the more a survey on it will cost you.
- O Fees increase with the thoroughness of the survey you choose – a valuation survey; homebuyer's report; building survey; specialist survey will be increasingly expensive.
- O Mortgage lenders and surveyors all have their own scales of charges.
- O Price quoted may include or exclude VAT at 17.5% – if not included, you must add this on.
- O Unless you need a valuation for mortgage purposes, there is no legal requirement for you to have a survey done at all.

HSBC SURVEY FEES 2005			
Value of property	Valuation Survey	Homebuyer's Report	Building Survey
£75,000	£125	£285	£460
£100,000	£135	£310	£500
£150,000	£155	£335	£545
£200,000	£175	£385	£625
£250,000	£195	£435	£660
£300,000	£225	£485	£725
£400,000	£265	£560	£835
£500,00	£325	£635	£885
£600,000	£385	£710	£1,035
£700,00	£435	£785	£1,185
£800,000	£485	£835	£1,285
£900,00	£515	£910	£1,385
£1,000,000	£535	£985	£1,485
These fees include VAT			

Arrangement, Application or Acceptance Fee

Charged by a lender for arranging a mortgage, typically around £250 to £300. Different mortgages from different lenders will have different fees, and some may have none at all.

Lender's Legal Fees

The legal fees charged by your lender's solicitor are payable by you. They may be added on to the amount you borrow, and thus become part of your mortgage repayments.

Bank Charges

Electronic transfer of purchase price and fees from your account to your solicitor's account is done under the CHAPS system. There is a charge of around £18 for this.

If you pay by cheque from your personal bank account, there would normally be no bank charges, but the cheque would take up to seven days to clear so you would have to take the funds from your account a week early and you would lose any interest during this period. On a large sum of money, this may be more than £18, so it may prove quicker and easier – and no more expensive – to use CHAPS.

If the money is paid by cheque from a business account there will be bank charges on the transaction, and it will still require up to seven days to clear.

Factor's Fees

If you are buying a property which is subject to factor's fees or a management charge, you will be asked to pay a 'float' at the time of settlement, payable through your solicitor who will then disburse the relevant amount to the factor. This float varies, but typically will be between £100 and £300.

In addition, there will be further annual charges to pay, depending on the size of the flat, its quality (which, as a rough guide, can be assessed on the council tax banding) and the services provided. As an example, in 2005, a two-bedroom flat in the West End of Glasgow, with a council tax banding of F, had factor's fees of around £800 per year; while a one-bedroom flat in Glasgow City Centre with a council tax banding of E had factor's fees of around £500 per year.

Note that these fees include buildings insurance.

Buildings Insurance

If you are taking out a mortgage, you are legally required to fully insure the property against structural and other damage for the full term of the loan. The annual premium you pay depends on the area in which you live, the size and type of the property and the insurance company.

Some mortgage lenders offer their own insurance, or a policy with an insurance company they work closely with. You have no obligation to take this and can arrange your insurance elsewhere. It is sensible to get quotes from a number of insurance companies.

Life Insurance

Endowment mortgages require you to take out a life insurance policy to pay off your mortgage in full in the event of your death. Again, the lender may offer to arrange life insurance, but you can arrange the necessary cover elsewhere. It may save you money if you shop around for the most competitive quote.

Part IV

WHAT HAPPENS NEXT

SERVICES

MAKING THE MOVE

BUILDING OR RENOVATING

MAKING MONEY FROM YOUR PROPERTY

SERVICES

CHAPTER SUMMARY

- There are several electricity, gas and telephone suppliers in competition with each other, so shop around for the best deal.
- They all bill customers quarterly and charge a fixed service charge in addition to the cost of actual consumption.
- When you move into your new home you should contact the suppliers to set up accounts with them.
- Mains gas is not available in all rural areas. Bottled gas is used in these regions.
- Good central heating is important, as it gets very cold in Scotland.
- In rural areas, where electricity cuts are not uncommon, it is sensible to have a back-up form of heating and cooking if possible.
- Oil fired central heating is normal where mains gas is not available.
- Water and sewerage services are supplied only by Scottish water.
- If you have a septic tank it should be emptied regularly to work most efficiently.
- Refuse collection and disposal are free.
- Insurance premiums vary depending on where you live.
- If you employ staff, you are responsible for paying their tax and National Insurance contributions to the Inland Revenue.

UTILITIES

There are many companies supplying electricity, gas and telephone services, some specific to Scotland, others UK wide. It is a very competitive area with all the companies looking to increase their market share, so you may find it profitable to shop around for the best deal. Many of the bigger fuel companies are now able to supply both gas and electricity, and some are getting into the telephone market too, offering a certain level of free telephone calls as an incentive to join them. If you look at their websites you will find them offering various discounts and one-off savings if you switch some or all of your services from your existing supplier.

Whoever they are supplied by, electricity, gas and telephone are usually billed quarterly, and there are numerous ways of paying:

○ Online through the company's website, using a credit or debit card.
○ At any bank, using cash or cheque.
○ By post, using a cheque.
○ Via internet or telephone banking services.
○ By telephone using debit card.
○ At a post office, using cash or cheque.
○ Using direct debit.

There may be discounts for paying online or using direct debit. If you choose to use monthly direct debits, your consumption will be assessed and a regular monthly amount set. As this evens out the fluctuations of fuel bills in the winter and summer months, it is a useful budgeting tool. The amount you pay will be reassessed every six months or so, to ensure your payments are neither too low nor too high in relation to your actual consumption.

You may be given the option of 'paperless billing' where you view your bills online and they are not sent through the post. There may be a discount of around £5 per year for choosing this option.

All the utilities levy a standing charge in addition to the cost of actual consumption. This is added to the quarterly bill, or included in your direct debit payments.

When you move into your new home, you should contact the supply companies to ensure that you do not pay for electricity, gas or telephone calls used or made by the previous owner or tenant. They will ask you to read your electricity and gas meters and ring through the reading. Then they will set up a new account in your name, unless you wish to change to another supplier in which case you will need to contact them. This can usually be done by phone or through their website.

Meters are sometimes situated inside the property, sometimes outside in a secure box which you and the supply company can access with a special key.

If your new home has been empty for some time before you move in, services may have been disconnected in which case you may have to pay a reconnection charge.

Gas

Mains gas is available in all urban areas, but many rural areas do not have piped gas. Although mains gas may be available in your town or your street, it may not necessarily have been run into your home. If you wish to have it piped in you should contact a gas supply company to discuss the cost of being connected to the mains.

In areas which have mains gas, most central heating systems are gas-fired as they are generally the most efficient and cheapest to run. A good heating system for your house is essential as it can get very cold in Scotland – not just in the winter months.

In rural areas, many people use bottled propane or butane gas (usually Calor Gas), particularly for cooking. Some suppliers will deliver to your door, or you may collect it yourself from local shops. If you do use bottled gas for cooking or heating, you must ensure that any appliance is specially adapted to use the correct fuel.

Any tradesman who comes to your home to fit, service or adapt gas fittings, appliances or supply, must have Corgi (Council of Registered Gas Installers) registration. This will be prominently displayed in any advertising, so if a gas fitter doesn't display it, assume he is not registered and find another one.

Electricity

The electricity supply throughout the UK is 240 volts AC, 50 hertz (cycles), single phase. Electrical plugs have three flat pins and should be fitted with a 3, 5 or 13 amp fuse depending on the wattage of the electrical equipment. If you buy a plug from a shop, it will have a 13 amp fuse in so you will have to replace this if necessary. Although some equipment from Europe or the US could be used with adapters, it is safest to buy new equipment in the UK.

Many light fittings use bulbs with push-in 'bayonet' fixings, but the current trend in houses is to have recessed ceiling lights, or spotlights, which mainly use screw-in bulbs, some with reflectors, some without. There is an increasing range of environmentally friendly long-life bulbs which last far longer than an average bulb. Although they are much more expensive than a standard bulb, it is claimed that they save you much money in electricity in the long run. There is a bewildering range of bulbs required for modern light fittings, which vary in type, size, shape, wattage and so forth, so do make sure you take the old bulb with you when you go to buy a replacement one.

You may suffer occasional power cuts in remote areas, particularly during periods of bad weather. The Highlands and Islands are particularly prone to them. From time to time you may be informed in advance of planned power cuts, due to maintenance work. If you are buying a home in an at risk area, it is wise to retain an open fire or install some other form of back-up heating, such as bottled gas portable heaters. Keeping a portable camping stove handy can also be a boon at such times, if only to boil up a kettle on.

If you need some electrical work doing in your home, it has to be performed by a qualified electrician or, if you wish to do it yourself, you are legally obliged to tell the Building Control department of your local council first. They will inspect the work and give you a certificate if it's okay. You *do not* need to tell your local authority's Building Control Department about:

- ◯ Repairs, replacements and maintenance work.
- ◯ Extra power points or lighting points or other alterations to existing circuits (except in a kitchen or bathroom, or outdoors).

Gas and Electricity Supply Companies

British Energy: 3 Redwood Crescent, Peel Park, East Kilbride G74 5PR; ☎ 01355-262000; www.british-energy.com.

Npower: Customer services ☎ 0845-070 9494; www.npower.com.

Powergen: PO Box 7750, Nottingham NG1 6WR; www.powergen.co.uk.

Scottish Hydro-Electric: PO Box 7506, Perth PH1 3QR; ☎ 0845 300 2141; www.hydro.co.uk

Scottish Power: Spean Street, Glasgow G44 4BE; ☎ 0845-270 6543; www.scottishpower.com.

Scottish and Southern Energy: Inveralmond House, 200 Dunkeld Road, Perth PH1 3AQ; ☎ 01738-456000; www.scottish-southern.co.uk.

*Calor Gas:*Customer Services ☎ 0800-626626; www.calorgas.co.uk. This website has a searchable database of UK suppliers. They also offer gas cylinder telephone ordering through Calor Gas Direct, ☎ 0800-662663.

Oil

In areas where there is no mains gas, most central heating systems are oil-fired. Oil supply companies deliver oil in large tankers, from which they fill up the householder's storage tank situated outside the property. Before deciding to install such a system, you first need to ensure that the tanker can reach you. If you live on a very narrow road, or access is required across an unsuitable bridge, this may be difficult.

Oil Supply Companies

BP Oil: Witan Gate House, 500/600 Witan Gate, Milton Keynes MK9 1ES; ☎ 0845-303 3377; www.bp.com.

Highland Fuels: Affric House, Beechwood Park, Inverness IV2 3BW; ☎ 0800-224224; fax 01463-710899; www.highlandfuels.co.uk.

Gleaner Oils: Head Office, Milnfield, Elgin IV30 1UZ; ☎ 01343-557400; fax 01343-548534; www.shell.com.

Water & Sewerage

Scottish Water is responsible for all water and mains sewerage services in Scotland, the only one of the utilities which is not open to deregulated competition.

Domestic water and sewerage charges are based on the council tax banding of the property, unless you choose to have a water meter fitted, in which case you pay a fixed standing charge and your actual consumption is measured on a meter and charged accordingly. Contact Scottish Water if you would like them to fit a meter.

Water charges for the year are included on your annual council tax bill, and paid together with your council tax on a monthly basis.

Mains sewers run through all urban areas and many rural areas. In remote areas domestic waste is discharged via a septic tank which must be of an approved design and be tested to ensure it operates to the required standard for the area. If you have a septic tank, no sewerage charge is included in the water rates. The local authority will have a septic tank disposal service and they will empty the tank on request. You can arrange with them to have your tank emptied regularly – every year or two is normally adequate – in which case there may be a reduction on the charge.

Scottish Water: PO Box 8855, Edinburgh EH10 6YQ; ☎ 0845-601 8855; www. scottishwater.co.uk.

Refuse Collection

All residential properties have a free weekly refuse collection, run by local authorities and paid for through the council tax. In most areas, each house is supplied with a large wheeled refuse container called a 'wheelie bin'. If you live in a flat, there will be a central collection point where residents put their rubbish, and it is removed from here on a weekly basis by the binmen.

Telephone

The telephone system throughout Scotland has been upgraded over recent years, with the aim of allowing all residents to have access to new high speed and hi-tech telephony systems by the end of 2005. At the time of writing the authorities seem to be on course to hit this target, but there are still some rural areas where, although broadband is theoretically available, the lines running into their houses are overloaded and need replacing, so their ability to actually use their broadband connection may be temperamental.

Most telephone lines are owned and maintained by British Telecom (BT). In some urban areas, telephone services are provided through cable TV networks, but there are many areas of Scotland where cable is not available.

If your new home was previously occupied, there will almost certainly be a phone line already installed and you need to ask BT or the cable company to re-connect you and allocate you a telephone number. If you wish a new or additional line to be run into the property, there is a standard charge of £174.99.

If you are located in a remote area and the line has to be run in from a connection point some distance away, the cost of connection could be higher than average. You may be able to claim compensation from BT if there are any major delays in getting your phone line connected.

Although BT provide most of the infrastructure, you can obtain your calls via a number of other telephone companies. The way you pay your bills depends on the type of company they are:

- *Direct access* companies (such as cable companies) provide physical telephones lines which connect to the telephone network. You pay line rental and call charges to them.
- *Indirect access* companies redirect your calls over their own network, and you pay call charges to them, line rental to your direct access company, such as BT.

There are numerous mobile phone companies operating across the UK. Mobile phone coverage in Scotland has improved greatly in recent years but is still not complete, especially in remote areas. The topography of the land and the lack of mobile telephone masts can mean that reception is patchy is some areas.

COST OF RUNNING YOUR HOME

It has been estimated that, on average, Scottish homeowners spend nearly one fifth of their incomes on running their homes. The average annual amount they paid in 2004 for council tax, power, insurance, telephone bills, water supply, mortgage interest, electrical appliances, goods and services and toiletries was £5,479.

This is higher than the percentage of income spent by homeowners in England and Wales, largely due to higher than average council tax and fuel bills and lower average incomes.

SECURITY

The likelihood of having your home broken into varies greatly depending on whereabouts in the country you live. Generally, the more remote the area you live in, the less likely you are to be the target of thieves. Within towns and cities, there are 'bad' areas and 'good' areas. Insurance companies reflect these probabilities in the price they charge to cover your house and its contents against loss due to criminal acts. If your home is in a high risk area, your premiums will be higher than for a similar property in a low risk area.

To provide extra security it is wise to have locking windows, a burglar alarm and security lights fitted. Such tactics may also bring down your insurance premium – in some cases, they may be a requirement of getting insurance cover in the first place.

If you let a holiday cottage or have a second home, which will be empty for parts of the year, the insurance company may add extra requirements and the premiums may be correspondingly higher. For instance, they usually require that if the property is empty for more than a thirty day period, the electricity and water should be turned off.

Even today, when the possibility of crime is accepted as part and parcel of modern life, there are still large areas of the Highlands and Islands where people routinely leave their house doors and cars unlocked, secure in the knowledge that they will be safe.

Housesitters

Some people who leave their homes empty for long periods of time employ housesitters to live in the house while they are away. This has several advantages. It means minor maintenance of the house and garden will be carried out while you are away, and if you have pets you cannot take with you, they will be cared for in your absence. Keeping the house occupied year-round may also mean your insurance premiums are lower.

Housesitters are normally unpaid, but they get free lodging while they live in your house. There are a number of websites where potential housesitters advertise themselves.

www.housesitworld.com/uk.

www.housecarers.com.

STAFF

There will almost certainly be local people who will provide their services for a few hours a week as cleaners, gardeners or 'odd job' men, while you are in residence or away. Adverts in local newspapers or in local shops are the best way to track down such people – they may advertise themselves, or you could put a 'wanted' ad in yourself.

Tax & National Insurance

If they are working just a few hours per week, and provide the same service to other people as well, it is normal to pay casual workers by cash or cheque at an hourly rate. They are then classed as self-employed and it is their responsibility to declare their earnings to the Inland Revenue and pay any tax and National Insurance contributions (NICs) required by law.

This is not to say that everybody is as honest in their dealings with the Inland Revenue as they should be – many casual workers are happy to be paid cash in hand, and take their luck as to whether the Inland Revenue find out. Some of them may also be claiming unemployment benefit at the same time. This is all strictly illegal and if you suspected this to be the case, you would be morally – and almost certainly, legally – bound to tell the authorities. In such cases you would be best not employing them in the first place.

If, however, you employ somebody for a substantial number of hours each week, or employ a caretaker for your property who lives on the premises, the Inland Revenue would look suspiciously at any claim that he/she was self-employed, and would probably argue that you should be classed as their employer. In this case you must issue your staff members with weekly or monthly payslips, calculate their tax and NICs under the PAYE system, deduct the appropriate amounts from their wages, and pay these amounts to the Inland Revenue. In addition you, as their employer, must pay an addtional amount of NICs on their behalf.

References

If you take on any domestic staff, it is wise to take up references from former or exist-ing employers. If it is a local worker who does odd jobs, gardening or cleaning, a few discreet local enquiries will soon help you decide whether he/she is a good, reliable worker.

Agencies

In cities or towns you may find it easier and safer to go to a domestic employment agency to find such staff. Then you should have the security of knowing the workers have been vetted first, and the agency should provide you with references for them. There would be a fee payable to the agency.

Illegal Immigrants

There is no doubt that some people looking for casual work do so because they are illegal immigrants and do not want their names to come to the notice of any official agencies such as the Inland Revenue.

MAKING THE MOVE

CHAPTER SUMMARY

- **Removals.** Customs forms must be completed for any household furniture, goods and personal effects you reign into the UK.
  - There is no customs duty or VAT to pay if you have owned them for more than six months.
  - International Customs clearance can take up to two weeks.
  - Choose a removal firm which is a member of a British or international trade body.
  - If your new home is difficult to reach with a large van, tell the removal company.
  - You can store your belongings in large depots for a weekly charge.
  - Removal costs quoted by different firms vary greatly.
  - Insurance should be taken out to cover your goods in transit and in storage.
- **Cars.** You may need to pay duty and VAT on your car is it less than six months old and you will be using it in the UK for more than six months.
  - Cars in the UK are comparatively expensive to buy.
- **Pets.** There are stringent health regulations on bringing pets into the UK.
  - Under the PETS scheme cats and dogs from qualifying countries are issued with a pet passport which allows them to enter or re-enter the UK.
  - The whole process takes up to six months.
  - Pets without a passport must stay in quarantine for six months on arrival in the UK.

REMOVALS

Customs regulations

When transporting household furniture, goods and personal effects into the UK, you must complete Customs Form 3 for each shipment you send. So, if you are sending some items by air and some by sea, a separate form must be completed for each.

If you are using a professional removal firm to transport your goods, they will send you the relevant customs forms to complete. If your goods are sent unaccompanied, you will be sent the forms to complete once they arrive in the UK.

Previously owned and used household goods and personal effects are allowed into the country free of any customs duty or tax. They must have been in your possession and used abroad for at least six months before your arrival in the UK. All items less than six months old are subject to both duty and VAT, and you should bring with you any receipts/invoices for any such items.

There is a list of prohibited goods which cannot be brought into the UK, including such things as controlled drugs, firearms, obscene material, plants and plant products, most animals and birds, whether alive or stuffed, and certain articles derived from protected species, such as ivory, fur skins and reptile leather. For the full list, see www.omnimoving.com/customsinfo/uk.html.

Antique items over 100 years old are not liable to duty, but you must be able to prove their date of manufacture and declare the age and value of the goods to Customs in advance of importation.

If you are bringing household goods from elsewhere in Europe, Customs clearance is usually very quick. However, International Customs clearance takes longer – allow up to two weeks.

Further advice on importing personal effects and goods into the UK may be obtained from *HM Revenue & Customs*: Portcullis House, 21 India Street, Glasgow G2 4PZ; ☎ 0845-010 9000; http://customs.hmrc.gov.uk.

Removal Firms

International. Removal companies can be found on the internet, and in classified telephone directories, either in the United Kingdom or in your home country. To ensure that you are covered by guarantees of safe delivery, and have some means of receiving compensation if things go wrong, you should only give your business to members of the International Federation of Furniture Removers (FIDI). Many national trade bodies – such as the British Association of Removers (BAR) – are themselves members of FIDI. Membership is a guarantee that they work to the FIDI Accredited International Mover (FAIM) quality standard.

TIMESCALE

Allow as much time as you can to arrange the date of transit with a removal firm – the longer the notice you give, the more likely they are to be able to deliver on exactly the date you require.

Delivery Time to Scotland	From
2-5 days	Continental Europe.
4 weeks	USA East Coast.

---

6 weeks	USA West Coast.
6 weeks	Far Eastern Countries.
8 weeks or more	Australasia.

United Kingdom. If you are moving to Scotland from elsewhere in the UK, choose a firm which is a member of the British Association of Removers (BAR). Get several quotes – prices can vary enormously to move the same consignment. You will need to provide a comprehensive list of all the items you wish them to carry, or the company may visit you to make their own list.

Although most removal companies will move items anywhere on the UK mainland, some companies may charge excessively for long distance moves. Large companies with branches throughout the UK, or Scottish companies, are generally the best choice for removals to remote areas of the mainland or the islands.

Special Requirements. Most removal firms will pack your items for you if you wish. There is an additional fee for this, so do include this request in any quotations you ask for. Alternatively, you may choose to pack yourself. Some removal companies will supply boxes of various sizes – they may allow you a certain number of free boxes, and charge you for additional ones.

You must inform the removal firm if any items are particularly large or heavy, such as a piano. They may insist that four men are available to move a piano. If you cannot arrange for two strong men to help move it into your new home, you may have to pay for four men to travel all the way. An advantage of using a large firm which has depots around the UK is that they would normally provide any additional help from the local depot, which should cut down on the cost.

Inform the removal company of any difficulties of access to your new home. If, for example, it is on a narrow, single-track or unmade road they may need to use a smaller van. Again, if they have a northern depot, they would transport your belongs in a large van most of the way, and transfer your goods to smaller van(s) at the nearest depot.

Storage. If you are moving into temporary unfurnished accommodation while house-hunting or waiting for your house purchase to go through, you may need to put your belongings into storage for a period of time. Many, but not all, removal firms do have storage depots, usually in or near large towns or cities. A weekly charge is made for storage, based on the quantity of goods you have stored.

Try to look ahead and be as certain as you can that anything you store will not be essential for the foreseeable future. Although you may expect your house purchase to go through in a few weeks, things can go wrong and you might find yourself without essential papers and the like for months. If you do need to access any items during the storage period you will be charged an additional fee to have the container opened. It is best to arrange to have your belongings stored as near as possible to your new abode. This is most convenient if you do need to gain access at any time. It may also cut down on the cost when you finally have your belongings delivered to your permanent address, although the cost of transporting your goods a further distance from your original home would be correspondingly more, so there may be no saving overall.

Cost. The costs of packing, removals and storage can vary tremendously from one company to another, so do get several quotes before deciding which firm to use. Provide as precise a list of the items you wish to have moved as you can, so the quote they give you is accurate.

When asking for quotes, you need to provide the addresses of both properties, the one you are moving from and the one you are moving to. If your belongings are going into storage while you stay in temporary accommodation, you may not have a final delivery address for the second part of the move. In this case, any quote you are given can only be provisional until you have a definite address. Note that if you are moving to a flat, you may be charged more if you are moving to a top floor rather than a ground floor flat.

Insurance. Generally, removal firms provide only limited liability insurance. This covers you for any loss or damage caused by the firm's negligence, but not for loss or damage which is out of their control. There will also be a limit on the amount of their liability – Pickfords, for example, have a limit of £40 per item – which will not be enough to cover many items. Customers should therefore take out their own insurance which covers full risks on the full value of any items moved. You may find that your house contents insurance covers your household goods while they are in transit, but they would probably not be covered while in storage. Most insurance companies will quote you for insurance of your household effects while in transit and/or storage.

Storage companies will also offer you insurance for the period of time while the goods are in store, but it is the customer's responsibility to ensure that the insurance covers the full value of the items stored.

Value for Money. Having the entire contents of your home moved is a very expensive business – you need to budget a minimum of £2,000 if you are moving from England, far more if from anywhere further afield – so you need to consider very carefully just how many of your belongings you wish to take with you to Scotland. It is wise to cut the amount of furniture to the minimum, unless it is very valuable or impossible to replace. If you are downsizing, it is just a waste of money to move everything north, only to find that 50% of it won't fit in your new home. It may work out more economical to sell or dispose of much of your furniture before you move, and buy new or second-hand furniture when you arrive. If you can also 'weed out' other smaller items, such as books, kitchenware and so forth, which you rarely if ever use, you will streamline the whole moving process, cut down the cost, and have a far less cluttered house when you arrive in Scotland!

Large 'flat-pack' furniture chain stores, such as IKEA or MFI, are a good place to buy comparatively cheap but reasonably good quality furniture. There are currently IKEA stores only at Glasgow and Edinburgh, whereas MFI has branches throughout Scotland. Auctions are good for second-hand or antique furniture. There are household and better quality auctions held throughout Scotland on a regular basis.

When making your decision, do bear in mind that the further from the central belt you move to, the further you will have to travel for a wide choice of furniture and delivery costs on it will be correspondingly higher. Although Inverness and Aberdeen have fairly large shopping centres and the choice of goods is growing, they both still feel a little behind the times so you may be disappointed with the selection of furniture available.

Useful Addresses

International Federation of Furniture Removers: www.fidi.com.

British Association of Removers: 3 Churchill Court, 58 Station Road, North Harrow HA2 7SA; ☎ 020-8861 3331; fax 020-8861 3332; www.bar.co.uk. The website includes a searchable database of BAR members, national and international.

Pickfords Ltd: Heritage House, 345 Southbury Road, Enfield EN1 1UP; ☎ 0800-289229; www.pickfords.co.uk. Includes a branch locator listing over 100 branches throughout the UK.

Britannia Greers of Elgin: The Depository, Edgar Road, Elgin, Moray IV30 6YQ; ☎ 01343-542229/545307; fax 01343-541426; www.greers.co.uk.

Britannia Movers International: 23 Kilbirnie Place, Tradeston Industrial estae, Glasgow G6 8QR; ☎ 0141-221 0001; www.britannia-movers.co.uk.

The Overseas Moving Network International: www.omnimoving.com. A large international company, with members in 60 countries, working to FIDI/FAIM standards.

Search for removal firms throughout Scotland on www.yell.co.uk.

IKEA: www.ikea.co.uk.

*MFI:*www.mfi.co.uk.

Search for auctions throughout Scotland on www.bbc.co.uk/antiques.

IMPORTING YOUR CAR

Most private vehicles can be imported free of duty for a period of less than six months. For a period of more than six months, there is no duty payable as long as:

- ○ The owner is moving their normal home to the UK and has lived for more than twelve months outside the EC.
- ○ The vehicle was not obtained under a duty or tax-free scheme (except for

diplomats and members of some government organisations).

O The owner must keep the vehicle for their personal use and not sell, lend or hire it out within 12 months.

You must complete a C104A customs form, which must be supported by copies of your passport, utility bills to prove you have resided previously in another country, your car insurance policy and a purchase invoice.

If the motor vehicle is under six months old you will have to pay the full rate of duty and VAT, which works out at approximately 29% of the car's value.

Once you have paid any tax or duty, and if everything is in order, Customs will give you a clearance form and registration instruction. Take these, together with proof of car insurance, to the nearest Department of Transport Vehicle Registration Office. Here the vehicle will be licensed, a road tax disc will be issued and car registration plates supplied.

Motor vehicles are comparatively expensive in the UK, even though prices have come down in recent years, so it may be cheaper to import your car rather than buy a car in the UK. Even where your car is less than six months old and you have to pay import duties and tax, it would probably still be cheaper than selling up, then buying the same make and model of car from a UK outlet.

IMPORTING PETS

If you wish to bring family pets with you to Britain, there are stringent regulations involved, with hefty fines, or even the possibility of the animal being destroyed if you do not comply with all the requirements. You need to start the process of preparing to bring your pet with you many months in advance, or you may find that it cannot travel at the same time as you do.

The Government department responsible for all aspects of importing animals into the UK is the Department for Environment, Food & Rural Affairs (DEFRA).

The Pet Travel Scheme (PETS) allows dogs, cats and ferrets from specified countries and which have undergone a certain procedure to ensure their health, into the UK without the need to go into quarantine.

The whole process of health checks and documentation can take up to six months, and cost around £200-£300. However, this is far less expensive, and less traumatic to owner and pet, than the previous quarantine regulations. Once a pet is issued with a passport, its owner needs to ensure it is kept up to date by taking the animal to the vet for boosters by stated dates. If these procedures are followed, there will not in future be a need for a blood test or a six month wait to take your pet in or out of the country, so it is important to keep these dates in your diary.

PETS Routes. Even if your pet has a pet passport, there are still restrictions on the route you use to bring it into the UK. You can only use specific approved routes and transport companies, which are frequently amended. For the current list see www.defra.gov.uk.

Quarantine

Animals which are not from the qualifying countries or are not otherwise eligible for entry under PETS must be detained in quarantine for six months. The animal's owner should choose where this will be from a list of authorised premises available from DEFRA. The cost of keeping a pet in quarantine is £900- £1,500 for cats; £1,500-£2,000 for dogs.

You or the quarantine premises should complete Form ID1 'Application for a licence to import a dog or cat for detention in quarantine'. Once completed, send the form to one of the following addresses:

For animals which land and clear HM Customs in England or Wales: *Defra*, Quarantine Section, Area 211, 1A Page Street, London SW1P 4PQ; ☎ 020-7904 6222; fax 020-7904 6834

For animals which land in England but are transhipped to Scotland for clearance by HM Customs, or which land directly into Scotland: *SEERAD*, Pentland House, 47 Robb's Loan, Edinburgh EH14 1TY; ☎ 0131-244 6181/6182; fax 0131-244 6616

Form ID1 is available from these addresses, or may be downloaded from the DEFRA website www.defra.gov.uk.

Authorised Quarantine Premises

There are only three authorised quarantine premises in Scotland.

Aquithie Boarding and Quarantine Kennels & Cattery: Kemnay, Inverurie, Aberdeenshire AB51 9PA; ☎ 01467-643456; fax 01467-642616.

*Edinburgh & Lothians Kennels:*Seton East House, Longniddry, Lothian; ☎ 0131-665 2124 or 01875-811478; fax 01875-814553.

Milton Quarantine Kennels: Milton, Dumbarton G82 2UA; ☎ 01389-761208; fax 01389-734648.

Dangerous Dogs

In Great Britain, some breeds of dogs are prohibited and it is illegal to bring them into the country. Pit bull terriers, Japanese tosas, dogo Argentinos and fila Brazilieros brought into the country may be seized and destroyed.

BUILDING OR RENOVATING

CHAPTER SUMMARY

○ **Builders.** An experienced building contractor will save you much time and effort by organising your house build or renovation.
  ○ Try to get background information on local firms and get at least three quotes for the job.
  ○ Visit the building site regularly to keep the builders on their toes.
○ **Doing It Yourself.** You could save up to one third of the costs by being your project manager.
  ○ Make sure you have enough time to give the project your full attention, or it could be a false economy.
○ **Plans.** You can hire an architect or plan drawer to draw up plans; your builder may have plans you can adapt; or you can download them from the internet.
○ **Restrictions on Development.** In some designated areas or on certain buildings there may be restrictions on the type of building work you can do.
○ **Renovate or Re-build?** It may be cheaper to knock an old building down and build a new one, than to renovate the existing structure.
  ○ The planning office may insist that you renovate rather than replace a building.
○ **New Build.** VAT is not charged on new buildings.
  ○ Builders normally ask for stage payments during the build.
  ○ Never pay large amounts of money to a builder before the work is completed.
  ○ All new homes must have adequate disabled access.
○ **Planning Permission.** Most building work or renovations need planning permission.
  ○ In addition, you also need a building warrant. Some small jobs which don't need planning permission do need a building warrant.

> O Building work must comply with Scottish Building Standards and conditions imposed by local authority departments and other official bodies.
> O **Grants.** There are a number of grants available to assist in renovating or building a new home.

There seems to be a positive mania in the UK for property renovation. Certainly there are dozens of programmes on UK television about some aspect of property – whether selling, buying, renovating, redecorating, interior design, building your own home, or full-scale property development. This has largely been stimulated by the property boom over recent years, as people have seen the money they could potentially make from their properties.

Scotland is no exception to this mania, and there may in fact be more opportunities for property renovation, and the potential for a larger return, than in other parts of the UK. There are many substandard houses throughout the country, a fact recognised by local authorities, which have a number of grants for improving properties to bring them up to habitable standard. In both rural and urban areas, the old housing stock is in the process of being brought back to life, whether by professional developers or individual owners who have bought a run-down property and are investing time and money into renovating it into their perfect home, with the added benefit that this will maximise the return on their investment if and when they come to sell in the future.

The crofting system is built on the premise that tenants, and latterly owner-occupiers, have the right to build their own house on their croft, so the preference for building one's own house, rather than buying an existing house, is built into the social fabric. When incomers buy a croft, there is usually some form of dwelling or agricultural building on the land, which is ripe for renovation or, if too far gone, knocking down and replacing with a new house.

Because the general level of house prices is lower, but rising faster, in Scotland than in England, and because there is competition from potential incomers for the relatively few rural properties which come up for sale in the Highlands and Islands, if you do decide to renovate a run-down or derelict property, or build from scratch, there is a practically cast iron guarantee that it is a wise investment for the future. It is difficult to see that it could ever lose money as long as you take good advice, do the job well and build a resaleable property.

HIRING A BUILDING CONTRACTOR

The simplest option, whether renovating an existing property or building new, is to employ a building contractor to do the whole job. He will give you a price for the entire job (although this may be subject to variation as you go along) and arrange for the right tradesmen at every stage of the job to come on site and complete the necessary tasks. Timing is a very important part of the process, as the electrician generally needs to come in after the plumber has fitted pipes and so forth for the heating, but before the plasterer and decorator have been to finish the walls; and there's no point the roofer turning up either before the roof trusses are erected, or before the roof tiles have been delivered by the supplier. Depending on the size of the building company you use, they will either have their own teams of labourers and tradesmen, or they will sub-contract the skilled work, such as plumbing and electrical work, to tried and tested self-employed tradesmen they work with regularly.

Before choosing a building contractor, you need to do some homework. There is no shortage of building firms, even in rural areas, so it is rare that you will find only one company that can do the job. Ask around, if possible, to find out what local opinion of the local building firms is – although bear in mind that everybody will have their favourite, not necessarily based on the quality of the work. They might be related to one builder, for example, so be biased one way or the other. Look at other new houses or renovations which have been done in the area, and find out who did the ones you like – and the ones you hate.

Armed with this background information, you should then try to get quotes for the job from at least three firms. Normally the best way to do this is to arrange a site meeting with the builder, so he can see the terrain where the house will be built, or the state of the property you wish him to renovate.

Unless you already have full plans drawn up for your dream house, at this stage it can only be a ball-park figure. It is wise not to be totally price driven – don't automatically go for the cheapest quote without looking at other factors. Local opinion might be that builder A is more expensive than builder B, but that the quality of his work is better and he gets the job finished more quickly. Or you might learn that builder C is notorious for quoting low to get the job but adding lots of 'extras' on as the job progresses, so the build ends up much more expensive than you budgeted for.

In an urban area, it is far harder to get this background information just by asking around. The best approach here is to check the local papers and telephone directory for firms; or ask the estate agent and/or solicitor involved in the purchase of your new property or plot if they know of any building firms. (They are unlikely to officially recommend anybody, but may give you the contact details of some firms they know of.) When asking for quotes from these builders, ask them if it's possible to have a look at any similar jobs they have done previously. If they are cagey about doing so, it's a warning sign – if they are proud of their work, they will be delighted to show it off to you!

Once you have firm plans for your building or renovation project, then you need to get a firm quotation from the builder of your house. Agree in advance a cost for the build, and get down in writing, in as much detail as possible, exactly what work and materials this includes. If you do get a fixed quote, you will need to allow some leeway to take account of extra expenses which the builder could not have foreseen, or for changes, additions or upgraded specifications you decide to introduce. Do agree in advance that any such amendments or extra charges must be discussed and agreed with you first, and a price given for it. Although this may slow down the work, it is essential for budgeting purposes.

Whichever building firm you choose, and wherever they are in Scotland, you will rarely find they turn down a job because they are too busy. But if you've done your homework and chosen a reputable firm, they inevitably will be very busy. The consequence of this is that, in order to get the job, they may agree that it will be no problem to get the work finished before Christmas, or in three months, or in six months – whatever seems to suit you best. So they start the job, and get the work underway, to a stage where you're committed to them completing the project. Then they have a habit of disappearing for days or weeks at a time to do another job they're working on – with another customer who is equally convinced they will be in their new house by Christmas. The moral of this story is, by all means employ the contractor which suits you best, but don't expect it to be finished exactly when you hope for. And accept that fact that all the other contractors are almost certain to work this way too.

If it is absolutely essential that the job is finished by a certain date, you could try introducing a completion guarantee clause into the contract, where the builder is obliged to pay penalty fees if the job is late being finished. It may be easier to get a large builder from an urban area to agree to such a thing, but a small rural company probably would be very reluctant because they couldn't afford to stand the extra cost if things went wrong. You would almost certainly have to pay a premium on the price of the build in the first place. And any clause they put in the contract would doubtless be hedged about with provisos, such as saying that the rate of work is weather-dependent. And the weather is a big factor in any Scottish build – with the unpredictable climate, one thing which is predictable is that at some stage during the build there will be days or weeks of rain which make certain parts of the work impossible to complete during that period. This will inevitably delay all the later stages which can't be started until the previous stage is finished.

One thing which may work better than a completion clause is to ensure that you are regularly on site yourself to make sure that the workers are actually there and working, and that the work they do is as you requested and up to standard. Giving them too free a hand is not generally a good thing. The builder's ideal customer is one who gives him carte blanche to get on with the job at his own pace and without regularly coming to see what work has been done. If this is your own laid-back style, fine – but you may need to accept that when your house is finally complete, you turn up to find that details of the external or internal appearance or fixtures and fittings are not what you had originally specified. And there will always be a 'good reason' forthcoming why this was so. In order to avoid any nasty surprises, and to 'encourage' the builders to stay on site for longer than three hours a day, make it a habit to turn up regularly, unannounced.

> **Sharon Blackie suffered from not being close at hand to oversee the renovation of her croft cottage**
>
> *I was lucky enough to choose a builder who ended up completing it just one month late. I have since heard some real horror stories about west coast builders, so I didn't do too badly. Generally the standard of workmanship was fine. However, I wouldn't recommend the stress of trying to manage a renovation project of this scale from the other end of the country. Inevitably when you call them builders want to make you go away happy and so there's a tendency, shall we say, to be over-optimistic about progress... I remember coming up to check on progress precisely one month before I was about to quit my job, move out of my rented accommodation and arrive with all my worldly goods – and none of this was reversible – and finding that I had no electricity, no water and no septic tank. I had external walls and windows but no interior walls and no staircases. The builder had sworn on the telephone that everything was on schedule. It wasn't a happy time!*

Another reason for keeping a close eye on progress is that, however carefully you have planned the house initially, there will inevitably be points along the way where you change your mind about some aspect of its layout or the fittings. Regular discussions with the builders will allow them to make these amendments as they go along, and also give you a quote for any additional cost involved.

THE PROPERTY DEVELOPER'S MANTRA

It will always cost more and take longer than you planned for.

DOING IT YOURSELF

As a rule of thumb, the cost of any building or renovation project breaks down into roughly 1/3 labour, 1/3 materials, 1/3 to the contractor. So if you decide to act as your own project manager, in theory you should immediately save 1/3 of the cost. If you can also do some of the work yourself, this will cut it down still further.

Of course, there are other things to take into account. You will need to have the time available to organise the project as well as additional time if you will be labouring or doing any of the more skilled jobs. If you are in full time work this means that the time you can spend on the build is very restricted so it is only worth contemplating if there is no pressure for a specific completion date. If, however, you can commit yourself full time or for a good portion of the week to the building project you could save yourself quite a lot of money as well as having the satisfaction of really being 'hands-on'.

Bear in mind that if you hire a contractor they can probably source materials and tradesmen more cheaply than you can. They are also more skilled at the project management side of the build which can be a complicated process. One of the most important things to get right is the timing of deliveries of materials and ensuring that the right tradesmen are available at the right time. If a delivery is delayed for any reason, so the tradesman you have booked for a specific day arrives but there are no materials for him to work with, not only have you lost time, you may also have to pay for a day's work as well as arranging for him to come back once the materials do arrive. A contractor who finds himself in this position can always send his workers off to do another job until the materials do arrive, but as an individual you won't have this luxury.

Approach the hiring of tradesmen for specialist work in exactly the same way as hiring a contractor (above). Ask around for recommendations and get several quotes before offering the job to anyone.

If you are doing it yourself, it is very important that you get the advice of somebody aware of Scottish Building Standards because any work you do must comply with these, and if it does not you may be required to put right anything you have done incorrectly.

Get the local authority Building Standards department involved at an early stage. Call one of their officers out for a site meeting before you submit your plans and he/she will be able to give you advice on what will and will not be allowed. They may also come and inspect the work at regular intervals during the project, although the responsibility is left to the architect or builder to ensure that standards are complied with during the build. When the house is finished, you should apply for a completion certificate. Before this is granted, the Building Standards officer should come and inspect the work to ensure that the requirements of the building warrant have been complied with.

You should also arrange a site meeting with a Planning Officer as they too will have various requirements you would need to comply with before planning permission or a building warrant for the work is granted. See below for more about this.

Scottish Building Standards Agency

There have been recent changes in the building standards in Scotland. In November 2004 a new agency, the Scottish Building Standards Agency (SBSA) was launched, charged with the responsibility of ensuring all new, extended, renovated and converted buildings meet safety and environmental standards. Their website gives plenty of advice and information about the new regulations. It also has downloadable technical handbooks explaining the requirements for domestic and non-domestic buildings. These are in the form of a number of pdf files, which are in some cases very large. The website is www.sbsa.gov.uk.

The two Handbooks are also available in loose-leaf format within a folder and come with a companion CD-ROM containing the full PDF copy of the text. Copies may be obtained from The Stationery Office (www.tsoshop.co.uk) and all major bookshops, details and pricing as follows:

- **Domestic Handbook** £50.00 ISBN 0 9546292 2 1
- **Non-domestic Handbook** £50.00 ISBN 0 9546292 3 X
- **Both Domestic and Non-domestic Handbooks** £80.00 ISBN 0 9546292 4 8

Bill Herbert decided to take the do it yourself approach

In 1999, I had the chance to buy a small, stone cottage right by the side of a loch in Wester Ross. Because I knew the people who owned it, and because they were locals who don't put a great value on old cottages, it was offered to me cheap – £35,000, to be exact.

The vendors weren't naive though. It was in a pretty parlous condition. It was damp to the point of squishy, it was infested with woodworm, mice and rot, it had an old, rusty tin roof, and it had no septic tank – the raw sewage simply emptied into the loch, or would have done if the outfall hadn't been blocked.

But, ever the optimist, and on the strength of having done lots of DIY and basic renovation jobs on other houses I had lived in, I bought it.

The thing that really persuaded me to buy it was that the land on which it stood was not croft land. The cottage was an old cotter's (estate worker's) cottage. It had a large garden, which I saw had potential, and it was in a magnificent location. I went for it.

Experience has taught me that the first two things to sort out in any property are the roof and the drainage. I decided to retain the tin roof, which was basically sound, and simply 'spliced in' new sections where the rust was too pronounced. I painted the whole roof with red Hammerite (metal paint). My feet felt like budgerigar's claws after spending day after day on roof ladders and, as I recall, the weather was so hot that the paint was drying as I applied it. My neck was the same colour as the roof by the time I had finished!

Next: the drains! This was just backbreaking work. The cottage was built into the side of a hill and there was no room to get a machine in there, so it was pick and shovel and barrow and blood and sweat and many oaths. But I did it, and the results were immediate. A combination of sound roof and new drains meant the old cottage started to dry out before my very eyes (helped along by a dehumidifier of powerful proportions).

At this point, you might well ask why I didn't get a builder in to do the work. Well, to be blunt, I had seen how West Coast builders operated – their slowness to start and, even worse, their slowness to complete, plus I needed to save money, so I reckoned I could do most of the work myself more quickly and for a fraction of the cost. I was proved right.

The biggest job I tackled, though, was the removal of a huge tree, branch by branch, from the top, using only a small chainsaw. The tree was overshadowing the cottage and threatening to wreck it with its roots which had already invaded and destroyed the land drains. This job alone took me two months and at the end of it, I had muscles in my spit!

The inside of the cottage proved relatively easy. I knocked down a partition, non load-bearing wall, to open up the whole of the ground floor. I rebuilt the staircase, removed the fireplace, installed a wood-burning stove, knocked off the old rotten plaster from a gable end wall and re-pointed it, and so on. Working inside to music from the radio and with heat and power available made it almost a pleasure.

I drew the line at DIY-ing, though, when it came to installing bottled gas to the kitchen, re-wiring part of the cottage, and installing a new toilet and sink. In any case, these latter jobs needed synchronising with the installation of a septic tank, which was the only job I had to get the local builder to do. The other jobs were done by self-employed local tradesmen – much more controllable than the builders .

In the end, the most troublesome part was indeed, as I had feared, getting the builder to do what was required of him with regard to the septic tank. I began to develop a pathological hatred of all builders, not without justification.

Oh, I nearly forgot. The actual renovation process, even dealing with the builder over the septic tank, was child's play compared with getting planning permission for the building alterations and the installation of the new sewage system. Everybody and his dog, it seemed, had to be consulted, and everybody and his dog raised some objection/observation or other which I needed to take account of – SEPA, Roads and Transport, neighbours, the crofters' common grazings committee, the estate, the Planning Officer, Building Control.... the list seemed to go on and on. But I got there in the end.

Would I do it again? Not on your life! Once is quite enough for any man, I think, unless you are a tradesman. But I'm glad I did it and was pleased with the outcome. I sold the place last year and made a lot of money and, here's the best thing – I managed to get planning permission for a house in the garden which I had spotted had so much potential! That increased the selling price of the cottage by over £40,000 on its own.

Would I recommend it to others? Of course I would. If you are young enough, have a little experience of good quality DIY-ing and have the time to do it, anybody can do it. It's not rocket science, as they say.

PLANS

Whether you are renovating or extending an existing building, or building a new one from scratch, you will need to obtain either Planning Permission or a Building Warrant before the work can go ahead, and in most cases you will need both.

There are various approaches you can take to getting your plans drawn up. Firstly, if you have a very good idea of what you want, you can draw them yourself. The details required to apply for planning permission are, however, quite specific, so it may save you money in the long run if you employ a professional to draw up final plans on the basis of your sketch. If the first set of plans you submit with your planning application are not complete with all the specifications required, you may need to resubmit them and also pay an extra fee, so it is best to get it right the first time.

A qualified architect will draw up plans for you on the basis of your instructions. He/she should also advise you on which of your ideas are workable, which will be wildly expensive, and which won't get through the planning system, either because they do not comply with general SBSA standards or because they fall foul of local planning restrictions. Because there are local differences, it is sensible to employ a local architect who will be aware of what is and is not acceptable in the area.

Try to negotiate fees with your architect first. They can be expensive. Find out what hourly rate he/she charges and get an estimate of how many hours' work will be involved. Some architects charge a percentage of the final cost of the build, sometimes as much as eight per cent of the total cost – which on a £100,000 house is a hefty additional cost.

You may also go to a 'plan drawer' who can draw up plans for a house or a conversion project in a form acceptable to the planning department. If you want a unique, one-off, individually-designed house, this is not the place to go – you would have to employ an architect for something new and original. But if you want a standard type of house, a plan drawer is likely to work out far cheaper.

Another alternative is to ask your builder to design the house for you. They will have plans of previous houses they have built, and you can choose one of these standard designs. Or use that as a basis, and the builder can make any amendments to the basic layout you require.

There are also other sources of standard plans, most notably the internet. With the boom in self-building throughout the UK, and indeed world-wide, there are now a number of websites with plans for a variety of different types of home, some offering them free, others for a charge. There are also books of outline home plans of many styles of houses. These can be a great source of inspiration, but treat them just as a starting point to add your own requirements, and always ensure that they comply with SBSA requirements.

Finally, there is now software available which allows you to draw up your own plans on your home computer or online.

Sources of Plans

Internet Home Plans: www.ihomeplans.net.
Swift Line Design: www.swiftlinedesign.co.uk.
Archlectic Design: www.web-nexus.com/archlectic.
The New Home Plans Book, Murray Armor & David Snell (Ebury Press, 2003.)
500 Best Selling Home Plans, Bob Doyle (Sunset Books, 2003.)
Online Home Design Tool: www.plan3d.com.
Punch Software: www.punchsoftware.com.

RENOVATING A PROPERTY

So, you have come across a neglected or derelict building for sale in an ideal location. How do you decide whether to renovate the property or to knock it down and build a brand new building on the site? The first thing to do, before deciding whether to buy at all, is to consult the local planning office. Ask a planning officer to visit the site with you and he/she will advise you, in principle, on the probable views of the planning department to development on that site.

This is very important, because you may discover that the site, being sold by a local owner to an unsuspecting incomer, would be most unlikely to get planning permission either to renovate the existing building nor to build a new one. Every area in Scotland is subject to a Local Development Plan which specifies areas which may be used for different purposes. If it is not designated for residential use, you would have a big fight on your hands to persuade the Planning Department that an exception should be made for you.

The Development Plan also takes account of areas which have environmental or heritage designations, some of which again restrict or forbid any form of development. If, for example, the site is in a protected coastal strip, you would be highly unlikely to get planning permission.

The Scottish Environmental Protection Agency (SEPA) has the power to place stringent conditions on any development in certain environmentally sensitive areas, and the local Planning Office always ask for their views on any planning applications. So it may be wise to contact them also to discuss your plans in principle.

These restrictions do not only relate to rural areas, although the environmental designations are more likely in the remoter areas. But within urban areas, historically important parts of a town or city may be classified as conservation areas, which can restrict the type and extent of development you may wish to do.

DESIGNATIONS WHICH MAY RESTRICT DEVELOPMENT

- National, Regional or Country Park.
- World Heritage Site.
- National Nature Reserve.
- National Scenic Area.
- Natural Heritage Area.
- Site of Special Scientific Interest.
- Area of Great Landscape Value.
- Shellfish Loch.
- Conservation Area.
- Listed Building.

These are the main designations which may affect your proposed development, but there are many more. For further information see:

- National Heritage Designations in Scotland: A Guide (The Scottish Office.) www.scotland.gov.uk/library/documents-w4/nhd-00.htm.
- Historic Scotland: www.historic-scotland.gov.uk.
- Scottish Natural Heritage (SNH): www.snh.org.uk.
- Scottish Environmental Protection Agency (SEPA): www.sepa.org.uk/regulation/ index.htm.

Although all this may sound somewhat draconian, these restrictions do relate to specified areas – although it must be said that within the highlands in particular large areas can be subject to a succession of these environmental designations. Even within these regions, if the land falls within an existing residential area and there is a building already on the site, whatever state of repair it is in, you would in most cases be allowed to renovate or rebuild on that site. You would need to seek the views of the Planning

Officer as to whether there would be any restriction on the size of the building you could construct – i.e. would it be restricted to the footprint of the existing building or could you extend it beyond those bounds?

The Planning Officer should also be able to advise you on whether there would be a specific requirement for you to renovate rather than demolish the structure and start again. If there is a substantial part of the building still standing and it is in the traditional vernacular for the area, they may prefer you to renovate rather than rebuild.

This can make a substantial difference in the cost of your project. If extensive restoration of the existing stonework or brickwork is required in order to make it stable, this may prove very expensive. And another important consideration is that any renovation or conversion of an existing structure – even where as little as one wall of the original building remains – attracts 17.5% VAT on materials. New buildings are, in contrast, exempt from VAT.

Aside from any government regulations which may affect your project, you also need to be confident that the property is suitable for renovation. The costs involved may be excessive for the value you will add to the building. Even the most idyllic location may not be enough to compensate for the heartache and financial strain involved in buying what may prove to be a moneypit. You need to look at the property with a developer's eye to spot potential problems such as cracks, damp, old wiring, dry rot, woodworm and decide whether they are fixable.

NEW BUILDINGS

Many of the comments made above in relation to renovating a property also apply to new buildings. In addition, there are other things to take into account when planning and costing your build.

When you are renovating an existing building which does not comply with all the latest Building Standards you are unlikely to be told to introduce these except in relation to any extension you are making to the building. If you are building a new home all SBSA regulations must be adhered to. If your house is being planned and built by a reputable architect and builder you can rest assured that they will take all the relevant standards into account. If you are managing the project yourself, however, you must ensure that you are aware of the new standards and comply with them. (See above for further information.)

Another requirement of all new homes in Scotland is that they include disabled access, even if you intend to have no disabled persons living or visiting there. They must be designed to be 'barrier free' and must:

- Be easily accessible from the road or parking area.
- Have adequate space, wide enough corridors and suitable doors for wheelchair users to move around easily.
- Allow wheelchair access to essential rooms such as the bathroom and kitchen.

- ○ Have a toilet or bathroom on the ground floor.
- ○ Allow easy access to all fittings and controls such as light switches, plug sockets and heating controls.
- ○ Leave room for a stairlift to be installed, if the house has stairs.

Planning permission for your house may include conditions regarding car access to the property. If, for instance, it is accessed from a local authority road, they will have regulations regarding sightlines – i.e. the distance you can see along the main road in both directions as you exit your property – and the radius of the turning into your driveway. They may also stipulate the material used to surface the first few metres of the entrance and driveway.

Hard standing for vehicles, or a garage, must be included in the plans for the house if they are to be constructed at the same time. It is sensible to include these in the first place even where you think you may add a garage later but haven't yet decided, or can't yet afford to. If you apply separately later for planning permission for a garage, you will have to pay a whole new set of fees and go through the often slow planning process again.

Builders normally ask for 'stage payments' during the progress of the building of a new home – and sometimes during renovation work if this is extensive and therefore involves large sums of money. This means that they will ask for payment of a proportion of the total cost at specific stages of the build, for instance, once the basic structure is built; then when the windows and doors go in; when the inside is partitioned; and finally when all the interior and exterior work is completed. Self-build mortgages also pay out money in similar stages, so you need to ensure that the money the builder asks for at any stage is no more than the amount the mortgage lender will allow you at that stage of the build. You should clarify with the builder before he starts whether and when he will require stage payments. If the money for any particular stage is not forthcoming, because of a delay in the lender releasing money for example, your build may go on hold until the money is paid.

It is foolhardy to agree to pay large sums of money to the builder in advance of any work, so negotiate with him that stage payments will be made at the end of any particular stage of the build. As mortgage companies normally pay stage payments at the start of the various stages, this will mean you never need to keep the builder waiting for his money and the job can continue without a halt. If for any reason you fall out with your builder along the way, as long as you have only paid for work done to date, you can find another builder to continue the job and pay him similarly as each stage is completed.

It is worth saying again, do not pay money upfront to the builder. It is not unknown for unwise customers to trust their builder enough to pay the full sum long before the build is completed – and lo and behold, they are never seen or heard from again, leaving the customer in the nightmare position of having a part-built house and no money to pay for another builder to complete the job. Be warned!

PLANNING PERMISSION

Most new development, whether a complete new building, or an extension to, renovation or conversion of an existing building, require permission from the local authority before the work can commence. It is very important to apply as early as possible, because it can take some time for a planning application to go through the system. The local authority have the legal right to insist that any work started before it is granted be demolished or put back to the condition it was in before.

There are some small works which do not require planning permission, which are known as 'permitted development.' These include such things as:

- Some internal works to existing buildings.
- Erection of small rear extensions below a certain size.
- Garages and greenhouses.
- Installation of oil tanks.
- Provision of hard surfaces in gardens.
- Installation of satellite dishes.
- Erection of fences.

Your architect or builder should know whether planning permission is required for any particular job, but if you are in any doubt, consult the local authority Planning Officer.

Applying for Permission

Normally, your architect or builder would act as your agent and would apply for planning permission on your behalf. However, there is no legal requirement for them to do this. You can choose to apply on your own behalf, which may make the process slightly cheaper. However, if there are any difficulties which arise with regard to your application, and any amendments are required, you would need to discuss them with whoever drew up your plans, and they would have to amend them. As they should know the planning system in far more detail than you, it may simplify the process, but you are left at the mercy of the slow speed at which builders and architects often work. If you apply on your own behalf, all paperwork will be sent direct to you so you are always aware of the progress of your application. You cannot always assume that your agent will move things through as quickly as you would, especially if they are busy with other jobs.

There are two main forms of planning permission:

- **Outline Planning Permission:** You should apply for this where you wish to know whether a development is acceptable 'in principle'. This is the best approach to take where, for example, you are arranging to sell a plot of land for residential purposes and you want to ensure that the local authority will allow a house to be built on it by the purchaser. If the outline application is approved, full planning permission must be sought before anything can actually be built.

○ **Full Planning Permission:** Here the application contains all details of the proposed development, with detailed plans of the actual house you wish to build.

Where a building is currently used, or has been used in the past, for some other purpose, you will normally need to apply for change of use permission. For instance, when you are renovating a cottage to turn it into a shop or restaurant, or indeed, vice versa.

Documents Required

For both outline and full planning permission you need to submit the following documents to the local authority:

○ An application form.

○ Location map(s).

○ Scale drawing(s) showing the site and what is required (more detailed for full permission).

○ A fee (see below).

○ You must serve a notice on all neighbours with adjoining land informing them of your application.

Your local authority will tell you their exact requirements. Some of them have the application forms available for download from their website.

The local planning department have up to two months in which to reach a decision on the application. During this time the application is publicised in local newspapers and the views of neighbours and relevant organisations such as SEPA, the local authority Roads Department, and the local Community Council will be sought. Neighbours and others with an interest in the area have the right to submit their observations, objections or support for the project. If you expect some local objections, it is a wise move to muster some of your local contacts to send in letters stating their support and/or lack of objections to the build as this will help to counteract the negative comments.

Comments or objections to planning applications can only be made on specific grounds – the effect of the development on the value of your neighbour's property, the loss of his view, or the mere fact that he doesn't want anybody building there, are not normally allowable planning considerations.

Relevant observations touch on matters such as:

○ The impact on adjacent properties and the local area:

- ○ Noise, nuisance and smell.
- ○ Daylight and privacy.
- ○ Visual appearance.

○ The impact of traffic movement:

- ○ Increased traffic.
- ○ Road safety and access.
- ○ Parking problems.
- ○ Effect on pedestrians and cyclists.

○ The needs of the area:

- ○ Employment.
- ○ Commercial, social and community facilities.
- ○ Opportunities for leisure and recreation.

Some of these are more relevant to permission for a commercial development, rather than a residence, but if you wish to run a business from your home they would be taken into consideration.

Although the local authority are obliged to respond to your application within two months, this does not mean that it will take no longer than this for your permission to be granted or denied.

Bill Herbert found this out the hard way

I applied for outline planning permission to put a house in the large garden of my cottage. The application went in on 29th July 2004. Just at the end of the two month period of grace, I was contacted by the planning office to say that my application had been considered but no decision could yet be made because SEPA wished to set some conditions regarding the type of septic tank which was appropriate, as it would discharge into Loch Ewe, a shellfish loch subject to very stringent water quality standards. So although they had stuck to their statutory requirement of replying to me within two months, neither SEPA nor Planning hurried themselves to make a decisions after that. Permission was finally granted on 24th March 2005, almost nine full months after my original application!

When planning permission is granted, it will be subject to certain conditions laid down by the local authority or other organisations such as SEPA, whose views are always sought. Many of these are standard conditions and relate to such things as ensuring no ground water flows onto a public road; that vehicle access to and from the site can be undertaken in a forward gear; and that approved septic tank drainage is used. Other conditions will include such things as the appearance of the house: in the Highlands, for example, this is almost certain to include the requirement be of 'traditional design' and for the walls to be white or off-white in colour (i.e. no avant garde architect-designed nonsense!)

If permission is not granted, or if conditions are imposed which make your project unworkable, you have the right of appeal, which must be lodged within six months of a refusal date.

If outline permission is granted, full permission must be sought within three years and the development must be started within five years of the date the outline permission was granted. Where the original application was for full permission, the project must be commenced within three years. If for any reason you cannot start the development within these time constraints, you must ensure you reapply to the local authority before the permission lapses, and in most cases, the original decision would not be overturned unless there had been a substantial change in status of the local area. Once permission has lapsed, you have to start the whole process again from scratch, and this time permission might not be granted. The safest course is to make absolutely certain that some work is started on site before the time limit, even if this is just getting the footings dug or foundations laid. Then the permission stays in force without time limit.

BUILDING WARRANTS

In addition to planning permission, where required, you will need a building warrant giving permission for any work you propose. These are issued by the local Building Standards department once they are satisfied that the proposed work complies with SBSA regulations. Again, there are a few exceptions where building warrants are not required, which include some, but not all, of the exemptions from planning permission (see above). However, some internal works or alterations to an existing building, which may not require planning permission, may still require a building warrant. This includes such things as window replacements or knocking through a wall in the house. In some cases where you wouldn't normally require a building warrant, you may need one for some aspect of the work. e.g. You don't need a warrant to attach a conservatory to your house, but if you wish to create a new door in the existing house to allow access to the conservatory, you would need a building warrant before you could construct the doorway.

You must submit an application form to your local authority plus detailed plans for the proposed work, plus the required fee, which is charged on a sliding scale based on the cost of the work (see below). This fee is substantially more than the planning application fee because it includes the cost of several inspections during the course of building works, a final inspection and issue of a completion certificate. Again, you may be best advised to ask your architect or builder to act as your agent and apply for a building warrant on your behalf. Where you are also applying for planning permission, the two should be applied for in conjunction.

The average time taken for a building warrant to be issued is four weeks, but it may be longer for complex buildings. A warrant is valid for three years from the date of issue. If you have started but not completed the work within that time you can apply for an extension to the warrant period, as long as the application for extension is made before the expiry of the warrant.

The work undertaken is subject to checks by the local authority while work is in progress, to ensure that the terms of the warrant are being complied with. They will not, however, comment on the quality of the work nor supervise the builders employed. This is the responsibility of the architect, the building contractor, or yourself if you are the project manager.

Once the work is completed it is your responsibility to submit a completion certificate, a form for which is available from your local building standards office. They must establish that the work complies with the warrant and if satisfied, they must then accept the completion certificate, or refuse it, within 14 days.

PLANNING/BUILDING WARRANT APPLICATION FEES 2005

For a new house:

Outline or full planning application	£260
Building warrant	100 sq. m. single storey house, £546
	(sliding scale based on the cost of the works)

For a house extension or alteration:

Outline or full planning application	£130
Building warrant	typical 24 sq. m. extension, £294
(calculated on a sliding scale)	

Change of use:

Planning application	£260
Building warrant	£40

SEPTIC TANKS

If you are building or renovating in a rural area where no mains sewage is available, one of the most problematic areas, and potentially an expensive matter, is the provision of a septic tank. Over recent years, thanks to EU legislation, ever more stringent specifications have been introduced. Septic tanks which were previously approved are no longer deemed suitable for the purpose in some areas where the ground does not allow for the distillate from the tank to be speedily absorbed. In these areas, new houses will be granted planning permission if they specify a more expensive form of septic tank termed a 'sewage treatment plant' which can process waste more efficiently.

Anybody who has a septic tank which discharges into a water course (allowed under certain specific conditions) must be issued with a 'Consent to Discharge' by the Scottish Environmental Protection Agency (SEPA). If you are buying an existing house which already has a septic tank, it is advisable to ask your solicitor to obtain any discharge consent from the previous owner. If there is none, you should insist that the vendor take steps to obtain one, otherwise you may find yourself inheriting a problem which might put you up against the might of SEPA if they deem you are not complying with their regulations. This is a situation which is especially likely to arise if you propose to do any renovation or conversion work on the house which will involve the local authority in consultation with SEPA.

In addition to the hassle and time delay, the requirement to install an upgraded septic tank can add several thousand pounds on to the cost of the project.

In order for a septic tank to work correctly, there must be adequate space to fit in the pipe work, septic tank and soakaway, about 20 metres. If you cannot fit this on your land, you may have to make an agreement with a neighbour to put it on his land. Where your property is close beside a roadway, you may also find that you need to run your pipe work under the road and place your septic tank on the other side. In such a case, you must employ a builder or other contractor who is qualified to carry out this work – he must have taken a special course and been issued with a certificate to show he is an approved contractor. In addition, you must apply to the local authority for permission to dig up the road, for which there is a fee of around £200.

GRANTS

There are a number of grants available to assist in renovating or building your new home. These are some of the main ones:

Repair & Improvement Grants

Paid by local authorities to help towards the costs of upgrading properties to bring them up to a tolerable standard and/or a good state of repair. Grant aid may be available towards the cost of repairs to roofs, downpipes, eradication of dry rot; installing a water supply, bath or shower, and replacing lead drinking water supply pipes; adaptations for disabled people and care and repair for the elderly. Level of grant payable is worked out on the basis of the cost of the works and the income of the applicant. For further information, see the booklet *Housing Grants,* available from Scottish Executive, Housing Division 2, Victoria Quay, Edinburgh EH6 6QQ, or downloadable from the website: www.scotland.gov.uk.

Lead Tenancies Scheme

Run by Communities Scotland and designed to bring empty properties back into good condition and residential use. If you, as the owner, agree to lease the property to a housing association, they can access a grant of up to £22,000 to improve the property and bring it back into residential use. The grant is £1,100 per year for every year the owner leases it to the housing association up to a maximum of 20 years. The housing association sub-lets the renovated property to a tenant, and the owner is paid rent by the housing association for the duration of the lease. Although this means you cannot occupy the property until the end of the agreed period of lease, it is a good way of earning income and capital growth for a period while you cannot occupy the house – for instance, if you are thinking ahead and wish to retire to Scotland some years hence. Further information from Communities Scotland, Thistle House, 91 Haymarket Terrace, Edinburgh EH12 5HE; ☎ 0131 313 0044; www.communitiesscotland.gov.uk.

Croft House Grant Scheme (CHGS)

Available to a crofting tenant, or an owner occupier of a croft who was previously the tenant and became the owner within the last seven years. A grant may be given to provide assistance towards improving an existing croft house or building a new one. For further information contact *Crofters' Commission*, Castle Wynd, Inverness IV2 3EQ; ☎ 01463-663403; www.crofterscommission.org.uk.

Other Grants

There may be other grants applicable to you in specific situations. for an exhaustive list of the options see *Guide to Housing Options,* www.communitiesscotland.gov.uk.

CONSTRUCTION

Walls

Over 60% of houses in Scotland are constructed using a timber-frame which is then surrounded by breeze (cinder) blocks which are finished with a protective concrete rendering, called 'harling'. This compares with only six per cent in England, where brick and concrete construction are the norm. The timber frames are generally made from sitka spruce, a plentiful and renewable supply of which is available in Scotland. Some specialist firms design, supply and construct beautiful oak framed houses, but these are far more expensive. Internal walls are normally formed using plasterboard on wooden frames.

Stone-built houses are the traditional style in the Highlands, because the stone was once plentiful. However, today there is less stone available and it is also an expensive option. Some local stone also proves to be water permeable, so it can lead to dampness, and you may find you need to have your beautiful stones covered with harling to keep the house dry inside.

Windows & Doors

UPVC (plastic) window frames and doors were a very popular option, due to their modern look and ease of maintenance, but the tide has turned and people are tending to choose wooden ones. There is no doubt that a well-maintained wooden window or door, whether painted or varnished, is far more aesthetically pleasing, and on a house with any age, they are far more in keeping with the traditional look. Softwood frames and doors are much cheaper than hardwood ones, but they will deteriorate more quickly, and the additional cost of maintenance and/or earlier replacement may mean they don't save you money in the long run.

In a country as cold as Scotland you should always opt for double-glazed windows. They make a significant difference to the heat-retaining properties of a house and thus save money on your heating bills.

Roofs

Pitched roofs are a must: everybody knows it rains a lot in Scotland, so you are asking for trouble if you go for a flat roof which does not allow the water to run off easily. This inevitably leads to problems of dampness and leakage. If you cannot avoid having a flat roof over either all or part of the building, the extra cost of having the flat surface fibre-glassed is money well spent.

As well as being wet, Scotland is very windy, especially in the north west. Tiles on your pitched roof need to be securely fixed down, and builders in these areas will nail down each individual tile, a practice which a builder imported from England may not adhere to.

When Jane Farres moved into her house in Wester Ross, she asked her neighbour why her stone-built house was so different in appearance from the surrounding houses

'Och,' said the neighbour, 'That's because the English couple who had the house built brought up a team of builders from Cheshire. He only had one arm, the head builder, but that's by the by. Anyway, I told him the roof wasn't steep enough, but he wouldn't listen. And I told him that he should make sure each and every tile was securely fastened down. But he wouldn't listen.

So eventually they finish the house and the English couple move in. A few weeks later, the first storm of the winter comes along. And within half an hour, the wind's got under those tiles, lifted them up and half of them come crashing down.

Aye, the English couple weren't best pleased. When the storm passed through, they called in a local builder to replace the lost tiles Highland style – and nail down every single tile still intact. I didnae say I told you so. I didnae need to!'

Planning requirements

Local planning offices have their own requirements regarding the appearance of houses, and the materials used, in their areas. They like to retain the traditional look for the area, so you may not be allowed to build the steel and glass temple of modernism you hanker after.

This is almost certain to be the case if your house is in a National Park or Conservation Area. The external appearance of the house will have to adhere to very strict guidelines, although you will probably be allowed to do whatever you like inside, as long as it complies with building standards.

Listed Buildings

Even more stringent restrictions will probably be put on you if you are renovating a listed building, and this will affect both the external and internal appearance of the building and may extend to what you can do with the grounds also. In addition to planning permission and building warrants you will need listed building consent for your proposed works.

You may be required to use certain materials, such as cast iron drainpipes and gutters rather than plastic, hardwood window frames, traditional lime mortar and so on, all of which will add to the cost. You may also be required to use approved conservation builders to work on the renovations.

Land Drainage

When renovating an old property in a place as notoriously wet as Scotland, the main problem you will come across is likely to be damp. However, this is one of the most easily remedied problems. Digging ditches and installing land drains to allow the water to run away from the walls of your property should solve the problem and keeping the building well-ventilated and warm, plus the use of a dehumidifier, should eventually get rid of any residual damp.

Porches

In an exposed area, make sure you know which direction the prevailing wind comes from. That is the side of your house which needs most protection from the weather. Adding a porch to an external door, ensuring that it opens in the lee of the wind, will do much to keep your house draught free.

> **Caroline Deacon found this out for herself when she bought her house in Inverness**
>
> *It was a four bed, two garage detached newly built bungalow. We added another study and conservatory, and then after we moved and discovered the westerly winds, we added a porch!*

Heating

Wherever in Scotland you build or renovate, you will need some form of efficient permanent heating. You will find you need this on for at least part of the day for most of the year – sometimes even in the middle of summer.

Central heating systems generally provide hot water as well as heating, either via radiators on the walls, through wires run under the floors, or a mixture of both. Underfloor heating is very popular at present, and is reported to be very efficient. However, as the heating wires are concreted in under the floors, if something should go wrong with it the cost and mess involved in digging up floors to effect repairs, with the additional cost of replacing the floor and floor coverings, may make it a less attractive option.

Wooden Floors

Not long ago, most home owners in Scotland aspired to fitted carpets in most rooms in their home, as a reaction against the traditional pattern of wooden floorboard with rugs on. Fashion has come full circle now, and the current trend is for wooden or laminate (imitation wood) flooring in homes. There are some unforeseen drawbacks to having so many hard floor surfaces in your home. The main one is noise – it has been found that walking on a carpet is 22 decibels quieter than walking on a wooden floor. This is a particular issue for flat dwellers, as people living below a flat with wooden floors do report high levels of noise from footsteps overhead.

Another thing to bear in mind when you have domestic pets is that their claws can damage the flooring – and they may also be unable to get any grip on the floor and so spend much of their time 'skating' about the house. This may be amusing to watch, but the average dog or cat probably doesn't really enjoy that form of locomotion!

Gardens

If you want to create a garden round your new home, the plants you can grow and the best layout for the garden depends greatly on whereabouts in the country you are. If you are in the south of the country, in an inland, sheltered area, the plants which will be both appropriate to the landscape, and best suited to the climatic conditions are going to be quite different from those which will thrive in an exposed west-facing garden on the edge of a sea loch in the north west Highlands. However, even in the most apparently inhospitable areas, beautiful gardens have been created – some world famous, such as Inverewe Garden in Wester Ross. As long as shelter is provided against the prevailing westerly wind, and the plants chosen are salt tolerant and thrive in frequently wet conditions, you too can produce your own stunning garden.

An in-depth discussion of the subject is beyond the scope of this book. The following books give inspiring and practical advice on gardening in Scotland.

Scottish Plants for Scottish Gardens, Jill Hamilton (Mercat Press, 2000). Scotland boasts a great diversity of over a thousand indigenous plants, any of which make a welcome addition to any Scottish garden.

Some Branch Against the Sky: The Practice and Principles of Marginal Gardening, G.F. Dutton (Timber Press, 1997). The author explains the general principles of marginal gardening and their specific application to a nine-acre garden he built in the Scottish Highlands.

A Garden in the Hills, Katherine Stewart (Mercat Press, 1995). Gardening in a crofting area in the 1950s.

The Scottish Gardener, Suki Urquhart (Birlinn, 2005). Looks at 60 private gardens in Scotland and considers how Scottish gardening has been shaped by the climate, conflicts and changing fashions.

Protected Trees

If you have trees on your land of any great age you may find you cannot fell, or even prune, them without permission. Local authorities make tree preservation orders (TPOs) to prevent certain trees or woodlands from being felled, lopped, topped, uprooted or otherwise wilfully damaged without permission from the planning office. They are most common in urban or semi-urban areas, and may be applied to protect a tree or woodland for the public's enjoyment.

Garages

Given the Scottish climate, it is worth considering including a garage for your vehicle when submitting plans for your house. You may not actually need planning permission to add one later, provided it falls within certain parameters of size and location, but it will cost you no extra to put it on your original application.

If, like most other people, despite your good intentions the car rarely finds its way inside the garage even in the worst weather, a garage serves as a very useful outside storage and work space.

MAKING MONEY FROM YOUR PROPERTY

CHAPTER SUMMARY

- **Bed & Breakfast.** If you are in a popular tourist area you can make a good income from offering B&B accommodation in your home.
  - If you can accommodate no more than six people, you do not need to inform the authorities.
  - Any income should be declared to the Inland Revenue.
- **Guest House/Hotel.** Larger properties are classed as guest houses or small hotels and there are local authority regulations to comply with.
- **Holiday Lets.** Self catering accommodation is very popular, especially between Easter and October.
  - In rural areas, weekly lettings are normal, but in urban areas shorter lets will bring you more business.
- **Long Term Lets.** Tenants pay their own council tax and domestic bills.
  - Have an official lease drawn up to give you and your tenants legal protection.
  - Local authorities or housing associations rent housing from private landlords in areas where there is a shortage of social housing. This is a source of risk-free income and may allow you to access improvement grants.
- **Advertising.** The most efficient and cheapest form of advertising is on the internet.
  - If you advertise with VisitScotland you must pay to have your accommodation graded under their Quality Assurance scheme.
- **Running a Business.** It is easy to set up a small business in your own home.
  - There are business grants and loans available from public bodies and banks. You must produce a detailed business plan if you need funding.

○ A self-employed sole trader with a low turnover pays low rates of National Insurance and income tax.

○ If you need to alter or extend your home for your new business you may need to apply for planning permission.

○ **Selling On.** There is a high demand for housing in Scotland, so you are unlikely to lose money if you sell your property after a few years.

○ Redecorate your home and make cost-effective improvements to maximise the price you achieve.

○ You can sell your home privately or through an agent.

BED & BREAKFAST

The most obvious way to make money from your home, if you have one or more spare bedrooms, is to offer bed and breakfast accommodation. This can bring in some extra income, especially during the summer season, and if you are in a popular holiday area, this can be quite substantial. In areas of the country such as Aviemore, Edinburgh or Glasgow the potential income is greater because tourism in these areas is pretty much all year round.

In other areas of the country too the tourist season is getting longer. Although June to August is still the most popular time for Scottish holidays, and the period when you should be aiming to attract most of your guests, people's holiday habits have changed and off-season short breaks are more popular than ever. Those who still like the traditional two-week holiday in the summer tend to go to sunnier climes for their 'main' holiday, but will perhaps have an additional week in Scotland in Spring or Autumn when it is less busy.

The basic B&B in a family home is less popular than it once was, because there are far more guest houses and hotels which offer a higher standard of facilities, including private bathrooms and lounges. With many people feeling that an en suite bathroom in their own home is a necessity, rather than a luxury, they are less inclined to share bathroom facilities than they once were and are happy to pay extra for them. So those B&Bs which have en suite facilities do far better business than those which do not.

There is no 'official' definition of when a bed and breakfast becomes a guest house, and when that becomes a small hotel, but the VisitScotland categorisations are a good guide to the essential differences between them.

○ *B&B:* In most cases, a private house that offers bed and breakfast. B&Bs will normally accommodate no more than six guests, and may not serve an evening meal.

○ *Guest House:* Usually a commercial business, with normally a minimum of four letting bedrooms, some of which will have en suite or private facilities. Breakfast is available and evening meals may be provided.

○ *Small Hotel:* Will normally have a maximum of 20 letting bedrooms and a minimum of six, the majority with en suite or private facilities. It will have a drinks licence (sometimes a restricted one) and will serve breakfast, dinner and usually lunch. It will normally be run by the owners and reflect their personal style.

The income you can generate depends greatly on your location and the facilities you provide. If you are on a main tourist route, offer en suite facilities and extra services, you can still attract healthy numbers of guests. The downside here is that you can guarantee that many of your neighbours will also be offering B&B so you will have far more competition than if you are off the beaten track. In the latter case, you should have less competition but will probably need to spend more on marketing so people know you are there.

Current prices charged vary quite widely, but on average you can charge around £20-£25 per person per night for bed & breakfast; £25-£35 for a guest house; £35-£50 for a small hotel.

The beauty of offering bed and breakfast in your own home is that there are no regulations you need to observe and nobody to inform. You can just put a sign up in your garden, and away you go. You should declare any income you make to the Inland Revenue. Any money you spend in relation to running your business – the costs of bed linen, foodstuffs for breakfasts, advertising, phone calls, laundry and so forth – can be offset against any tax you owe, so it is well worth doing this. If you are large enough to be classed as a guest house, and you start operating as a commercial business, you should inform the local authority. They may require you to satisfy fire safety and food hygiene regulations, and look at your access and car parking provisions, to ensure that there are no road safety implications.

RENTING OUT

Holiday Lets

If you will not be using your property full-time, a healthy income can be made from letting it out to tourists. There is plenty of demand for holiday accommodation, and if the property is advertised well, you should be able to pick up bookings throughout the year. In rural areas, the biggest demand is between Easter and October, reaching a peak in July and August. Christmas and New Year are popular too, especially if you have an open fire, something which people wanting a winter break generally look for, dreaming of long winter evenings by a crackling fire.

In the cities, particularly Edinburgh and Glasgow, there is a less noticeable tourist season as they attract visitors all year round. Holiday cottages are usually rented for a week at a time, but to maximise your bookings for a city flat it is sensible to let it out by the night so you can attract people on short breaks for leisure or business reasons.

The properties that let most easily are, in rural areas, old-style cottages rather than new built modern houses or chalets, as tourists are looking for a taste of tradition. However, inside the quaint old cottage, they demand a high level of comfort and modern equipment and fittings in kitchen and bathroom. In the cities, apartments close to the centre are very popular, while other tourists prefer to stay outside the city in a comfortable house, with easy access by car or public transport into the centre.

If letting out your home, aim to provide comfort and quality. Make sure it is warm, comfortable and well-equipped with plenty of hot water. If you are catering for families, extras such as books, board games, videos and computer games go down well with both parents and children.

If you are living in your home full-time, but would still welcome some extra income, consider putting a caravan or chalet in the grounds if you have space. Alternatively, when looking for your ideal home, look for properties which have a cottage, or outbuildings which could be converted into holiday accommodation, in the grounds. This is an astute investment which will bring you both regular income and capital growth.

If you do not occupy your property full-time, you may get a discount on your council tax rates. For some years there has been a country-wide 50% discount for second homes, but this has now been amended and individual councils are allowed to charge higher rates of council tax on second homes. The Highland Council, for example, concerned about the lack of housing for local families, in part due to the large number of second homes and holiday lets in the region, now charge up to 90% council tax on these properties, and wish to scrap discounts altogether in coming years.

You should have no difficulty employing somebody locally to clean the property, change linen and so forth between lets. Asking amongst your neighbours, or putting an advertisement in a local paper or shop, is probably the most effective way of finding somebody. In holiday areas you may find that there is a small local enterprise which has a team of staff who look after a number of holiday properties for their owners, and will also undertake to welcome guests as they arrive, hand over keys and show them around the property, plus deal with any problems they may have during their stay.

Long Term Rental

If you are buying a property for an investment, or will not be occupying it for some time, a long term rental may be a better solution. Although the rents you can ask per week are far lower than for a holiday rental, you do not have the added expense and inconvenience of taking bookings or cleaning the property at least once a week between bookings. In addition, long term tenants are responsible for their own council tax and domestic bills while living in your property. You would generally only be liable for buildings insurance, contents insurance if it is let already furnished, and general maintenance of the property.

To give yourself the greatest legal protection, you should have an official lease drawn up for your tenants to sign. The normal form of lease, which gives you and your tenant the best legal protection, is the short assured lease under would you would normally let your home on a six month lease, renewable every six months if agreed by you and your tenant. A standard lease which you can amend to suit your own requirements is available at www.pastures-new.co.uk. Alternatively, a solicitor will draw up a lease for you. For further details about leases and legal protection, see *Renting A Home*.

Leasing to Social Landlords

It is acknowledged that there is a shortage of affordable housing throughout Scotland, partly as a result of the conservative government's introduction of council and housing association tenants' 'right to buy' their properties at well bellow market value. Consequently, much of the stock of social housing has now passed into private ownership.

Somewhat ironically, in many cases the only way councils and housing associations can now fulfil their commitment to providing housing for those in need is to lease properties from private landlords to let to homeless individuals and families – often these properties being council houses which have passed into private ownership having been purchased in the past through the right to buy scheme!

Most local authorities have such a scheme, called variously residential, private sector, or rural leasing schemes. Under these leasing schemes, the council, or a housing association on their behalf, will lease a property for a period of at least five years, on a sliding rental scale depending on the size, type and condition of the property. They then sub-let to tenants in need of housing. Rental is paid to you by the council or housing association quarterly or six-monthly in advance, and is guaranteed even when the property lies empty. Although the rent is generally lower than you could charge if you let privately, the council or housing association takes on all costs including buildings insurance, routine repairs and maintenance.

Nick Robertson bought an ex-council house in the north-west Highlands in 1999

I bought it as an investment and decided to let it to the Highland Council through their Rural Leasing Scheme. I signed it over to them for seven years, and in 1999 the annual rental I received from them was £2,304.48, paid in advance in two six-monthly instalments. I had no additional costs to pay and the rental went up year on year. Now, six years later, the annual rental is £2,799.84 and my accountant tells me that few such risk-free investments would have given me an equivalent return during the period. The rental has paid for the loan I took out to help finance the purchase of the house, plus giving me a small profit in recent years. In addition, I estimate the house has more than doubled in value. I have now to decide whether to extend the lease for a further period when it expires in May 2007, or whether to sell and realise the capital. Either way, it has proved an excellent, hassle-free investment. Highly recommended!

If you have an empty property in need of renovation or upgrading, and do not wish to live in it for at least five years, you may be eligible for up to £22,000 worth of grant under the Lead Tenancies Scheme. Here you let the property to a housing association and they can then claim £1,100 of grant per year, for up to 20 years, to bring the house up to habitable standard and put housing association tenants in. In addition to the house being improved for you, you also receive rental income from the Housing Association for the duration of the lease. For further details see *Building or Renovating*.

ADVERTISING

If you wish to set up as a B&B, or are hoping to get holiday bookings in your property while you are not using it, the most effective way of advertising it nowadays is on the internet. If you have your own website, for the comparatively small cost of setting it up, it is constantly available for the whole world to access.

If you don't have your own website, there are many accommodation websites where you can advertise your property. Some of these are free, others charge varying amounts to advertise for a year or longer. Some also offer to produce your own mini-website, and this may be an attractive option if you don't want the expense or bother of setting one up yourself.

VisitScotland is probably the focal point for Scottish tourism – it is almost inevitable that anybody who isn't familiar with Scotland will start by contacting the tourist board, whether via the internet, by phone or by post. If you advertise your property with them, you will guarantee an instant large audience. If you do wish to advertise through VisitScotland, however, you will, in addition to paying their advertising fees which start at well over £100 per year for a B&B or holiday cottage, have to pay to have your property graded as they will not advertise any accommodation which is not part of their Quality Assurance scheme. An inspector will come to examine your property and, if it reaches their minimum standards, will award one to five stars depending on the cleanliness, ambience, hospitality, accommodation service and food, as appropriate. This will cost another £100 plus, so you will have to pay over £200 for a year's advertising with them. However, this does entitle you to advertise in their printed Where To Stay guides as well as on their website, www.visitscotland. com.

If you are offering specific services to a niche market – perhaps you want particularly to attract mountain climbers, or retired people, say – you could try advertising in magazines aimed specifically at these people.

Another alternative is to advertise with a holiday letting agency, private firms who offer much the same services as VisitScotland, generally including their own grading schemes. They take a percentage of your rental income as their fee for advertising properties in their glossy brochures and on their websites, and dealing with bookings for the owner. Fees can be as much as 33.3% of your income, which means you may have to set your rental higher than your competition in order to make it worth your while, which could affect your booking levels.

An advantage of going with an agency is that they will take over most of the administrative work for you and can take online credit card bookings, which is particularly useful if you are living abroad when you are not in Scotland.

Long term rentals can also be advertised on the internet, on a personal, commercial or local community website. Local papers and shops are a good place to advertise – most people looking for a home to rent in a particular place will be in the area already so a local outlet is probably the most efficient and cheapest way to find a tenant.

VisitScotland: Information line ☎ 0845-2255 121; www.visitscotland.com.

Hoseasons Holiday Cottages: ☎ 01502 502588; www.hoseasons.co.uk.

Country Cottages Online: www.countrycottagesonline.com.

Letting Web: www.lettingweb.com.

There are also a number of books which list holiday accommodation, and you can usually pay to advertise in them.

The Munro Baggers Bed and Breakfast Guide: Accommodation for Walkers in the Highlands of Scotland, Angus Johnson (Prune Publications 2005).

British Bed and Breakfasts (Alastair Sawday Publishing 2005).

The Hidden Places of Scotland, James Gracie (Travel Publishing 2004).

RUNNING A BUSINESS FROM YOUR HOME

If you wish to run a small one-person business from your own home, there are few legal barriers put in your way. The Scottish Executive are keen to encourage small enterprises and if you have no need to apply for money to fund the business, in the form of loans or grants, you can advertise your business and start trading without the need to notify anyone in advance.

If you need some funds to get the business going, try approaching your bank for a loan, or your local Scottish Enterprise Company or local authority for a grant. In either case, you will be required to produce a detailed business plan, and Scottish Enterprise may require you to attend a short course to introduce you to the basics of drawing up a business plan and running a small business, before they will decide whether to fund you in any way.

Contact the Inland Revenue and inform them that you are self-employed and running a small business. If your turnover is low, you pay special low rates of National Insurance contributions. Keep a record of all your income and outgoing during the tax year, which runs from April 6th to April 5th the following year. You will be sent a tax form to complete on which you enter all your figures for the year. Tax allowances for money spent to operate your business are fairly generous, and you may find you end up paying very little, or no, tax, especially in the early years while your business is getting off the ground. If you operate the business from your home you can claim a percentage of your household costs, such as electricity, gas, water, insurance, council tax and so forth as business expenses.

If you employ staff, you must d`educt income tax and National Insurance contributions from their wages and send these off to the Inland Revenue. They will send you a small business package which contains detailed instructions, tables and forms to allow you to calculate the payments. Increasingly the system is being automated, and calculations and payments can now be made online.

Once your turnover reaches £60,000 in a year, you must register the business for VAT and start charging this on all your sales. This threshold figure rises by a few thousand pounds each year.

Ideas for Businesses

There are three main approaches to deciding what sort of business to run and where in Scotland it would work best:

1: Businesses supplying locally-based services. If you have already bought your home, any business you run must be suitable for the local area. Look for a gap in the local market and consider whether there is a customer base for that particular service.

> **The author moved to the Highlands from England in 1994**
>
> *It wasn't an easy process finding a house to buy while I was living hundreds of miles away and had two young children to bring up. It also didn't prove easy to find out from a distance about the schools available in different areas, or the Scottish house-buying system, and so forth. I realised that there were many other people wishing to move to Scotland who had similar difficulties, and there was nobody in the Highlands offering services to help these people. So I set up 'Highland Dreams', the first Highlands-based relocation agency providing information, advice and assistance to people to ease their journey north. I set up a website and it was instantly popular with people looking for a hand to hold to ease them through the process of relocating.*

2: Businesses which rely on your personal skills and talents. A move to a new country is an ideal opportunity to make the most of your creative or physical talents. There are artists, craftsmen, alternative therapists throughout Scotland who have made their abilities the basis of a thriving business.

> **Sharon Blackie**, *a qualified psychotherapist who had worked in large corporations for many years, moved to a seven acre croft in the north west highlands and now runs her one-woman business Metamorphia, providing psychology-based workshops and services for individuals, groups and organisations. She encourages participants to use storytelling and other expressive therapies to bring about creative change and transformation in their lives.*

> **Robert & Lynn Howard**, *talented artists and sculptors, built a workshop and shop onto their home and support themselves selling their work to visitors to the area and also supplying other retail outlets through Scotland.*

3: Knowledge-based businesses which are not dependent on locality. These include occupations such as writing, editing, indexing, proof-reading, website design and other computer-based services which are marketed over the internet and can be carried out from anywhere in the world.

> **Englishwoman Joanne** *went on a tour of the Highlands and Islands, fell in love with the country, and wrote up her experiences on her own website. This proved so popular with readers across the world that she started designing websites for them, with a particular bias toward those with a Scottish theme. Today she is living in Inverness and has a full-time Scottish web design business, while her own website has developed to become one of the best sources of information about Scotland on the net.*

BUSINESS IDEAS

Tourism	accommodation, sightseeing tours, provision of outdoor activities, painting/photography holidays, ancestry research.
Food & drink	cafe, restaurant, hotel, bar, specialist food production.
Retail	arts & crafts shop, specialist food shop, general store, post office, antiques shop, bookshop.
Computer services	hardware and software design, website design, support and repairs for home and business computer users.
Alternative therapies	aromatherapy, psychotherapy, chiropractic, massage, yoga.
Trades	builder, plumber, hairdresser, gardener, decorator, odd jobs.
Freelancing	writing, editing, proof-reading, data input, indexing, translating, technical authoring, abstracting, distance teaching, graphics, illustration, web design, programming, music composition.
Property Services	estate agency, managing holiday properties, lettings agency, relocation agency.
Audio/Visual	photography, videography, producing CDs and DVDs.
Animals	kennels and catteries, horse riding school or trekking centre, alternative therapies for animals.
Music	recording. composing, playing or singing at pubs, hotels, dances, weddings etc.
E-commerce	buying and selling through internet auctions, Scottish travel site, Scottish weddings agency, marketing your business.
Consultancy	providing professional advice in your sphere of expertise.

Planning Permission

If you need to make alterations or additions to your home to accommodate your business, you may need to apply for planning permission. If the additions are just an extra room to act as an office, this would be classed as a domestic addition and would need no more than basic planning permission. However, if you wanted to extend your kitchen to produce chutneys and jams commercially, for example, you would almost certainly have to comply with food hygiene and building standards regulations relating to food premises. If you buy a building specifically to run your business from, you will have to apply to the planning office for permission for change of use, unless the building was used for the same purpose previously.

If the premises will be open to members of the public, parking provision and health and safety considerations will be taken into account and conditions applied to ensure that you observe the regulations.

The rules are different for different categories of business. Providing tourist accommodation in particular is relatively free of legal constraint. If you buy a small cottage and let it out for self-catering, there is no requirement to apply for permission, whereas if you buy the same cottage and turn it into a small café or shop you have to obtain permission for change of use.

For further information on all aspects of running a business from your own home, as well as buying an existing business, see Live & Work In Scotland (Vacation Work Publications, 2005).

SELLING ON

You may buy a home in Scotland with the intention of spending the rest of your days there, but circumstances change, and you may find yourself wishing or needing to sell up sooner rather than later for a variety of personal or financial reasons. Even if you do end your days in the house, your estate will pass to your next of kin and they may decide that they wish to sell it on.

Or you may buy a place in Scotland intending to stay there for a limited time, or go into it purely as a business venture, to renovate it and sell it on.

Whatever the circumstances, there is such a demand for housing throughout Scotland, especially in the more upmarket or beautiful areas, that as long as the house has not deteriorated during your ownership it is most unlikely that you would make a loss on it. In recent years, the property market has been so buoyant that owners have made huge profits on their properties. As discussed earlier in the book, the market is currently slowing considerably, but all the indications are that it will be a 'soft landing' and that a crash in prices is unlikely to occur, so even if you can't rely on making a huge killing from your sale, you should be able to make a reasonable amount of profit.

However, if renovating or redecorating a property, it is important to ensure that you don't go overboard with adding your own design statements. Although you may love them, you will severely restrict the number of buyers who feel the same way about your architectural or interior design vision. If you do redecorate before putting your house up for sale – always a good idea – go for a light, bright but neutral effect which will appeal to the widest range of buyers.

Your property also needs to fit within the range of prices generally achieved for property in the area. Estate agents will tell you that each street of houses has an upper price limit, and if you extend or renovate your house to a level which takes it right out of that price bracket, you will find it very difficult to sell at above that ceiling price. This is less of a problem in a rural area where properties tend to be individually priced and a mansion worth half a million might sell easily, even where more modest houses along the road are selling for less than half that price.

If you have lived in your home for many years before you sell on, you will undoubtedly make a profit just by virtue of the ongoing inflation in house prices over time. But in order to maximise the amount you can get for the property it is sensible to look at it with an objective eye and try to see it the way a prospective buyer would. An estate agent will advise you, if it is difficult for you to take this detached approach.

The kitchen and bathroom you have had for years and are quite happy with, may look old fashioned to a prospective buyer, carpets may look shabby, paintwork and wallpaper may look tired. Buyers will take into account the price of putting these things right when making an offer for your house. However, it is important that any improvements you make will not cost more than the value they add to the house.

INCREASING THE VALUE OF YOUR HOME

Estate Agents' recommended top ten improvements	Average value added
1. Loft conversion	£12,359
2. Adding an extension	£11,915
3. A conservatory	£10,891
4. New windows	£7,464
5. New kitchen	£3,925
6. New bathroom	£2,976
7. Redecorate living rooms and bedrooms	£1,947
8. Resurface drive	£1,365
9. Re-carpet house	£1,249
10. Garden decking/patio	£1,213

Capital Gains Tax

If the house is not your main residence, you will be liable to capital gains tax on any profit you make on the property. See *Finance* for an explanation of the rules and tax rates.

Selling Through An Estate Agent

Estate agents or solicitors will take control of all aspects of putting your house up for sale and advertising it. First arrange for them to come and value your house. This valuation is free, so it is sensible to get three valuations and choose the company which either promises to get the highest price for your house or the one which impresses you most with their terms and professionalism.

Just because an estate agent values your house highly doesn't necessarily mean they can achieve that price – they may value it an unrealistically high price to get your business, and then later suggest you drop the asking price because there isn't enough interest.

They will photograph your property and advertise it for sale through various outlets, including the internet, newspaper advertising and property details available from their offices and sent to house-hunters. They should also supply you with a For Sale board to put up outside your property.

They will arrange appointments to view the property with prospective buyers and will show them round if you prefer not to do it yourself. They will also deal with queries about the property from prospective buyers, and act as a go-between when you and a buyer are negotiating a final price. They will also be involved if a closing date is set. However, when sealed bids are submitted, it will be your solicitor who will deal with these, even where an estate agent is the selling agent.

For these services they will charge a fee which is a percentage of the selling price – 1.5% to 2.5% is average. If they do not succeed in selling the house, there is no fee payable.

For more information on the selling process, plus a list of Scottish estate agents and solicitors, see *Finding Properties for Sale* and *Purchasing, Conveyancing & Fees*.

Selling Your Own Property

You can save money by selling your home privately. Decide what asking price to set by looking at similar properties for sale in the area and setting your price on the basis of what they are asking. It is also a good idea to get a number of valuations from estate agents. They will make no charge for this.

Once you have set your price, produce your own sales particulars – pick some up from an estate agent to see what details to include. Include photographs of the interior and exterior of the house and grounds. Include measurements and a brief description of all the rooms and outbuildings.

If you have your own website, put the full details on there. If not, there are many property websites which you can advertise on. Adverts on these sites range from a few words to a full page with lots of text and photographs. For a basic entry you may not have to pay anything at all, with charges increasing depending on the amount of information and number of pictures you include. There is a list of property websites in *Finding Properties for Sale*.

In addition, advertise in local newspapers and shops, and put a For Sale board up outside your house. Make sure that you keep your house neat and tidy all the while it is up for sale, as you may have people drawing up outside your house 'on spec' asking to view it there and then.

If you are selling it yourself and receive enough interest that you feel you want to set a closing date to encourage a bidding war, you should then involve your solicitor to ensure that this is all carried out in a legal fashion. Your solicitor will take over the conveyancing from the point when you accept an offer on your property.

Appendix

PERSONAL CASE HISTORIES

PERSONAL CASE HISTORIES

CAROLINE DEACON

When did you move to Scotland and for what reason?
We moved in July 2003 because we wanted to downsize.

Where did you move from?
Surrey, England.

Where did you move to?
Inverness.

How old were you and your family at the time?
The children were 11, 9 and 7, we were 42 and 45.

Why did you decide to relocate to Scotland?
We reckoned it would be a cheaper lifestyle, and we have always liked the country. There was also an element of going back to family roots.

What made you decide on the Inverness area. Did you consider any other areas?
Yes, we considered other rural areas such as Cornwall and north-east England, Stirling, Perth as well as Edinburgh. We had very specific priorities:

- We wanted to move at that time before our eldest started secondary schooling.
- We wanted to find somewhere in a town or city where the kids could have access to everything teenagers wanted, where they could go out and about under their own steam without having to be ferried everywhere by car. So it had to be in a town centre with facilities. We also wanted it to be safe to allow the children to go out and about on their own.
- We wanted good state schools nearby.
- We wanted a town where housing was cheap, not more than half the price where we were – we had a maximum budget to spend if we were to have enough money left over from the sale of our property in the south east to al-

low us to work part time or even not at all.

○ We wanted good transport connections to London so we could continue to work part time or consultancy.

○ We also wanted a place where we already had some connections – family or friends.

So Edinburgh was out because house prices were too expensive. Cornwall was out because the travel connections to London were not good enough. North east England was too rural and did not fulfil the town requirements for the kids. We were left with Stirling northwards, and in fact Inverness had the best travel connections with the south east, having the sleeper and planes. Also we had family connections and knew the area. Finally we were able to buy a new house within the budget in the catchment area for schools we liked, and in reach of the town centre.

Did you find the property buying process straightforward?

No – we wanted to know we had something definite before we sold up down south. So we spent some time looking at houses and putting in offers, but we kept getting outbid. It was awkward to keep flying up and looking at places, as we had to do this separately, and then we would not get the place. Finally we found an estate about to be built, and we were able to secure a house not yet built for £100 deposit, which would be ready around the time we wanted and would be within our budget. Then we had to sell our house which took longer than expected – the sale kept falling through etc. We still had not sold before I had to move up with the kids in order to allow them to start school, while my husband Mark stayed down south to sell the house – which was pretty scary, but we did eventually sell it for the amount we needed that autumn.

How long did it take to find a property, have your offer accepted, and finally take possession?

We put the £100 deposit down in March 2002 and the house was finished in November when we had to pay the balance. Then we had builders in to change it – adding an office and conservatory – so it was finished in Feb 2003 and we then moved up when school broke up in July.

Describe the property you bought. Did you need to have any renovation work or similar done on it? If so, were you happy with the work done for you by tradesmen?

Four bedroom, two garage detached bungalow, new build. We added another study and conservatory, and then after we moved and discovered the westerly winds, we added a porch! We had fantastic tradesmen – the building company who built the house was brilliant and then the additions were done by a recommended local builder who was fabulous.

What job(s) were you doing previously?

I am a freelance writer, and also work partly for the National Childbirth Trust. Mark is chief financial officer for a fund management company in the city of London.

Did you have set ideas on what you intended to do (work and community) when you moved to Scotland?

I intended to continue as before, as I worked from home and the NCT work involved travel anyway. Mark wanted to go part time. We both wanted to be at home more with the kids and to aim to work only when the children were at school.

Has it turned out as you visualised or are you doing different things than you intended?

It is largely as we planned. I am travelling more than I thought for work, but actually happy with that at the moment as it keeps me in contact with friends down south. I could alter that balance fairly easily. Mark is now only working six days a month in the south which is brilliant.

How have you and your family settled?

Mostly fine. My youngest has taken the longest and still misses her old friends, but the boys settled more quickly than I expected, and they have made lots of friends which I also did not expect to happen so quickly and easily. I thought there might be some anti-English feeling which there has not been. I did think they would be more interested in the outdoor life than they are – perhaps if they had been a bit younger they would have benefited from that aspect, but actually they enjoy the freedom.

On balance, are you glad you made the move?

Yes, very much so.

Have you any advice for others thinking of buying a house in Scotland?

Those who are thinking about it need to plan carefully, be really rational about it, and be quite clear about budgets and stick to these. It would be easy, I think, to be swayed by a lovely house or a lovely area into buying something you couldn't quite afford – but remember that if you are having to work then incomes up here are far lower than in the south, and you don't want to move and then have to slave away to finance your lifestyle. So keep your objectives in mind, and don't be panicked into buying something you can't really afford. You also need to have a clear list of what you need and stick to that too.

SHARON BLACKIE

When did you move to Scotland and for what reason?

It was all tied up with a desire to escape from corporate life and seriously change my lifestyle. I wanted solitude, scenery, clean air and mountains.

Where did you move from?
I made the decision to move when I was working in Macon, Georgia in the USA. While I was waiting for the croft purchase to be completed and for the house renovations to begin, I was based in Winchester.

Where did you move to?
I decided to move to the Ullapool area, and ended up on the shores of Loch Broom about 12 miles from the village.

How old were you at the time?
40 when I decided to move; 42 by the time it actually happened.

Why did you decide to relocate to Scotland?
Two reasons. First, my family is from Edinburgh and I've always considered Scotland to be home, even though I've never lived here full time.

Second: I originally decided to move to the Highlands as a first-year (Liverpool) University student spending her first summer vacation working as a waitress/receptionist in a hotel in Drumnadrochit, on Loch Ness. I loved it so much that I almost never went back to University! However, it was to be another twenty years before I actually made the move.

What made you decide on the Ullapool area. Did you consider any other areas?
I chose Ullapool basically by sticking a pin in a map of Scotland. From my previous stay when I was 19 I knew that I'd loved the western Highlands, but I had no fixed ideas really. I'd never been to Ullapool but it looked (from an office in Macon, Georgia!) as if it had all the right ingredients: sea, mountains and remoteness; and yet it was situated on a major road to Inverness which is only just over an hour away.

Eventually it turned out that Ullapool happened to me rather than that I specifically chose it. While I was still working in America and thinking about the possibility of moving, a business colleague from the UK paid a visit. I had been told by other colleagues that he'd recently bought a house in the Highlands. I told him that I was looking for a place too; he asked me where. I told him that I thought I might like to live in a tiny little place he'd probably never heard of, called Ullapool. It turned out that not only was his own house in Ullapool, but the son of the people he'd bought it from had a ruined croft-house by the lochside for sale.

Did you particularly look for a croft? Were there special requirements you had to satisfy in relation to crofting law?
I didn't specifically look for a croft: it just so happened that I found one. However, I definitely wanted an older property with at least an acre of land.

The croft at the time I offered to buy it was still part of Dundonnell estate, and rented by the crofter from whom I was to purchase it. To do this, it was necessary that he purchase the croft from the estate, thus becoming an 'owner-occupier' of the croft. (Crofting law grants any crofter the right to buy their croft from the landlord at what is usually a tiny, token amount). At that point I could purchase it from him and in turn become the 'owner-occupier'. However, if a crofter buys his land from the estate and then sells it on to someone else within five years, there is a provision that 20% of the proceeds is payable back to the estate. This provision applies only to land, not to property on the croft. For that reason we split the purchase so that I bought the ruined croft-house and a small piece of garden at once, and the rest of the land purchase is to be completed five years later.

Did you find the buying process straightforward?
I found it bizarre. I was particularly astonished to receive a letter from my solicitor one day telling me I now owned the house. I told her I couldn't see how I possibly could, as I hadn't signed any contract! I have to admit that I was fairly horrified to discover that this isn't required in Scotland; the letters exchanged by solicitors on behalf of the purchaser and the vendor represent the contract. I never did see any of those letters before the purchase was completed. Moral: you really need to be able to trust your solicitor, or insist on seeing the letters to make sure everything is clear before you send the money!

Apart from this, it seemed fine.

How long did it take to find a property, have your offer accepted, and finally take possession?
Difficult to answer this as it wasn't a conventional purchase – I hadn't been looking for property before this came along, and the time-frame for moving in was dependent on my job situation as well as the necessity to organise building work. However, in effect it was two years.

Describe the property you bought. Did you need to have any renovation work or similar done on it? If so, were you happy with the work done for you by tradesmen?
The property is an old croft house with two rooms downstairs, two upstairs in the roof space. It was derelict and in effect came down to the four exterior stone walls: everything else had to be replaced. Then an extension was added, effectively doubling the size of the property.

I was lucky enough to choose a builder who ended up completing it just one month late. I have since heard some real horror stories about west coast builders, so I didn't do too badly. Generally the standard of workmanship was fine. However, I wouldn't recommend the stress of trying to manage a renovation project of this scale from the other end of the country. Inevitably when you call them, builders want to make you go away happy and so there's a tendency, shall we say, to be over-optimistic about progress... I remember coming up to check on progress precisely one month before

I was about to quit my job, move out of my rented accommodation and arrive with all my worldly goods – and none of this was reversible – and finding that I had no electricity, no water and no septic tank. I had external walls and windows but no interior walls and no staircases. The builder had sworn on the telephone that everything was on schedule. It wasn't a happy time!

What job were you doing previously?
Running a research and development centre for a major multinational.

Did you have set ideas on what you intended to do (work and community) when you moved to Scotland?
Yes: I intended to go back into practice as a psychologist, and I retrained as a clinical hypnotherapist too. I also intended to continue with some corporate consultancy work and, ultimately, wanted to give myself time to try my hand at fiction writing.

Has it turned out as you visualised or are you doing different things than you intended?
Yes: pretty much as I'd imagined.

How have you settled?
Very well. I'm fortunate to have a very friendly and supportive community around me. It's a great mix: incomers from a wide range of nationalities as well as the born-and-bred crofters. They all mix together wonderfully well. One of the major pleasures is seeing all of these very different people of such different ages and backgrounds mix together so well at the very regular parties that happen up and down the road, when people come along with their grannies, kids and dogs!

On balance, are you glad you made the move?
Yes. Wouldn't change a thing and intend to stay.

Would you recommend it to others?
It doesn't suit everybody. To the extent that I've seen people move here and then change their minds, much of it seems related to the weather – especially the often poor summers and the very long dark winters. I love winter here, but lots of people find it very depressing.

And perhaps one other thing: as a psychologist I find that I treat a lot of people who move here thinking that you just have to be happy and well in a place as beautiful and as peaceful as this: that the enormous change of location and lifestyle will be the answer to all their problems. It rarely is, for the very simple reason that, wherever they go, people take themselves with them! If someone is prone to stress or depression, they'll find something to be stressed or depressed about up here just as they did wherever they came from.

On the other hand: if you're prepared to work at making changes in yourself (as well as in your surroundings) then this is an environment that is definitely conducive to doing that.

CHARLIE WHITTAKER

Charlie bought a flat in Glasgow city centre in 2005 to let out for holidays and short breaks.

What made you decide on Glasgow city centre. Did you consider any other areas?
The two prime areas to live in Glasgow are the West End, where I already live, and the city centre. I had some spare cash and wanted to invest it. It seemed to me that property has been a sound investment for as long as I can remember and so I started looking for property within my price range in both places.

Two factors swung it the city centre's way. First, I rather liked the idea of city centre living and, of course, with a property there I always had an eye on the fact that I could use it myself now and again. Secondly, because I don't want the potential hassle often associated with a long-term tenant – friends of mine have had horrendous experiences with them in their properties – I calculated that the tourist market would be more inclined to city centre stays than the West End. On balance, that calculation was probably right.

Did you find the property buying process straightforward?
Absolutely easy and very quick. Not surprisingly, one or two things crept out of the woodwork, so to speak, but these were mainly concerned with a bit of a technical issue over whether the property was new when I bought it or whether it was pre-owned. What appears to have happened in this case – and I have since discovered it is common practice – is that a consortium bought the flat 'off plan', hung onto it for maybe a year or so, then put it back on the market to make a quick buck without any expenditure. The flat was fine (still is), but the 'newness' or otherwise of the flat had consequences for guarantees on white goods, for example, and also who paid an outstanding bill for repairs to the lift which had been required prior to my purchase of the property.

But, on the whole, the buying process was pain free, if that can be said about the purchase of any property anywhere.

Were there any problems?
Well, as I have said, the problems were minor and, in fact, the whole process taught me quite a bit about how to make money out of property without doing anything at all. The practice of buying 'off plan', then selling again some months later in a rising market seems a far better wheeze than developing or renovating existing property. But, it does require spare capital, of course.

How long did it take to find a property, have your offer accepted, and finally take possession?
It was very quick. I moved to Glasgow West End in early May 2005. I started looking for additional property in June and completed the purchase of the city centre flat by 8th July.

Describe the property you bought.
It's a one bedroom apartment in a converted Georgian sandstone building in the Merchant City quarter of Glasgow city centre. It is very near to George Square.

Access to the building is controlled by locked gate and locked internal doors. There is a lift. I suppose there are about 40 or 50 apartments in the block, many of them being one bedroom. It is extremely quiet inside the complex, almost hotel-like.

The flat itself is, for all intents and purposes, brand new. The lounge is open plan, looking out over a main street, with a fitted and rather nice kitchen at the rear. My one complaint about the kitchen is that there is a paucity of storage space but that isn't a problem for short-stay tenants.

The bathroom is stunning – all black slate and white suite. There is a shower over the bath. It would have been preferable to have a separate shower but that's just the way it is.

The bedroom is at the rear of the property and overlooks a rather grotty courtyard which means that it is quiet at night. I have stuck really nice and very expensive transfers on the bedroom windows to mask the grot of the courtyard. It works well.

The rooms are accessed by a stylish hallway, off which there is a large storage cupboard containing the hot water tank and all the bits and pieces one needs in such a property. Heating throughout is by wall-mounted, thermostatically-controlled electric radiators, and very efficient they are too.

Did you need to decorate or furnish it in a particular way to suit the customers you were aiming at?
I aimed at a 4-5 star grading standard as determined by the Tourist Board. I wanted to attract foreign tourists looking for quality accommodation. I also had an eye on the visiting businessman market so I have installed a wireless broadband connection. Another niche market for the flat is that of newly-weds because of my connections with a weddings agency.

So, the flat had to be comfortable, attractive and, if I can put it this way, gently seductive in tone. I have original art on the walls, intriguing curios here and there, and the bedroom is best described as a tasteful boudoir! The whole thing is eclectically modern.

How do you market it?
Internet and Tourist Board. I have my own website and also advertise on the wedding

agency websites. I have only recently decided to advertise with the Tourist Board in an attempt to kick-start the letting business.

Has it turned out to be a good investment?
I am sure so. Even though the property market is experiencing a 'soft landing' generally, such is the speed of redevelopment of the Merchant City and Glasgow generally that I feel confident the capital value of the flat has already risen significantly. It will not fall.

Does it bring you a good income?
Not yet, but the signs are good. I have a few bookings already although the flat has only been marketed for a month or so and I am still tinkering with the price structure and the marketing strategy; I think my income expectations were overly-optimistic to start with and I over-estimated the willingness of the market to pay high prices for city centre comfort and convenience. I'm sure it will work though and, given 12 months or so, bring in a good income stream.

Glasgow is a great city with huge potential for growth in the tourist market and furnishing and preparing the flat for its purpose has been fun. I'm ashamed to admit that I love staying there so much I am almost reluctant to let it out to strangers. But needs must!

INDEX

Complete guides to life abroad from Vacation Work

Live & Work Abroad

Live & Work in Australia & New Zealand £12.95
Live & Work in Belgium, The Netherlands & Luxembourg................... £10.99
Live & Work in China £11.95
Live & Work in France.. £11.95
Live & Work in Germany £10.99
Live & Work in Ireland... £10.99
Live & Work in Italy... £11.95
Live & Work in Japan £10.99
Live & Work in Portugal... £11.95
Live & Work in Saudi & the Gulf... £10.99
Live & Work in Scandinavia.. £10.99
Live & Work in Scotland... £11.95
Live & Work in Spain £12.95
Live & Work in Spain & Portugal... £10.99
Live & Work in the USA & Canada... £12.95

Buying a House Abroad

Buying a House in France £11.95
Buying a House in Italy.. £11.95
Buying a House in Morocco.. £12.95
Buying a House in New Zealand £12.95
Buying a House in Portugal.. £11.95
Buying a House in Scotland £11.95
Buying a House in Spain £11.95
Buying a House on the Mediterranean £13.95

Retiring Abroad

Retiring to Australia & New Zealand £10.99
Retiring to Cyprus.. £10.99
Retiring to France... £10.99
Retiring to Italy £10.99
Retiring to Spain £10.99

Starting a Business Abroad

Starting a Business in Australia.. £12.95
Starting a Business in France £12.95
Starting a Business in Spain.. £12.95

**Available from good bookshops or direct from the publishers
Vacation Work, 9 Park End Street, Oxford OX1 1HJ
☎ 01865-241978 * Fax 01865-790885 * www.vacationwork.co.uk
In the US: available at bookstores everywhere
or from The Globe Pequot Press (www.GlobePequot.com)**